THE WAR NORTH OF ROME

June 1944–May 1945

By

THOMAS R. BROOKS

Foreword by Senator Bob Dole

SARPEDON
New York

Published in the United States by
SARPEDON

© 1996 by Thomas R. Brooks

ISBN 1-885119-26-7

Published in the UK in 1996 by Spellmount Publishers Ltd.

Library of Congress Cataloging-in-Publication Data

Brooks, Thomas R.
   The war north of Rome, June 1944–May 1945 / by Thomas R. Brooks ;
foreword by Senator Bob Dole.
      p.   cm.
   Includes bibliographical references and index.
   ISBN 1-885119-26-7
   1. World War, 1939–1945—Campaigns—Italy.   I. Title.
D763. I8B76   1996
940.54'245—dc20   96-17257
                                                                CIP

10 9 8 7 6 5 4 3 2 1

MANUFACTURED IN THE UNITED STATES OF AMERICA

To the men of Company G,
85th Regiment, 10th Mountain Division,
who were killed in action.

Contents

Foreword

By Senator Bob Dole

Back in the early days of World War II, General George Marshall was asked if America had a secret weapon for winning the war. And he said, "Yes, our secret weapon are the best darned kids in the world."

Those words were true then—and they have been true in Korea, Vietnam, the Persian Gulf, and wherever freedom has been at risk this past half-century.

Like countless other Americans, I had the opportunity to defend freedom alongside the "kids" of my generation. It was for me, as it was for so many others, the defining experience of my life.

I don't know how a kid from the plains of Kansas ended up in the 10th Mountain Division, but when I arrived in the Po Valley in late February of 1945, I found myself in terrain unlike anything I had seen back home.

Late winter and early spring can be pretty cold in the Apennine range. Digging trenches was one way to stay warm. Dodging sniper bullets was another. Like soldiers anywhere, we killed more time than anything else. We waited for mail from home. We sweated out news from the front. Men lay flat on their bellies for hours, peering through a twenty-power scope at enemy soldiers on a nearby ridge.

By the first week of April 1945, Hitler's Germany was on the brink of collapse. Operation CRAFTSMAN was devised to bring about Germany's surrender as quickly as possible.

Beginning in the rugged hills around the village of Castel D'Aiano, forces spearheaded by the 10th Mountain Division would leapfrog the mountainous spine of central Italy. If all went well, Bologna would be snared and the Po Valley secured, clearing the way for Mark Clark's Fifth Army to chase the retreating Germans to—and perhaps beyond—the Brenner Pass.

While we waited for the weather to clear so our attack could begin, we received word that Franklin Roosevelt had died. Many of us shed some tears over the loss of our commander-in-chief, but we had little time to grieve.

Two days later, in the midst of battle, I felt a sharp sting in my upper right back, and my life was changed forever.

I have always considered myself fortunate, because I came home from the war. Many who served beside me in Italy did not.

I thought about these "kids" in the summer of 1994, when I returned to the hills of Italy and the beaches of Normandy as part of the events marking the 50th Anniversary of D-Day. I thought about their courage and the sacrifice they made.

As my fellow veterans and I talked, we reflected on what we had accomplished. And we spoke with pride about the fact that since the end of World War II, America has been the leader of the Free World.

And then we wondered whether our children and grandchildren will be able to make the same claim.

Given the challenges facing our country today—a staggering deficit . . . an ever-growing government . . . a loss of the values that made our country what it is . . . dictators and tyrants unafraid to use terrorism . . . will those reading this book 10, 20, 30 years from now still be able to say that America is the leader of the Free World?

I am committed to ensuring that they will, and I know as we go about our work, the men and women of America will always take heart from the courage of those who fought "The War North of Rome."

Washington, D.C.
1996

I

ROMAN TRIUMPH

Rome fell on June 4, 1944. All that day and the next, Allied soldiers streamed through the city, tasting briefly the pleasures of their Roman triumph before trudging on toward their next objective, somewhere to the north.

News of the triumphant entry into Rome, flashed around the world by cable and wireless, made headlines and dominated radio broadcasts. "All roads from all over the world led to Rome today," Herbert A. Matthews reported in the *New York Times*. "We must give thanks to God for the favors we have received," Pope Pius XII declared from a balcony looking over Piazza San Pietro. "Rome has been spared. Today she sees salvation with new hope and confidence. This day will go down in the annals of Rome."

President Franklin D. Roosevelt over a nationwide radio hook-up observed that Rome marked "one up and two to go." He also warned Americans: "The way ahead is hard." Prime Minister Winston Churchill sent his compliments to the Allied forces in a personal telegram to Field Marshall Sir Harold Alexander, adding: "It certainly seems that the position which your armies occupy and the superiority they enjoy in the air and in armour give favorable opportunities by further rapid action of inflicting more heavy losses on Kesselring's disordered army, so that their retreat to the north may cost them dear." The capture of Rome, as Churchill remarked to Alexander earlier, "is a vast, world-wide event, and should not be minimized."[1]

Two days later, Allied forces landed in Normandy. CBS broadcaster Eric Sevareid was at work in the building set aside for the press by the military when a BBC man ran in and shouted: "Eisenhower has announced the invasion of France! It's official!" Every typewriter stopped, Sevareid later recalled. "We looked at one another. One or two shrugged their

shoulders and went back to work; most of us sat back, pulled out cigarettes, and dropped our half-written stories about Rome to the floor. The
'play' had suddenly been taken away from the Italian campaign . . . we
had in a trice become players without an audience"[2]

Though correspondents would soon pack up and leave for more
newsworthy fronts, the soldiers would remain to fight on for another
eleven months. The fall of Rome was followed by sweeping runs north to
the Arno and to Rimini on the Adriatic, but in the autumn the combat
soldiers of the American Fifth and the British Eighth Armies would suffer the consequences of fighting on a downgraded front. America's political and military leaders persisted with plans for the invasion of southern
France, draining Allied forces in Italy and dissipating all chances for the
destruction of the Wehrmacht south of the Alps.[3] Germany would reap
the agricultural and industrial riches of the Po valley until the last months
of the war.

The decision to invade the Italian mainland was made at a conference of
the Allied Combined Chiefs of Staff in Quebec, in August of 1943. The
capture of Sicily, completed on the 17th of that month, after 39 days and
31,158 casualties, had secured the Mediterranean. It was the logical conclusion of the African campaign. The invasion of Italy, however, need not
have necessarily followed. General George C. Marshall, Chief of Staff of
the U.S. Army, was opposed. "Cross-Channel operations for the liberation of France and an advance on Germany," Marshall told Sir Alan
Brooke, "would finish the war quicker." Marshall had even wanted an
invasion of western Europe in 1943. Then the United States would be free
to concentrate on Japan. Marshall, too, viewed Churchill's insistence on
a Mediterranean strategy—the "soft underbelly" of Europe—as an effort
to shift the Allies away from a head-to-head Western Front campaign.[4]
He also feared that all secondary fronts "were operations [that] invariably
create a vacuum into which it is essential to pour more and more means."[5]

Churchill carried the day, tempting President Roosevelt and, ultimately, Marshall with "the great prize" of Italy. One more push, the
British Prime Minister argued, would take a demoralized Italy out of the
war. The occupation of the Italian mainland would give the Allies much-
needed air bases for attacks on southern and eastern Germany as well as
the oil fields of Rumania. The overthrow of Mussolini on July 25, 1943
by conspirators led by Marshall Pietro Badoglio and King Victor

Emmanuel raised the ante, suggesting that Italy might be gained with little trouble. Churchill clinched his argument with the irrefutable point that as all were agreed that an invasion of France could not be mounted until the spring of 1944, the Allies could not in the meantime suspend offensive operations while the embattled Russians were fighting some 156 German divisions. The correct strategy for 1944, Churchill told his Chiefs of Staff, was an Italian campaign "with option to attack westward in the south of France or north-eastward towards Vienna. . . ." Marshall reluctantly endorsed limited operations on the Italian mainland in the expectation that German weaknesses would enable Allied forces to press on to Rome and beyond.[6]

On September 3, 1943, Italy surrendered and British and Canadian troops crossed the Straits of Messina. British paratroopers occupied Taranto on the Italian heel six days later. The Germans disarmed the Italians on the same day and the Americans landed at Salerno, south of Naples. Here the Germans were ready and in a fierce battle nearly dislodged the attackers. The beachhead nonetheless was secured by the 18th of September and the Germans began a phased withdrawal. The British Eighth Army took Bari on September 22 and the Foggia airfields at the end of the month. Naples fell to the Fifth Army on October 1. By the 15th, the Americans had made a bloody crossing of the Volturno River, north of Naples. The Germans dug in along the Gustav Line, ten miles deep in places, which ran behind the Garigliano and the Rapido Rivers in the west and across Monte Cassino and the central mountains to the Sangro in the east.

Field Marshall Albert Kesselring had been given command of the Italian theater in November after making the case to Hitler that the geography of Italy lent itself well to north–south defense. His brilliant and flexible tactical measures soon forced the Allied advance to a miserable crawl. The British Eighth Army crossed the Sangro and breached the Gustav Line to take Ortona after a week's intense fighting on December 27. The American Fifth Army suffered enormous losses clawing its way through the Mignano Gap on the approaches to Cassino, and by the end of the year the Allied forces were exhausted. Veterans of World War I's Western Front termed the Italian campaign almost as unpleasant as Flanders. This war was a chaos of rain-soaked plains, snow-choked mountain passes and freezing nights. The costs to the Allies were high. The First Canadian Division, for example, victors at Ortona, lost 164 officers and

2,101 men in December alone. Isolated units worked in rugged terrain in what correspondent Eric Sevareid called "slow, spasmodic movement from one patch of silence to another."[7]

The war that winter south of Rome foreshadowed that of the following winter in the Northern Apennines. Bleak stone villages perched on ridges overlooking the two roads to Rome served the Germans well as defense outposts. From the heights, the enemy laid down a murderous fire of shot and shell on men struggling up stony ravines to elevations of 1,500 feet with packs laden with ammunition and supplies. Foxholes were only scratches in the stony soil, men flat on their stomachs, building parapets of loose stone for protection. What General Alexander called the difficult "ridge and furrow" country in the Eighth Army sector to the east offered few chances for decisive success to an Army attacking across the grain of the country. "The further north we pushed our advance the more numerous and close together were the river lines," he added.[8] Frequently flooded, rushing river waters washed away hastily erected bridges, leaving front-line troops without food or ammunition. Sodden soldiers shivered through the night as clothes froze, leaving men sleepless, hungry.

"The Gustav line," said Hitler, who in any case hated to yield territory, "must be held at all costs for the sake of the political consequences which would follow a completely successful defense. The Führer expects the most bitter struggle for every yard."[9] And that the Führer got in full measure from the men of the Wehrmacht. To break the winter deadlock, the Allied Supreme Command decided to employ its vast naval and amphibious superiority in an end run around the Gustav Line—a landing at Anzio, a coastal resort, in the German rear. This, it was hoped, would precipitate an enemy withdrawal from Cassino, followed by a breakthrough on to Rome 33 miles to the north. The Germans were indeed caught by surprise and American and British troops landed without opposition, establishing in two days a beachhead seven miles deep. Major-General John P. Lukas, commander of the U.S. VI Corps, then called a halt, ordering his troops to dig in until the tanks and heavy artillery were landed. It was a near-fatal mistake, though perhaps an understandable one.[10] Churchill grumbled from distant London, "I had hoped that we were hurtling a wildcat onto the shore, but all we got was a stranded whale."[11]

Kesselring responded adroitly. At first the Germans put together ad hoc units, stopping soldiers in the vicinity coming or going on leave and sending them to the beachhead. Within days, however they had brought up three divisions across bridges the Allies believed destroyed and shortly thereafter pinned Allied troops on the open, rocky beaches with an additional five divisions. After a German counterattack failed to drive the Allied forces off the beach, both sides settled down to a siege that lasted three grim months. The Gustav Line, too, held throughout the long bitter winter in the face of repeated Allied assaults.

The final offensive against the Gustav Line opened on May 11, 1944, along a twenty-mile front from the sea to a point east of Monte Cassino with the U.S. II Corps on the left, the French to their right, the Canadians in the center and the British and Poles on the right ready to outflank the venerable Benedictine monastery, which had been bombed to rubble earlier in the year. The shattered ruins of Cassino fell to Polish troops on May 18. The Canadians reached Pontecorvo and the breakthrough was well underway when British and American troops broke out of the Anzio beachhead on May 23. The French proved the value of mountain troops by their thrust through the massifs of Aurinci and Lepini. The U.S. II Corps and the VI Corps, out of Anzio, joined hands on May 25 and the race for Rome was on.

The Germans, however, were able to stall their advance, digging in around Valmonte on the Caesar Line south of Rome. The Allies were unable to break through until the bulk of the U.S. Fifth and British Eighth Armies caught up with one another at the end of the month. Controversy has attended General Clark's decision to focus on the capital instead of enemy formations in the field. In any case, Kesselring found himself with time to extricate his Tenth and Fourteenth Armies intact. Hitler authorized withdrawal from Rome and the Germans fell back to fight another day.

For the foot-weary soldiers of the U.S. Fifth Army, the first "barbarians" to take Rome from the south since Belisarius' Household Knights entered the Asinarian Gate in 536, the fall of Rome afforded a brief respite from the rigors of combat. A patrol from the 88th Division's Reconnaissance Troop was the first unit to enter the city, but the 1st Special Service Force was the first to penetrate the heart of Rome in strength to secure the five bridges over the Tiber north of Ponte Margherita. While seated on a rock in order to observe his troops enter the city, General Geoffrey Keys, Commander of II Corps, came under sniper fire. He was urged to get down to safety. "Go away," he told an anxious officer, "this is the first quiet spot I've seen in weeks.[12] Passing through the city at night, General Fred L. Walker, commander of the 36th "Texas" Division, remarked on the eerie near-silence, no sound but the tramp of marching feet and the low whine of truck motors. Then, as "we moved along the dark streets we could hear the people at the windows of the high buildings clapping their hands."[13]

Rumors were rife within the city as the Americans approached and entered through the city gates. Peter Tompkins, an OSS officer who had established a spy network within Rome, noted: "Germans are leaving in a pathetic state, some are trying to get away with cars that no longer have tires, driving on the rims. One motorcyclist had a flat tire but went right on. Some were on bicycles, but the most pathetic were the ones on foot who had been walking so long they could hardly stand." Nonetheless Romans were alarmed on hearing that the Hermann Goering division, falling back, intended to move through the city. As Tompkins and several of his friends walked through their neighborhood and wondered if the Germans would try to hold out within the city, or succeed in blowing up the bridges over the Tiber, they noticed several excited children. A girl came tearing across the piazza, shouting, "They're at San Paolo." How do you know? she was asked. "Because one of them gave a man a can of meat and beans."

"To the others," Tompkins said, "this sounded like a rumor, or a trick to get the partisans to come out in the open, but I knew damned well it was the truth. If they had said tanks and guns and American uniforms, I might have doubted it, but not meat and beans. Only a G.I. could be dishing out those goddamn 'C' rations to the populace."[14]

Stony-eyed from the fighting south of Rome, the dusty and tired G.I.'s moved through the city. Harold L. Bond, an aide-de-camp to the Assistant Commander of the 36th Division, Brigadier General Robert Stack, recalled the deserted early-morning Roman streets. "The air was clean and fresh, and the slanting beams of the rising sun shone orange-yellow on the buildings as we passed. Then, out of nowhere seemingly, people began to appear, Romans in their bathrobes and nightdresses, cautiously, a few at a time, and then more and more. Someone started cheering, and very soon the streets were lined with people, clapping, calling gleefully to one another, shouting. We waved back to them, smiling, but kept moving at the same speed straight on."[15]

The 36th got snarled in a huge traffic jam near the Vatican as MPs tried to straighten out the tangle in the midst of wild crowds of cheering Romans. Others, too, found the city streets confusing—as tourists, even with their guidebooks, can attest. Colonel James C. Fry, Regimental Commander, 350 Infantry, 88th Division, assured by one of his officers, "We are generally moving in the right direction, but I haven't any idea where we are," noticed an ancient pile in the moonlight, and said: "Good Lord, that's the Colosseum." Before the day was over, Italians would delight in the story of the G.I., who on seeing the Colosseum said, "Jeez, I didn't know our bombs were so powerful."

As the troops moved deep into the city, the crowds thickened. "The Germans had obviously departed," Fry comments in his book *Combat Soldier*, "and the Romans were ready to indulge in a celebration." Colonel Fry, trying his best to sort out a mix-up at a crossroad, observed, "My young officers and men were quite evidently more interested in the young ladies about them than in the success of our mission. Wine bottles were being passed around freely and occasionally a jeep was seen with a 'signorina' among the passengers." One battalion commander and his staff were located in the Hotel Excelsior, drinking champagne with Italian hosts, who, in Colonel Fry's phrase, "were now anxious to be identified as friends of the Americans."[16]

Fry sounded a cautionary note echoed by soldiers who wondered how many among the cheering crowds had hailed Mussolini, or had been Fascists or German sympathizers. Some soldiers did not make it through the city. Two American units mistook one another for the enemy in the darkness of the first night and engaged in a brief fire fight. One man was killed, several wounded including General Robert T. Frederick, commander of the 1st Special Force. And there were those caught by enemy rearguard sniper fire, who, John P. Delaney reported, "lay crumpled and twisted in the pathetic shapes that the newly dead assume. . . . Around their bodies, small groups of silent civilians stood watch until the GRO [Graves Registration] details took over." With understandable bitterness, the 88th Divisional historian adds, "And from the bar of the Grand Hotel, one war correspondent so forgot the men who had died to make possible his entry into Rome, that he filed a first story to the States describing how pleasant it was to have his favorite bartender remember him and his favorite drink after all the long years of occupation."[17]

Unfortunately, the liberation of Rome was marred by acts of violence. Eric Sevareid and several other correspondents overheard a burst of tommy-gun fire in the police headquarters and entered "just in time to see several tough-looking young men, wearing the banner of their underground political group, dashing down a corridor, firing blindly. . . . There was a frightening look in their eyes, an expression of sheer bloodlust and hatred. The rat hunt was on. This was not like war; this was a personal matter, and they were out to kill for the sake of killing. . . ."

Vigilantes were in operation at every corner, Sevareid adds. "They were smashing in the plate glass of shops that presumably were owned by Fascists or German sympathizers. A terrified man ran out of one, his hands in the air. He was slugged and kicked and went stumbling through the street with blood running down his face. . . . I tried to tell myself that these present victims had done frightful things to countless others, that savage oppression must result in savage release. But it remained a sickening thing to see."[18]

American soldiers, too, were not all well behaved. A.W. Ovenden, a soldier with the 1st Special Service Force, noted in his diary: "It's June 5th and the British and French are pushing through Rome in huge numbers. The city is completely taken over, people were very happy. Now the boys are drunk, raping women and disgusting the Italians who are becoming repelled. The British stand out as the neatest looking soldiers." And Peter Tomkins was unhappy over his first experiences with American and British generals. "The mentality of some of these senior officers was incredible," he said. "The first thing they wanted us to do was to provide women for them."[19]

Bill Mauldin expressed another gripe in one of his mordant cartoons, showing Joe and Willie in Rome on pass being directed to the Catacombs for a room. In *Up Front*, he adds: "It was always a little infuriating for the dogfaces to take a town away from the Germans by dint of considerable effort to be treated royally by the liberated inhabitants and given the golden key to the city, and, after moving on farther, to come back to that town and find everything changed. . . . All the liquor has been drunk and the pretty babe who kissed the dogface tearfully as he liberated her is already going steady with a war correspondent."[20]

But for the day, while the passage through Rome lasted, for most G.I.s it was a wonderful experience. "Talk and laughter filled the streets," Robert H. Adleman and Colonel George Walton recalled "Crowds swarmed over the tanks, throwing flowers and kissing the men. The older women sobbed and everyone pressed forward with wine and fruit and whatever else they could find as gifts for the soldiers. . . . Grimy, unkempt, with the mud of the mountains still on many of their uniforms, the young men discovered that the role of conquering hero was very much to their liking. That night all of Rome saluted them as liberators and, evidently, genuinely meant it. . . . Many a young G.I. got 'lost' that night in the company of an adoring signorina. There wasn't a whorehouse in Rome that did not have a line outside it, and even those infantrymen not searching for sexual release found pleasure in just being guests of an appreciative Italian family and sleeping that night between clean sheets and on a soft mattress for the first time in months."[21]

General Mark Clark, commander of the American Fifth Army, entered Rome early in the morning of June 5. He, too, lost his way. He had scheduled a meeting with his corps commanders on the Capitoline Hill but wound up in St. Peter's Square. A priest gave directions to the Campidoglio and introduced himself, saying, "I like to help American boys." The general replied, "My name's Clark." The priest turned away, then did a double-take, General Clark?" In one of those coincidences that surely delight Clio, the priest was Father Hugh F. O'Flaherty, a monsignor from Killarney, who had organized a network to help Allied escaped prisoners of war.

The meeting in the Piazza del Campidoglio, designed by Michelangelo in 1536 and one of the world's most beautiful and majestic squares, turned into an impromptu press conference, to the chagrin of the assembled commanders. Clark made a brief statement, but he neglected to salute the Eighth Army and the other units who had lost so many men in opening the way to Rome and at that moment were pushing the Wehrmacht northeast of the Tiber. General Keyes was charitable: "The thing was staged, there's no question about it. . . . But I can understand General Clark. He wanted to make sure that Fifth Army got the glory. I don't think that it was intentional that he left the British and French out. But it did kind of hurt them." Most correspondents later reported a feeling of embarrassment, even disgust. What Clark said was: "This is a great day for the Fifth Army and for the French, British and American troops of the Fifth who have made this victory possible." General Lucian K. Truscott, Jr., who as commander of IV Corps had planned the breakout at Anzio, wryly commented, "I reckon it was, but I was anxious to get out of this posturing and on with the business of war."[22]

The G.I.s, perhaps, were not quite so anxious, but get on with the war they did. By the morning of June 5, Rome had been secured and most of the Fifth Army was drawn up along a twenty-mile front, running from the mouth of the Tiber, southwest of Rome, to the river's junction with the Aniene, northeast of the city. The 1st Special Service Force held the bridges and the 3rd Division along the Aniene prepared to enter the city as garrison troops. As the Fifth Army liberated Rome, advance units of the French Expeditionary Corps were working through the mountains below Tivoli and the tanks of the South African 6th Armored were leading the Canadian advance into Paliano to the southeast. Other Eighth Army units were on the way to Subiaco and Avezzano in the central Apennines. On the Adriatic, at Pescara, the Germans began withdrawing to conform to their general retreat north to their next defensive line along the Arno, and the British prepared their pursuit.[23]

During the night of June 4, the U.S. 1st Armored crossed the Tiber and by morning of the 5th had reached Rome's western limits. An exultant General Truscott radioed General Ernest N. Harmon, "Push on to Genoa, if you want to." The Blue Devils' 913 Field Artillery Battalion set up in the Pincio Gardens and became the first artillery to fire from Rome. At first, the G.I.s moved warily north out of the city. "We were momentarily expecting enemy resistance," Colonel Fry recalled, "and I advanced the regiment with the greatest caution." His men were moving along Route 2 up a sharp incline from the Tiber when the regiment ran into its first firefight north of Rome on the ridge line. Its front was marked by a scatter of substantial villas. They reached the top mid-morning to overlook a fertile valley about a thousand yards in width. Machine-gun and mortar fire held up their advance until, joined by tanks, the infantrymen cleared out the enemy from the orchards and vegetable plots ahead. The crossing of that first valley north of Rome, Fry says, was relatively easy, "yet a substantial number of men were killed or wounded among the grape arbors that sunny day."[24]

The war north of Rome had begun. The fighting men had Germans to chase and it was clear as the troops thrust north that the Wehrmacht was not going to allow them to advance without making it as difficult as possible. For the combat soldiers, as Harold Bond put it at the end of the first day, "what seemed like a few minutes of pleasure in the city of Rome was now just another dream. They were faced with the coming of darkness on a battlefield, with the usual unknowns about the location of the enemy to the north and west. All the old fears of death coming suddenly and unlooked for in the chill and quiet of the night came back, and soon there would be another hill to climb, another German strongpoint to be taken. On this night the infantry would have the same old cold rations for their fare, while behind them they left a city wild with rejoicing, people dancing in the streets, laughter and gaiety everywhere."[25]

CITATIONS

[1] Matthews, *New York Times,* June 5, 1944, p. 1; Pope Pius XII, President Roosevelt, *New York Times,* June 6, 1944, p. 1; Churchill, *The Second World War,* Vol. V, pp. 610 and 608.

[2] Sevareid, *Not So Wild a Dream,* p.417.

[3] At the Teheran Conference, in November 1943, Stalin, too, pressed for an attack on southern France, ostensibly to draw German troops from OVERLORD (codename for the cross-channel invasion of France). According to the minutes, Stalin argued "that after the capture of Rome the troops thus relieved might be sent to Southern France...eventually [to] meet in France the main force of OVERLORD from the north." Stalin also wanted to frustrate Churchill, who favored the Italian campaign as getting Allied forces further east in Europe.

[4] General Albert Wedemeyer, Marshall's "planner," remarked of the "soft-underbelly": "The terrain was against it." He favored a cross-channel invasion in 1943 while the Wehrmacht was preoccupied deep in the Soviet Union. A 1943 invasion might enable Allied forces to reach into the heart of Europe before Hitler could react. Wedemeyer would have scratched the Mediterranean campaigns to provide needed manpower.

[5] Cray, *General of the Army,* pp. 396 and 430–33; Wedemeyer, *Wedemeyer Reports,* p. 229.

[6] Ibid, p. 387 and p. 410; Howard, *The Mediterranean Strategy in the Second World War,* p. 45.

[7] Sevareid, *Not So Wild a Dream,* p. 388.

[8] Sheppard, *The Italian Campaign,* p. 164.

[9] Jackson, *The Battle for Italy,* p. 183.

[10] Lucas remembered all too well the failure to establish the Salerno beachhead properly. That landing, as a result, was a near thing. But Anzio was not Salerno: The Germans were not waiting on the high ground with heavy artillery. Nonetheless, Lucas' caution ought not be condemned out of hand. He had cause, certainly, and, as Frank Sinatra sings in one of his ballads, "The Monday morning quarterback never loses a game."

[11] Churchill, *The Second World War,* Vol. V, p. 488.

[12] Adleman & Walton, *Rome Fell Today,* pp. 253–54.

[13] Fisher, Jr., *Cassino to the Alps,* p. 220.

[14] Tomkins, *A Spy in Old Rome,* pp. 338 and 339.

[15] Bond, *Return to Cassino,* p. 189.

[16] Fry, *Combat Soldier,* pp. 110–11.

[17] Delaney, *The Blue Devils in Italy,* p. 97.

[18] Sevareid, *Not So Wild a Deam,* pp. 412–13.

[19] Adleman & Walton, *Rome Fell Today,* pp. 266 and 268.

[20] Mauldin, *Up Front,* pp. 163 and 164.
[21] Adleman & Walton, *Rome Fell Today,* p. 259.
[22] Clark, *Calculated Risk,* pp. 355–56; Adleman and Walton, *Rome Fell Today,* pp. 272–73; Trevelyan, *Rome '44,* pp. 319–20.
[23] Fisher, *Cassino to the Alps,* pp. 220–21; Shepperd, *The Italian Campagn,* p. 276.
[24] Fisher, *Cassino to the Alps,* p 220; Fry, *Combat Soldier,* pp. 111–14.
[25] Bond, *Return to Cassino,* p.198.

II

THE SPLENDID ADVANCE

Most of the soldiers on the front lines in Italy on June 4 missed out on people dancing in the streets though they did experience a letup in the fighting as the Wehrmacht fled northward in disorder. An exuberant Churchill telegraphed General Alexander on June 9: "All our information here goes to reinforce your estimate of the ruin you have wrought on the German armies in Italy. Your whole advance is splendid, and I hope the remains of what were once the German armies will be collected."[1]

Nineteen German divisions had been involved in the fighting to the south of Rome in May. Three were destroyed; most of the rest were retreating in disarray. On June 5, Lieutenant General Sir Oliver Leese, commander of the British Eighth Army, ordered: "We now have the enemy disorganized and on the run. He must gain time and try to delay us by stubborn rearguard action, demolitions and minefields. We must drive him on, keep him moving night and day. Every hour gained, every German killed or captured, brings nearer the annihilation of the German Army in Italy."[2]

The terrain north of Rome offers fewer defensive advantages as the peninsula broadens, attaining a width of some 140 miles at the latitude of Lake Trasimeno. The Tiber, which flows south out of the Umbrian highlands, formed the general boundary between the Fifth and Eighth Armies and the two retreating German Armies, the Fourteenth confronting the American Fifth in the open country to the west and the Tenth facing the British Eighth in the difficult mountain country to the east. The central Apennines curve eastward, then swing to the northwest to reach the sea north of Leghorn (Livorno) and the Arno River. In the northern Apennines, Field Marshall Kesselring planned to establish a new winter line—the Gothic Line—which would run from Marina di Carrara on the

Ligurian Sea, along the southern edge of the mountains above Pistoia through the Futa Pass (between Prato and Bologna) and then east to Pesaro on the Adriatic. Kesselring, however, needed time for completion of the Gothic Line defenses. He also had to cope with Hitler's orders to stand and fight.

In the event, circumstances decided for Kesselring's delaying strategy, which was a variation of that employed in the 3rd century Punic War by the Roman general Quintus Fabius Cunctator, who wore down the Carthaginian armies by a series of delaying actions. Kesselring's Fourteenth Army was in rough shape and he planned to shift sufficient forces from the Tenth Army, which had escaped north over the Aniene River, east of Rome, virtually intact. He also hoped to stall the Allies' advance along a temporary covering position, the Dora Line, centered on Viterbo and running from Tarquinia on the coast through Orte on the Tiber and then to Narni, directly north of Rome. Failing that, the Wehrmacht would fall back for another delaying action on the Trasimeno Line, a series of defensive positions running from just above Grosseto through the mountains near Radicofani and Chiusi, bracketing Lake Trasimeno, passing above Perugia and extending on to the coast along the Chienti just below Macerata and Ancona. North of the Trasimeno Line, Kesselring counted on falling back through a series of minor delaying positions to the Arno River, where his forces would make a last stand before withdrawing into the Gothic Line for the winter.

On the day Rome fell, the Royal Natal Carbineers, a regiment of the South African Sixth Armoured Division, dominated the high ground to the south and southwest of the village of Paliano, some twenty-odd miles southeast of Rome. Communications with the artillery were not good. Unable to call up artillery shots, the Carbineers watched enemy tanks, vehicles and guns streaming away in retreat. Lieutenant John Beaton of the Carbineers recalled: "It was just maddening to see the stuff going by. . . . We did all we could to get in touch with someone who could shoot it up instantaneously, but it was no use. It was too late." As for the weary Germans, they were no doubt amazed as well as relieved at the lack of Allied air interference with their withdrawal.[3]

Paliano was the first Italian hamlet liberated by the South Africans. The Cape Town Highlanders pursued the Germans across the lateral road north of the town. By then, the South African artillery had located the German lines of retreat and shelled the German infantry and vehicles withdrawing to the northwest. The South Africans were ordered to bypass Rome on the east, cross the Tiber over a bridge just north of the city and advance along the ancient Via Flaminia (Route 3) to Narni, 53 miles away from Rome. The shift was essential to the pursuit of the Germans, but the South Africans lost valuable time in the shuffle.

It was essential to secure a bridge that crossed the Tiber where Routes 3 and 4 nearly converge north of Rome. The South Africans sent a flying column of infantry and tanks forward. The column was held up first by masses of French and American traffic along Route 6, then by an armored battle. As Neil Orpen remarks in his history *Victory in Italy*, the American division involved was "most uncooperative." As it turned out, the bridge had been taken by the Americans but was destroyed during the night. To add insult to injury, the South Africans were held up at pistol point by an American MP. An American general had ordered a halt and, although Major General W.E. Poole appeared to argue for passage, the South Africans had to withdraw. "An exasperating waste of precious time followed," Orpen wryly states, "as Divisional Headquarters negotiated to get the division through Rome." It was but one of many similar hitches experienced by American Fifth and British Eight Army units as the splendid advance got underway.

The South Africans, however, got to enjoy their share of liberation. The Natal Mounted Rifles leading the advance were greeted by cheering Italians who threw flowers on the tanks. Their route was well posted and, Orpen notes, the South Africans, after the initial balls-up, were "impressed with the excellent traffic control, but what held the attention of the troops even more was the beauty of many of the women. Well-dressed and well-groomed, the Romans were in striking contrast to the southern peasants the South Africans had previously seen."[4]

Once out of Rome, the Natal Mounted Rifles picked up speed on the Via Flaminia against light resistance. On their right, sounds of fighting were heard from the British 6th Armoured Division front, centered on the Via Salaria. To the left, clouds of smoke and dust bore witness to German opposition to the Americans' 88th Division. Under fire from small arms, two 75s and two Mark IV specials, the South Africans knocked out the antitank guns and destroyed a tracked vehicle, five civilian-type cars, a water truck, two troop carriers and a motorcycle. Twenty-two enemy soldiers were killed and 24 taken prisoner at a cost of one Sherman and one Stuart out of action, four other ranks killed and three wounded.

Castelnuovo di Porto, some 18 miles north of Rome, became the first "inhabited locality" north of Rome liberated by the South Africans. "The atmosphere," according to Orpen, "was more like that of a fiesta than war, and the vehicles were soon flower-bedecked by pretty girls who poured 'vino' down the throats of the thirsty men." Before dark on June 6, the leading elements of the South African Armoured Division were 31 miles north of Rome, just below Civita Castellana, their column strung out for miles along the road.[5]

The division, Orpen writes, "was disposed as nearly as it was ever likely to be to the 'copy-book' formation of an armored division in the advance, with reconnaissance screen of Honeys, Shermans and infantry troop carriers ahead of the main body to gather intelligence of the enemy's movements and dispositions. With the big headquarters armored command vehicle in the lead, the main body of tanks from the armored brigade was strung out down the road behind the screen, fanning out across the country where possible, with the fast-moving motor battalion ready for immediate action."[6]

The movement of the South Africans was, to one degree or another, typical of those first days of pursuit of the Germans north of Rome—even though the Springboks had plunged ahead of the American 88th Division on their left and the British 6th Armoured on their right. On the Adriatic, the British Eighth Army V Corps deliberately dawdled so as not to accelerate the German withdrawal—in hopes that the Eighth Army's advance would prompt the Germans to yield the Adriatic port, Ancona, without a fight, as well as to economize in bridging equipment and transport needed by the main bodies of the Fifth and Eighth Armies. Elsewhere, however, the advance was rapid, meeting Churchill's expectations for a "splendid advance."

By noon of June 7, a motorized battalion of the 168th Infantry, 34th Division, had cleared Civitavecchia, 38 miles north of Rome on the Tyrrhenian coast. (The captured port, badly blocked by enemy demolition experts, was partially opened and in use by Allied supply units in four days.) "Old Ironsides," the U.S. 1st Armored Division, too, was on the move along coastal roads and inland towards Lakes Bracciano and Vico, working in task forces with units of the 34th, 36th and 45th Infantry Divisions. Colonel Maurice W. Daniel's Combat Command A was held up for three hours near Vetralla by a rearguard of the 3rd Panzer Grenadier Division, long enough to enable the enemy to evacuate the town. Viterbo, northeast of Civitavecchia, with its airfields, was only seven miles away but was within the adjacent II Corps' zone of operation. Major General Ernest N. Harmon, Old Ironsides commander, however, was not, in historian Ernest Fisher's phrase, "overly respectful" of such boundaries when opportunity beckoned. From his Piper Cub, where he kept a close watch over his advancing troops, he ordered Daniel to go on into Viterbo. After a brief delaying action on the night of June 8, the enemy abandoned that city before daylight when a unit of Daniel's Combat Command entered it.[7]

The 85th and the 88th Divisions headed almost due north on June 6 from Rome in the zone assigned to II Corps between VI Corps on the coast and the British Eighth Army east of Highway 3, the ancient Via Flaminia. General John B. Coulter leapfrogged his 5th Custer Division (the 85th) regiments up Highway 2. Strewn along both sides of the Via Cassia was the wreckage of war—bombed-out guns, tanks and assorted vehicles. The fleeing Germans had grabbed anything with wheels for flight—old trucks, motorcycles, ambulances, Italian buses, bicycles. South of Viterbo, the town of Monterosi was taken without a shot.

The highway to Viterbo wound through gently rolling country. "One could look for miles across the rich pasture lands and olive groves and here and there a patch of woods to the far-off mountain ranges, purple in the sunset," a Division historian wrote at the end of the war.[8] Some sharp fights developed wherever the Germans set up a delaying position on a hill or a bluff, but the delays were insignificant as the prisoners came in droves. Among them were rifle-toting cook and baker school students. By nightfall on June 8, the Custermen were within six miles of Viterbo—which was about to fall to the 1st Armored. They had pursued the enemy 46 miles beyond Rome after being in action for nearly sixty days, and were relieved on June 9 by the 3rd Algerian Infantry Division of the French Expeditionary Corps.

The crossing of the first valley north of Rome had been relatively easy for the 88th Division. Over the next few days of pursuit, the enemy forced the Blue Devils to do most of their fighting at night. "During a daylight advance the enemy resistance would suddenly melt," according to Colonel Fry of the 350th Regiment, "and then as our men began to move more rapidly, we would get caught by machine-gun fire from new positions farther to the rear. . . . During daylight there was time for reconnaissance. . . . [D]uring darkness the advance would be resumed. No one ever got very much rest." Moving along secondary roads east of Highway 2, the advance of the weary troops was, in Colonel Fry's judgment, "too slow and too cautious to be effective."

On one moonlit night, Fry recalled, "One could see for miles across the vineyard-lined fields." Fry went forward to coordinate a two-in-the-morning jump-off. "I walked in front of [my jeep], scolding and begging the officers and men about me to move from the road. Completely exhausted, they lined both sides of the narrow path, their heads, free of helmets, lying in the ruts. Perfectly indifferent to what might happen to them, they snored peacefully. Sometimes I bent to lift a man's head with my hands, other times I put my toe beneath a neck to lift an individual aside."[9] Little wonder then that the Blue Devils welcomed relief from the French on June 11. They would have a month for rest, recreation and retraining.

Along the coast, the 36th "Texas" Division (VI Corps yielding to IV Corps) took over the advance from the 34th on June 9 with Grosseto, a provincial center sixty miles northwest of Civitavecchia, their objective. The men of the 36th wore their "T-Patch" proudly, tracing their history back to 1835 and the Alamo, when the 141st Regiment was formed. Originally composed of Texas National Guardsmen, its three regiments—the 141st, 142nd and 143rd—were mobilized at Camp Bowie, Texas in November 1940. Under Major General Fred L. Walker, the division landed at Salerno on September 9, 1943, where, in the words of historian W.G.F. Jackson, its "superb training" and "many acts of great bravery made up for its lack of battle experience."[10] That winter, however, the 36th failed to cross the Rapido because of lack of time for adequate preparation. The "Bloody River" effort reduced the 36th to the strength of one regiment.

On May 30, 1944, the much-battered but replenished 36th had made a stunning breakthrough in the center of the Alban Hills at Velletri, just 24 miles south of Rome. While one regiment held the Germans at Velletri, the other two scaled Mount Artemisio, assisted by engineers and followed by tanks, to break the German front. The Fifth Army had swept into Rome and the 36th, moving through moonlit streets to the clap of hands, crossed the Tiber and headed north. Early in the morning, the 142nd was fired upon at a turn in the road five miles outside Rome and was pinned down for most of the day. By late afternoon, the German roadblock was wiped out and the 36th plodded on. Later, near Lake Bracciano, the 36th assault battalion ran into a company of 200 bicyclists, recently hurried from Denmark to slow the Allied advance. It was crushed before it could fight, providing veterans of the 36th one of those quirky war stories that lighten reunion recollections.[11]

After relieving the 34th, the 36th moved north along the coast. Highway 1 passes through a defile just east of Orbetello, where the Umbrian Hills stretch to the coast. The defile had been incorporated into the enemy's Dora Line, the first of Kesselring's fall-back positions. More important, Orbetello lay at the mainland end of a causeway to rocky Monte Argentario and its port, Porto San Stefano, with its large liquid storage facilities. The Allies were running short of fuel, a shortage aggravated by a fire in the Fifth Army dumps near Rome.

At dawn on June 11, the Texans were halted by automatic weapons and artillery fire stabbing at their lead units in the early light. In the dim visibility of early morning, the Texans deployed across Highway 1 and the 2nd Battalion of the 141st worked up 700-foot Capalbiaccio Hill to flank German outposts. Before they could accomplish that task, the Germans infiltrated the wheat fields east of the high ground to overrun the 2nd Battalion's lead company. The Texans were forced to fall back to the base of the hill. Reinforced by a battalion from the newly committed 361st Infantry of the 91st Division and with an assist from 36th Division artillery, the 2nd fought back up the hillside. By dawn of the 12th, they were on top of Capalbiaccio, overlooking the enemy roadblock along the highway. The 1st Battalion of the 141st mounted an attack up the road and the Germans were forced to yield the Orbetello defile, falling back towards Grosseto.

Porto San Stefano was captured that night with its fuel storage facilities still intact. Italian engineers "failed" to carry out German orders to destroy them. An Italian diver afterward led American engineers to the underwater mines placed in the deep moats surrounding the fuel tanks. Clearing the harbor of sunken ships and repairing damaged docks, however, took until July 1, when the first Allied tanker docked. The port then became the main oil terminal for the Fifth Army.

The 36th had breached the Dora Line on the coast!

So far, to June 11, casualties for the Fifth Army had been exceptionally light, each division seldom exceeding a daily average of ten wounded or killed. Once they cleared Orbetello, the men of the 36th moved north, the infantry across the hills and the tanks through the narrow valleys.

Engineers constructed footbridges during the night of June 12 to enable the infantry to cross the Albegna River, five miles north of Orbetello. Heavy fire from the village of Magliano and the hills to the north halted the advance of the 142rd Regiment. Staff Sergeant Homer L. Wise of L Company boarded a tank, cleared a machine-gun stoppage while exposed to enemy fire and then sprayed the German positions with the weapon. For this and his fearless leadership of his platoon, which enabled the 2nd Battalion to secure a foothold on the outskirts of the Magliano, he was awarded the Medal of Honor. Lieutenant Charles Graham climbed a ladder to gain entrance into the walled town. That afternoon and on into the night, the infantry fought from house to house, street to street. The fall of Magliano opened a road enabling the division to outflank Grosseto from the southeast.

The 143rd Infantry moved up astride the coastal highway. It took the 2nd and 3rd Battalions five hours to drive the enemy from the high ground north of Bengodi, capturing fifty prisoners and five artillery pieces. Opposition, however, slackened as the Germans fell back toward Grosseto with the 36th in steady pursuit. Sporadic machine-gun and mortar fire harassed troops working across the small streams and drainage ditches in the valley of the Ombrone. Fortunately, there were few casualties.

As the 143rd waited until dark to cross a ford east of the main road, one battalion entered Grosseto unopposed. On the right, the 361st Infantry at Istia d'Ombrone waited anxiously through the night as engineers built a footbridge. Enemy artillery pounded away as the men crossed in daylight. By early afternoon on the 16th, three battalions had crossed the river and seized the high ground beyond.

Task Force Ramey, on the 36th's right flank, had been held up since the morning of the 14th by the Germans south of Triana, a small walled town 22 miles east of Grosseto. General Ramey ordered his troops—elements of the 1st Armored, the 91st Reconnaissance Squadron, the 141st Infantry and the 59th Field Artillery Battalion—to clear the neighboring villages. Their line of communications threatened, the Germans now withdrew from their strongpoint at Triana. The 36th advanced on a 15-mile front to secure the high ground southeast of Highway 73. Task Force Ramey then cut Route 73, ten miles north of the coastal highway, and paused to await relief by the First Armored. In ten days, IV Corps had advanced 22 miles against a stiffening rearguard action. As it prepared to cross Route 73 and hit the Trasimeno Line, intelligence officers identified prisoners from the crack 16th SS Panzer Grenadier Division. Kesselring had committed his reserve.

Task Force Ramey had maintained contact with the Fifth Army's right wing, General Juin's French Expeditionary Force. The expectation that they would soon be landing in France may have dampened French exuberance. Why die now, when France was so close? Yet the French were fighting in the mountains over the worst terrain in the Fifth Army sector.

Juin formed a Pursuit Corps of the First Motorized Division and the 3rd Algerians, which darted around Lake Bolsena with commendable speed. To cover a developing gap between the French and the Americans, the French commander committed another task force based on the 1st Group of Tabors and the First Moroccan Infantry. By nightfall of the 17th, the French had progressed some 15 miles north of Lake Bolsena and, over the next three days, gained another ten miles in the face of vigorous resistance and worsening weather. (In a separate operation, the French captured the island of Elba, off Piombino.) On June 20–21, the 2nd Moroccan Division relieved the First Motorized Division, withdrawn to Naples in preparation for the invasion of southern France. With the 3rd Algerians on their left and the 2nd Morrocans on their right, the French prepared to cross the Orcia River and strike north astride Highway 2 towards Siena. By June 20, the Fifth Army had raced halfway up its zone between the Tiber and the Arno. Ahead, however, along the Trasimeno Line, Kesselring was finally ready to turn and fight.

Meanwhile, to the east, the British Eighth Army maintained its "splendid advance" on a two corps front through the rugged mountain country flanking the Tiber. XIII Corps' 6th South Africans and the British 78th, in tandem, headed north to Orvieto and the west side of Lake Trasimeno as X Corps' British 6th and 8th Indian drove north towards Perugia and the eastern side of the lake. To move on Orvieto, the South Africans had to swing west from Civita Castellana through Vignanello–Vallerano and Viterbo. Taking advantage of heavy brush and well-placed Panzerfaust antitank weapons, mortars and snipers, the Germans slowed the South African advance. When a roadblock on the Fabrica–Vignanello road pinned down the Natal Mounted Rifles, Sergeant Bruce Gordon "reversed back" and, gaining "crest clearance," silenced an enemy antitank gun, helped a wounded man onto his tank under fire and pulled out with the wounded. Silencing enemy infantry with hand grenades and machine-gun fire, Gordon enabled his troop to extricate itself from a hot spot. He was awarded the Military Medal for gallantry under fire.[12]

Viterbo, already in the hands of General Harmon's 1st Armored, its narrow streets encased in a triangle of sturdy medieval walls, soon became jammed with troops as the South Africans came in from the southeast and the French and Americans entered from the southwest. The confusion reflected a boundary shift between the Fifth and Eighth Armies, units of the former veering northwest just outside the city. The South African artillery temporarily had to cease firing because of the difficulty of distinguishing between friend and foe. More than once General Poole had to leave his jeep and could only get forward on the seat of his Provost Escort's motorcycle. A large number of British prisoners of war had been liberated along with Viterbo, and General Alexander visited the town to tell them that the South Africans were the spearhead of his advance and would remain so—at least as far as Florence.[13]

Once outside Viterbo, the South Africans moved north astride a road east of Montefiascone towards Bagnoregio and Orvieto. Kesselring now committed the German 356 Infantry Division, recently arrived from Genoa under Generalmajor Rohr. Though the German troops were still raw and rather poorly trained, they were backed by elements of the 4th Parachute and 362nd Infantry Divisions. That stiffened the Wehrmacht defenses. On reconnaissance, first light June 10, the lead Natal Mounted Rifles tank under Lieutenant Howard Butcher, who had fought through Abyssinia and the desert campaign, was knocked out, its commander killed along with two crew members. Another tank fell victim to an enemy antitank gun. One man was captured and died of wounds; five others were also wounded before a Special Services Battalion Squadron came to their rescue.[14]

Sporadic firefights slowed the South African advance to a crawl. On their left, the French occupied Montefiascone, a rugged hilltown near Lake Bolsena. The enemy set up an antitank screen along an east–west railway running through Grotte San Stefano. To turn the enemy's left flank, the Special Services squadrons were ordered forward.

The Rhodesians of C Squadron were at breakfast when they got the call to action, and mess tins and mugs were abandoned "with contents unfinished." At midday of June 10, South African artillery fire pummeled German defenses in the vicinity of Grotte, knocking out five 88s, sixteen 50mm tank guns, three machine guns, a Mark IV tank, four Mark IIIs, "and many of the infantry also." By 2000, the Special Services tanks had run out of gas and ammunition but they had broken the enemy defenses along the high banked railroad by a daring run along the road under a railroad bridge. The South Africans had also captured Celleno, another hilltop village, which overlooked the road north to Bagnoregio and Orvieto.[15]

Bagnoregio, the birthplace of Saint Bonaventura, sits on a high bluff overlooking the approaches to Orvieto. Machine-gunners and snipers were posted at the windows of the houses perched at the edge of the town's forbidding cliffs. It had rained the night before and Bagnoregio was lost in a foggy haze as the Scots Guards advanced with the Natal Mounted Rifles in support. Pretoria Regiment tanks accompanied the Scots as enemy Grenadiers were attacking along the road from the west to Bagnoregio. In the gorge beneath the town, the South Africans left their vehicles and pushed through the undergrowth. A German outpost captured some prisoners when the Grenadiers attempted to cross a mined wooden footbridge. Lieutenant G.W. Lamb led a party of South Africans hand-over-fist up the lower terraces, surprising the Germans and releasing the prisoners.[16]

Overall, the day did not go well for the South Africans. While the mist saved the tanks, the Germans poured artillery, mortar and small-arms fire into the infantry crouched in the gullies beneath the town. While the South Africans were held up, the British 78th Division captured Civitella, a hilltown to the southeast. During the night, the German 356th Infantry Division was relieved by the 10th and 11th Parachute Regiments. On the 12th, General Poole ordered a divisional attack— French troops were to take Monterado on the western approach, the 11th South African Armoured Brigade would seize the ridge west of Bagnoregio and the 24th Guards Brigade would attack frontally while the 12th South African Motorized Brigade outflanked the objective from the southeast.

Clausewitz has remarked on the uncertainties of battle; and, indeed, it was the unexpected that turned the tide at Bagnoregio. Both sides had assumed the town to be unapproachable on the east. But some Royal Natal Carbineers spotted an approach up the almost-perpendicular walls of the gorge below the ridge linking Bagnoregio with Civita, a tiny hamlet a kilometer away. The Carbineers scaled the wall west of a blown-up bridge.

At one stage, two lead climbers, Corporal D.P. Smith and Private E. Pollock, had to be boosted up the slope. A German counterattack forced the small detachment back on a ledge where the South Africans huddled through the night as the enemy lobbed grenades from above. In the morning, more men climbed the cliff and soon a whole company held the high ground east of Bagnoregio. Their sudden appearance threw the enemy into confusion and they began to withdraw. Civita fell to another company of Carbineers. The Coldstream Guards entered Bagnoregio from the south to meet them. At 1300, the church bells pealed the liberation of the town. Two hours later, on June 13, the tanks of the Prince Albert Guards were within three miles of Orvieto.[17]

Orvieto rises precipitously some 65 feet above the Paglia plain on a flat-topped block of volcanic tufa. Its streets are narrow and winding, flanked by houses made of tufa stone or basalt. Olive trees and vines flourish in the countryside, and from the south Orvieto appears a Gibraltar-like fortress. It dominates the area as it had since it first became an Etruscan stronghold. It was essential to German lateral communications between sectors east and west of the Tiber.

Kesselring, fortunately, had completed his regrouping before the Allied advance reached Orvietto, boosting the strength of his Fourteenth Army front with the transfer of the 26th Panzer and 29th and 90th Panzer Grenadier Divisions from the Tenth Army zone east of the Tiber. As Orvieto no longer remained essential, the Wehrmacht began withdrawing to the hills commanding the Paglia plain from the north. By noon on June 14, the South Africans cleared Orvieto of the last of the German rearguards. Two days later, the 6th Armoured was held up on Highway 71, twenty-two miles north of Orvieto, at Chiusi, another former Etruscan stronghold surrounded by massive walls high on a hill southeast of Lake Trasimeno.

To the right of the South Africans, the British 78th Division crossed the Paglia at Orvieto without opposition, although the Royal Inniskilling Fusilliers lost one of their subalterns to the enemy—temporarily. As John Horsfall, historian of the Irish Brigade tells the tale, the young officer "was probing ahead on a motor bike and had the ill luck to pile into a whole platoon of *Jaegers* who were just packing up their kit by the roadside. The

German lieutenant in charge of the *Zug*—aged nineteen—then carted off his newfound friend into the mountains for forty-eight hours, until they eventually collided with one of our posts, and the Inniskilling escaped in the confusion. The subaltern, Foster, said there was nothing wrong with those young men, and they seemed to have got on splendidly together. He brought one of them back with him—his erstwhile custodian."

The Irish Brigade headed up Route 71 north of Orvieto in pursuit of the retreating enemy, reaching the Morrano Ridge on June 14, just as the Germans sought to regroup. The ridge was a typical rearguard position, commanding the highway beside "a series of horseshoe bends where the road heaved itself over the shoulder of the opposite hill with an unfordable river, the Chiani, between them." Horsfall adds that the Germans were "much disorganized" and caught out by the rapidity of the Irish Brigade's approach. "They were just not ready for us and as we came within range we were met only by scattered and ill-aimed rifle shots."

After an hour's fire fight, the Morrano Ridge was taken, along with a half-dozen prisoners, two or three wounded and several others who had been killed. Although the Germans still tried to garrison Morrano, the Royal Artillery and Irish Brigade riflemen fended them off. The Trasimeno Line lay just ahead.[18]

East of the Tiber and to the right of the 78th Division, the British 6th Armoured moved by day; the British infantry, by night. The Wehrmacht's LI Mountain Corps skillfully exploited the terrain, forcing the British tanks to inch along valley roads. It took the British tankers five days to cover the thirty miles from Passo Corese to Terni. There, they were held up two days by a blown-away bridge across a deep gorge just outside the town. By the time they crossed the gorge, on June 15, the Germans had withdrawn to Perugia.

Ten miles east of Lake Trasimeno, Perugia was a major German supply dump. Von Vietinghoff, the Tenth Army Commander, had chosen it as the hinge of his forward defensive zone. After crossing the Nera River at Terni and Narni, the British resumed their advance with the 6th Armoured in the lead. Twenty miles north of the Nera, southeast of Todi, halfway to Perugia, the British ran into stiff opposition. To bypass it, the 6th Armoured swung west, where sappers (engineers) bridged the Tiber. The terrain on the west bank favored the tanks, and, moving rapidly, the 6th closed to within six miles of Perugia by nightfall on June 17. Three days later, the British liberated the university city.

Now, however, heavy rains transformed the countryside into a quagmire. The enemy was determined to give battle along a line that extended across the Italian boot from a point between Grosseto and Piombino on the Tyrrhenian Coast some 110 miles north of Rome, east to the Adriatic five miles north of Pedaso, a town on the coast south of Macerata. The "splendid advance" had drawn to a close.

NOTES

[1] Churchill, *The Second World War*, Vol. VI, p. 84.
[2] Anders, *An Army in Exile*, p. 185.
[3] Orpen, *Victory in Italy*, p. 49.
[4] Ibid., p. 54.
[5] Ibid.
[6] Ibid., pp. 54–55.
[7] Fisher, *Cassino to the Alps*, pp. 239–40.
[8] Schultz, *The 85th Division in World War II*, p. 109.
[9] Fry, *Combat Soldier*, pp. 114–17.
[10] Jackson, *Battle for Italy*, p. 112.
[11] Huff, *A Pictorial History of the 36th Division*, p. 76.
[12] Orpen, *Victory in Italy*, pp. 62–63.
[13] Ibid., p. 64.
[14] Ibid., p. 65.
[15] Ibid., pp. 66–68.
[16] Ibid., pp. 70–71.
[17] Ibid., pp. 69–76.
[18] Horsfall, *Fling Our Banner to the Wind*, pp. 132–36.

III

SMILING ALBERT

Field Marshall Albert von Kesselring kept his headquarters as long as possible after the fall of Rome at San Oreste. some 22 miles to the north, on the western edge of Monte Soratte just off Highway 3—the historic Roman Via Flaminia. By remaining at the front Kesselring hoped to inspire confidence. "I was still in direct contact with units in the line at Viterbo on 6 and 7 June," he later affirmed. From his aerie, he had a stunning view of the valley of the Tiber to the north and over the approaches to the first of his possible defense lines in the mountain passes to the west, from Civita Castellana to Viterbo. In the aftermath of the Allies' "undeniable victory" in taking Rome, he attempted to persuade himself "that after weeks of bloody fighting the troops might succumb to the demoralizing influence of a capital city—only an exceptional strong and ruthless discipline could force the pace uninterruptedly." Though ever the optimist, Kesselring is quick to add in his memoirs that he did not really believe it, "nor did I make my plans on this assumption."[1]

Hitler, on November 6, 1943, chose Kesselring as Commander-in-Chief of the Italian theater over Field Marshall Erwin Rommel. At first, Hitler favored Rommel, who wanted to fall back and defend "the line of the Apennine mountains." Joseph Goebbels, Nazi propaganda minister, noted in his diary just after the Italian surrender two months before that the "Führer hopes we can withdraw and build up a first line of defense at that point. It would, of course, be a good thing if we could remain in Rome. But in Rome our flanks would be too long and too vulnerable. We would always be in danger there."[2] Rommel feared Allied landings up the Italian boot would trap the Wehrmacht. Kesselring argued that the Italian peninsula was best defended with the least troops at its narrowest point—south of Rome. Moreover, Allied bombers would be held farther back from industrial targets in southern Germany and northern Italy. Also, by holding the Winter Line, invaluable time would be secured for the construction of an impregnable Pisa–Rimini Gothic Line. At a briefing on August 31, 1944, a year after his selection of Kesselring, Hitler shrewdly observed: "I have been justified in my decision to leave Field Marshall Kesselring down there [in Italy]. I reckoned that politically he was an incredible idealist, but that militarily he was an optimist, and I don't believe you can be a military commander unless you are an optimist. Within certain limits I think Rommel is an extraordinarily brave and able commander. I don't regard him as a stayer."[3]

"Smiling Albert,"[4] 58 years old in 1944, was a brilliant choice on Hitler's part. Kesselring came from the solid Bavarian middle class— farmers, brewers and vine growers. His father was a town councilor and a teacher. "I wanted to be a soldier," he says in his memoirs; "indeed I was set on it, and looking back I can say that I was always a soldier, heart and soul."[5] He joined the German Army in 1904, served on the Western Front for two years in World War I and transferred to the Luftwaffe in the 1930s. He became Goering's Chief of Staff in 1936 and commanded the Air Fleet in the invasion of Poland, in the Blitzkrieg across France and during the Battle of Britain. In 1941, he was sent to the Russian front, but was then recalled to take part in the campaigns of North Africa, Sicily and Italy as field commander. As Douglas Orgill neatly sums up the man: "Defeat, which destroyed Rommel, was a spur to Kesselring."[6]

At San Oreste, Kesselring's most pressing problem was, in his words, "the appalling deterioration of the Fourteenth Army's plight." Its plight was exacerbated by Kesselring's refusal to budge from his decision "to keep the battle out of Rome." The bridges over the Tiber were left intact because of their historical value—Kesselring was an ardent Italophile— and because they carried essential pipes and cables. Retreating German troops complained that they were at risk because of Kesselring's determination to spare Rome. Kesselring acknowledged this, at least indirectly, when he asserts in his memoirs that his decision "entailed the abandonment of a defense line along the Tiber to the sea and along the Aniene as far as Tivoli." These "intrinsically excellent" positions were "simply unhinged" by the Allies, who, on entering Rome, then used them as starting points for their attack north. "Instead of defending the river line for several days," Kesselring observes, "our best hope was now to halt the enemy for a short while north and on either side of the city."[7]

Much to Kesselring's relief, Von Vietinghoff's Tenth Army managed to check the British Eighth's drive north in the rough country east of the Tiber. The British, Kesselring said, "were being remarkably cautious."[8] Still, late in the afternoon of June 7, a reconnaissance squadron of the South African Imperial Light Horse Kimberly Regiment investigated several burning buildings on the upper slopes of Monte Soratte. Kesselring's headquarters group had already fled. The next day, South African sappers searched the Gibraltar-like labyrinth of tunnels and uncovered huge dumps of enemy stores, including a warehouse of excellent sherry and French wines and an operations room. Intelligence officers unearthed several maps, one depicting the Gothic Line (*Gothemstellung*), the first use of that tag for the network of defenses between Pisa and Rimini. Another useful find was a map of the axes of retreat for enemy divisions.[9]

On June 12, General Frido von Senger und Etterlin, commander of XIV Panzer Corps—then positioned to stabilize the crumbling front created by the rapid advance of U.S. IV Corps up Route 1 on the Tyrrhenian coast—was ordered to Fourteenth Army Headquarters. With his high forehead and great beak of a nose, Von Senger had the look of an austere hawk. He was a Catholic from Baden in Bavaria, a Rhodes scholar at Oxford just before World War I (where he had fought in the trenches of the Western Front), and he was a career soldier.

In 1940 Von Senger had commanded a motor brigade in northern France. He had also served as chief liaison officer to the Franco-Italian Armistice Commission in Turin. Then, in 1942, he commanded the 17th Panzer Division in an abortive effort to relieve Paulus' encircled army at Stalingrad. Back in Italy—a country that he came to love—he organized the German defenses of Sicily, extricated troops from Sardinia and Corsica, and then succeeded in holding off Allied attacks on Cassino until that front cracked in May 1944.

Von Senger, who in fact had little sympathy for the Nazi or Fascist regimes, was not happy with his present assignment. He informed Kesselring, who was at the June 12 meeting: "[T]he forces at my disposal were quite inadequate for the task which had been assigned to me." In the attempt to reinforce the troubled Fourteenth Army, Kesselring had appointed a new commander, General Joachim Lemelsen. Von Senger had been assigned two "so-called" Luftwaffe Field Divisions and the 162nd Turkomen Division.

The Luftwaffe divisions consisted of redundant air force personnel, some recently arrived from occupation duty in Denmark. They were not,

Von Senger said, battle-worthy. The 19th Luftwaffe Division was disbanded during the withdrawal. The other, whose officers were former cavalry officers, did better but it, too, was later disbanded. The Turkomen Division was composed of former Russian prisoners from Soviet Turkestan led by German officers and non-coms. Under fire, Von Senger says, they frequently ran away "but could be easily re-assembled and led forward again." Von Senger wanted to fall back to the Gothic Line, pointing out that so long as he lacked efficient divisions the front was in danger of disintegration.[10]

The conference at the Fourteenth Army Headquarters lasted several hours and Von Senger thought that Kesselring and Lemelsen "took up too much time" on unimportant details, even discussing the operations of individual pairs of tanks. The meeting, he concluded, "was more in the nature of an inquiry."

Kesselring, indeed, was seeking information. He had received disturbing orders from the Oberkommando der Wehrmacht (OKW), the German Army High Command. Hitler ordered him on June 9 to "stand and fight." Even so, Kesselring, as he remarks in his memoirs, had to operate "as I thought necessary in the light of my own more accurate knowledge of the situation." Taking a leaf from Quintus Fabius Maximus, the Roman dictator during the Second Punic War known as Cunctator—the Delayer—Kesselring's strategy called for avoiding great battles, gathering reserves arriving from the rear and from the side (the Tenth Army), both armies "contesting every step of their retreat" and stopping up the gaps. "The main thing," he noted in his memoirs, was "to surmount our momentary weakness, to pull out our battered divisions and to rest and re-equip them."[11]

The situation was not quite so hopeless for the Germans as it may have appeared from Allied command posts. From the Allies' point of view, "the splendid advance" was still going forward despite momentary setbacks. But in Kesselring's view, the Allied High Command *aided* his plans for delaying actions at Lake Trasimeno and along the Arno. The Allies, he said, "failed to seize their chances." Instead of exploiting the seam—a weak one, as it turned out in retrospect—of the two German Armies, the Allies spread their forces over the entire front. Their air force was not sent to smash helpless targets, especially in the back area where roads and villages were jammed by supply columns and troop movements. The feared tactical landing in the Wehrmacht's rear never took place. From

Kesselring's viewpoint, the "remarkable slowness of the enemy's advance and the subsequent hesitation of the French Expeditionary Corps eased the situation." As Kesselring moved "here, there and everywhere by day and by night," he felt reassured in his assessment of the situation. "[T]he fighting power of even the most sorely battered elements of the Fourteenth Army was not broken."[12]

Hitler reiterated his command to halt the retreat at the latitude of Lake Trasimeno. On July 3, Kesselring with his operations chief, Colonel Dietrich Beelitz, flew to the Führer's Headquarters at Obersalzberg in Bavaria. Hitler lectured the two officers for nearly an hour. "The only area which offers protection against the enemy's superiority and restricts his freedom of movement," Hitler declared, "is the lower gut of Italy."

Kesselring's reply, by his account, was short and heated: "The point is not whether my armies are fighting or running away. I can assure you they will fight and die if I ask it of them. We are talking about something entirely different, a question much more vital: whether after Stalingrad and Tunis you can afford the loss of yet two more armies. I beg to doubt it—the more so as, if I change my plans to meet with your ideas, sooner or later the way into Germany will be opened to the Allies. On the other hand I guarantee—unless my hands are tied—to delay the Allied advance appreciably, to halt it at latest in the Apennines and thereby create conditions for the prosecution of the war in 1945 which can be dovetailed into your general strategic scheme." According to Kesselring, "Hitler said no more—or rather he muttered few words which, according to Beelitz, were not uncomplimentary. Anyhow, I had won my point."[13]

And so he had. The remainder of the war in Italy would be fought on Kesselring's strategic terms. As Von Senger succinctly puts it: "Before occupying a new main battle line that is to be held for some time, it is essential to involve the enemy in considerable exertions, thereby weakening him and preventing him from at once launching a spirited attack across the new obstruction. If the defender breaks off a successful defensive battle, he will gain time and can the more easily settle into the new defensive line."[14]

Historian W.G.F. Jackson, who was wounded while fighting with the British Eighth Army in its thrust towards Florence, makes the point that while the Apennines north of Rome looked on the map like an impenetrable barrier against which the Germans could be pinned, in fact, "they provided an excellent escape route." There were roads and tracks for a

withdrawing army, he pointed out, yet the hill routes and mountain passes were easily defended by rearguards. "They served the double purpose
of escape and protection for the exhausted German divisions"[15]—an
advantage that Kesselring exploited to the fullest. Von Senger eventually
got his "efficient divisions"—the battle-strained 3rd Panzer Grenadier
Division, then the outstanding 26th Panzer and 90th Panzer Grenadier
Divisions.

Payoff by the Cunctator tactic was soon evident. Von Senger provides
the evidence: "During the twelve days following the capture of Rome on
June 4, the Allied Fifth Army had moved forward 140 kilometers—a rate
of advance that amounted to the pursuit of a defeated opponent. When
XIV Panzer Corps took charge, the rate of advance was slowed down to
thirty kilometers in the week from June 16 to 23 and to another thirty
kilometers during the subsequent three weeks."

While Kesselring worked out his basic strategy, the Allies engaged in a
final wrangle over the Italian campaign, a discussion that began on June
7 and lasted until August 8. It was one of the most significant strategic
debates of the war between American and British policymakers. American
and British differences over the conduct of the war had first surfaced at
Casablanca in January 1943 and were papered over at the Teheran
Conference eleven months later. Here, as Churchill has said, the "design
for final victory in Europe had been outlined." The Allies agreed on the
invasion of France. But, Churchill noted, "we still wielded powerful forces
in the Mediterranean, and the question had remained, 'What should they
do?'" Capture Rome and advance to the Pisa–Rimini line, was the answer,
"and there hold as many enemy divisions as possible in Northern Italy."
The Americans pressed for a full-scale invasion of southern France, code-
named ANVIL and, later, DRAGOON—with Stalin's support. He was delighted at the opportunity to prevent the British from using Italy as a base
for a thrust into both Austria and the Balkans. He had his own postwar
plans for those regions. Churchill acceded, as he had other fish to fry—
"although I contemplated other ways of exploiting success in Italy."[16]

The fall of Rome presented Churchill with an opportunity to press
again for a "dagger" thrust at the "soft underbelly" of Hitler's Europe.
Should we go on with ANVIL or should we make a new plan? Alexander posed
this question at the end of May when he telegraphed Churchill: "You will
have heard of fresh enemy divisions which are on their way here. I hope

our tap will not be turned off too soon as it was before [when Alexander had to yield divisions for the Normandy invasion], and prevent us from gaining the full fruits of our present advantageous position."[17]

Plans for ANVIL were well underway when Harold Macmillan, the British Minister Resident in North Africa, jotted in his diary on June 17: "The problem of the future of Alex and his armies is a grave one. It seems a terrible pity to entrust a difficult operation in southwest France to untried French and American generals, and to leave unused or break up the armies of Italy, which are now a great fighting instrument, confident in themselves and their commanders."[18]

Macmillan may have underestimated General Lucian K. Truscott, a hard-nosed and seasoned commander, who was preparing the Seventh Army for the invasion of southern France. Truscott had the pick of the Fifth Army (essentially VI Corps) and he chose well—his own crack 3rd Division, garrisoning Rome until relieved for the invasion; the Texan 36th, still in the field north of Rome; and the 45th, withdrawn for beachhead training just after the fall of Rome. Ranger battalions and the top-notch Japanese-American 442nd Combat Team rounded out his choices. The four divisions of the French Expeditionary Force were also assigned—for obvious political reasons. The French, however, remained available for the early phase of the splendid advance. Still, the loss of the Moroccan Mountain Division and the Goumiers—who had proved their worth in the mountains south of Rome—was particularly grievous because Alexander hoped to use their hard-won expertise in the Apennines.

Field Marshall Maitland Wilson, Allied Supreme Commander in the Mediterranean, had already recommended launching ANVIL/DRAGOON on August 15, when Alexander pressed his alternative plan. In a telegram on June 18 to Churchill, Alexander cited 30,000 German prisoners taken since the fall of Rome and argued that Kesselring's armies were a "beaten force but not yet eliminated from the field." The Germans, he said, intend to hold the Apennines with the equivalent of ten to twelve divisions on a front of 180 miles. "Against this, I can, provided I have left to me intact my present force, amass such a powerful force of fresh divisions, tanks, guns and artillery as will split the German Army in half and eliminate the German forces in Italy." Nothing would prevent Allied forces then, he said, from marching on Vienna unless the Germans send in at least ten or more fresh divisions. Should that be the case, Alexander concluded, "I understand it is just what is required to help OVERLORD. I believe we have here and now an opportunity of delivering such a defeat on the German Army as will have unpredictable results and such a chance must not be missed at this stage of the war."[19]

Churchill needed little convincing, and General Maitland "Jumbo" Wilson told the Combined Chiefs of Staff on June 19 that the best contribution to the common cause would be to press forward to the Po with all possible resources. South Africa's Prime Minister, the highly respected Field Marshall Jan C. Smuts, entered the debate, throwing his support to Churchill and the British high command. General Eisenhower then stepped in and stated that ANVIL/DRAGOON was the best way to support his advance into Europe: a major storm in the Channel had wrecked the American "Mulberry" harbor on the Normandy coast. Marseilles could be quickly captured and would furnish a route north to join the battle for the Ruhr. The American Chiefs of Staff reply was, in Macmillan's words, "brusque"—even "offensive." The conflict between the Allies, as Churchill remarked, could only be resolved between himself and President Roosevelt.[20]

Churchill telegraphed an appeal to Roosevelt on June 28: "Our first wish is to help General Eisenhower in the most speedy and effective manner. But we do not think this necessarily involves the complete ruin of all our great affairs in the Mediterranean, and we take it hard that this should be demanded of us." He reminded the President of the strategic importance of Istria and Trieste in northeastern Italy. He suggested that the Bay of Biscay with its major port, Bordeaux, was closer to the United States than Marseilles and could be quickly seized, making it easier to replenish and reinforce Eisenhower's main assault troops than an invasion in southern France. "It is better to have two ventures than three," Churchill argued. "Let us resolve not to wreck one great campaign for the sake of another. Both can be won." Roosevelt, still currying favor with Stalin, insisted on what he called "the grand strategy" of Teheran, one that called for (1) exploiting OVERLORD to the full, (2) "victorious advances in Italy" and (3) the invasion of southern France. He reminded Churchill that Stalin had favored ANVIL and held that other operations in the Mediterranean were of lesser importance. He even went so far as to suggest that Stalin should serve as arbiter of the dispute.[21]

Churchill was clearly upset by the President's reply. In *Triumph and Tragedy* he italicizes, as if with an angry stroke of pen or pencil, those bits of Roosevelt's telegram that disingenuously or deliberately distorted what

Churchill had proposed. After the withdrawal of five divisions, Roosevelt declared: "The remaining twenty-one divisions, plus numerous separate brigades, will certainly provide Alexander with adequate ground superiority." This in the face of Allied intelligence reports that Hitler had issued orders for the Gothic Line to be held at all cost must have added to Churchill's irritation with American notions of strategy. "I cannot agree," Roosevelt wrote, "to the employment of United States troops against Istria and into the Balkans . . . For purely political reasons over here ['44 was a presidential campaign year], I should never survive even a slight setback in 'Overlord' if it were known that fairly large forces have been diverted to the Balkans."[22]

"No one involved in these discussions had ever thought of moving armies into the Balkans," Churchill remarks, adding that Istria and Trieste were clearly strategic and political positions of great importance. Alexander, General Mark Clark and the British Chiefs of Staff, moreover, were flexible on the possible deployment of Allied forces in Italy after moving into the Po Valley, willing to turn to France or Istria as the opportunity arose. General Wilson was ordered to proceed with ANVIL/DRAGOON on August 15. Churchill, as his physician Lord Moran notes in his diary on August 4, was distraught. When the good doctor remarked that the war seemed to be going well, he burst out: "Good God, can't you see that the Russians are spreading across Europe like a tide." The American landings in the south of France [Dragoon] were the last straw, Moran notes. "He can see 'no earthly purpose' in them: 'Sheer folly,' he calls them. He had fought tooth and nail to prevent them. . . . [B]ut the Americans would not listen."[23]

However distraught Churchill may have been, as Lord Moran avers, "you cannot get him down." By early August the German forces around the Normandy bridgehead had begun to crumble; Allied forces approached the Loire River, cutting off the Brittany peninsula.

Churchill made one last attempt to divert DRAGOON to the southwest coast of France. Such a move, he telegraphed Roosevelt on August 6, "by taking the shortest route right across France" would be "decisive for Eisenhower's victorious advance." In the hopes that presidential aide Harry Hopkins would help convince Roosevelt, he spelled out in greater detail his argument that "Bordeaux could be obtained easily, cheaply, and swiftly." Marseilles, he pointed out, was 500 miles away from the main battlefield "instead as almost upon it at St. Nazaire." Moreover, as

Churchill believed, at Marseilles "the turn-around from the United States is about fourteen days longer than the straight run across the Atlantic."

Hopkins' reply, in Churchill's words, "was far from comforting." Churchill then visited General Eisenhower at Portsmouth in a futile attempt to gain his support. Roosevelt settled the matter in a short message on the following day, August 8: DRAGOON would go forward. Churchill telegraphed Roosevelt: "I pray God you may be right. We shall of course do everything in our power to help you achieve success."[24]

Although mention of the invasion of southern France is to anticipate events in the campaign north of Rome, the Allies' decision was to have a profound effect on the fighting to come. While Kesselring was gaining eight divisions from elsewhere in Europe, the Allies in Italy would lose seven to DRAGOON. The 45th was attached to the invasion-bound Seventh Army immediately after the fall of Rome. The 3rd American Division was withdrawn from patrolling Rome on June 17. Ten days later, the 36th Division at Piombino (164 miles north of Rome) was withdrawn to Salerno for retraining. Two French divisions were withdrawn between June 24 and the first week in July. French troops entered Siena on July 3; then the remaining divisions continued to advance over twisting mountain roads until their front stabilized just ten miles south of the Arno. (Before relieved by the British on June 22, the French were to suffer over 8,000 casualties on their drive north of the capital.)

The First Special Service Force, the Rangers, began amphibious training south of Salerno on July 1. The 442nd Combat Team remained in Italy until the end of September. The Allies in Italy also lost a good number of service troops and equipment to the invasion of southern France. The withdrawal of troops to the south for refitting and training as others moved north caused no little confusion. The 12th Tactical Air Force was moved to Corsica in mid-July to support DRAGOON. According to Harold Macmillan, DRAGOON deprived the Allied armies in Italy of seventy percent of their air support.

The landings in southern France took place on August 15; orders for the assault on the Gothic Line were given on the 16th. As grievous as the loss of air power, men and material to DRAGOON was the very idea that in Allied planning the Italian front had been downgraded. Macmillan visited General Alexander's advanced headquarters on Lake Bolsena on August 5. "I found the general as agreeable as ever—a little tired, and of course a little disappointed." The "interference" of DRAGOON, Macmillan notes, has been great in terms of material. "But," he adds, "it has also affected morale—both the remaining Americans and the Eighth Army feel that something has gone out of the campaign. And this a little was reflected even in General Alex's resilient and controlled temperament."[25]

NOTES

[1] Kesselring, *A Soldier's Record,* pp. 204–205.

[2] Goebbels, *The Goebbels Diaries,* pp. 343–44.

[3] Warlimont, *Inside Hitler's Headquarters,* pp. 383–84.

[4] Douglas Orgill, who commanded a troop of Sherman tanks in Italy, reports in his book *The Gothic Line,* "To British soldiers, with their knack of summing up the salient points of personality of a commander, Kesselring was known as 'Smiling Albert.'" S.L.A. Marshall, who served as Chief Historian of the European Theater, says his staff dubbed Kesselring "Smiling Al," largely because of his unfailing good humor—"smiling, dignified, unembittered"—even in the face of his death sentence (later commuted).

[5] Kesselring, *A Soldier's Record,* p. 3.

[6] Orgill, *The Gothic Line,* p. 12.

[7] Kesselring, *A Soldier's Recod,* p. 204.

[8] Ibid., p. 205.

[9] Orpen, *Victory in Italy* , p. 56.

[10] Von Senger, *Neither Fear nor Hope,* pp. 259–61.

[11] Kesselring, *A Soldier's Record,* p. 206.

[12] Ibid.

[13] Ibid., p. 207.

[14] Von Senger, *Neither Fear nor Hope,* p. 265.

[15] Jackson, *Battle for Italy,* pp. 243–44.

[16] Churchill, *The Second World War,* Vol. VI, pp. 57–58.

[17] Ibid., p. 608.

[18] Macmillan, *War Diaries,* p. 468.

[19] Ibid., p 470.

[20] Macmillan remarks in his *War Diaries* that he left a meeting with Churchill just after the American reply had arrived with the strong impression that, given the U.S. contribution to the European campaign, the British would have to yield. "We can fight up to a point, we can leave on record for history to judge the reasoned statement of our views, and the historian will also see that the Americans have never answered any argument, never attempted to discuss or debate the points, but have merely given a flat negative and a somewhat Shylock-like insistence upon what they conceive to be their bargain."

[21] Churchill, *The Second World War,* Vol. VI, pp. 64–65; see also App. D, pp. 716– 23.

[22] Ibid.

[23] Moran, *Diaries of Lord Moran,* p. 173.

[24] Churchill, *The Second World War,* Vol. VI, pp. 66–71.

[25] Macmillan, *War Diaries,* p. 498.

IV

TRASIMENO

Lake Trasimeno, the largest stretch of inland water in the Italian peninsula, lies between the valleys of the Tiber and the Chiana. Surrounded
by rolling Umbrian hills, "fields the colour of dirty gold with patches of
vegetable green," in Raleigh Trevelyan's perceptive phrase,[1] vineyards and
olive orchards, Trasimeno is fifteen miles west of Perugia and some 110
miles north of Rome. Its shores are flat, dotted by crenelated castles and
scythe-like inlets bordered by thick reedy beds. During the Second Punic
Wars, in 217 B.C., Hannibal slaughtered 15,000 Romans in a famous
Carthaginian victory on the plain at the northwest end of the lake near
the tiny village of Sanguineto, "a name of blood from that day's sanguine
rain."

Kesselring hadn't a prayer of emulating Hannibal, but he had regrouped his Tenth and Fourteenth Armies to good effect. As the Allies
pushed past Orbetello on the Tyrrhenian coast and moved towards
Orvieto in mid-June, Kesselring ordered his Tenth Army to resume the
defensive at Trasimeno. "I realized, of course, that it would be a mistake
to try and force a decision in this region, but it was vital to gain time to
complete the defense lay-out of the Apennine front."[2]

The Germans did not have much time to develop a position organized in depth. But they did remarkably well within a matter of days, digging field fortifications supported by antitank guns well situated in forward positions and backed by mortars and rockets in the critical 30-mile
sector flanking Trasimeno. The 334th Infantry Division straddled
Highway 71—the only road capable of bearing the traffic of an armored
advance—along the west side of the lake. Part of the 1st Parachute
Division, the Herman Goering and the 356th Divisions completed the
German defenses, running from the hills southwest of Trasimeno to little
Lake Chiusi, across the Chiana Valley, and including the hilltowns of

Chiuso and Chianciano.

The weather had turned foul on June 17 as the South African 6th Armoured on the left and the British 78th Division on the right pushed north along Highway 71. Heavy rains turned roads and fields into quagmires; tanks and trucks churned earth into sludge. Fighting continued in isolated pockets. Mired-down tanks, however, were unable to reach infantry objectives. Two platoons of the Natal Grenadiers charged and took dug-in enemy positions within the tiny village of Le Piazze, west of Highway 71 on the South Africans' approach to Lake Chiusi. The only road to Le Piazze soon became a morass and vehicles had to be freed from the muck, one after the other. Enemy fire from the brickworks in the village pinned down the infantry and at dusk the two platoons had to be withdrawn. In that day's fighting, the Natal battalion lost eight killed, six wounded. During the night, the enemy evacuated Le Piazze in a typical fallback.

"For twenty-four miles we squelched through mud towards the front line," South African Lieutenant John Smallwood noted in his diary.[3] John Horsfall, with the Irish Brigade to the east of the South Africans, thought the water-sogged terrain "the foulest bit of Italian hill country that I had seen so far." His temper was not much improved by his feeling that his outfit had just made a bad mistake. "Our men," he wrote in his account of the Irish Brigade, "were as hard now as men ever could be, but there were not a lot of them left." None of the rifle companies as they moved up towards Trasimeno were more than seventy strong; Horsfall's beloved Royal Irish Fusiliers [the Faughs], however, he adds, alone in the brigade were still in reasonable fighting condition. They were attached to the 78th Division's Reconnaissance Regiment, leading the way north along Highway 71, the Romans' Via Cassia, towards Trasemeno. They fought several sharp encounters en route, catching in one a Wehrmacht mortar detachment on the move and leaving twenty-five of them on the ground.

A Faugh patrol entered Citta della Pieve, a hilltown with medieval walls and a 14th century fortress commanding a crucial point on Highway 71, overlooking the Chiana Valley. As Horsfall wryly notes, "the bottleneck there was self-evident." It was, he adds, "extraordinary that the Faughs were not kept together just then. The whole battalion ought to have pitched into the town, not just a detachment."

As it was, the patrol stirred up a hornet's nest and the Wehrmacht's crack 1st Paratroop Division were back into town in no time. By nightfall, "they had it in strong grip, and they missed killing our divisional commander by a whisker." (Major General Charles Keightley came forward to look over the situation and a German sniper shot his field glasses out of his hands.) The enemy defence of Citta della Pieve delayed the attack on Trasemeno by several priceless days. "I have often thought it affected the whole course of the war," Horsfall avers, "for if the Faughs had secured it as they easily could have done at the outset, the 78th Division would have piled in to the enemy at Trasemene three days earlier—before they were ready—and probably rolled the whole lot up in the process." Horsfall concludes that the "incident" at Citta della "perfectly reveals a classic 'what might have been'."[4]

There is no question but that the time gained from the slowing Allied advance was put to good use by the Germans. They had established their first truly coherent defensive line north of Rome. It was not quite so well defined on the west above Piombino and inland below Roccastrada to above Radicofani, overlooking Highway 2. But Kesslering had managed to regroup the Tenth and Fourteenth Armies. Seven of the eight armored or mobile divisions that had been east of the Tiber after the fall of Rome were now positioned between Trasimeno and the Tyrrhenian Sea. Though the coastal region remained the vulnerable flank, the Germans outnumbered the the Fifth Army two to one. On the Eighth Army front, centered on Trasimeno, the terrain favored the defense with its forward edge in a line that ran from the southern end of the lake through Chiusi and Sarteano to the northern slopes of Monte Cetona. The British were some 200 miles in advance of their railhead, which precluded reinforcements— the South Africans and the 78th Division had gone forward on June 20 to engage the enemy.

The South Africans literally had to haul themselves out of the mud to proceed. Leading elements of the Kimberly Regiment secured Stazione di Chiusi, a railroad stop, with little difficulty. A patrol climbed the road into Chiusi itself but was driven back out. Listening posts were placed on the outskirts of the hilltown but when the mists lifted on the morning of June 21 they discovered that they were overlooked by enemy observation posts in the church tower to the right front and the *fortezza*, or, castle, to the left.

The South Africans withdrew to the railroad station area. The covering platoon stumbled into a minefield and eleven men were wounded. Lieutenant G.A. Hoskins, an artillery observer, managed to get through with a jeep and a wireless set. By mid-morning, although under almost continuous concentrated mortar bombardment, he directed fire from South African guns, for the rest of the day. Though the guns fired to good effect on enemy vehicles within the town, the South Africans were held up by well-placed enemy units. By one count, no fewer than 17 Spandau machine guns and two Nebelwerfers were located in the area close to where the road climbed up into Chiusi.[5]

Chiusi, one of twelve cities of the ancient Etruscan Confederation, established some seven centuries before Christ, sits on a hill some 360 feet above its approach road and a little over a mile from Stazione di Chiusi, at the junction of the Arezzo and Siena railway lines. Lars Porsena, he who swore by the Nine Gods, set forth from (then) Clusium to attack Rome in 508 B.C. where Horatius held the bridge over the Tiber in a heroic stand immortalized by British historian Macaulay. A ruined 12th century fortress and a Romanesque cathedral built almost entirely of Etruscan and Roman fragments and a campanile, which rises above a huge antique cistern, overlook the vast Etruscan necropolis that surrounds the town. Though it was a drab place in 1944, it provided the Germans with the strongest natural defensive position in their line. Kesselring wanted it held as long as possible.

Confusion, if not a god of battle, is surely one of its hazards—as the South Africans were soon to discover. Corps headquarters wanted Chiusi cleared, to open the main road for further advances up the ChianaValley. Unfortunately, Stazione di Chiusi was not on the 1:250,000 maps being used by the 6th South African Armoured Division. When reports came back that Chiusi railway station had been taken and patrols sent forward, few realized that the station was not a *stazione centrale*, or even a stop at the edge of town.

The Capetown Highlanders were ordered to attack Chiusi on the night of June 21 from the east at 2300. Lieutenant Colonel O.N. Flemmer, the battalion commander, had observed the shelling of Highway 71 in the afternoon, but ordered his men forward in the belief that the Kimberly Rifles had already been through the "village" of Chiusi, which he understood was "not strongly held." To add to the confusion, the Kimberly Regiment was not consulted, nor had they been told that the Highlanders were to pass through their lines. Moreover, apparently little weight was given to intelligence that Chiusi was occupied by a battalion of the Hermann Goering Division, with two companies forward, supported by artillery and Nebelwerfers. When the lead platoon of Highlanders met a Kimberly carrier section near the railroad yard, it gathered that Chiusi was held by the "customary" light rearguard elements.

But Chiusi had not been properly reconnoitered, nor had its approaches been scouted for suitable tank routes. According to Neil Orpen, the South African 6th Armoured historian, "There is no indication that the Highlanders spoke to any of the men who had actually tried to enter Chiusi."

The three Highlander companies had to struggle forward on foot over soggy ground, under shellfire, and across ditches and canals to cross their line of departure forty-five minutes late at 2345. The slopes before Chiusi were lined with 12-foot terraces dotted with gaunt, twisted olive trees eerily silhouetted against the flash of shells and mortar rounds. A prisoner said that the town was held by 300 infantry. A company in the lead reported at midnight that the attack was going well though it was slowed down by the terrain. While climbing the twisting road to Chiusi, it was challenged by a sentry, "*Wer da?*" The Highlanders hit the dirt as flares lit the night with shocking brilliance. Grenades were lobbed down from the terraces above and machine guns opened up on all three sides.

The flares burned out and in the darkness another platoon came forward to relieve the men pinned down beneath a twelve-foot terrace. For reasons known only to the enemy, hostile fire then died down and Lieutenant E.P. Hardy's platoon climbed the terrace on one another's backs. Bren guns silenced grenade-tossing Germans dug into two shelters on the next terrace. Enemy machine guns quickly zeroed in on the Highlanders, killing one and wounding several others. Very lights flared, and once again the South Africans were pinned down.

In another of war's oddities, two men joined the Highlander platoon, but by the time it was discovered that they were Germans, they had apparently realized their mistake and disappeared before anyone could shoot. While the rest of A Company was pinned down by a counterattack, Hardy's platoon advanced through the gardens on the outskirts of Chiusi and entered the town near a small square where the Teatro Communale, a theater used as a movie house, stood across the road from a two-story winery with a large cellar and vats below ground.

Working forward in the darkness, the Highlanders could barely make out a bulky shape dominating the square. They crept closer, until they realized that the "shape" was a tank—a Tiger or a Panther. Lacking any antitank weapons, Hardy's men rolled grenades under the tank, which rumbled out of the square. So far, A Company had suffered only six casualties; at 0257, it reported its position consolidated in the theater and two adjoining houses, with one platoon in the castle. The Engineers reported that the road to the town was clear though heavily sniped. All seemed to be going well, with two Highlander companies forward and one in reserve. However, a prisoner from the Sturm Battalion of the Goering Division revealed that Chiusi was held by three companies. A Company confronted the German center while the rest of the Highlanders outside of town were held up by heavy gunfire.

Dawn broke, cold and misty. In the murky half-light, the Highlanders picked off a number of Germans moving around the square. A Panzer rumbled in and began firing point-blank at the building where the South Africans crouched for cover. Within twelve minutes, Harding's men suffered a dozen more casualties. At 0540, Corps signaled the 6th SA Armoured: "Please give us some news of Chiusi." At 0815, Hardy's gallant band reported some success at sniping with brens and rifles at enemy infantry crossing the tops of buildings some 500 feet away. Panzers hammered away at the theater; 75mm shells, Spandau and enemy rifle fire added to the din, choking dust and smoke. When a German paratrooper clambered on a tank and called, in English, for surrender, Corporal R. McGregor fired on him and others on the back of the tank to such good effect that the Panzer withdrew.

An hour later, Company A reported that the enemy had broken into the Teatro Communale and were on the stairs to the dress circle. Two Germans were killed and the rest wounded. But the end was in sight.

"Blasting a gap in the walls with guns and machine guns," a Highlander history records from eyewitness accounts, "the Germans brought the roof of the theatre collapsing onto the courageous defenders, and it became impossible to see through the dense dust and smoke. Fire broke out within the building itself, all the officers and many others were wounded, and the situation was desperate. Sergeant Campbell ordered all who were not wounded to follow him down the stairs. Fighting their way into the street they ran almost straight into a tank. There was no possibility of escape, and the gallant little band of survivors from the cinema was forced to surrender. Battalion HQ had lost all contact with 'A' Coy."

The Highlanders kept on trying to oust the Germans from Chiusi. D Company, advancing in single file as the enemy lobbed grenades from up above, managed to get into the town, but only barely—in the face of enemy tanks and infantry. Lieutenant A.M Caro's platoon gained cover in a house on the main street but could not hold the position. Corporal Jimmy Ferguson volunteered to remain with the wounded and Caro withdrew. He and two others—all three wounded—reached Battalion Headquarters.

By 1000, the Highlanders' reserve, Company B, was also falling back under heavy enemy fire. Tanks that might have eased the situation were immobilized midday by a pelting rainstorm that turned the Chiana Valley into a morass of mud. Hot meals and ammunition were sent forward by jeep. The 11th South African Armoured Brigade reported that it was still trying to drive the enemy out of Chiusi. It was, Orpen tells us, a forlorn hope. Two platoons of B Company, supported by stationary Shermans, never got beyond the high ground some 1,000 yards short of Chiusi. "The attack had been a failure," Orpen notes sadly, "and the South Africans had suffered their first reverse in Italy."[6]

General Poole decided that his troops had best outflank Chiusi. While the Capetown Highlanders had battled over the town, there had been some progress on their left, where South African tanks and British infantry had begun to move through Cetona along the ridge-running road to Sarteano towards Chianciano Terme (whose waters are taken internally for liver complaints and used for baths). Rain and demolitions made for heavy going. Nonetheless, the British 24th Guards Brigade passed through the South African motorized brigade with little difficulty—only to be pinned down by enemy fire in the hills just beyond Cetona.

At dawn on June 23, the Scots Guards, backed by the South African tanks, machine guns and mortars, attacked the ridge line ahead. At first, the right-flank company met with light resistance, but before the day was over was held up well below the summit. By skillful expoitation of the ground and with South African supporting fire, the right flank achieved its objective by 0900. A counterattack at midday was broken up by South African Shermans. Early on, the next day, a Scots Guard patrol reached the summit. It had been abandoned but the Guards had lost six killed and twenty wounded in the fighting on the slope the day before. Sarteano, too, had been abandoned. The Coldstream Guards walked into town and were greeted by its citizens waving homemade Union Jacks and offering the weary soldiers flowers and wine.[7]

Beyond town to the northwest, the Guardsmen on top of "Castle Hill," overlooking the provinces of Umbria and Tuscany to the north, could see Germans digging in along the Astrone, a river running through a deep valley on the south side of the Chiusi–Chianciano Terme road. The Grenadier Guards suffered sixty casualties from enemy shellfire as their patrols sought a crossing over the Astrone. Then, Brigadier Archer Clive ordered his Scots Guards around to the left over yet another hill, 846, near the Pietraporciana farm.

"Here it was," the Scots Guards' history says, "that the perfect understanding and confidence between the tanks and the Guardsmen was born." As well it might be, for the attack on June 26 was a remarkable display of infantry–tank coordination. Almost three German companies were dug in overlooking the advance of the Scots Guards. When the infantry were pinned down, the tanks charged over the hilltop, driving the enemy back and quelling their Spandaus.

The Guardsmen charged, and at mid-morning were consolidating their position. The South African tankers withdrew for "a brew of tea" and were enjoying the moment of respite when the enemy counterattacked. The tanks quickly formed a defensive circle but were unable to make out the enemy infantry infiltrating among the bushes on the slope, nor were the tanks able to depress sufficiently to fire to good effect. Two South African machines then charged down a narrow track, firing as they went, then withdrawing, before the astounded enemy could react. Another pair of tanks repeated the performance. In three daring dashes, the tankers killed some 40 Germans and wounded another 60. By evening, the Guards were firmly in position and in contact with the French forces to the left.[8]

As the Guards pressed on towards Chianciano Terme and the town of Montepulciano, the British 4th Division's Reconnaissance Regiment reached the shores of Lake Chiusi to the right and some three miles to the north of the town. Because holding Chiusi was no longer tenable, the Germans withdrew early on June 26.

Demolitions, extensive mining, booby traps and shellfire slowed the South Africans, who now pushed north from Chiusi. The SA engineers did yeoman's work in clearing up. In a single month, they had built 50 bridges, constructed 40 bypasses and filled 111 craters. On the road to Acquaviva, one section of engineers was pinned down for four and one-half hours, losing a bulldozer, a jeep and a scout car. A sniper shot

Lieutenant M.P. Pearse through the ear, which brought the casualties in the three South African Engineer squadrons to 63 for the month.[9]

Chianciano Terme was cleared by the Coldstream Guards and a troop of South African tanks on the morning of June 28. That night, an infantry patrol entered Montepulciano, a charming hilltown noted for its wines. Mayor Bracci and his wife produced wine to go with biscuits provided by Major Derek Cardiff of the Guards in order to celebrate the arrival of the Allies. The road to Acquaviva was secured against light opposition. South African tanks and the Scots Guards swept left to avoid extensive demolitions through Monticchiello and Pienza, moving northeast again towards Sinalunga.

By dawn on the 30th, the 11th South African Armoured Brigade was advancing in two columns through the Chiana Valley, the Hermann Goering Division contesting the ground between Gracciano and Valiano. The Guards advanced to within three miles of Torrita di Siena and forced a general German withdrawal. The British and South Africans were soon moving into the heart of the Chianti country.

On the South African right, two British divisions also made progress—but not without heavy fighting. By the evening of the 20th, the two forward brigades of the 78th Division had been badly mauled. Coming out of the hills above Citta, the 36th Brigade met heavy opposition in the low rolling country between Lakes Chiusi and Trasimeno. At Vaiano, a mile east of Lake Chiusi, the British were driven back by a heavy counterattack. The 11th Brigade, coming up on the Trasimeno shore, attacked the Sanfatucchio Ridge in an attempt to outflank the German defences around Vaiano.

"Perched up in the castle of Montalera," John Horsfall later recalled, "the entire Trasimeno sector spread out below us like a model landscape, with the lake as the centerpiece. As a battlefield it hardly seemed real. Even . . . the cotton wool puffs of shell explosions [that] were rising continually in those hillocks where we knew the Lancashire Fusiliers were hanging on by their eyebrows."[10]

The setting for the battle of Sanfatucchio was, in Horsfall's phrase, "typical." "The Germans looked down, we looked up," as one soldier put it; Horsfall comments, wryly, "the enemy . . . had a view of the landscape like that of a billiard table from above."

Two infantry regiments, the 754th and 755th of the Wehrmacht's 334th Division, amply backed by artillery, antitank guns and self-propelled 88s, held the village of Sanfatucchio, with its towering church and bell tower, as well as a scatter of fortified hamlets and farmhouses on the Pucciarelli Ridge running north, parallel to the shores of Trasimeno to the valley of the Pescia. West, towards Vaiano, a jumble of ridges and wooded thickets provided additional cover for the enemy. The main-line railway lay between the British and German fortifications, a handy line of departure for the attack launched by the Irish Brigade at 0730 on June 21.

Brigadier Patrick Scott's orders were simple. He told Horsfall: "You capture Sanfatucchio and I will push the others on through you as soon as you have opened that door for us." The 17th Field Artillery laid down smoke on Sanfatucchio to enable the infantry to swing around the town through folds to the west for an assault on the town from the rear backed by a dozen tanks from the Canadian 11th Armoured Regiment. Outflanking the town had the added advantage of keeping free of the handful of Lancashire Fusiliers still engaged with the enemy.

Dense smoke saturated Sanfatuccio but the bell tower, looming above the murk, served the Germans well as an observation post. Allied infantry and tanks came under heavy shellfire as they crossed the rail line. E Company commander Ronnie Boyd reported an hour later that "matters were going as planned" but that "the enemy were possessed and fighting like maniacs."

At the battalion observation post, Horsfall reports, little could be seen of the fighting along the ridge ". . . as the dust clouds thickened— only the flash and spume of the shell explosions, and black streaks of smoke spiralling slowly upwards above the holocaust beneath." At 1030, E Company, supported by one or two tanks, had blasted its way into the first building block of Sanfatucchio. Most of the enemy was killed by the tank fire and of the few prisoners taken hardly one was unwounded. The Canadians lost several tanks to German 88s but managed to get the rest into town, where the Rifles were fighting down the main street, house by house. By one o'clock, German resistance in Sanfatucchio collapsed. "The relief was indescribable," says Horsfall, whose command tank had just entered town, "and seeing our gasping soldiers one sensed it immediately." Sprawled riflemen of both sides were scattered down the main street among the dead and badly injured. But haggard and dust-covered, "Our riflemen could still give a thumbs-up as soon as they saw us."

Four 3-inch mortars were set up in Sanfatucchio's central square and began laying down fire on the Rifles' next objective: a cemetery and other targets to the north. Before the day was over, the sweating mortar men would shoot off over two thousand rounds of high explosives and the mortar-base plates would be driven down until only about a foot of their snouts would be visible above ground level. Before the Rifles could drive the Germans out of the cemetery and nearby wheatfields, however, a resolute German infantry platoon had to be driven out of the town's church. After two hours, that building was pulverized by the Canadian tanks and taken over by the British riflemen, beefed-up by the remains of the tank troops, whose machines were now down to one survivor.

With the church in British hands, the Germans counterattacked, rising out of the wheatfields like Confederates charging Cemetery Ridge. Despite heavy mortar fire—a hundred rounds or more—they came on, crowding up against the shattered church walls. The Rifles were out of grenades, but the Germans heaved stick grenades with such vigor that they overshot the men crouched on the opposite side of the wall. An eager German warrant officer peered over it to check on the results. A surviving Rifles subaltern did likewise, but with better luck, knocking back the enemy platoon commander with a pistol shot at a range of less than one foot. The loss of their officer demoralized the German infantrymen, who immediately surrendered, tossing their rifles over the wall. Others, farther back, bolted.

Utilizing artillery fire and the remaining tanks with considerable skill, Horsfall directed his lead companies forward along the Pucciarelli Ridge and the lakeside slopes. Though the Rifles cleared several houses on the ridge, the enemy mounted at dusk yet another counterattack under a storm of shellfire. As the battle raged, Horsfall comments, "I knew we had failed. We had broke in but not through, and the enemy had given in nowhere." His three rifle companies had suffered heavily and most of the Canadian tanks were lost.

The Rifles' sister battalion, the Inniskillings, attacked Pucciarelli village that evening but the Germans held fast. Vicious street fighting continued all night long. John Kerr, the Skins' commander, had his headphones parted in a burst from a German Schmeisser. The Irish Brigade position was touch-and-go as sporadic fighting continued through the night. June 21 had been a costly day for the Rifles: six officers and over seventy NCOs and riflemen lost. Nine tanks and half their crews were gone, too. The three forward companies were each scarcely stronger than a platoon. The Germans had held, but sixty were dead and another sixty or so were taken prisoner. A jeep convoy brought up hot meals for the exhausted soldiers. Mess Corporal Telfer, with a touch of British panache, served dinner to the battalion officers. He had draped a damask table cloth over upturned wine casks and set a table with silver—Kesselring's silver liberated by the Rifles earlier in the month.[11]

All the next day, June 22, the Irish Brigade and the Germans disputed possession of Pucciarelli. Captain Cullen's machine guns were set up in the second story of a convenient building, but German infantry stormed through the floor below. Cullen unshipped one of his guns and used it, in Horsfall's phrase, "like a pneumatic drill" against the Germans beneath. When a self-propelled gun began to blow the building to bits, the machine-gunners moved out in a hurry. In the morning, the Rifles, backed by tanks, resumed their attack on Pucciarelli Ridge in an attempt to clear out the remaining German strongholds. They closed the gap between themselves and the Inniskillings in the village. By nightfall, their positions were stabilized with the loss of twenty more men and a gain of twenty-eight prisoners.

BBC war correspondent Eric Linklater visited the Rifles' headquarters and found: "In the ruins of what had been a little country church about a half-dozen soldiers were sitting on a pile of rubble. Partly buried by the fallen stones were the torn vestments of the priest, blue silk and purple, and from a shattered glass case a wax figure of St. Anne, I think, in a dusty black dress leaned towards the door in an attitude of surprise. On the rubbish heap in front of her there were . . . clips of ammunition, the splintered butt of a rifle and fragments of web equipment. The soldiers were dirty and dishevelled and their cheeks were grey, partly with dust and partly with the weariness of battle. They had fought hard for the church and for the low walled cemetery beyond it . . . I said to them, 'I suppose you're feeling very well pleased with yourselves' . . . 'Feeling bloody sorry for ourselves' was the answer I got. I looked at the speaker with new respect and . . . recognized the voice of the British infantry. They were proud . . . and because of their pride they would presently buckle on their dirty equipment and take up their newly cleaned weapons."[12]

The following day, June 23, was relatively quiet as the men of the 78th Division and the Canadian tank crews girded themselves for the next phase: an attack on the German line along the Pescia, a sluggish and shallow stream seeping east to Lake Trasimeno. Colin Gibbs's platoon was out front by about a half mile at the apex of an isoceles triangle that made up the Rifles' perimeter. His position on Montemara was isolated, but dominated the terrain ahead. Offered a chance to withdraw, Gibbs pointed out that this would yield a key position to the enemy. Unhappily, it was also the point where the opening barrage had to start. "It has good cellars," Gibbs told Horsfall.

And so it came about, Horsfall comments, "that an Irish Rifles company commander with a subaltern, a handful of NCOs and thirty-odd riflemen elected to stay in their posts when the whole of their division's artillery put down their wrath upon them."

When it fell at 0530 the next day, the Faughs bypassed the bulk of the enemy garrison at Montemara. Gibbs's platoon took seven direct rounds, but only a handful of his men were hit—only a few seriously. The rest engaged the enemy, which was stunned by Gibbs's 6-pounders, and captured eighteen Germans. The Faughs pressed on, supported by Canadian tanks; then the 5th Buffs of the 36th Brigade took the lead to cross the Pescia.

The Rifles, on the left flank, cleaned up around the tiny hill hamlets of La Villa and Badia on the 26th. Horsfall reports that one of his companies was down to twenty men, two others had thirty, and the fourth, fifty. A hundred and eight of his men had been hit in four days' fighting—three times that number since the onset six weeks earlier. Of the enemy, he says, "accurate assessment was rarely possible but the Rifles had captured three hundred and buried nearly as many." On the 24th, the German 334th Division lost two hundred prisoners and withdrew, badly shaken, to the high ground north of the river.[13]

Thunder rumbled overhead, lightning flashed and the rain poured down as the sappers of the 36th Brigade repaired a demolished bridge in Pescia. Tanks were mud-bound on the morning of the 25th, so the Royal West Kents and the Argylls of the 76th Division advanced without armor for a thousand yards. The Germans had reinforced the Casamaggiore Ridge above the road running west from Castiglione del Lago to Gioiella, a village in the hills east of the Chiana Valley. Heavy enemy fire held up the Kents and Argylls short of the ridge. The 76th was ordered to consolidate its positions.

The next day, the 10th Infantry Brigade of the 4th Division (supported by Canadian tanks) resumed the attack in a flanking maneuver on Gioiella, taken after a sharp clash at midnight. The 2nd Cornwalls crossed the valley and broken ground to reach the top of the Casamaggiore Ridge under heavy fire, while the 76th's Surreys took the village. The Bedfords of the 4th Division led the atack off the ridge, heading north to the open country beyond. The 76th, in reserve, waited for a counterattack. "It never came," 78th Division historian Cyril Ray later observed, "because the whole strength of the Trasimeno position had rested, as in Hannibal's day, in the Sanfatucchio feature. Once that had gone the position was bound to crumble."[14]

The British Eighth Army had broken the back of the Trasimeno Line, taking seven hundred prisoners in eight days of savage fighting. German positions to the west were also crumbling, but the Wehrmacht had gained invaluable time. As Kesselring put it: "The fighting at Lake Trasimeno from the middle of June to the middle of July satisifed my tactical requirements."[15]

NOTES

[1] Trevelyan, *The Fortress,* p. 205.
[2] Kesselring, *A Soldier's Record,* pp. 206–207.
[3] Orpen, *Victory in Italy,* p. 83.
[4] Horsfall, *Fling Our Banner,* p. 140 and pp. 136–37.
[5] Orpen, *Victory in Italy,* pp. 88–92.
[6] Ibid., pp. 86–104.
[7] Ibid., pp. 107–109.
[8] Ibid., pp. 110–13.
[9] Ibid., pp. 114–15.
[10] Horsfall, *Fling Our Banner,* pp 142–43.
[11] Ibid., pp. 146–63.
[12] Ibid., p. 169.
[13] Ibid., pp 180–83.
[14] Ray, *Algiers to Austria,* p. 150.
[15] Kesselring, *A Soldier's Record,* p. 209.

V

AREZZO GAP

The Romans, who had a good eye for military strongpoints, chose Arezzo as a military station to serve the Via Cassia, the main highway from Latium to the mid-section of the Arno River. Arretium, as they called the city, had been one of the more important of the twelve cities of the Etruscan Confederation, long a Roman foe and subsequently an ally.

The city sits on a hill nearly a thousand feet high (971.5 ft.), overlooking the Chiana Valley to the east and south, and the Casentino, the 300-square mile elliptical basin of the Upper Arno, to the north. It is also overlooked by mountains on three sides. Although the military center was later smashed by barbarians, the old Roman layout may be traced along the curving Via Garibaldi. Home to the artist Piero della Francesca, the poet Petrarch, the playwright, pimp and talented blackmailer Aretino, the deviser of modern musical notation Guido Monaco, and before them all, Maecenas, the patron of Horace and Virgil, Arezzo was of tactical importance to the Germans and the Allies as the war north of Rome approached the Arno. Its walls, castles and Romanesque/Gothic buildings centered on a crucial road junction. Its potential as a railhead and supply base was recognized by the Allies and their foe alike.

The British "splendid advance" north of Rome had ground to a halt on June 20 in the Umbrian hills north of Perugia and some ten miles southeast of Lake Trasimeno. As XIII Corps' spearhead, the 78th Division fought up the east side of the lake, while the British X Corps made little progress in terrain well suited to the Germans' defensive needs.

On June 24, General Leese regrouped his forces for the drive on Arezzo and Florence. He withdrew the British 6th Armoured from General McCreery's X Corps to give General Kirkman's XIII added weight for its thrust towards Arezzo twenty-eight miles ahead. At daybreak on June 29, the Germans gave way along the XIII Corps' twenty-mile front as the 6th Armoured prepared to advance along the Corps' axis, Highway 71, with the 4th Division in the center on the Chiana canal and the South Africans to the west, alongside the Fifth Army's right flank.

The Germans as they withdrew took good advantage of the hilly terrain in a zone ten miles deep around Cortona and Castiglion Fiorentino east of the Chiana Valley. Rearguards and snipers among the farm buildings gave the British a bad time. The 4th and 78th Divisions gained only two or three miles a day.

Then the advance resumed, as the Germans fell back along Highway 71. British patrols entered Cortona unopposed. The British 6th Armoured on July 4 ran a gauntlet of fire from a ridge overlooking the highway from the east to Castiglion Fiorentino, a walled market town ten miles south of Arezzo. Minefields north of town stopped the tanks.

To the west and the northwest, the 4th Division crossed the Siena road and climbed the hills about Civitella della Chiana and San Pancrazio. On the right of the main thrust, the 2nd Kings took Tuori; to the left, the 6th Black Watch, with Italian partisans, fought for five hours to capture Monte Altuzzo. The Derbyshire Yeomanry crossed the Siena road near the head of the Chiana Valley, but patrols working the southwestern slopes of Monte Lignano discovered the enemy in force on the heights. The Royal West Kents stormed Al'Omo, an isolated hill at the center of the German line, which now ran along the dominating heights between Monte Castiglione Maggiore, overlooking Highway 71 from the east south of Arezzo to Castello di Brolio, some twenty miles west of the city. The enemy had the advantages of good observation and open fields of fire.

On the eve of his twenty-first birthday, July 6, Subaltern Ralph Trevelyan considered his position with a ruefulness born of his experience at Anzio, where he had been wounded by a German grenade. "I don't think even now," he noted in his diary, "I really fear death, or the process of dying. It is only the thought of whether or not I shall acquit myself honourably tomorrow or not that obsesses me."

Trevelyan had just rejoined his company of the Rifle Brigade and had been asked to lead the next day's attack on Castiglione Maggiore because he was "fresh." Spandau Ridge, his platoon's objective, was a portion of the massif just above Castiglione Fiorentino that overlooked Highway 71 from the east. As it turned out, Trevelyan was to be leader of the second wave. Little else was involved that night, he remarks, "than a stiff climb up a mountain under an aching load of weapons, picks and shovels. Our denims clammy with sweat, we hauled ourselves in single file along the valley up the side of Maggiore." The full moon limned the rocks "like strokes of crayons." The ground was rocky, and when they dug in the infantrymen had only parapets of stones for protection.

Day broke with a barrage—friendly mortar fire much too close for comfort, and enemy Spandau fire as the sun climbed in the cloudless July sky. The next night, a counterattack drove Trevelyan and his men off the crest of the ridge. Re-forming the remnants of his platoon, Trevelyan clambered back onto the crest, where the moonlight had "turned the rocks into great contorted bergs of silence." A mortar crumped behind the lines. Soon shrapnel spat all around the platoon. Trevelyan threw himself into a shallow trench where he was half buried by stones and broken pieces of rock. During a brief lull, he became aware of shouted commands and the cries of wounded—in German.

The company had withdrawn, and he and his men were caught in a counter-barrage. The only thing left was to make a run for it. When the next lull came, Trevelyan jumped up and "the whole world cracked open in a sheet of flames. There was a noise like a dinner gong ringing inside my head. My face was all stocky and hot liquid streamed into my eyes. . . . staggered downhill, my left arm felt numb and loose—I was quite unable to lift it when I tried to wipe my eyes." He reached battalion headquarters with the support of two men. "Everything was swimming, slipping; high up on Maggiore I could just hear the first bursts of automatic firing."[1] Maggiore was finally secured a day or two later.

XIII Corps had not quite appreciated the strength of the German positions around Arezzo. At the center of the front, intelligence reports indicated that the German 15th Panzer Grenadier and 1st Parachute Divisions had been reinforced, as had the Herman Goering Division to the west. The 305th Infantry Division with a battle group of the 9th held Monte Lignano and the mountains to the east. From the left front, to the west, where South African tanks had ground to a halt in the Chiantian hills, to the steep sides of Lignano and Maggiore, where British infantrymen held precarious ground in the face of fierce counterattacks, the entire British advance slowed to a stop during the first week of July. British tanks reached a point about a mile south of the junction of Highways 71 and 73, but could get no closer to Arezzo, only three miles away. XIII Corps had drawn ahead of X Corps, leaving its right flank—a mountainous area without roads—exposed. The King's Dragoon Guards and the 1st/60th Rifles were withdrawn from the 9th Armoured Brigade, attached to X Corps, to form a flank guard, Sackforce.

X Corps had been slowed by German resistance in the difficult country north of Perugia, where only infantry could be deployed. For a week after the fall of the city on June 20, the 6th Armoured—then with X Corps—and the 8th Indian Division attempted to break through the German lines—to no avail. After the 27th, when German lines west of Lake Trasimeno crumbled, the enemy began to fall back along the banks of the Tiber. The 10th Indian Division relieved the 6th and 8th Divisions to take up the pursuit of the withdrawing Wehrmacht.

Two roads, one on each side of the river, run north through the mile-wide Tiber Valley. Market towns had grown up around old castle sites and fortifications that were usually on a bend or a loop of the river every ten miles or so. High on the ridges and saddlebacks, tiny villages clustered around churches whose towers offered observation over miles of country-side. Spread out over a fourteen-mile front east of the Tiber and another ten miles to the west, more than halfway to Lake Trasimeno, the Tenth Indian Division was assigned the 3rd Hussars, 12th Lancers, King's Dragoon Guards and troops of the Royal Horse Artillery.

The Division's advance began on July 1 against light opposition; still, it was heavy going. The troops worked against the grain of the ground. As the divisional historian put it: "Uphill, downhill, ford a stream, uphill, downhill, ford again."[2] Along the Tiber, the King's Own and the Punjabis cleared a number of villages, brushing aside snipers and rearguards in the surrounding woods and orchards. By July 2, the Indians were within reach of the enemy's first layback positions, ten miles north of Perugia on Monte Corona, a thickly wooded pinnacle, and Monte Acuto, a bald-pated sugarloaf.

A long night march surprised the Germans, who, on the morning of the 3rd, threw back the Baluchi company that had seized Acuto. The Gurkhas held the crest of Corona in the face of a similar attack. The capture of Cortona, west of Trasimeno, threatened to trap the enemy on the Indian front. The Germans hastily withdrew, pausing seven miles north on the River Nestore. This disengagement marked the end of easy going for the 10th Indian Division.

On the night of July 2, the King's Own tangled with the Germans in a little village of Pierantonio at a cost of 3 officers and 33 men, of whom

12 were killed. The village, perched at a junction of the many lateral valleys east of the Tiber, was taken the next day after a concealed approach
march from the west. Umbertide, a sprawling factory town of yellow-and-
gray-walled house a few miles to the north, was left undefended by the
Germans. A Punjab patrol pushed on and encountered the enemy at
Montone, five miles to the north, on a peak above the Tiber Valley.

The village and a north-running ridge were held by a battalion of the
114th Jaeger Division. Sikhs and Mussulman infantrymen battled across
the open countryside in the afternoon heat and up the open southern
spur to the village. From the rear, the King's Own charged with bayonets
from the hillside above Montone. They had encircled the town the night
before in a twelve-mile night march across the ridges and ravines that
characterize the terrain east of the Tiber. The Jaegers, however, did not
quit, and it took several hours of street fighting to dislodge the enemy.
Twenty Germans were killed, sixty-five prisoners taken. The British suffered nineteen casualties.

On July 8, the 4th Indian Division assumed the 10th Indian
Division's responsibilities west of the Tiber, north of Umbertide. It was
the 4th's task to force a way over the mountains to XIII Corps' front
below Arezzo. Meanwhile, on the right, the 12th Lancers pushed far into
the mountains until they were some twenty miles from the Adriatic. Two
mobile columns, formed on July 2, continued this advance on to Gubbio
and Fabriano. The 4th Indians' two forward brigades quickly established
a four-mile front along the Nestore, which fed the Tiber from the west. A
Gurkhas patrol commanded by Jemadar Pirthilal drew first blood when it
attacked, with kukris (curved foot-long knives) drawn, an enemy observation post on an isolated knoll. Six Germans were killed and one prisoner taken at the cost of one broken nose.

The Gurkhas crossed the Nestore under the bright light of the moon,
on the night of June 10 and gained the 2,500-foot summit of Monte
Civitella. The Royal Sikhs swung west and climbed a narrow, steep,
wooded spur that rose 2,000 feet in less than 3,000 yards. The next morn-
ing, they turned farther west to storm Monte Pagliaiola. Sepoy Kartar
Singh single-handedly destroyed three machine-gun positions, killing five
Germans before falling fatally wounded. He was awarded a posthumous
IOM. Another company of Sikhs pushed on to take 3,500-foot Monte
Favalto. Its crest overlooked Palazzo di Pero in a loop of Highway 73,
which runs at that point between Arezzo and Sansepolcro, skirting the

massive Poti Alps. In Indian hands, this would pose a serious threat to the Germans in Arezzo from an unexpected direction.

Before mounting an assault on the Potis, it was essential to strengthen the 4th Division line to the east. On July 11, the Gurkhas crossed Troppo Ridge and explored the valley of the Aggia, a stream two miles north of the Nestore. Tanks in support bogged down in the soft gravel of the stream bed. The infantry continued on to the Monte Santa Maria Tibernia Ridge, east of high Favalto. A German counterattack on the night of July 9–10 at a cost of 25 casualties failed to oust the hillmen.

Santa Maria Tibernia was a picturesque walled village perched farther east on an isolated pinnacle overlooking the Tiber Valley. Divisional artillery laid down heavy fire that wreathed the village in smoke. Under its cover, the Royal Sussex passed through the Gurkhas to encounter brisk resistance. Company A lost its company commander, Major D.H. Brand, said to have been "a gallant officer with a fine fighting record." The Germans then withdrew and a patrol was sent forward to the northeast to seize Monte Cedrone, a lookout which blocked the advance of the 10th Brigade along the west bank of the Tiber below.

German counterattacks at dusk on July 13 were repulsed, but the Royal Sussex platoon on Cedrone was withdrawn—its position was deemed precarious. Meanwhile, on the east bank of the Tiber, the Punjabis advanced through continuous harassing fire from German mortars hidden in the numerous ravines in the hills overlooking the river. Promano, above an eastward bend of the Tiber, was taken.

The next hamlet, Santa Lucia, was part of a defensive line hinged on the massive Monte della Gorgacce to the east. While two companies circled the mountain position, another made a feinting attack along the only track leading to the ridge. Deceived, the enemy on Della Gorgacce broke when the rush of attackers came from an unanticipated direction. The Baluchis mounted an attack on Monte Cedrone from the southwest at 0200 on July 15. Heavy and accurate defensive fire caught the infantrymen just after they crossed their starting line. Mule trains stampeded in the darkness, dragging and tossing their handlers in all directions. The Baluchis were recalled. But the next day, the Durhams had the good fortune to assault Cedrone as the Germans were undertaking a relief.

By then, the 4th Indian Division held a more or less stable line from Monte Cedrone to Monte Favalto. From Monte Civitella, they could observe German traffic east and west on Route 73 along the Cerrone

Torrent, between Arezzo and the Tiber Valley. While German movement was subjected to harassing fire, the Indians faced the problem of crossing the valley of the Cerrone and attacking the towering crests of the Poti Alps ridges, seven miles to the northwest of the Indian line and five east of Arezzo. To their immediate front was an obstacle course that would have daunted Hercules: wooded razor-backed ridges, deep clefts, and a boulder-strewn valley. With the aid of a spotter plane, a line was drawn on the map that defied common sense. It was estimated that it would take ten days to construct a primitive roadway over that terrain.

The work began on the morning of July 14, when, as a unit history put it, "a cross-section of the United Nations had assembled in this wild spot."[3]

Central India Horse provided cover. Italian labor companies cut the undergrowth and plied pick and shovel. Canadian explosive squads blasted boulders and rocky outcrops. British sappers bulldozed a rough track. Bombay and Madras sappers and miners completed the roadway. In 28 hours, Jacob's Ladder was open from Monte Dogana on the left of Favalto to within two miles of Palazzo del Pero, the closest spot on Highway 73. Before the job was finished, Major Patterson and Lieutenant Murray of Central India Horse drove over the two remaining miles to Palazzo di Pero on collapsible parachutist motorcycles. They arrived in time to greet a New Zealand armored car entering the town from the west.

XIII Corps' advance had stalled at the Arezzo Gap, a defile less than three miles from the city where Route 71, running north from Cortona to the valley of the Upper Arno meets Route 73, the Arezzo–Siena–Sansepolcro highway. The British 6th Armoured gained a foothold on Monte Lignano and Monte Castiglion Maggiore south of Arezzo and east of 71, but they were unable to clear the enemy from the crests. The 4th Division and the South African 6th Armoured could make only very little progress through the hills west of the Chiana Valley to the part of the Arno that ran west of Arezzo. Further, XIII Corps' right flank was exposed, though the Indians were closing in and had taken Monte Favalto on the 13th. The Xth Corps, however, was not in a position to undertake an assault on Arezzo unless its projected attack on Sansepolcro was abandoned, or the weary 8th Indian Division was recalled to the front. The 2nd New Zealand Division was ordered forward to open the Arezzo Gap.

Four days were needed to move the New Zealanders two hundred miles from a rest area in the Liri Valley to the front. It was, a battalion history records, "a rough and dusty journey through a countryside much like New Zealand, with fences and with reapers and binders working on the farms." The men were awed by the damage, however. As B.C.H Moss noted in his diary, at a railway station, "a whole concentration of loco-motives and railway rolling stock had been beaten up by the RAF. Numerous craters were squarely in the middle of the track and the rails were bent back like baling wire. . . . One or two [locomotives] had been ripped open like tin cans. . . . Most of the coaches and trucks were burnt out while others were shattered by the explosion of their contents." As the New Zealanders closed in on Arezzo, the country became a good deal more rugged, with peaks rising 2,500 to 2,800 feet. Grape vines and olive trees flourished on the lower slopes, an occasional line of elegant cypresses giving way to ash trees higher up.[4]

Intelligence reports indicated that the 15th Panzer Grenadier—its 115th Regiment held the western slopes of Monte Lignano—and 1st Parachute Divisions in the center had been reinforced. The German Tenth Army gave orders that the 305th Division was to hold firm on Monte Lignano while the balance of its units (reinforced by troops from the 94th Infantry Division) occupied a front over a stretch of mountains running southeastwards. As the New Zealanders traveled north, the Royal Artillery bombarded the German lines, and the RAF made an average of a hundred sorties a day. The task of the New Zealanders was to clear and occupy the heights from Monte Catiglione Maggiore to Monte Lignano while the 4th British and 6th South African Armoured Divisions on the left, west of the Chiana Canal, diverted attention by gunfire and active patrolling.

The capture of Monte Favalto by the Indians endangered the German left flank. General Herr, commander of the 76th Corps, told the Tenth Army that the 305th's troops on the left were "in an untenable position, and must draw back and lose control of the commanding heights. That may mean that the Corps cannot hold on for long in the rest of the sector"[5]—which included Lignano. The Division thinned out its endangered salient on the night of July 12–13 and abandoned Monte Castiglione Maggiore, its southern tip, altogether. The New Zealand 26th Battalion that night relieved the Argyll and Sutherland Highlanders on the lower slopes of Monte Maggiore.

On the right, an Italian reconnaissance force occupied the high ground to prevent enemy infiltration from the east. At dawn, a three-man patrol climbed the mountain and found it unoccupied. The patrol pushed along a high saddle to Poggio Cavadenti, also unoccupied. The day passed quietly, the New Zealanders occupying the crest of Castiglione Maggiore. In the evening, two platoons were sent to occupy Cavadenti and met an enemy patrol. Surprise, says the battalion historian, "was mutual but the New Zealanders were the first to recover." One German was killed, three taken prisoner; two escapees were believed wounded. The platoons dug in; they were hit by heavy mortar fire during the night, but shelling eased off towards morning. Only one man was hit.

The 26th Battalion accomplished its mission with little difficulty. The next day, when C Company moved to occupy Monte Opino, with peaks about two miles north, it was fired upon, but artillery fire brought to bear drove off the enemy. While the company was digging in that evening on the nearer peak, the Germans counterattacked and forced one platoon to withdraw 80 yards. The other two remained in position. When the artillery forward observer called for fire, the rounds fell short, causing four casualties, including two killed. However, the Germans failed to press their advantage. On the 15th, the situation remained unchanged. A B Company patrol sent northwest of Cavadenti just before dawn tripped over a machine-gun nest. Patrol leader Corporal Brick opened fire, killing one German. Two others of the enemy were wounded and taken prisoner. But other German machine guns opened up. Private W. Parker lobbed grenades at one while his comrades provided covering fire. Driving the prisoners ahead, the patrol raced downhill and across the open ground back to Monte Cavadenti.

While the 26th Battalion was occupied in taking Monte Castiglione Maggiore and the neighboring high ground, the 24th and the 25th Battalions were to clear Monte Camurcina and Monte Lignano. An advance platoon of the 24th was told that Colle de Luca, one of Camurcina's two peaks, was either unoccupied or lightly held. At dawn, July 14, Second Lieutenant K.S. Crawshaw's platoon set out to discover whether this was so.

Two hundred yards from the summit, the lead scout was fired upon. Crawshaw ordered his two leading sections to encircle the enemy, but they were pinned down along with the reserve section, which attempted to assist. Company C sent forward another platoon but it came under fire and withdrew down the ridge. Crawshaw's men beat off an enemy attack but lost two killed, five wounded. They then withdrew at the cost of three more killed and one wounded. The two platoons consolidated their positions below Colle de Luca the rest of the day.

Meanwhile, the 25th Battalion had relieved the King's Royal Rifles a few hundred yards southwest of the crest of Monte Lignano. The Rifles had been "pretty badly knocked about," according to Private J.M. Shinnick of the New Zealanders. "[T]wice Jerry had got amongst them with patrols while his continuous mortaring took a heavy toll, for the positions, held as they were in a thick plantation of pines, were subjected to a type of low air-burst as the falling bombs exploded on contact with the branches. They had lost over 50 percent casualties in four days."[6] The New Zealanders were understandably anxious to get on with their attack. Zero hour was set for 0100 on July 15, when the artillery barrage opened up after a thunderstorm.

C Company moved off first, 40 minutes later, followed at ten-minute intervals by A and D, working up a narrow ridge. "The terrain was such that the start line could only be reached by scrambling on hands and knees in single file," Shinnick recalled. The artillery had been cautioned, because of the precipitous terrain, "[C]are will be taken in computing correct Angle of Sight for individual guns during fire plan."

C Company was held up by supporting shellfire. "We . . . commenced to move forward up the steep face of the feature," Shinnick's account continues. "It was terribly rocky and often it was a case of helping one another over the obstacles. . . . [A] few [shells] came over . . . causing no casualties though often the blast knocked us flat to the ground. First opposition was from a Jerry fox-hole, but we silenced it and pressed on over the rocky terrain until we encountered the next opposition. Another Jerry strong point was left in silence. . . . We made the crest on which was a very badly shattered building and we occupied it. . . . Prisoners were now being taken. . . . We wirelessed back that the position had been taken and to lift the barrage but it continued to whittle away at what poor protection we had."[7]

A Company encountered little opposition. Two or three machine-gun posts were wiped out. Platoon Lieutenant Liddell reported that "[e]nemy resistance was not strong after artillery stonk. Several badly laid Teller mines . . . no casualties as wires were too slack." D Company passed through A Company and on to its objective, a ridge running westward of the main peak, and was held up for a time but was in position by morning. By daybreak on the 15th, the New Zealanders held Monte Lignano.

Their casualties in the Battle of Arezzo totaled 116, including 37 killed. During the day they were mortared and shelled by the enemy. Between 1300 and 2140, there were also six reports of friendly supporting fire hitting the forward companies. A Battalion report gives 14 such instances, which caused 16 casualties, including two men killed. The other two New Zealand battalions also complained of "short-shooting." When the 24th moved up to finally clear Monte Camurcina in the early morning on July 16, it experienced little difficulty. In a supporting attack to its right, B Company of the 26th found hilltop 844 deserted. But just as it wirelessed success, the lead platoon reported being shelled by 25-pounders. The firing ceased after frantic messages reached the artillery—but not before two men had been killed (one, "Cpl. Fred Tyson, a popular NCO who had done so well at Cassino"[8]) and one wounded.

At 0930 on the 15th, the Chief of Staff, Tenth Army, told the Chief of Staff, 75th Panzer Corps: "We must accept the loss of M. Lignano. . . . The withdrawal to the next line will take two days. A strong rearguard immediately north of Arezzo will hold on for a day." The Army Commander then explained what had happened to the Army Group: "This penetration on 15 Pz. Gren Div.'s left, which has led to the loss of Lignano, was caused by a strong attack with a purely limited objective. I don't like it because the enemy shelling is so heavy down there that I don't want to mount a counterattack, which would be very costly. On the other hand, from Lignano the enemy can see right to Arezzo. That is a point in favour of . . . [the] plan to withdraw."[9]

The British 26th Armoured Brigade drove through the Arezzo Gap on the morning of the 16th and occupied the city. During the remainder of the day, British and New Zealand troops dashed along west and northwest roads and crossed the Arno where it flows west before turning northwest towards Florence. The Indians took the high peaks of the Poti Alps on July 17. The battle for Arezzo was over. The city would soon serve as the Eighth Army's administrative center and as a roadhead for operations in the Northern Apennines—from which a force of some thirteen divisions could be sustained.

But Kesselring had gained ten more days for bolstering the Gothic Line at a relatively low cost. XIII Corps netted only 165 prisoners during the ten-day battle.

NOTES

[1] Trevelyan, *The Fortress,* pp. 196–210.
[2] India, Defence Dept., *The Tiger Triumphs,* p. 86.
[3] Ibid., p. 107.
[4] Kay, *From Cassino to Trieste,* p. 100–102.
[5] Ibid., p. 103.
[6] Puttick, *25 Battalion,* p. 449.
[7] Ibid., p. 455.
[8] Norton, *26 Battalion.* p. 414.
[9] Puttick, *25 Battalion,* pp. 458–59.

VI

THIS SUMMER BATTLE

"In this summer battle," General Frido von Senger later recalled of the fighting in Tuscany, "I was torn between the grim prospect of defeat and the sheer beauty of my surroundings." To reach his divisions fighting desperate rearguard actions as they fell back from the Ombrone to the Cecina, the XIV Panzer Corps commander had to move at night and by a roundabout route through the towns of Volterra and Siena. One night the car carrying his Chief of Staff, Colonel Schmidt von Altenstadt, crashed. The Colonel's lacerated muscles required treatment in Germany (where he died of thrombosis the day before his discharge from the hospital). "My staff of Cassino days was no more," Von Senger lamented. Then, more lamentable, his son Ferdinand was wounded for the eighth time, gangrene developed and the young man's arm had to be amputated.

When he passed through Siena, Von Senger sought a few moments of relief from the vicissitudes of war in the charms of this 14th-century city. He regretted the inaccessibility of the Trecento paintings—hidden away for the duration—but found some contentment in "the wonderful freshness" of the Pinturicchios in the Cathedral Library. "The moment for the final gathering of the rearguards," however, could not be delayed for "the nearer the XIV Panzer Corps came to the Arno, the fiercer was the fighting."

Von Senger hoped that he could put up a delaying defense along the Cecina River, which flows some fifteen miles west, from just below Volterra to the Tyrrhenian coast. The terrain in the sector was so-so for defensive purposes. The hills to the north, however, afforded the Germans an extensive view of the country to the south as well as cover for the German rear. The wooded crests and the orchards and vineyards on the seaward slopes were in full leaf, and provided XIV Corps with concealment. The withdrawal of significant elements of the Allied air force for the invasion of southern France also was, in Von Senger's phrase, "a considerable relief to us." Moreover, some of the low-lying areas north of the Cecina were sufficiently open for armored operations.

In the wooded country south of Volterra, the monster Tiger tanks could only operate on the roads, of course—and Italian partisans succeeded in blowing up bridges and erecting effective barriers of hastily felled trees. An immobilized Tiger could only be hauled out of danger by another Tiger. Even slightly damaged tanks were lost under these conditions.

Von Senger, an experienced tank commander, protested in vain against the squandering of irreplaceable armor. Though the Wehrmacht infantry, defeated and demoralized, considered tank support indispensable, it did not, according to Von Senger, enjoy close cooperation with the tankers, who often gave up the fight for inadequate reasons and became immobilized for minor technical faults. As a consequence, the German infantry and tanks acted independently. South of the Cecina, Von Senger observed, "the losses among our ranks were painfully high." One day, late in June, on the heights north of the Cecina, he saw for himself "how at a distance of two kilometers ahead of and below me dozens of enemy tanks were preparing to attack."[1]

General Mark Clark characterized the post-Rome phase of the Italian campaign as "a very fluid period which did not present any definite pattern other than a pursuit to the Arno River." There was plenty of stiff fighting, as Clark observed, but there were no large battles such as those that preceded the fall of Rome at Anzio, Cassino and among the Alban Hills.[2] The Fifth Army's briefing called for a vigorous advance on Leghorn (Livorno), the last remaining port on the Tyrrhenian coast.

Above Grosseto the coastline runs northwesterly and the Fifth Army's IV Corps front broadened, allowing room for the deployment of two full divisions. Corps commander General Willis D. Crittenberger believed with good reason that the Germans would concentrate on defense of the coastal plain while relying on the rugged Tuscan Hills inland to slow down the Allied advance in the interior. Crittenberger decided that armor could force the Wehrmacht back through the hills, freeing the coastal corridor of German observation and of flanking artillery fire. Once the hills were cleared, coastal Highway 1 would be open for a dash to Leghorn.

General Harmon of the 1st Armored was not happy with his assignment and protested that hill country was no place for tanks—a sentiment shared by General von Senger. Unlike the rolling hills south of Viterbo, where the 1st Armored had scored a stunning success, the Tuscan Hills were filled with steep-sided ridges ranging from 1,500 to 2,000 feet in height. There were no first-class roads and few second-rate ones, and there was a jumble of trails and footpaths. Roads twisted through narrow defiles and S-curved up and down the heights. Masonry houses lined narrow streets in the towns and villages scarcely a step away from narrow door-ways. There was little room for maneuver for more than a tank or two at a time. Opportunities for delay by enemy demolition, therefore, abounded. It was, as 1st Armored historian George F. Howe put it, terrain "as difficult as any ever faced by an American armored division."[3]

Nonetheless, Harmon tackled the task with his customary zest. The 361st Infantry (less one battalion) was assigned to the 1st Armored's Combat Command A. This was the first contingent committed to combat from the 91st Division then arriving in Italy. They had participated with the 36th Division in the drive north of Tarquinia to Grosseto and Roccastrada, but had little experience working with tanks. On June 22, Harmon committed Combat Command A on the right, along secondary roads running roughly north–northeast of Grosseto through Roccastrada, Torniella, Chiudino and to Highway 68 along the Cecina south of San Gimignano. To the left, some 18 miles from the coast, Combat Command B with the 6th Armored Infantry Regiment (less one battalion) worked its way north along a secondary road through Massa Marittima, Pomerance and the Cecina slightly west and south of Volterra. Tanks and infantry worked in small task forces to achieve flexibility and mobility. But American hopes for a fast-forward offensive were frustrated by the German response.

Fourteenth Army commander General Lemelsen beefed up XIV Panzer Corps with all available reserves. The 1st Armored combat commands had hardly begun to roll when General Harmon decided he needed more power. In the early afternoon of the first day, he committed Task Force Howze from his reserves to the center. Colonel Howze's troops made the best gain of the day—five miles towards the hilltown Montieri. Antitank fire to the right slowed Combat Command A to an advance of two miles, while Combat Command B made even less progress after suffering heavy losses from an enemy ambush south of Massa Marittima.

The enemy exploited the terrain with considerable skill. Highway

73, the main axis of advance for Combat Command A, crosses the Farma River about three-quarters of a mile northwest of the village of Torniella. The enemy demolished the bridges there, and, as the approaches are too steep and the water too deep for tanks, Combat Command A's advance came to a halt on June 24 under heavy fire. The enemy also held the hill-town Scalvaia, overlooking the river from the northeast. 361st infantry-men waded the river and secured the high ground on the other side. But before the engineers could build a bypass and the tanks could move, the Germans had to be cleared from Scalvaia.

When Company C of the 361st advanced on Scalvaia the next morn-ing, the Germans allowed the forward platoons to pass and then attacked the weapons platoon in the rear. When the company withdrew, seven wounded men were left in no-man's-land, with little cover.

Company medic Bruce K. Turner crawled through intense fire to administer first aid. He made his way from one man to another and, as he reached the last one, he came face to face with a German—who ordered him to raise his hands. Turner pointed to his medical brassard and continued to dress the wounded man's wounds. Fortunately for Turner, a burst from a machine gun sent the German to cover. The American moved the wounded man to a ditch and remained with him for the rest of the day under machine-gun, rifle and mortar fire. After dark, he returned to the American lines and led litter squads to pick up the wounded.[4]

The next day the 361st cleared Scalvaia and Combat Command A resumed its advance. By then, the 1st Armored managed an average advance of five miles a day over the next four days. Infantrymen cleared the enemy from around blown-up bridges and roadblocks. Engineers then followed, as did tanks, on the alert to knock out machine-gun nests and enemy armored vehicles. (The record of the 16th Armored Engineer Battalion points up the importance of engineers to successful combat in difficult terrain.) The battalion swept more than 500 miles of road for mines, disarming two new types; then it bulldozed through the rubble of eleven towns, improved eight fords, repaired twelve bridges, constructed 37 steel treadway bridges and built or graded some 150 miles of bypasses. Tankdozers, new to Italy, proved to be of enormous value to the advanc-ing troops.

Though the Germans exploited the terrain with great skill, their tanks, too, were inhibited. Moving northeast out of Prata towards

Montieri, a Task Force Howze column was held up by a German tank around one of the many bends in the road. Colonel Howze climbed a nearby hill to get a look at the enemy. Gazing through a pair of captured German field glasses, he later wrote, "I thought I could reach out and pat it [at a distance of 200 yards and 30 feet below]. I swung my vision left along the road and there, looking like another beached 10,000-ton cruiser, was a second Tiger. Both of these creatures had their guns leveled directly at the bend of the road where it rounded the nose [on which Howze stood]. And in the turret of each stood the tank commander, visible from the waist up, and clad in the black German tankers' uniform."

While he expected the Tigers to swing their guns—"I watched [them] with all the happy anticipation with which a bird watches a cobra"— and blow him off the hill, Howze gave orders for an attack. The infantry platoon moved onto the high ground flanking the tanks; when the lead M10 Tank Destroyer heard the infantry open up, it was to wait thirty seconds, then dash forward around the bend and paste the first Tiger. The medium-tank platoon would follow and engage any visible target. A bazooka gunner on the hilltop with Howze would fire, on his order, and cue the infantry to open fire. The lead German tank commander, Howze recalled, "seemed suspicious," frequently scanning the woods to his left through his binoculars. At one point he appeared to fix his glasses on Howze and "we seemed to stare fixedly at one another for a long half-minute."

The bazooka gunner scored a direct hit on the front plate of the Tiger—a remarkable shot at 200 yards. The projectile did not penetrate the buttoned-down tank, but it must have shaken up the crew, for its movements became lumbering and awkward as it tried to get out of the ditch and onto the hardtop. Though the infantry opened up, the TD did not move until Howze scrambled off the hill and ordered it forward. While the lead Tiger was hit repeatedly, nothing penetrated its armor. The crew panicked, however, and was cut down by the infantry when they tried to escape.

Lieutenant Carl Key tried to head off the second Tiger, but a group of buildings—including a hanger-like warehouse with doors open at both ends—obscured his vision. Key, however, could see a stretch of the road over which the tank had to retreat if it were to escape through the shed. He cut loose with a couple of rounds, raising a cloud of dust in the shed and an astounding racket. He then did some blind shooting. When the dust settled, he saw that the tank had fled. Howze's troopers found another abandoned Tiger the next morning; it had thrown its track in the mud as the result of two bogies that may have been hit by Key's blind firing. Still, as Howze readily acknowledged, who could be certain?[5]

And so it went as June drew to a close. Combat Command B rolled inexorably north, taking Gerfalco, Monterotondo, Fosini, Castelnuovo and Pomerance. The tanks passed through the valley of the Lardarello, where the Germans had blown gaps in the pipes used to carry volcanic steam to surface electric-power plants. The escaping steam made the area sound like one of Dante's regions of hell.

The Command crossed the Cecina north of Pomerance on July 1 and seized the high ground north of lateral Highway 68 and four miles southeast of Volterra. On CCB's right, Task Force Howze was held up by enemy artillery fire at Mazzola and troops reinforced by the 90th Panzer Grenadiers. Harmon had to commit the last of his reserves to dislodge the enemy, who yielded after throwing back seven separate assaults. Seven miles to the southeast of Howze, Combat Command A tackled fortified Casole d'Elsa. It took four days of bitter fighting, numerous casualties and the loss of six medium tanks, three light tanks and two tank destroyers to capture the town on July 4.

Though the thrust of the 1st Armored denied the enemy the use of Highway 68, its position under the frowning heights to the north around Volterra was precarious. Nonetheless, the exhausted tankers, armored infantry and the troops of the 361st Regiment held their ground until relieved by the 88th Division. During its three weeks' advance from Grosseto, the 1st Armored had suffered heavy losses in equipment, including seventy medium and light tanks, but it had destroyed fifty German tanks, including thirty Mark VIs

Crittenberger's hope that the 1st Armored Division's operations in the Tuscan Hills would threaten the German coastal flank and prompt a withdrawal was only partially realized. The Germans did fall back initially along the coastal corridor above Piombino, towards the Cecina and lateral Route 68. But Kesselring also beefed up the defending XIV Panzer Corps under Von Senger with the newly arrived 16th SS Panzer Grenadier and the 19th Luftwaffe Field Divisions. General Charles W. Ryder's 34th Division, reinforced by the Japanese-American 442nd Combat Team, relieved the 36th northeast of Piombino on June 26.

In Bill Mauldin's descriptive phrase a "grizzled outfit," the Red Bulls had been the first American division to go overseas in World War II. It was originally a National Guard outfit drawing men from the central states of Iowa, North Dakota, South Dakota and Minnesota. By the time it entered the line north of Rome, however, having lost men on the beaches, deserts and mountains of North Africa at Gafsa, Faid Pass, Kasserine, Sidi Bou Zid, on the beach at Salerno, crossing the Volturno, along the canals of Anzio-Nettuno and in the breakthrough to Cisterna, it was an All-American division, drawing replacements from all the U.S. states and territories. In the end, the 34th logged more combat time than any other division in Europe. Yet, as Mauldin pointed out, ". . . it never got much publicity because it was seldom involved in glamorous affairs such as taking a major city or disastrous ones such as the Rapido River crossing, which decimated the 36th at Cassino." The 34th was, as Mauldin summed it up, "a classic footslogger division. Every company had four or five characters who had managed to survive from the beginning . . . mostly Joe and Willie types."[6]

With the 133rd Infantry on the left, astride Highway 1, the 442nd Combat Team in the center and the 168th Infantry on the right, the Red Bulls attacked on June 27 and moved to within 15 miles of Route 6—a gain of some six and a half miles. The 133rd Infantry captured San Vincenzo, where Highway 1 borders the coastal village's long beach, and crossed the Bolgheri River; on the third day it approached the Cecina. The 168th, preceded by a superbly accurate barrage laid down by the 175th Field Artillery, took hill after hill to capture Monteverdi on June 28. The footsloggers then entered Bibbona, with its panoramic view of the coast, and joined the 34th Reconnaissance troops in Montescudaio, which overlooks the Cecina inland, some eight miles east of the river mouth. Intense enemy fire disrupted an attempted crossing of the Cecina, which succeeded when maps and overlays disclosing enemy deployment were discovered on a prisoner.

The Nisei 442nd meanwhile advanced on Suvereto, a walled town rising some 300 feet to dominate the flat country running to the sea, only to be held up by fierce resistance just before noon of the first day. F Company's commander ordered his mortar squad to take out a particularly bothersome German gun, but the terrain afforded no cover. Gunner Pfc. Kiyoshi K. Muranaga volunteered to man his mortar alone. His third round landed directly in front of the German gun position. Before he could fire again, the enemy gun crew scored a direct hit, killing Muranaga instantly.

However, Muranaga's accuracy apparently unnerved the Germans, who withdrew. The 442nd then renewed its attack on Suvereto, but was unable to move beyond the town in the face of enemy fire from the village of Belvedere to the north, some 400 feet above Suvereto. Scouts in the command car preceding General Ryder—who was on a personal reconnaissance up the road west of Belvedere—were ambushed and captured. Ryder and his aides hit the ditches alongside the road and crawled back to the third scout car.

Lieutenant Colonel Gordon Singles, commander of the veteran 100th Battalion, was ordered to infiltrate the enemy's position and attack Belvedere. He had no time for reconnaissance, so he and his company commanders huddled over their maps and worked out plans for the attack. He decided to push off in a line of companies with B and A flanking the fortified village to the east and C in reserve. B Company reached a high point to the northeast that the enemy had neglected to cover, and the 1st platoon seized Belvedere after some sharp house-to-house fighting.

A Company now began a sweep north along the main road to Sassetta while B Company's 3rd Platoon captured a German company command post in a house on the secondary road running northeast. As the platoon consolidated, a Mark IV opened up from a nearby olive grove. A bazooka team worked its way forward to within thirty yards of the tank under the covering fire from Pfc. Henry Y. Nakamura's BAR. Taneyoshi Nakano scored a direct hit with his first bazooka shot, blowing up the tank and killing its crew. The tank explosion also killed bazooka squad leader, Staff Sergeant Grover N. Nagaji and stunned gunner Nakano.

The 2nd and 3rd Battalions advanced under a curtain of mortar fire and drove the remaining enemy into the guns of the waiting 100th. The 442nd suffered only one dead and eight wounded in the attack on Belvedere, while the enemy lost 17 killed, 20 known wounded, 86 captured. The Nisei also captured 8 trucks, 19 jeeps, 13 motorcycles, two antitank guns, 3 self-propelled guns, two tanks, two command cars, 2 halftracks, one 81mm mortar, and one battalion and one company command post. The 442nd seized Sasseta six miles to the north the next day, pushing on another six or seven miles through Castagnetto to the Bolgheri River, where it was relieved by the 135th Infantry on June 29.[7]

When General Ryder decided to commit his reserve, he ordered the 135th Infantry to swing east to envelop the enemy's defenses along the coast south of Cecina. The river, at that time of the year, was scarcely more than a trickle, easily fordable in most places. But the high ground overlooking the 135th's sector—four miles east of the coastal highway— was held by the outstanding 26th Panzer Division. On June 30, at dawn, Company E crossed the river; but when the battalion sought to reinforce the bridgehead, heavy fire from the high ground pinned the men down. Another attempt was repulsed with the loss of nine Sherman tanks.

The two surviving tanks withdrew to the south bank, leaving the infantry huddling in its foxholes through the long day. The next morning, on July 2, air and artillery support paved the way for a crossing by the entire regiment. By nightfall, the 135th had begun to expand the bridgehead.

Cecina is that anomaly of Italy, a modern city founded halfway through the last century when land reclamation made it possible to reoccupy an area that had been marsh since the Middle Ages. Though the area had been drained, it was still interlaced with small canals and ditches, as well as covered with olive groves, vineyards and open fields.

Von Senger believed that "any prospect of prolonged resistance on this line was illusory."[8] Nonetheless, the Germans were determined to hold Cecina and block the Americans from Leghorn as long as possible. A regiment of the tough 16th SS Panzer Grenadier Division—the Reichs-führer SS—and elements of the 19th Luftwaffe Field Division bracketed Highway 1 as it entered the city and crossed the river. The 133rd Infantry had made its way to within two miles of the city without serious difficulty.

In the late afternoon of June 29, the 3rd Battalion was held up by fire from small arms and self-propelled guns and a counterattack from west of the highway. Shortly before midnight, Company K led the battalion's dash up the road but was caught in an ambush among the orchards and vineyards and was badly cut up. The 3rd Battalion attack was renewed at daybreak the next day with the support of a platoon of tanks.

Engineers calmly cleared a profusion of mines. The Red Bulls were within 300 yards of Cecina when a counterattack almost succeeded in cutting the lead company off from the rest of the outfit. As it was, Company I had to back up a mile down the road. The 2nd Battalion had been halted by the enemy about a mile to the southeast of the city. Colonel William Schildroth then committed his reserve, and for three hours the 1st Battalion inched its way forward northwest between the other two blocked battalions. Six enemy guns were captured, but the attackers failed to dislodge the Germans from their positions.

At 0300, the 133rd renewed its attack, the 2nd Battalion driving north and the 1st moving northwest across the 3rd Battalion front. Although the Germans were preparing for a withdrawal the next day, they put up a stiff fight. By morning, the 2nd Battalion cracked through the 19th Luftwaffe's positions to reach the river on the 133rd's right flank. Tanks and infantry wheeled west and entered the eastern outskirts of Cecina and at the end of the day occupied most of the city. Five Mark VI tanks and an infantry platoon counterattacked but were beaten off. Cecina was secured. South of the town, enemy rearguards resisted stubbornly for most of the day, holding the 1st Battalion to within 500 yards of Cecina. By evening, however, the worst was over and the 1st and 3rd Battalions made their way through minefields to the river.

Cecina was one of the costliest battles fought by the Americans between Rome and the Po Valley. The 133rd lost 16 officers and 388 men killed, wounded or missing in action. With its beachheads north of the Cecina secured, the 34th Division was now ready for its final drive to Leghorn, twenty miles up the coast.

The British were now in the valley of the Upper Arno, moving towards Bibbiena, north of Arezzo, down the Arno and through the Chianti country towards Florence. The French Expeditionary Corps, which formed the Fifth Army's right flank, had earlier, on June 21, attacked north astride the ancient Via Cassia, Highway 2, the 3rd Algerian Infantry Division on the right and the 2nd Moroccan on the left. For the next five days, the Germans held the French to a two-mile Corps gain along a twenty-nine-mile front centered on the Orcia River, a westward-flowing tributary of the Ombrone. The river was fordable, but the enemy had the advantage—although the hills rising to the east could be bypassed and the Upper Ombrone Valley, running towards Siena, formed a path around that western end of the line. German troops from the 20th Luftwaffe Field Division, the 4th Parachute and 356th Grenadier Division were bolstered by elements of the 26th and 29th Panzer Grenadier Divisions. Crossfire from well-placed automatic guns raked the Orcia. Dug-in soldiers were backed by a larger concentration of artillery than so far committed by the Wehrmacht north of Rome. The opposition was formidable.

Moreover, French morale was uncertain. They had learned that they would soon be withdrawn for the invasion of southern France. As the FEC approached the Orcia, its 1st Motorized Division was taken off line to prepare for Operation ANVIL. General Clark noted in his diary that General Alphonse Juin, commander of the French forces in Italy, had "performed magnificently"; yet Juin had heard nothing from his government, though he "received indications that [left] him and his staff depressed."

Juin, apparently, was out of favor with General de Gaulle, who had come into power, and it was clear he would not have the honor of leading his men into France. Juin also opposed the withdrawal of his troops from Italy. "It is shameful," he told Clark, "that after this victory in Italy [the capture of Rome] we will not be allowed to exploit it." It was a great pity about the withdrawal, he added. "This will cause the loss of the battle of Italy because it is in the plains of the Po Valley that we must destroy the German reserves. History will judge this decision severely. . . . Well, events turn out as they do."⁹

The French moved out in the early hours of June 22 and by noon the entire area centered on the Orcia Valley was aflame. Heavy fire halted crossings at two bridges, although the outlook was brighter at the end of the day to the west, where the 1st Group of Tabors made contact with the 1st Armored.

The Tabors moved five miles northeast, along the south bank of the Ombrone, where resistance was less than that to their right. On the morning of the following day, the 4th Moroccan Infantry edged forward, but by noon the 2nd Moroccans on the right flank were blanketed by enemy artillery. Several enemy aircraft—the first seen in many days—strafed Highway 2 south to Radicofani. But there was little movement and much fighting along the French front. Then, Juin decided to exploit the German weakness on his left flank. General Guillaume's Goumiers were reinforced by the 4th Moroccan Spahi armor, and forded the Ombrone the morning of June 24. Side by side with the American 1st Armored, the French swept north, unhinging the enemy line. By the end of the next day, the Guillaume Group cleared the area west of the Ombrone and crossed the Farma, a tributary of the Ombrone. At noon, the 8th Moroccan Infantry crossed the Orcia west of Highway 2, and later the 3rd Algerian Division crossed on the left. By the 26th, the French were across the Orcia and on the way towards Siena—at a cost of 972 casualties.[10]

The French approach to storied Siena was constrained by General De Gaulle's assurance to Pope Pius XII that his troops would spare the city. To cut off the enemy inside the city—which General Juin judged the best way of limiting possible damage—the French deployed in a series of flanking and bypass maneuvers. Such tactics took time, but they also applied pressure on the Germans to abandon Siena.

Before dark on June 26, American armor had outflanked Monticiano, where General von Senger had suffered some of the blackest moments of his war, and forced the enemy out of the valley to the northwest, enabling the Guillaume Group to make good progress that night. On the following night, the 7th Algerian Infantry contested the Germans for Monticiano. On the right, the Moroccan Infantry advanced on San Quirico, a hilltop town located between the Orcia and Asso Valleys on Highway 2. Everywhere along the French front the German line began to yield.

The pursuit became a pincers movement, the 3rd Algerians attacking towards Siena from the southwest and the 2nd Moroccans from the southeast. Although the Germans were dropping back towards the Arno, delaying parties were left behind to ensure that the French did not have an altogether easy run to Siena. Tiny Pienza, birthplace of Pope Pius II and the very model of a Renaissance city, fell to the French on the morning of June 28. Stubborn enemy rearguards fought desperately to slow the French advance.

The Moroccans gained control of the lateral road Monteroni d'Arbia–Asciono on July 1 but were unable to dislodge the enemy from Asciono during a day's bitter fighting. Monteroni, however, was cleared and the advance resumed. The 8th Moroccans dashed across Highway 73, and that night halted three miles east of Siena. By then, enemy convoys were reported running north from the city.

The left pincer, too, began to squeeze the Germans. An all-day battle at Casanova enabled the Goumiers of the Guillaume Group to push into the hills north of Highway 73. Though the Group met fierce enemy resistance covering the German withdrawal from the area, they seized Simignano, southwest of Siena, to secure the left flank as the French closed their pincers. By midnight, June 2, forward elements of the French

Expeditionary Force were at the crossroads south of the city. By 0630, July 3, Siena was in French hands.

On the city's Porta Camollia, where a vast Florentine enemy army was once put to flight by prayers to the Virgin and a sunrise Sienese sortie, there is an inscription *Cor magis tibi Sena Pandit*. "Siena opens her heart to you." Which Siena certainly did on July 3rd. By noon, the French Tricolore flew above the ancient Palazzo Pubblico, the most pleasing town hall in the world.

NOTES

[1] Von Senger, *Neither Fear Nor Hope,* pp. 262–64.
[2] Clark, *Calculated Risk,* p. 378.
[3] Howe, *First Armored Division,* pp. 354–55.
[4] Robbins, *The 91st Division,* pp. 41–42.
[5] Howe, *First Armored Division,* pp. 357–60.
[6] Mauldin, *The Brass Ring,* p. 229.
[7] Shirley, *Americans: The Story of the 442nd Combat Team,* pp. 33–36.
[8] Von Senger, *Neither Fear Nor Hope,* p. 262.
[9] Clark, *Calculated Risk,* pp. 379–80.
[10] United States Army, *Fifth Army History,* Vol. VI, p. 71.

VII

WAR OF POSITION

The "war of position" along the Arno began with the fall of Leghorn on July 19. Kesselring had gained precious time at Trasimeno, Arezzo and along the Cecina. Each day gained enabled the Germans to further reinforce the Gothic Line along the high peaks of the Northern Apennines some twenty-five miles north of the Arno River. On July 1, as the British broke through the Trasimeno Line and the Americans approached the Cecina River, Kesselring called his army commanders to a conference at his headquarters near Florence. There he announced a change in tactics—a modification of the OKW's strategic guidelines, which had called for maximum resistance along successive defensive lines.

"It was my objective," he wrote in his memoirs, "to put up a longer resistance on narrow and better located fronts." Hard-pressed troops must vacate "at speed," he told his commanders, "unfavorable sectors"— which meant falling back on a delaying position on a line running from Pisa on the Ligurian coast along the Arno to Florence and over the mountains to the Metauro River and the Adriatic. Kesselring gave orders to prolong "the delaying action in the country immediately covering the Apennines, holding the Arno for a while." Florence, "which [he] wished to spare," was to be bypassed, although her bridges would not be spared (nor her citizens left unscathed). Delay along the Arno would gain time to improve the Gothic Line and make possible a smooth withdrawal into the Northern Apennines.[1] As Von Senger remarked, the Arno covered "the length of our line [and] gave the German forces the feeling of security that they so badly needed." To their front, "the field of fire was open and at many points the river was an obstacle to tanks."[2]

"The whole art of war," Wellington once said, "consists in getting at what is on the other side of the hill." General Alexander may well have had this, or something like it, on his mind when he declared in a dispatch to Clark: "I intend to penetrate the Gothic Line roughly between Dicomano [an agricultural center on the Sieve, a major Arno tributary, about 15 miles northeast of Florence] and Pistoia." It was "essential," Alexander continued, that these two centers be secured "quickly." He also suggested—typically Alexander's orders were issued as "suggestions"— that the best way to cross the Arno would be "to force a passage somewhere between Empoli and Pontedera and then develop two thrusts, one on Pistoia and the other on Lucca." The valley of the Arno would serve as a base for the assault on the Apennine German stronghold. Alexander said he appreciated that the Fifth Army had been greatly reduced in strength and that three out of its four remaining divisions were battle-weary and that the 1st Armored was being reorganized. Still, he insisted, Clark had left "sufficient troops to force the Arno . . . [and] play a part in the attack on the Gothic Line in the area north of Pistoia in conjunction with the Eighth Army's attack further east."[3]

At the beginning of July and the start of the final drive for the Arno, the 34th Division was north of Cecina on the left flank of the American IV Corps, ready to attack with the 88th Division going on line to replace the 1st Armored above Highway 68. The French Expeditionary Force had taken Siena and was engaged in a bitter fight for Colle di Val d'Elso and Poggibonsi at the junction of roads fanning out in a "V" to Empoli and Florence. The British X and XIII Corps had branched out above Arezzo, the former working up the Arno Valley east of the mountain mass of Pratomagno towards Bibbiena and beyond to Dicomano, while the latter wheeled down the Arno towards Florence. The "war of position" was about to open.

Coastal Highway 1, the main axis of the Allied advance from Rome, changes its character above Cecina to wind north with abrupt drops to the sea on one side and steep hillsides above. Rosignano Marittimo, some nine miles north of Cecina and nearly three miles inland from the sea off Highway I, sits on a hill that offered the Germans a commanding view of the approaches from the south, almost to the 34th Division's line of departure. With its closely built stone houses and its massive medieval castle on the summit at the center, Rosignano was a natural choice for a major stronghold south of Leghorn. There Von Senger placed key units of the 26th Panzer Grenadiers, a division that had fought fiercely to hold Cecina. He also deployed the 19th and the 20th Luftwaffe Field Divisions on the high ground—the flanking ridges bracketing the main approaches to Leghorn and Pisa that rose to peaks of over 1,500 feet seaward and over 2,000 to the east. From strongholds in this confined and rugged country, the Germans were positioned to rake advancing American troops with a deadly flanking fire.

East of the coastal range and Highway 1, a secondary road, Route 206, runs through a valley flanked by yet another high ridge line. It parallels a lesser road five miles to the east, which passes through Riparbella, Castellina Marittima, Pastina and Lorenza to join Route 206 below Collesalvetti on the southern edge of the Arno Valley. General Crittenberger committed the bulk of the 34th Division to a thrust along these two roads towards Pisa, bypassing Leghorn and leaving it isolated.

The 804th Tank Destroyer Battalion and the 34th Cavalry Reconnaissance Troop advanced along the coastal highway. By outflanking Leghorn, Crittenberger hoped to threaten the enemy's route of withdrawal. That, he believed, would cause the enemy garrison to abandon the key port facility. To beef up the 34th, Crittenberger added the 442nd Regimental Combat Team, the 804th Tank Destroyers and the 363rd Regimental Combat Team (the second of the newly arrived 91st Division's units committed to combat). When General Ryder launched the advance on Leghorn from the Cecina River line on the morning of July 3, he commanded 36,000 men, nearly triple the number called for by a divisional table of organization. It was an impressive array of troops.

The Red Bulls moved out at dawn on July 3, with the 135th and 168th Regiments working the flanking ridges and the 442nd attacking on a broader front in the valley between. The 135th made good time that day. Its 3rd Battalion reached the southern outskirts of Rosignano Marittimo by early evening. The rest of the regiment soon caught up, but the infantrymen were halted short of town by intense mortar and artillery fire. The men dug in for the night; the next morning, they literally inched forward and began to clear the hilltown street by street as the 26th Panzer Grenadiers hurled grenades into the narrow streets and fired rifles and burp guns from the upper stories of stone buildings. By late afternoon, the 3rd had beaten off a tank-supported counterattack and gained a foothold in the southern third of Rosignano.

On the night of July 5, as the 3rd Battalion held on in Rosignano, the 442nd's 2nd Battalion infiltrated the high ground east of the beleaguered Red Bulls. When the Germans discovered the Nisei dug in on their flank, they mounted counterattack after counterattack.

In his observation post, Staff Sergeant Kazuo Masuda of F Company spotted the German infantry as it opened fire. He crawled 200 yards through heavy fire to pick up a 60mm mortar tube and some ammunition. Back on post, he used his helmet as a base plate and single-handedly fired the mortar for twelve hours—throwing back two counterattacks on his own. Awarded the Distinguished Service Cross, Masuda was later killed on patrol along the Arno. Tech Sergeant Ted T. Tanouye, a Company K platoon leader, noticed an enemy machine gun going into action on his left. He killed three Germans and drove others back. Hit in the left arm by a grenade fragment, Tanouye raked an enemy trench with his submachine gun. To obtain more ammunition, he crawled twenty yards to a platoon mate; from there, he knocked out another enemy machine gun. His platoon seized their objective and Sergeant Yanouye organized its defenses before he allowed himself to be evacuated. He, too, was awarded the Distinguished Service Cross. Later, he died of wounds received in action along the Arno.

Two days later, on July 7, the 100th Battalion captured the town of Castellina, driving off a company of enemy infantry supported by a platoon of tanks. Over the next three days, the 442nd fought along the ridges and hills north to Pomaaia and Pastina. By nightfall, after taking Pastina house by house, the Nisei controlled the high ground east of Rosignano.

It took three days for the 135th to gain the northern edge of that town, fighting house by house all the way. A stubborn German rearguard held scattered strongholds on the north side for several days more. By noon on July 11, however, the city belonged to the 135th. Many civilians, unable to flee the city, were killed. Their bodies and those of the German dead were strewn throughout the city. Cremation became necessary to avoid the dangers of an epidemic.

The savage fight for Rosignano and Castellina was matched elsewhere on the 34th Division front. It took the 168th Infantry four hard-fought days to reach and capture the village of Castellino Marittimo, five miles east of Rosignano Marittimo. As the 168th mopped up that village, the 2nd Battalion of the 363rd Infantry moved on cone-shaped Monte Vaso, two and a half miles to the northeast. From the tip of the cone, the enemy could see anything that moved to the east and the south. The paved road running north to Chianni and on to the Arno Valley was a shooting gallery for the enemy's self-propelled 88s, mortars and machine guns. So long as the enemy held the position, the drive to the Arno would falter.

At five o'clock on the afternoon of July 6, the men of Company L and Company I climbed Monte Vaso's rough slopes, firing as they went. They then drove back an enemy counterattack. By the time they reached the top three hours later, the two companies were down to an effective strength of 77 each. As night closed in, the men scraped together piles of rock for cover. When six or seven rounds a minute of artillery and mortar fire began to fall at daylight, these pitiful piles of stone afforded little protection. Company L, aided by friendly artillery, drove back the first counterattack, but at a cost of 35 casualties. Some 200 Germans mounted a second attack, screaming "*Heil Hitler*" as they came. Several of the handful of men guarding the company's right flank began to waver. Staff-Sergeant Alexander M. Greig, jumped up, shouting, "Don't let the sons of bitches bluff you—let's get 'em." Four men joined him in a charge as the rest reopened fire—and the line held. Greig was awarded the Distinguished Service Cross posthumously; only two men survived the charge he led.

For a time, both friendly and enemy artillery and mortar fire came in so close that it was impossible to tell them apart. Another 200 Germans, their Mausers, pistols and submachine guns spitting, attacked Company I on the left flank of Vaso. Pfc. Rex W. Jewkes picked up a light machine gun from a wounded crew and moved over the crest. He set up so far forward that he came under fire from his own comrades; one BAR chewed down a clump of grass less than a foot away. His well-directed fire, however, was credited as a main factor in driving the enemy off, along with the ferocious hand-to-hand bayonet fighting of the rest of I Company. Radio contact was difficult because batteries then had a short life. Nevertheless, radio men discovered that a battery's life could be extended by placing it in the hot sun. But sun-heated exhausted batteries barely worked—a minute or so twice a day and not at all after dark. That night, the remaining soldiers were reduced to scavenging ammunition from the bodies and weapons of their dead and wounded buddies.

Logistics, a name as Eric Linklater remarks, that "aptly summarizes what all but a Quartermaster-General's Department find incomprehensible,"[4] is a military science, but in the mountains of Italy it often became a shambles. It was a long haul from the supply dumps south of Rome to the anfractuous hills that lie between the Cecina and the Arno.

Quartermaster trucks brought urgently needed food, water, ammunition and equipment as close as combat conditions would allow—behind Monte Vitalba in this instance. There, jeeps were loaded with supplies—a mixed load, so that if a vehicle was knocked out, no one item would be entirely lacking. At dark, drivers inched their Jeeps along obscure and rough trails as far as they could go. Carrying parties were hastily organized by battalion S-4s from Service and Antitank Company personnel, replacements, stragglers, mess sergeants, cooks, mail clerks, anyone who could serve as a strong back or as a guard. Each man moved out in single file loaded with cartridge bandoleers, machine-gun ammo belts, or with a dozen rounds of mortars, a box of K or C rations, a five-gallon water can, a replacement radio, extra batteries, wire, and whatever else was needed by the embattled infantry. Enemy artillery and mortar fire combed the draws and reverse slopes. Machine guns raked the ground and drove carriers to cover. Casualties mounted, and often the men had to drop their supplies and take up their guns and fight. Seldom did the carrying parties get more than ten percent of the supplies up to the front. The 363rd Infantry supply line was virtually stopped at Monte Vitalba.

By then, L Company was no longer effective as a fighting unit. The men were exhausted, thirsty and out of ammunition. It was hot and sultry on the mountaintop and the men would not eat whatever food they had—the rations only increased their thirst. I Company, which had lost 31 men wounded and 33 killed between 0830 and 1400, was not in much better shape. The decision to withdraw back to Hill 553, from which the attack was launched the afternoon before, was inescapable. But withdrawal was painful and slow.

Tech Sergeant/5 William A. Montooth, an extra cook and barber in Company L, had replaced a rocket-launcher man and had volunteered to act as a company observer. He killed twelve Germans during the first counterattack and accounted for five more in the second. As his comrades withdrew, he remained in position to cover the move. He ran from rifle to rifle left by the wounded, firing until the guns were empty. When further resistance became impossible, he carried wounded men over the top of the mountain to the reverse slope. He had been fighting for three days and nights with little food and less water. On the verge of collapse, Montooth finally reported to a battalion officer the location of the rest of the wounded so that the medics could find them. The young cook from

Sweetwater, Tennessee, was awarded the Distinguished Service Cross for his courage.

Three days later, on July 9, the 363rd Infantry attacked again and regained the ground lost on July 7. The Germans had begun to fall back, though small pockets of enemy soldiers—and enemy artillery—continued to exact a toll in dead and wounded men. On July 12, the Regiment was returned to the 91st Division, which was committed for the first time as an entire unit east of the north-running Era River.

The Powder River Division, a World War I outfit made up of men from the American West, had been reactivated in August 1942, at Camp White, Oregon. Its first objective in Italy was the hilltown of Chianni, some eight miles north of Monte Vaso. The Division was inserted between the 34th and the 88th Divisions to strengthen the attack along a widening front. While the 363rd advanced along rocky, winding mountain trails through a rough, scrubby land east of the Era and southwest of Chianni, the 362nd moved to take a key lateral road leading from the east to the town. Engineers cleared the mine-ladened Sterza Valley and the infantry made good progress until Company C came under a murderous grazing fire from several enemy machine-gun positions on a hill two miles southeast of Chianni. The lead platoon faced almost certain annihilation.

Sergeant Roy W. Harmon led his squad along a draw, seeking to neutralize the Germans from the right. As soon as his men were within range, they attempted to fire three haystacks near the enemy guns with tracer bullets, but with no success. Harmon ordered his men to hold their positions and he crawled, under fire, to within twenty yards of the first enemy machine-gun nest to set fire to the haystack at the enemy's front with a well-thrown phosphorus grenade. As the two machine-gunners fled, he killed them. Then, while machine-gun bullets kicked dirt all around him, Harmon crawled towards the next enemy position, nearly a football field's length away.

Wounded, he dragged himself to within twenty yards and threw another phosphorus grenade, killing two more Germans. He then dashed thirty yards towards the third machine gun, dropped to the ground and crawled into the face of enemy fire and was wounded again. He hesitated a moment, but kept on going, leaving a trail of blood. About twenty-five yards from the enemy, Harmon rose to his knees to throw his grenade. Enemy guns knocked him down. He rose again and threw his last grenade. Riddled with bullets, he died as his grenade fired the enemy position. His company was now free to advance. Sergeant Harmon was awarded the Congressional Medal of Honor.

That night, July 12–13, the enemy withdrew to the north. Partisans helped rid Chianni of some of its German occupants and reported that 400 to 500 of the enemy had left on the morning of the 13th. The 363rd's 3rd Battalion now sent in mop-up squads and bypassed the town. The mop-up teams met no resistance. The 91st continued its advance towards the Arno against scattered resistance. Meanwhile, the Red Bulls' 168th Infantry captured Casale, a village three miles north of Castellina, taking the last of the dominating hills that controlled the approaches to Leghorn. The two main strongholds of the German defensive line—Rosignano and the mountainous area to the east—were now in the hands of the Americans.

On July 16, Company K, 361st Infantry, 91st Division, entered Pontedera, an ancient fortress town at the confluence of the Era and Arno Rivers, then pushed on through enemy machine-gun and sniper fire to the south bank of the Arno, becoming at nine o'clock that morning the first troops of the Fifth Army to reach the river. That day, Von Senger moved his battle headquarters under a sweltering sun to the vicinity of Pistoia. General Crittenberger's tactics—outflanking Leghorn and threatening the enemy's route of withdrawal—were working, though no doubt not as rapidly as the Allies certainly wished.

East of the 91st, the 88th Division and the French Expeditionary Corps added their share to the growing pressure on the Germans to withdraw and yield Leghorn, Pisa and Florence. The 88th, refreshed and replenished after nearly a month in reserve, relieved the 1st Armored before Volterra on July 8. From that ancient Etruscan stronghold—a forbidding lonely eminence on the heights dividing the Era Valley to the north from the Cecina Valley to the south, the Germans had a commanding view of 15 miles in all directions. Through the artillery smoke drifting over the city, its medieval walls seemed to Blue Devil reconnaissance impenetrable, unbreachable by frontal assault up eroding slopes and crumbling cliffs. Fortunately, as Colonel Fry of the Blue Devils' 350th Infantry put it, Volterra was "merely a fortress island. It could be bypassed."[5]

That is precisely what the 88th did, enveloping the city in a scissor-like maneuver, the 349th Infantry attacking on the right and the 350th on the left. The fields around Volterra were heavily mined, however, and clearing the mines ahead of the infantry outposts was essential if the attack was to succeed. Corporal Orval Sullivan of Ontario, California, and 1st Lieutenant John P. Tuccei of Biloxi, Mississippi, were among the 313th Engineers assigned this perilous task.

They had not more than started when enemy 88s and self-propelled artillery forced them to take cover. After watching the exploding shells, they decided that the dust raised would shield them from enemy observation. So, working two to three minutes at a time, hitting the dirt every time a round came in, and taking advantage of the dust clouds, they cleared more than 400 yards of minefield for grateful dogfaces. Each was awarded a silver star. Artillery and chemical mortars "smoked" high-lying Volterra, enabling the Blue Devils to reach their initial objectives before dark, well within the time allotted in divisional plans. Volterra was soon encircled and the enemy withdrew. "Our casualties had not been light," Colonel Fry said, "but they were fewer than I expected."[6]

It was, nonetheless, as Fry said, "an old story of front-line operation, continuous hour-by-hour, day-by-day aggressive assault. Every yard would have to be bought by blood." The effects of the fighting were evident all about him as Colonel Fry moved up to a forward observation post west of the small city. Nine men lay dead, all in a row, in a small vegetable patch where a machine gun had cut them down. A stone building served as a combination command post and aid station. Chickens scratched in the straw as soldiers went about their business.

While Fry talked with his officers about the next phase of the fighting, the battalion surgeon, Captain Harold E. Reid, and an aide brought in a badly wounded man. They set the litter down among the chickens. Fry said, "That's a hell of a place to leave him" and suggested placing him outside. Before he died, Reid explained coldly, it would be "pretty damned unpleasant to listen to him. . . . There are a lot of boys in the next room who might be seriously affected by the convulsions he will go through and their chances of survival are none too good now." When the doctor left, Fry noticed, to his horror, that a chicken had begun to peck at the brains oozing from the boy's shattered head. He shooed the animal away and laid his handkerchief across the dying soldier's face.[7]

Northwest of Volterra sloping ridges branch off from the high ridge line that runs down into the Era Valley. The Blue Devils advanced through fields of vegetables, grapes and ripening grain north along the Era to the Arno. Each haycock, it seemed to the weary dogfaces, concealed an enemy machine gun. The enemy gave ground grudgingly, harassing the Blue Devils with artillery, mortars, Nebelwerfers and gunfire from well-prepared positions. Each day measured a small advance, with occasional significant advances as the Germans played out a cat-and-mouse defense. When the Germans caught E Company's 3rd Platoon (350th Infantry) in an exposed position, Tech Sergeant Steven Kasmyna crawled fifty yards to carry a wounded man (who subsequently died) to safety. He then returned to the fight, where another comrade was killed instantly by machine pistol fire from two Germans. By then, Kasmyna had run out of ammunition, so he slugged one Kraut unconscious and then chased the second until he was forced to take cover from machine-gun fire on his right. Undeterred, however, he managed to return to his platoon a bit later—with a prisoner.

War has many facets, many bitter and a few bittersweet. When Colonel Corbet Williamson, commander of the 2nd Battalion, 350th Infantry, tried to winkle the enemy out of several small hills jutting into his position, he asked for assistance from a tank destroyer unit. It was a simple operation: destroyers against machine guns dug in beneath several haycocks. But as the infantrymen closed in, the destroyers turned around and withdrew. A knoll that ought to have been taken without casualties was dotted with American dead.

Colonel Fry and Sergeant Clyde Pope stopped one afternoon to pick some corn in order to enliven the evening meal at that day's Command Post. As they were filling their helmets with the tempting ears, the air, in Colonel Fry's words, "was rent by the unmistakable screech of Nebelwerfers." Weighing 1,195 pounds, the German rocket launcher fired six rounds every 90 seconds at a range of two to seven thousand yards. The rocket clusters came in with a distinctive shriek. G.I.s tagged them "screaming meemies." Colonel Fry held his helmet over the back of his head as he lay in a convenient furrow. "When the last round arrived," he says, "we left the corn field as if the devil was after us."

He doesn't say whether or not he or Pope salvaged any corn, but one gathers that none was served at that evening's mess. On July 16, Fry's regimental command post was located in a charming house in Chizzano in the hills east of the Era. An artillery round had clipped a corner off a splendid living room, which contained a grand piano. Canvas covered the opening. As the evening's activity eased, Corporal Douglas Allanbrook, a talented pianist, and with a single candle flickering on the music stand, began to play. His recital, in Fry's apt phrase, "augmented the ghostly eeriness of a battlefield at night."[8]

Other, harsher notes dominated the battlefield as the Blue Devils fought towards the Arno. When I Company, 350th, was caught in a minefield near Trojano, medics Raymond E. Platt and Russell W. Redfern went from man to man to administer aid and then calmly evacuated the wounded. Medic Alfred Tavares recalls being shot at when attempting to reach a wounded man. He had friends "shot right in the head—right through the center of the Red Cross insignia painted on their helmets." When a lieutenant shot the sniper firing at Tavares, he surrendered, begging for mercy. "Some of the guys wanted to shoot him anyway," Tavares says, "but they let him live."[9] Germans at times took advantage of the Red Cross flag. One group of four approached carrying a litter apparently carrying a wounded man. There was a momentary cease fire. Suddenly, the Germans whipped off the blanket, which covered a machine gun, and opened fire, cutting down several GIs.

Initially in reserve, the 351st Infantry was committed on the Blue Devils left flank to take the Laiatico ridges east of the Era and northeast of Volterra. German artillery fire pinned down the approaching Blue Devils on the forward slopes. Pfc. Benjamin Barela, a G Company acting squad leader, managed to reach the hill top where with rifle and bayonet he killed seven, wounded two machine gunners and captured one prisoner. As the Divisional historian John P. Delaney put it, he "worked on him until the Kraut revealed enemy positions." Barela brought mortar fire to bear, then led his squad in an assault that netted 40 more prisoners. His company was then free to move up. H-Company T/Sergeant Frank McCormick, on reconnaissance for his machine-gun platoon, spotted enemy fire from a cave that killed an officer as three riflemen, unaware of the trap, continued their approach. McCormick dashed 35 yards to the cave, fired his carbine into it and demanded its occupants surrender. He got his answer in a hail of bullets. Grimly, he fired back. When he stopped 54 Germans filed out and dropped their weapons.[10]

The battle for Laiatico, however, was not over. Colonel Arthur S. Champeny relieved a battalion commander and reorganized his battered forces. On July 12, moving about 100 yards behind an artillery barrage, the 3rd Battalion attacked at night along the ridge running east from the hill town, Laiatico, to penetrate the Command Post of the 1st Battalion, 1060th Panzergrenadiers. The German CO was killed by grenades, 250

Germans were killed and 420 taken prisoner. By daylight, the 2nd Battalion had taken two hills and was at the southernmost edge of Laiatico. Artillery barrages caught both units at break of day but the attack was resumed and by 0300 on the 13th the Laiatico ridge was in Blue Devil hands.

On that day, the other two regiments moved abreast meeting scattered resistance as the 351st was checked in exploiting its capture of Laiatico. Then east of the Era, the 349th ran into tough opposition along what the troops dubbed "bloody ridge," barren slopes soon littered with its wounded and dead. By the 16th, the Blue Devils advance picked up speed as the Germans fell back. The next day the 349th was headed for Palaia, some seven miles from the Arno. Ahead, in San Miniato, close to the Arno with its superb vistas from the hills of Fiesole to the sea, from the Apuan Alps to the cliffs of Volterra, the Germans prepared for the oncoming Blue Devils by salting the streets and houses with mines and booby traps. To prevent the townspeople from spotting the mines and warning the GIs, the Germans locked them up in a church. Before they withdrew, they wheeled two tanks into position and fired point-blank into the huddled civilians. The battle-hardened veterans of G Company, 349th, who entered San Miniato that night, were sickened by the sight that greeted them. On the 18th, the 1st Battalion, 351st, attached to Task Force Ramey, captured Montaione, south east of Palaia. The next day Blue Devil combat patrols pushed on to the Arno to find that the enemy had crossed the muddy river.

East of the 88th, French soldiers, eager to liberate their beloved country, made their last contribution to the Italian campaign. After the fall of Sienna on July 3, the Germans retreated with the French Expeditionary Force hard on their heels. General Juin deployed two divisions, the 2nd Moroccan Infantry and the 4th Moroccan Mountain Division, along a fifteen mile front. (The Algerian 3rd Division was moved to Naples in preparation for the invasion of Southern France.) As the French moved northwest along a road net which fed Highway 2, the Germans decided to make a stand along lateral Highway 68 west of Poggibonsi to Colle di Val d'Elsa some twelve to fifteen miles from Sienna. Here elements of the 71st Panzer and the Turkoman Grenadier Divisions could guard critical Highway 68 and block the head of the Val d'Elsa, which forms a narrow path through the hills for twenty-five miles to the Arno. For four days the Germans held the French to a crawl. Though the 6th Moroccan Infantry and the 4th Group of Tabors seized Abbadia early on July 5, four miles south of the junction of Route 68 and Highway 2, after a day of stiff fighting, Highway 68 remained out of reach. Six enemy tanks in groups of two reinforced enemy troops at Sant'Andrea, about a mile south of Colle di Val d'Elsa. The 4th Mountain Division arranged a feint designed to draw the tanks away but the maneuver failed. A counterattack on Highway 2 pushed the 3rd Moroccan Spahis back some 1500 yards. But the 2nd Moroccans kept on pushing. The enemy, badly mauled, began a slow withdrawal. By 0300 on July 7, Colle di Val d'Elsa was in French hands and before evening all Highway 68 was behind them. The weary French troops continued their advance along winding mountain roads to Poggibonsi. General Juin's force stabilized its front roughly ten miles short of the Arno—from San Stefano to the Elsa and downstream to Certaldo—where they were relieved by troops from the 2nd New Zealand and 8th Indian Divisions on July 21st and 22nd. North of Rome, the French Expeditionary Corps sustained 43 days of arduous pursuit, inflicted heavy casualties on the enemy, and took 2,080 prisoners. The French suffered 6,680 casualties, including 1,342 killed and three hundred missing in action.[11] In a tribute to French gallantry, General Marshall—at the insistence of General Clark—personally pinned the Distinguished Service Medal on Juin, the first awarded to a Frenchman in World War II.

As the French consolidated their positions, waited on relief and the longed for return to France, the Fifth Army closed in on Leghorn. The 34th Cavalry Reconnaissance Troop and the 804th Tank Destroyers working up the coastal highway towards Leghorn, at the end, had little to contend with but destroyed culverts and scattered mines. To complete the envelopment of the city, General Crittenberger once again attached the 91st's 363rd Regiment to the 34th Division. It was to attack Leghorn from the east as the Red Bull's 135th attacked from the southeast at 0330, July 18. A weak German rearguard put up token resistance as their comrades slipped away during the night.

General Clark came up and gave the 363rd's column of dusty GI's a salute. At noon, Company B opened fire on a platoon of retreating Germans, inflicting heavy casualties. But Germans, manning three heavy machine guns, held the company down for forty-five minutes, killing three and wounding three others. Two miles south of the city German machine gunners caught the leading soldiers of A Company in an open area at the base of the wooded hill. Two men were killed and three more wounded. The Germans were soon flanked and knocked out with the aid of a tank.

Infantrymen then piled on tanks, jeeps and trailers and soon passed through groups of cheering Italians lining the streets and entered Leghorn at dusk on the 18th. The next day the Americans completed the occupation of the city without resistance. The 442nd's 110th Battalion moved to garrison the city. Leghorn's port facilities were second only to Naples', now 250 miles south of the front lines. It was a long haul overland for needed supplies. The port was essential to future operations beyond the Arno. The Germans were fully aware of the importance of the port to the Allies. Quay walls were demolished, masonry toppled into the water. Ships were scuttled alongside damaged piers and the harbor sown with mines. Moreover, Allied bombing had cut rail lines and created rubble that blocked streets in the port area. In a remarkable feat, Army engineers bridged over sunken vessels and extended the quays so that all cargo hatches could be worked without reversing the vessel. Two liberty ships docked on August 26, the first of many, only five weeks later.

General Clark entered Leghorn with the first 34th Division patrols. Wryly, he observed that the enemy had spent "more and more time thinking up new booby traps." By then, of course, demolition experts had accumulated vast experience with all kinds of hidden explosives but Leghorn, Clark reports, was filled with many new ones, "all of them tricky." The Germans "used articles such as chocolate bars, soap, a package of gauze, a wallet, or a pencil, which, when touched or molested, exploded and killed or injured anyone in the vicinity. Others were attached to windows, doors, toilets, articles of furniture, and even the bodies of dead German soldiers." Over 25,000 of these devices were found but not before hundreds were injured or killed.[12,13]

GIs could see the famed Leaning Tower of Pisa from various high points outside Leghorn. They also had a good view of enemy activity. The Arno enters the coastal plain near Pisa where the valley widens to fifteen flat miles. Numerous canals score the broad plain. Highway 1 alone crosses five large ones on its way to Pisa. As the enemy pulled back across the canals, they set off charges already laid under the bridges. On July 20 plans were made to secure the canal crossings and move on to the Arno and Pisa. The 363rd Infantry was to push up the coast and take Marina di Pisa and up Highway 1 to tackle the ancient city where Galileo once taught. The 442nd and Red Bulls' 168th Infantry were to parallel that attack on the right and slightly east of Pisa to secure the south bank of the Arno. While the latter regiments met with considerable harassing artillery and mortar fire, they reached the river on July 22 without serious opposition. But the 363rd found the going more difficult.

Under the cover of smoke, A and B Companies moved into position astride Highway 1 and at 1800 on July 20th started the drive to Pisa. The first canal was crossed over a bypass constructed and mined by the Germans. The bridge over the second canal, near the church at Stagno, was captured intact. (700 pounds of explosives were taken out from under the bridge the next day.) The rifle companies and the battalion Ammunition and Pioneer Platoon built foot bridges under enemy fire across the next two canals out of debris from blown bridges, rocks, planks and sandbags brought up for that purpose. Faulty demolition, which left bridge ends forming a V nosing into the canal at the center, eased the crossing of the last bridge. "With a little planking in the middle," Regimental historian Captain Ralph E. Strootman writes, "the battalion walked down one side and up the other without getting its feet wet."[14]

The infantrymen dug in that night north of the canals as the engineers began construction of bridges to keep supplies moving forward. Machine-gun fire in the vicinity of Stazione Tombolo slowed the attack the next day. Moving along a 6,000 yard front on the 22nd, the 1st Battalion resumed the push to the Arno west of Pisa. Shortly after midnight, despite constant artillery and machine gun fire, the Battalion was deployed along the south bank of the river. Two hours later, the 2nd Battalion opened its drive to the city. Small arms and machine-gun fire harassed the troops at the outskirts of the city at the airport and Cimitero Nuovo. By morning, the enemy had been forced to withdraw but not before flooding the canals. The flooding failed to halt the advance and the infantry continued on into Pisa meeting only sporadic sniper fire. On the left of the Regimental sector, the Germans held on to Marina di Pisa, home of the Fiat seaplane plant at the mouth of the Arno. The 2nd Platoon of the 91st Reconnaissance Troop reinforced by the 1st platoon, Company A, and heavy-machine guns from Company D, spent most of the night of July 22–23, fighting to clear the town of Germans.

By evening on the 23rd, the 34th Division and its attached units occupied the south bank of the Arno from the sea to a point about ten miles east of Pisa. (Over the next two days the Red Bulls were relieved by the 91st Division.) The Leaning Tower was across the river in that part of the city still occupied by the Germans. GIs hunkered down along the river banks joked that "our engineers will straighten that building up for them when we get across the Arno."

Enemy snipers, however, were active. Artillery and mortar fire killed two men and wounded nine others as the 363rd reorganized its position along the Arno within Pisa. Many GIs believed that the Tower was being used as an observation post by the Germans. Kesselring declared Florence an Open City on July 23rd and had ordered that the art treasures of Pisa and other Tuscan cities should not be harmed. A feature story in Stars and Stripes quoted an officer, who said Germans had been observed in the Tower. General Clark was pressured to order it shelled. He ordered an investigation instead. General Crittenberger reported that the officer said he was misquoted. "Observers with field glasses were seen in the tower on the morning of July 25." Crittenberger continued, "Although a close observation has been kept since then, no further observers have been seen in it and it is considered quite possible that the individuals originally sighted may have been in civilian clothes." Clark adds in his memoirs that he talked with civilians who had taken shelter in the nearby cathedral when the Americans crossed over the Arno and was told that the Tower was entrusted to an elderly caretaker, who escorted Clark up the Tower. "The only German who ever came into the Tower," he told Clark, "was Marshall Kesselring and he was a sightseer, just as you are."[15]

Kesselring, who "rather expected a rapid thrust across the Apennines beyond Florence," had inspected the Gothic Line high in the mountains in July and found "the positions better aligned and strengthened."[16] With understandable apprehension, the Germans waited for an Allied attack on the Arno front. Even as the Werhmacht moved into positions along the river, the German High Command wondered how long they should be held. Despite Kesselring's sanguine view of the Apennine redoubt, the Gothic Line was not ready. Von Senger, a skeptic, did not "fancy" fighting on a line "situated on a forward-facing slope" fully exposed to his enemy's view. For long stretches it ran through wooded terrain where trees had to be felled to create fields of fire, making defensive positions all the more conspicuous. "Experience had taught me," Von Senger adds in his memoir, "how easily such wooded positions, possessing a limited range of vision, can be lost through enemy infiltration."[17] Still, he conceded the necessity of yielding the Arno line, in no small part because Kesselring feared the damage that would be done to irreplaceable artistic and cultural treasures in the Tuscan cities—Florence, Pisa, Lucca and Pistoia—within the Arno Valley. Yet, the Arno constituted a natural defensive and delaying line before the Apennines. Moreover, the Germans still needed time to complete the Gothic Line defenses. Kesselring gave orders that Pisa and Florence were to be spared and directed that the Allies be forced to fight for every gain between the river and the edge of the Apennines. These orders, as Fifth Army historian Ernest F. Fisher, Jr., remarked, were "inherently contradictory"[18] as Florence, especially, was the key to the Arno position. Yielding the city made withdrawal inevitable all along the north bank of the river. As General Clark regrouped the Fifth Army across a 30-mile front from the Ligurian coast southwest of Pisa along the Arno to San Pierino, some 5 miles west of the Elsa River, the Germans waited.

NOTES

[1] Kesselring, *A Soldier's Record*, pp. 208–209.
[2] Von Senger, *Neither Fear Nor Hope*, p. 266.
[3] Clark, *Calculated Risk*, p. 386.
[4] Linklater, *The Campaign in Italy*, p. 18.
[5] Fry, *Combat Soldier*, p. 127.
[6] Ibid., p. 140.
[7] Ibid,. pp. 135–136.
[8] Ibid., pp. 151–152.
[9] Delaney, *The Blue Devils in Italy*, p. 114.
[10] Ibid., p. 109.
[11] Fisher, *Cassino to the Alps*. P. 281.
[12] The task of clearing mines was time-consuming, especially in and around Leghorn. The 10th Mountain Division, the last to enter the Italian Campaign, suffered its first casualties on January 6, 1945, when a bivouac area guard at Quercianella, just south of Leghorn, walked off his assigned route along a railroad track and stepped on a German "S" mine. He was killed as were seven others who, unwisely, rushed to his aid.
[13] Clark, *Calculated Risk*, p. 385.
[14] Strootman, *History of the 363rd Infantry*, p. 43.
[15] Clark, *Calculated Risk*, pp. 388-389.
[16] Kesselring, *A Soldier's Record*, p. 209.
[17] Von Senger, *Neither Fear Nor Hope*, p. 268.
[18] Fisher, *Cassino to the Alps*, p. 291.

VIII

OPEN CITY

While the Germans waited for the Fifth Army to cross the Arno, General von Senger's journeys to the front became less strained, "tours of inspection" rather than the laborious dodging of shellfire to reach observation posts under attack. On one such visit, the general's party climbed to a hilltown village with "a long view of the Arno valley." At full summer in Tuscany, as Von Senger recalled, "the green becomes darker; purple peaches and golden-yellow pears grow above the ripening vines and corn. The maize stands high as a jungle while the earth becomes more parched." High in that place it was a soldier's respite when the guns remained silent, the noonday peace undisturbed. "The background of the landscape turned more deeply blue," Von Senger remarks, "as in the paintings of Leonardo da Vinci." They had, he discovered later on consulting a map, been looking down on the Arno from the town of Vinci.

Despite the lull along the Arno, the German high command was not at ease. "Every prospect was forbidding," Von Senger mused as he considered the impending collapse of the Reich.[1] Closer at hand, he was painfully aware that the Gothic Line was not ready. Kesselring worried over "the latent flanking threat" as well as the need to hold the Allies back as the Todt Organization, with forced Italian labor, worked on the Apeninne redoubt. The possibility of another Allied landing in Italy behind the German lines had been a constant source of anxiety, however the Normandy invasion had eased these fears: the Allies could not possibly assemble the requisite amphibious tonnage in the Mediterranean for another major invasion. Still, as Kesselring observed in his memoirs, "tactical landings were always in the cards." The fall of Elba on June 17 was worrisome. "Otherwise," Kesselring queried, "what sense was there in capturing the place?"

As preparations for Operation DRAGOON got underway, German

intelligence officers gave equal weight to possible small-scale landings in both southern France and on the Italian Riviera. When German aerial reconnaissance reported two Allied convoys along the west side of Corsica on August 11, German staff officers considered that a portion of the Allied fleet might be en route to the Ligurian coast. Marshall Rodolfo Graziani's Italian-German Ligurian Army, which garrisoned the coast, was put on alert. Even after learning of the invasion of southern France, Kesselring expected tactical landings somewhere between Genoa and La Spezia, an Italian naval base fifty miles above Leghorn.[2]

Of more immediate concern, however, as the 363rd Infantry entered Pisa on July 23, was the British Eighth Army's thrust towards Florence. The German resistance along the Trasimeno Line had "satisfied" Kesselring's tactical requirements for delay. Nevertheless the best Wehrmacht motorized divisions were, in Kesselring's phrase, "strung out like a string of pearls" east of the Siena–Florence road. They, too, contributed to the slowdown of the Allied advance. But, as Kesselring conceded, by pinning down these valuable German troops "on this intrinsically uninteresting flank," the Americans contributed "largely to the success of the fierce Allied thrust between Siena and Florence."[3]

The last stage of this thrust opened on July 23, the day Kesselring declared Florence an Open City. He ordered his commanders to withdraw all but internal security forces from the city, the news of which was passed on to Allied commanders through the Vatican. General Alexander, though he was anxious to avoid fighting within the city, declined the opportunity to issue a similar declaration. More to the point, he did not doubt but that Kesslering would contest every defensible yard south of the "City of Flowers." Hitler had given orders that the line south of Florence was to be held as long as possible.

On July 21 German intelligence had noticed a buildup of Allied forces in the area south of Tavernelle, on Highway 2 some 23 miles north of Siena. Two days later Kesselring informed General Joachim Lemelsen, who had replaced General von Mackensen as commander of the German Fourteenth Army, that he believed an Allied attack was imminent. Late on the 23rd, the Fourteenth Army issued orders that the 1st Parachute Corps was to delay the Allies as long as possible. That evening, Fourteenth Army reported that the New Zealand and South African Divisions had attacked the center and left of the Paras in strength. "Very hard fighting took place, in which 4 Para Div particularly distinguished itself. Both sides lost heavily. All attacks were beaten off, and a decisive success was gained." General Alfred Schlemm, commander of the 1st Parachute Corps reported, "Terrible fighting was in progress on 4 Para Div's front; the division had New Zealanders opposite it."[4]

The New Zealanders, Alexander once remarked, were *"par excellence, the exploiters of a favorable opening on the battlefield."*[5] After the fall of Arezzo, the British XIII Corps, under Major General S. C. Kirkman, had swung northwest towards Florence. The South African 6th Armoured, with an assist from the 5th Grenadiers and the 1st Scots Guards, had fought through the lovely but difficult country along the western edge of the Monti del Chianti to the heights bracketing Greve. On their right, the 3rd Welsh Guards of the British 6th Armoured captured Castiglione Fibocchi, a village north of the Arno at the bottom of the "U" formed by the river as it flows south from the mountains, swings west, then north again towards Florence.

XIII Corps was strung out on a forty-mile front, which ran west from the Arno just above Arezzo to Castelfiorentino on the Elsa. The valley of the middle Arno appeared to offer the best terrain for an advance on Florence. But the hilly and wooded valley was dominated on the east by the rugged Pratomagno Massif. The ridges of the Monti del Chianti west of the Arno were comparatively gentle, but still afforded the Germans good defensive positions. The 76th Panzer Corps held the German line from the Chianti mountains across the Arno Valley and the lower tip of the massif, with five divisions. West of the 76th Corps, however, where the British were to relieve the French Corps, only two German divisions—the 356th and the 4th Parachute Divisions—covered the ten miles from the Monti del Chianti to Highway 2. Here, General Kirkman decided, he could make best use of the feisty Kiwis.

The New Zealanders went into action on July 22 when the 5th Brigade relieved two battalions of the 2nd Moroccan Division five miles or so northwest of Castellina in Chianti. On their left, the 8th Indian Division replaced the 4th Moroccan Mountaineers in the valley of the Elsa not far from of Castelfiorentino. As the Coldstream Guards and the South African tanks contested the high ground at Greve to the northwest, the New Zealanders stepped off from San Donato in Poggio towards Highway 2 and Tavernelle in the Pesa Valley.

This was Chianti country, where weather-beaten hamlets sat above terraced slopes planted with trellised vines or overlooked wheat fields and groves of gnarled olive trees. Twin lines of slender cypresses marked the driveways to handsome villas, whose farms were known for their Chianti Classico. Ancient stone walls enclosed narrow roads and nearby hills were often covered by a dark green matte of trees and undergrowth.

The German 4th Paras were said to be short-handed in infantry but they were well served by artillery, mortars and Tiger tanks. It was not ideal tank country, but both sides employed armor at every opportunity, the most feared weapon being the German 60-ton Mark VI. Though clumsy, the Tiger's armored plate—5.9 inches in front and 7.3 at the turret, compared to the Sherman's 2 and 3.2 inches—made it particularly effective in a defensive role. With their compact build and synchromesh transmission, the Shermans were indeed mobile and reliable. But the Sherman, with a 75mm gun and two 30-caliber machine guns, was outgunned by the Tiger with its 88 main gun and two 7.62mm machine guns. Small wonder then that the New Zealanders considered Chianti country Tiger country. As a regimental account puts it: "From the moment the Tiger appeared it became a kind of bogey, and the air was full of rumours of more and more Tigers lying in wait just ahead; just as in the desert every German gun was an 'eighty-eight,' so here every tracked vehicle heard over in German territory was a Tiger. The natural result was that, quite suddenly, the New Zealand tanks became more cautious than they had ever been before. . . . The high mutual regard of New Zealand tanks and infantry was in danger."[6]

But not for long. For although tankers, leery of mines and demolitions in country lanes and shallow watercourses, had to grope almost blindly among the trees and vines, they nonetheless held on to the respect of their comrades in the infantry. As historian Robin Langford Kay points out, and with good reason, "Policy was not to push on until the tanks were up."[7]

When B Company, attacking without tank support, attempted to take San Martino a Cozzi, a devastating fire forced the Kiwis back after their ammunition ran out. Since San Martino dominated a fork in the road, it had to be cleared before the New Zealand advance could be resumed to Tavernelle on the left and to Sambuca on the right. A renewed B Company assault, backed by artillery, mortar and small-arms fire from Divisional Cavalry armored cars, cost 30 casualties, including five taken prisoner. The initial attack had failed largely because of one of those seemingly inevitable foul-ups among the Allies. Several American Shermans were tucked up near San Donato but refused to assist the New Zealanders. The commander said he had been ordered "not to lose a tank or risk one." In fairness, it must be said that the Americans later ignored these instructions[8]; in one instance, when A Company was forced to withdraw in the face of a German counterattack along the road to Sambuca, the Americans joined a troop of New Zealand tanks to drive the enemy back.

The New Zealanders advancing along the axis of Highway 2 now drew level with the South Africans on their right flank. "The country was gently undulating and we went sweeping forward beneath the scattered olive trees," platoon commander R.T. Street said. "When a house, appearing through the trees, looked to house the enemy, the tanks blazed away with their 75s. . . . The enemy was on the run. Without the armour I don't expect we should have got very far."[9]

The New Zealanders made appreciable advances up the valley of the Pesa astride Highway 2, and in the valley of the Virginio. Tavernelle was entered without opposition, the Germans having faded back, but a mile and a half to the north "tank shells came whistling down the road [from Villa Bonazza]." New Zealand tanks, the Armoured Regimental report continues, shot up the villa and its grounds, "but this brought on a savage reaction from Jerry, and a Tiger tank beside a little cemetery on the right flank hit and burnt two Shermans in quick succession."[10] When a third troop of New Zealand tanks was brought into play, the Tiger left the cemetery and headed towards Highway 2. It was damaged beyond repair while trying to cross a gully and finally blown up by its crew. It was the first Tiger tank claimed by the New Zealand Shermans.

Hostile fire beyond Noce and around the Villa Bonazza held up the New Zealanders though the Tiger was now out of action. A machine gun posted at one of the villa windows spat to good effect. "We fixed bayonets and went down the gully and up the other side, pretty well worked up too," Sergeant P.W. Patrick, D Company 28 Battalion, later remarked. "The trees seemed alive with running men, and the yelling of the Maoris added to the din created by the shouting of the Jerries. We killed a few but the rest disappeared," apparently into the villa. "We searched," Sergeant Patrick added, "but found no one in it. It was a tremendous building and I remember a beautiful piano."[11]

The Maoris resumed their advance the next morning, July 24, making better progress on the left than on their right flank, where a Panther blazed away from the road. After some "nasty persistent shellfire," the enemy withdrew during the night. The move was part of a limited withdrawal to the Olga Line, which ran from Empoli on the Arno eastward across the 8th Indian front to San Casciano on the New Zealand front and Mercatale on the South African front. San Casciano, twelve miles south of Florence on Highway 2, was a center of communications located on commanding ground, and was expected to be heavily defended. Enemy fire from the town prevented Armcav—a composite force of Divisional Cavalry, armored cars, engineers and machine-gunners—from making any progress beyond the Terzona, a Pesa tributary about a mile and a half to the south. Tiger tanks and antitank guns were reported defending the town, which was shelled and twice raided, "spectacularly," by fighter-bombers.

On the New Zealand right, the South Africans were held up by enemy concentrations in the Mercatale area. With strong artillery support and tanks, plus sappers with a bulldozer, the 21st New Zealand Battalion advanced northwestward towards Montagnana, a village midway between Montespertoli on the 8th Indian right flank and Cerbaia on the Pesa.

On July 25, the Punjabis and Mahrattas were halted by enemy fire from a cliffside. Mortars hidden in Montespertoli played havoc with a company of Mahrattas in San Pietro, a tiny hamlet to the south. A Mahratta captain noticed that when church bells clanged once, the next flight of mortars hit the center of the village; on two strokes, a salvo fell behind the church; and on three, shells dropped in a dried watercourse. A search as well as a sentry posted in the belfry failed to frustrate the signaling, but when all the civilians in the hamlet were locked in a crypt the bells ceased. "Neither the enemy agent nor his ingenious method of ringing the church bells was ever discovered," an Indian historian tells us.[12] However, the 8th's columns in the Elsa worked north for eight miles against spotty resistance. The Punjabis occupied Montespertoli and by nightfall of the 26th the Royal West Kents were within two and a half miles of the Arno. The enemy then broke contact, and the Indians swept forward to reach the Arno east of Empoli on the evening of July 29.

Meanwhile, the New Zealanders entered Montagnana without opposition on the 27th. A patrol to nearby Montegufoni found the Sitwells' villa, which housed a veritable treasure-trove of Florentine paintings, undamaged. The villa, fortunately, was situated in a hollow, a position ill-suited for defense. Its only occupant, Cavalryman R.C. Cotterall reported, was "a gentle old Italian with the air of a Major Domo. We felt rather like barbarians in this house with its aristocratic atmosphere and we in our common army boots." Dozens of pictures were stacked around the walls and the largest was left leaning against a table. "This huge dark canvas commanded out attention. . . . I'm no art connoisseur," said Cotterall, "but I knew that this was Botticelli's *Primavera*. We were rather awestruck."[13] The Mahrattas, who took over, were perhaps less so. "A suit of damascened armour was topped by a shrapnel helmet," we're told by the Indian historian, "with a Bren gun detected in a stand of pikes and harbequeses."[14]

The New Zealanders were determined to break through the Olga Line by clearing Route 2 and making a frontal assault on San Casciano. The South Africans meanwhile consolidated their position around Mercatale after bitter fighting. The British 4th Division, blocked on the Arno, shifted west to take Meleto, a tiny village on the east side of the Chianti Mountains, and prepared to go up against Monte Scalari, northeast of Collegalle On the Adriatic, the Poles had taken Ancona on the July 18 and were pressing hard towards the Metauro and the eastern end of the Gothic Line. To fend off the Poles, Kesselring ordered the withdrawal of the 1st Parachute Division from the Pratomagno Massif. The growing threat to the Olga Line prompted another German fall-back to the Paula Line, the last of the Wehrmacht's delaying lines south of Florence.

When the New Zealanders crossed the Terzona on the morning of July 27, their tanks and other vehicles were held up by demolitions, but the 22nd Battalion infantry entered San Casciano unopposed except by sniper fire. Though the town had been abundantly booby-trapped and mined, a house-to-house search cleared out the snipers. From a tower in San Casciano, the New Zealanders could see Florence, with its plum-colored roofs, the Duomo and Giotto's Campanile.

The Germans were trading bodies for time, as each line yielded cost them lives and tanks. By the time of the German fade-back to the Paula Line, the Wehrmacht had gained a precious five days. As Eric Linklater noted, the enemy "showed a defensive genius that could be resolved into an elastic pertinacity, a masterly eye for ground, and the efficient tactical disposal of infantry, tanks and artillery in groups of mutual support."[15]

All this would have been to little avail had it not been for the tenacity of the German soldier. Some, of course, did surrender when hard-pressed or when they had just "had it"—as did a German corporal who came up a steep mountain path above Arezzo playing his mouth organ. "He was sure the English would not shoot him if they heard music," he told his captors. He was an eleven-year veteran who had fought in Norway and France and at El Alamein. His company commander was an idiot, he said, and he preferred to desert rather than serve under such a fool.[16] Most German soldiers, however, remained steadfast under the direst of circumstances, and even in the face of impending defeat.

Enemy morale, incredibly, remained high. In the Orca Valley as the Allies approached, Iris Origo, an Anglo-American married to an Italian landowner, noted in her Diary on June 16: "As to general morale, they [the German officers] are all quite frankly tired of the war and of five years away from their houses and families, appalled by the bombing of Germany, and depressed by the turn of events here and in France." Yet, she went on, there was not one "who [did] not still express his blind conviction that Germany [could] not be beaten, and their equally blind conviction in a terrible *Vergeltung* [revenge] against England." The Führer, she remembered, had promised it, and she wrote, ". . . he has never yet failed to keep his promises to his own people."[17] She continued, relating that Von Senger said that, in order to maintain morale among the troops, "those in authority had to give daily doses of propaganda on the need to hold out."[18] Nowhere, he added, was there "any sign of the disintegration that occurred in the First World War. The moral front was holding out while the military front was crumbling more and more."[19]

And it would do so until the very last. Kesselring, in recalling the July 20 plot against Hitler's life, remarks, "I have never come across any staff or unit in Italy where politics was discussed. The war was too hectic, the soldier too much aware of the obligations of his military oath, and the spell of Hitler's personality too ever-present and his criminal actions too little known for a conspiracy to prosper." Moreover, Kesselring adds, "As the youngest age-class—ardently devoted to Hitler through the Hitler Youth Movement—was absorbed into the services, the character of every formation had changed. . . . Their attachment to Hitler was genuine; they swore by the Führer and were ready to lay down their lives for him. [20, 21]

All along the Paula Line—running from Montelupo, at the confluence of the Arno and Pesa Rivers, across Highway 2 to Figline on Highway 69 in the valley of the middle Arno—German soldiers were prepared to give proof to Kesselring's observation. Above, the heights of the Pian dei Cerri, roughly at the center of the Paula Line, girdled Florence in a natural defensive pocket. From the crest of these rolling wooded hills, some over 1,000 feet high, the enemy could dominate both the Pesa Valley to the south and Florence and the Arno Valley to the north. To breech the Pian dei Cerri would be to take Florence. On the morning of the 28th, the Kiwis crossed the Pesa at Cerbaia, a critical crossroad, to establish two bridgeheads. This ended the first phase of their drive on Florence, however the German withdrawal to the Paula Line had concentrated their forces on a more narrow sector than before. The New Zealanders now confronted the 29th Panzer Grenadiers instead of the 4th Parachute Division.

The width of the New Zealand front was just sufficient to permit a two-brigade attack, and General Freyberg was confident that his troops would soon drive the enemy back and clear the way to Florence. Early on July 27 he discussed plans for the opening of a New Zealand club in the city. By evening, however, it was clear that the enemy was not to be disposed of that easily. More of a set-piece attack would be needed to replace the hitherto successful probing advances by single companies. Freyberg, according to Kay, apparently, "could not understand why the enemy had given up San Casciano." His attack plan was "modified and qualified and modified again in the usual manner."[22] The 4th Brigade was given a new line of attack northeast from San Casciano to Giogoli, avoiding the more formidable of the Pian dei Cerri hills, and on to the Arno through Galluzzo on Highway 2. The 6th Brigade was to tackle the Germans on the Pian dei Cerri heights.

The 8th Indians were now in position to protect the New Zealanders' left flank west of the Pesa. But the South Africans, under fire from guns on the high ground around Imprunetta, were held up along the ridge line east of the Greve. This left the Kiwi 4th Armoured Brigade about to push north of San Casciano with an unprotected left flank exposed to counterattack and fire from guns around Imprunetta.

From Cerbaia, several roads and tracks led into the hills. One ran northeast two miles to a tiny village, La Romola, and beyond to join the San Casciano–Giogoli road; above that, another ran up to the ridge between La Romola and San Michele; a third road to the north ran to San Michele, perched on a high hill overlooking Cerbaia and much of the surrounding country, and on, over the Pian dei Cerri. The 24th Battalion was ordered to drive on San Michele while the 26th took the high ground overlooking La Romola.

The attack opened on the night of July 27–28 as B Company of the 26th secured Cerbaia and A Company covered the bridgehead over the Pesa. On their left, the 24th Battalion's attacking A Company was delayed by shellfire, and crossed the starting line an hour and a half late, at about 0230. Moving towards San Michele, A Company had covered a thousand yards when Lance Sergeant A.E. New, a platoon section leader, ran into a machine-gun post near a house by the road. He opened fire with his tommy-gun, but it jammed. Undismayed, New attacked the enemy in the darkness with his fists, then escaped in the turmoil to warn his men. His platoon attacked while another cut off the enemy from the rear. Five Germans were taken prisoner and the New Zealanders moved ahead. Supporting tanks drew up and began bombarding San Michele, but they drew down such heavy mortar fire that the leading infantry had to fall back. They quickly fortified a nearby house against the expected enemy counterattack.

Although the 24th Battalion's A Company had been delayed by shell-fire, the 26th's C Company moved out on time. Handicapped by dark-ness and the lack of an adequate reconnaissance, Major G.T. Kain and his men followed a rough country road up a sharp and exposed ridge. Two enemy machine-gunners were taken prisoner. Somewhat puzzled by the absence of the 24th Battalion company—supposedly on his left—the Major decided to go ahead. The information that he had suggested the Germans had withdrawn.

At 0400, he reported that his company was some six hundred yards beyond his first objective, well up on the heights above San Michele and La Romola. Ordered to proceed, the Major decided to take no further chances and to wait for the supporting tanks to catch up. As the tanks began to roll, a voice called out, "*Buona sera*" ("Good evening"). Corporal E.C. Murphy, thinking that they were New Zealanders, asked who they were. Then, quickly, at the rattle of a bolt going home, Murphy charged into a trench, killed a German machine-gunner and wounded two other of the enemy. One of the wounded volunteered the information that there were others of his company in the vicinity. At 0500, the tank com-mander reported that he would not reach C Company before dawn.

C Company soon discovered that it was too far forward in an exposed position. Bombardment along the ridge at daylight drove the point home with a vengeance. Three tanks that had reached the area could find no cover and were blasted out of commission. Enemy fire was coming in from almost all directions—south, northwest, west and southwest. Major Kahn ordered his men to drop back and, as the German counterattack developed, the company ran in groups of two and three down the exposed slope. The wounded were evacuated to Cerbaia by jeep and the rest of C Company regrouped in a defensive position near the 24th Battalion's A Company.

The enemy counterattack seemed to pause while maintaining a steady fire across the entire front. But at 1915, A Company reported that it was "completely surrounded." At 1950, the Kiwis were "still fighting hard, position a little easier, tanks engaging SP guns and MG posts." Three hours later, the position was "still grim," but by then troops of the 6th Brigade with supporting tanks were on the move again.[23]

"The night [July 28 at 0100] was inky black," the 20th Armoured historian writes, "the road, which looked promising enough on the map, little better than a goat path." After six miles in six hours, the tanks and infantry were on a ridge above the Sugana Valley with La Romola high on the other side. Ordered to move down onto the flats below, the tankers did so, expecting little but "the odd MG post" in La Romola.

Trooper Bob Middleton wondered how he could get down a three-hundred-yard drop, zigging and zagging on a goat path scarcely as wide as his tank. "At each corner . . . it was necessary for me to hold back hard on the sticks, and push out the clutch, while the spare driver changed gear." In the valley, the troop opened up on La Romola, directly above the tanks, with their Brownings. There was no reply, "a deathlike quietness." Middleton's tank and two others were ordered forward, and halted by a four-foot vertical drop. The trooper hooked his elbows over the edge of the manhole for a look. A sheet of flame as blinding as a photographer's flash "at a dance back home," terrified the tank driver, who bailed out and took cover in the ditch. He raised himself for a look: all three tanks were ablaze. Running back to safety, he recalled, "I paused beside the old tank—the radiated heat was stifling—and on again as fast as I could go."[24]

Then, "suddenly like a broadside from a huge battleship," reported E.B. Patterson, a 22nd Battalion infantryman who witnessed the attack, "the whole hillside opened fire simultaneously—88mms, mortars, Spandaus, small arms fire—everything seemed to come out at once from the whole area of the hill opposite." In less than five minutes, B Squadron of the 20th Armoured Regiment lost one troop, a quarter of its fighting strength. An HE shell had exploded on the turret ring of Middleton's tank, killing the turret crew. Expecting a "brew-up," Sergeant Bell, who lost his right foot, ordered his crew to get out to safety. They refused and picked him up and ran through mortar and machine- gun fire for cover in a nearby ditch. Fortunately, Jerry honored the Red Cross flag on a Bren Carrier sent forward to rescue Bell. All that day and the next, hostile fire continued "intermittently heavy or light almost without let-up."[25]

Neither New Zealand brigade succeeded in capturing the high ground of the Pian dei Cerri in the initial attack. The Wehrmacht's Fourteenth Army reported, on the evening of July 28: "Fighting was extremely hard and confused, particularly on 29th Pz Gren Div's front, where the enemy forced a penetration this morning at Cerbaia. All further attacks . . . were beaten off with heavy casualties to the enemy." The 15th Panzer Grena-dier's counterattack north of Cerbaia "came up against fierce defense by the New Zealanders and extremely heavy shellfire, but attacked again and again and pushed the enemy back with very heavy casualties and equip-ment losses."

In the 4th New Zealand Armored Brigade sector, the 71st Panzer Grenadier Regiment "after stubborn fighting" beat off attacks "with heavy casualties to the enemy." (General Freyberg's diary records the expendi-ture of 17,900 rounds by medium and field guns during the 24 hours to midday on July 28.) The Germans claimed 18 New Zealand tanks and five troop carriers, knocked out "inside our lines," and the capture of two tanks, a gun and three more guns blown up. The Fourteenth Army report averred that the 29th Division "thus gained a complete defensive success against an enemy much superior in numbers. Its artillery and tanks (129 and 508 Panzer Battalions) gave it excellent support." Pleased, the report commended the division for "the staunchness and fanatical stubbornness of every man."[26]

The Germans, however, were worried. General Lemelsen, comman-der of the Fourteenth Army, reported on the 28th to Army Group C that the 1st Parachute Corps "could not continue to hold its present line unless it received fresh reserves, which Army did not have. . . . The high expenditure of the last few days was also causing ammunition to run out, as petrol was so scarce that ammunition could not be brought up in adequate quantities."[27]

The New Zealanders renewed their attack early in the morning of July 29, determined to take the high ground of the Pian dei Cerri. First, however, the 4th Brigade had to take La Romola, and the 6th, San Michele. Timed concentrations of artillery fire opened the way to the razor-backed ridge where a "mere clump" of houses scattered along either side of the road comprised the village of San Michele. Two Germans were killed, five made prisoner, in a house below the ridge.

Lieutenant F.J. Lea and his D Company platoon surprised the enemy occupying houses on the forward slope, killing six and capturing six at the cost of three men wounded. D Company then moved into San Michele without opposition, occupying the church at the northeast end of town as well as several other strongpoints. Here the Germans concentrated their fire and launched several counterattacks. A Mark IV firing point-blank drove the platoon into the crypt of the church early that morning. Trapped, the men decided that they had no choice but to fight.

Slowly but effectively, the village was reduced to rubble, a counterattack on the church being driven off. Private A.G. Swann, who had been knocked out in the shelling, awoke to see a Mark IV drawing up to fire. Grabbing an antitank gun, he fired four shots at a few yards range, forcing the tank to withdraw. German infantry made two more attempts to get in the church but failed to do so, and began to withdraw after 1100, leaving San Michele to the New Zealanders.

29th Panzer Grenadier Division casualties on July 29 were reported as 4 killed, 29 wounded, 22 missing. The New Zealanders later counted 47 German graves in San Michele. 24th Battalion's casualties on the same day were 4 killed, 18 wounded and 3 taken prisoner. "Terrific fighting took place," the German Fourteenth Army reported on July 29. "The enemy . . . was stopped at the village of San Michele by a series of counterattacks by our last local reserves. . . . Army advised Army Gp that the days of hard fighting, the heavy casualties and extreme exhaustion of the troops had considerably decreased the fighting value of 1 Para Corps, particularly 29 Pz Gen Div. Army was not in a position to give the Corps any more relief by narrowing down its sector any more, as 14 Pz Corps' sector was now so thinly held that any attack there could not be held without help from Army Gr or . . . 10 Army."[28]

While the New Zealander's 6th Brigade held San Michele, British fighter-bombers strafed the high ground to the north. Nevertheless, at the end of July, the Brigade was still hemmed in, the enemy fully prepared, it seemed, to fight it out on the Paula Line. The South Africans were held up on the southeast of the New Zealand right flank. From the high ground east of the Greve, the enemy enjoyed good observation and successfully harassed the 4th Brigade's salient below La Romola. A limited attack by A Company, 23rd Battalion, north of San Casciano into the ridges southeast of La Romola and west of the Greve and Highway 2 improved the New Zealand right-flank position. General Freyberg decided to concentrate on this salient, which offered the shortest route to Florence. The 5th Brigade opened its drive for the high ground centered around Faltignano to the north at 2200 on July 30. Three hours later the 4th Brigade started out for La Romola.

The 5th Brigade attack opened with a creeping barrage, 100-yard lifts every four minutes, fired by the three New Zealand field regiments and the 57th Field Regiment—the latter on loan from the British 6th Armoured Division. The 70th and 75th Medium Regiments were assigned concentrations on observed and suspected enemy positions. The 23rd and 28th Battalions each were backed by a half-squadron of 20th Armoured tanks. Opposition was slight, though the New Zealanders soon flushed two Tigers that had scored machine-gun hits on the turret of the lead Sherman but failed, "for some reason or other—including the obvious one that they may have run out of ammunition," to follow up their tracers with armor-piercing shells.

Tigers were active throughout the area that day. Though the infantry took Faltignano, supporting tanks could not come up and had to withdraw and circle around by another road. En route, the three Shermans were halted by an enemy SP gun and a Tiger, which set one of the tanks afire and killed its driver. Lieutenant M.W. Cross, whose tank had taken shelter behind a ridge, had "a dekko" and spotted the Tiger lying "beautifully camouflaged" below the crest. Flanking the enemy, he laid down "American smoke" and fired five or six armor-piercing shells at the surprised German tank, which withdrew—"much to our relief."[29] The two remaining Shermans and the infantry resumed their advance, killing some 20 of the enemy, capturing a German RAP and several prisoners. By the end of the day, the 5th Brigade had taken its initial objectives and had occupied the high ground around Faltignano and a mile north.

"Taken all around," the historian of 20th Battalion remarks of the attack on La Romola: "[I]t was a most confused night."[30] The enemy was on the alert, sparked awake by the attack opened three hours earlier on the right, and filled the valley below the town with a defensive fire. "The noise, dust and smoke were terrific," a 22nd Battalion platoon commander said, "and hardly seemed to increase when our own barrage opened up."[31] One of the infantry companies was caught in the friendly barrage. One tanker troop had to wait on a bulldozer and then was put on the wrong track by the engineers. "That was the last the troop saw of its infantry," according to the 20th Armored's history.[32] Mechanical troubles claimed one tank, while another got stuck when the road gave way. One infantry company was hard hit before it left the starting line; a platoon was reduced to a handful. Thickly planted grapevines on tightly strung wires slowed another company. Communications failed, and attackers were broken up into small, isolated groups. Infantry got too far ahead of tanks too soon. As an officer put it: "The wonder is how the attack succeeded at all, and how La Romola fell."[33]

Lieutenant I.L. Thomas' platoon reached the village first, knocking out at least two machine-gun nests and occupying a two-story building at the town's edge. It was joined at 0300 by another platoon, reduced to eleven men by shellfire. While searching the village after daybreak, the New Zealanders came upon what seemed to be an abandoned Tiger. Lance Corporal E.T.K. Dillon clambered on—"when up comes the lid. Before I could surrender, the German did, with three or four others."[34]

Driven to the rear, the tank "caused momentary consternation," as one may well imagine, until a New Zealander's head emerged from the turret. Antitank guns were brought up under fire to fend off possible Tiger-backed counterattacks. None developed, though the enemy shelled the forward positions all through the day. When a 17-pound-gun crew took refuge in a nearby house, a German patrol managed to render the gun useless and drive away the gun tower. By evening on July 31, the 22nd Battalion had La Romola well in hand. Its casualties numbered eight killed, 22 wounded and two missing; 21 enemy were taken prisoner and 40 to 50 reported killed.[35]

Before and during the attack on Faltignana and La Romola, the Fourteenth Army *War Diary* reports, ". . . about 50,000 rounds were counted in 29 Pz Gen Div's and 4 Para Div's sectors. This even surpassed the weight of fire during the heaviest days of the Cassino fighting."[36] The expenditure of ammunition forced a twenty-four-hour postponement of the next phase of the New Zealanders' attack.

While the Kiwis waited for ammunition to be brought up from a corps dump at Lake Trasimeno, a hundred miles to the south, the Germans fell back a mile and a half to the dominating Pian dei Cerri heights. Unfortunately, Brigadier Stewart, on a visit to his forward troops, was captured with a marked map in his possession. General Schlemm, commander of the 1st Parachute Corps, was pleased to inform his superior, General Lemelsen of the Fourteenth Army, that the Paras had "formed main points of resistance" to meet New Zealander thrusts.[37]

On July 31 and August 1, a hundred fighter-bombers attacked German strongpoints, forming up areas and gun positions. New Zealander guns opened fire at 2300 on August 1, and on their first lift twenty minutes later the infantry moved out with all three brigades forward. On the right, the 5th Brigade was frustrated in its efforts by a late start, a planning foul-up: artillery and infantry starting lines did not coincide, and this prevented the infantry from being close enough behind the barrage to catch the enemy while they were disorganized.

The enemy forced the Brigade into a defensive position short of its objective, the last hills covering one of the roads on which the Germans could withdraw tanks and transport. The 6th Brigade, the first off the mark on the left flank, took its objective by 0530. Smart work by tankers and antitank crews helped. While waiting for sappers to clear a minefield, the tanks blasted a house and several other German strongpoints to open the way to the Brigade's first objective. Later, when a German tank attacked, two antitank gun crew members fired one shot from their 17-pounder. It was "most spectacular," says an observer. "The shot hit just below the turret which was thrown six feet in the air and the tank split open, then a sheet of flame enveloped the lot, followed by the explosion of ammunition."[38]

The 4th Brigade started just north of La Romola, close behind the barrage that opened at 2335. Wireless communication was poor and one company seems to have overrun the barrage. "Though scattered and dazed," the 22nd Battalion account reports, "and hampered by wire— grapevines strung across the line of attack—the survivors pushed on."[39] At daybreak, La Poggiona—the village at the center of the New Zealand attack—400 open yards ahead, was still in enemy hands. Tankers silenced a nest of four Spandaus as the infantry crossed the open ground in an extended line. Halfway, the tanks stopped to lay down fire on the enemy as the infantry went up the steep slope, shooting as they went. The New

Zealanders overran La Poggiona and some distance down the other side.

Germans began to surrender, but unfortunately a green replacement panicked and fired a tommy-gun burst through an approaching German, whose hands were up. The Germans turned and ran downhill and the New Zealanders ran back to the top. The Germans counterattacked, and were repulsed twice. The third attempt succeeded in driving the New Zealanders back as by now they were nearly surrounded and running out of ammunition.

The attack on La Poggiona was renewed at 0600 on August 2. Artillery and fighter-bombers fired on the crest. Still, the infantry had to climb under enemy machine-gun fire and were mortared when they probed over the top. As the morning mists began to lift, firing fell off. By early afternoon, the New Zealanders had captured the eastern crests of the Pian dei Cerri hills. From one of these, Private J.M. Shinnick, C Company, 25th Battalion, recalled, "we had our first view of Florence some four miles away and nestling in the wide valley below us. It indeed looked beautiful still faintly haloed in a morning mist, with church spires and the outline of tall buildings rearing their architectural beauty in the sky."[40]

Though the New Zealanders had decided the battle for Florence, they were not to have the honor of being the first Allied troops to enter the famed city. That honor would fall to the South African 6th Armoured.

Pressure against the Germans was building all along the Eighth Army front. On the Adriatic, the Poles scarcely paused at Ancona, which fell on July 18, and were hard on the heels of the Wehrmacht, falling back to Senigallia, and the Cesano and Metauro Rivers. While the Poles fought up the coast, detachments of the Corpo Italiano di Liberazione and Maiella partisans pushed north in the hills to the west.

The advances up the Adriatic and in the drive to Florence forced the Germans to reconsider their defenses in the Upper Arno and Upper Tiber Valleys, some twelve miles apart in the rugged reaches of the eastward Apennines. Here, the Germans took advantage of the Pratomagno Massif west of the Arno and the desolate heights of the Catenaia Alps and the Della Luna Alps east of the Tiber. The German 305th Division, reinforced by six battalions, held the trackless heights of the Catenaia Alps in the center, with the 44th Division on its eastern flank and the 15th Panzer Grenadiers on its western. At the end of July, the British 4th Division had wheeled west to probe the Pratomagno and the 10th Indians had established a base in the Sansepolcro plain where the Tiber flows south out of the mountains. Both were in position to mount a converging attack westward towards Bibbiena.

Bibbiena, at the head of the valley of the Upper Arno ten miles north of the Indian lines, sits on a hill. Below its *centro storico* (historical center), which dates back to the Etruscans, the main north–south Highway 71 divides; one branch curves west at the northern end of the Pratomagno, then drops to where the Sieve meets the Arno some twelve miles east of Florence. The other branch bears northeast up a valley onto the main spine of the High Apennines. Bibbiena was a natural jump-off for an assault on the Gothic Line—on the crests ahead. Operation VANDAL, to take the town, was launched at 2130 hours on August 3. The 10th Indian was to storm the Catenaia Alps between the Arno and Tiber Valleys, while the 4th British tackled the Pratomagno Massif.

By daylight on August 4, the 10th's Mahrattas had marched four miles, climbed three thousand feet and secured the southern buttresses of the Catenaia Alps. Dawn, however, brought little respite as the Mahrattas then infiltrated a high saddle-back and fought towards Monte Castello, the highest crest—at 4,600 feet above the valley.

To exploit the advance, engineers worked furiously, building five miles of mule track in 18 hours, six miles of jeep track in 66 hours and five miles of tank track. On the summit of Castello, Gurkhas waited on a saddle-back for word to mount an attack on Regina, a bare bluff tucked into the crook of an easterly ridge. Elements of two enemy battalions crossed a ravine eight hundred yards behind the forward companies and dashed for the crest. The Gurkhas, out in front, retraced their steps, silent in the darkness, and fell upon the Germans at daybreak. "The hillmen went berserk," according to their historian, "hunting to the death, springing in with the stroke from behind trees, from out of the undergrowth. Screams rang through the woods as Germans fled until brought down; others knelt in the open glades with arms upraised imploring mercy. Few escaped."[41]

For the 4th Division, the operation opened well as the 1st/9th Gurkhas swept 2,000 yards along the base of the Catenaia Alps. The hillmen overran enemy outposts, killing 12 Germans and taking three prisoners at the cost of 21 casualties. The 1st/4th Essex, on their left, captured Falciano, 2,000 yards east of the Arno, while the 2nd Camerons secured the villages of Bibbiano and Monte Ferrato.

The Camerons' A Company seized Poggia del Grillo, a hilltop a mile to the north on the eastern arm of a V-shaped mountain that dominated the only road of importance leading into the Pratomagno. Two companies of the 115th Panzer Grenadiers counterattacked, overrunning a forward platoon and, using prisoners as a screen, assaulted the Cameron headquarters in a large farmhouse. German engineers blew in the doors with pole charges. Camerons and Germans fought to the death from room to room. Company commander Major Underwood was captured, but escaped when tank fire distracted his captors—he was the only survivor of three officers and sixty men. Grillo was recaptured, and held despite five counterattacks. The 4th Division had bitten deep into enemy territory, while the 10th held the crests of the Catenaia Alps. But the sector became a secondary front with the fall of Florence and a change in the Eighth Army's plans for the next phase in the fighting: a shift to the Adriatic.

West of the Indian sector, two British divisions in the valley of the Arno contested the Germans for every ridge and hamlet. The 4th Division tackled the westward heights, and on the afternoon of July 29 the 6th Black Watch stormed the crest of Monte Scalari and held it against five vigorous counterattacks. In the valley, the 4th's Reconnaissance Regiment broke the back of German resistance to take Figline on Highway 69, while the 4th's 61st Brigade drew abreast to the right. The British 6th Armoured worked a defensive flank east of the 4th Division.

From the first, on entering the Chianti country, the South African 6th Armoured (working with British infantry) had engaged the enemy only to find the Germans alternating between resistance and withdrawal—a skillful play of forces that delayed the Eighth Army advance on Florence. The South Africans caught their first glimpse of the city some twelve miles to the north late in the afternoon of July 20 from the summit of Monte San Michele, on the heights south of Greve.

On the heights bracketing Greve—Monte File to the left and Monte Domini on the right—the German 356th Division dug in with a fanatic determination to hold at all costs. The Coldstream Guards with a troop of Pretoria tanks went in after a fifty-minute controlled barrage against Domini. The Guardsmen charged, tanks behind, as the Guards' historian put it, "roaring up slopes such as the Sherman can hardly have climbed before or since."[42] By 1900 on July 23, the Germans were driven off the crest at the cost of 14 killed and 20 wounded Guardsmen.

Across the Greve Valley, the Witwatersrand Rifles, backed by tanks of the Prince Albert's Guard, captured Monte File in a stunning display of infantry and tank coordination. In the valley below, the Germans demolished what they could in Greve, leaving the town to the South Africans on the morning of the 24th.

On the next day, Pretoria tanks had exploited the northern limits of the Chianti range and the Guardsmen took 365th Battalion by sunrise to secure Monte Collegalle, the last of the Chianti hills above the road to Impruneta. German infantry supported by Tigers counterattacked and checked the South African advance there and near Mercatale on the heights to the west.

The weather was hot and dry on August, but New Zealander gains on the heights of the Pian dei Cerri Ridge on the left and the British 4th Division achieving Monte Scalari had broken the deadlock. Fighter-bombers ranged overhead, trouncing Impruneta with devastating effect. The next morning, Pretoria tanks and the Grenadier Guards entered Florence without opposition; the South Africans were moving down the valley slopes.

Within the city, the German Consul, Dr. Gerhard Wolfe, begged the General of the Engineering Corps and his staff to spare the bridges over the Arno. Florence had been declared an Open City; to destroy the bridges would be a sacrilege. In particular, Dr. Wolfe plead for the Santa Trinita, whose conception, he reminded the assembled officers, had been Michelangelo's. "The destruction of the Ponte Santa Trinità, of all the great works of art, will leave scars which are the hardest to heal and which will fill people's minds with hatred against the perpetrators," he insisted. A staff officer showed alternative demolitions plans that included the entire heart of the city. Another officer assured the Consul, "[A]t least the Ponte Vecchio [will] be spared." It was, after all, the Führer's *Lieblings-bruche*, his favorite bridge. Dr. Wolfe exploded, making the Florentine art lover's choice, "I'd rather save the Ponte Santa Trinità!"[43]

But the choice was not to be his. "We left Florence on the afternoon of July 28, with its hills covered with smoke from Allied guns and German explosives," he later recalled. "The enemy was still some two and a half miles away from the centre and might enter the town by nightfall. No one could tell what would happen."[44]

Cardinal Elia Dalla Costa, at the head of a seven-man delegation, made a last-minute plea for the salvation of the city, only to be rebuffed by Parachutist Colonel Fuchs, commander of the city's defenses. However, German Ambassador Rudolf Rahn met Kesselring at Recoaro, his staff headquarters, and told him: "Well, Field Marshal, I don't think you'd like to go down in history like that young Bavarian lieutenant who gave orders to fire on the Acropolis!" Irate, Kesselring slammed on the table a copy of General Alexander's "Special Message" to the people of Florence, which called on its citizens to "stand united" to prevent destruction of the bridges and other vital installations. The message was broadcast by the BBC on July 29 and disseminated by leaflets dropped by the RAF the next day.[45] Nicky Mariano, secretary to the noted art critic Bernard Berenson, was not the only one to react, as she noted in her diary, in anger and with scorn: "With what should this poor, peaceful, unarmed population prevent such military measures?"[46] Though the order to evacuate both sides of the Arno had already been given some 24 hours earlier, the proclamation surely risked revocation of Kesselring's Open City evacuation orders.

On July 31, the 1st Para Corps received written orders to prepare Operation FEUERZAUBER, which covered preparations for the destruction of all the bridges "in and near Florence," except the Ponte Vecchio, and houses on either side of that bridge were to be blown to make immediate access to it impossible.

At 1400 on August 3, the Germans ordered everyone off the streets under penalty of death. That evening, German soldiers withdrew from the Belvedere, an indication that they were about to yield the city, at least south of the Arno. Not long after "a formidable explosion," Ugo Procacci, a civilian who was in the courtyard of the Palazzo Pitti with a crowd of refugees, later recalled, "[E]verything seemed to crumble. . . . It seemed that the earth was trembling and that the great palace would be conquered . . . [F]rom every side glass and pieces of window rained on the crowd, and the air became unbreathable. Terror seized the crowd; a few began to cry 'The bridges, the bridges.' "[47]

South of the city, German rearguards had held up the New Zealand and South African advance in the vicinity of Galuzzo, but by first light on August 4 the Imperial Light Horse, Kimberly Regiment, occupied the commanding positions at the very edge of Florence. Italian partisans, historian Neil Orpen writes, offered to show General Poole a way into the city through the sewers, "but the idea did not appeal to the Divisional

Commander."[48]

Lieutenant J. Adamson, A Company, Kimberly Regiment, led a patrol of seven infantrymen, accompanied by Captain D.V. Jeffrey and a sapper of the 8th Field Squadron, and reached the Ponte Vecchio at 0430 on August 4. They found both approaches to the bridge, last rebuilt in A.D. 1345, blocked by debris. All buildings some 200 yards at either end had been destroyed. The Ponte alla Carraia had been flattened to water level; the three spans of the Ponte Santa Trinità were demolished.

The South Africans and, later, the New Zealanders were greeted with wine, flowers and kisses from joyous Florentines. German snipers and machine-gunners, however, continued to harass Allied troops from across the Arno. But no serious effort was made to cross the river, because the Allies did not want to make the city a battleground. Fighting continued in the loop of the Arno, east of the city, below Pontassieve. The Germans held the convent at Incontro but were finally dislodged by the 2nd Duke of Cornwall's Light Infantry. The British 4th Division then cleared the loop the following day, August 8. The Eighth Army's line on the Arno held from Pontassieve west to Fucecchio, where it met the U.S. Fifth Army.

On August 7, General Schlemn withdrew the last of his troops from Florence. Local partisans occupied the quarters south and east of the Mugnone Canal, which runs on the northwestern edge of the city. However Florence temporarily became a no-man's-land contested by roving bands of partisans and local Fascists. The Germans easily fended off the partisans along the Mugnone, but finally decided to abandon the canal line on August 17. That night, Indian infantry crossed over the Ponte Vecchio and fanned out to take over the entire city.

NOTES

[1] Von Senger, *Neither Fear Nor Hope*, pp. 267 and 273.
[2] Kesselring, *A Soldier's Record*, pp. 251-52.
[3] Ibid., p. 209.
[4] Kay, *Italy, Volume II: From Cassino to Trieste*, pp. 123–24, 126–27.
[5] Alexander, *Memoirs*, p. 40.
[6] Kay, *From Cassino to Trieste*, p. 119.
[7] Ibid., p. 124.
[8] Ibid.

[9] Ibid.

[10] Ibid., p. 125.

[11] Ibid., pp. 125–26.

[12] India, Defense Dept., *The Tiger Triumphs*, p. 114.

[13] Kay, *From Cassino to Trieste*, p. 134.

[14] India, *The Tiger Triumphs*, p. 115.

[15] Linklater, *The Campaign in Italy,* p. 333.

[16] India, *The Tiger Triumphs*, p. 110.

[17] Origo, *War in Val d'Orcia*, p. 206.

[18] This propaganda was often crude, but effective. Soldiers facing the newly arrived 10th Mountain Division in the winter and spring of 1945 were told that the elite division were killers and would take no prisoners.

[19] Von Senger, *Neither Hope Nor Fear*, p. 274.

[20] Allied insistence on an Unconditional Surrender also contributed to the German soldiers' determination to stand fast. No support whatever was given the July 20 conspirators, who were mocked and maligned as they died for taking on Hitler. B.H. Liddell-Hart, in *The German Generals Talk*, makes the point: ". . . 'blacklistening' to the Allied radio service was widespread. But the Allied propaganda never said anything positive about the peace conditions in the way of encouraging them to give up the struggle. Its silence on the subject was so marked that it tended to confirm what Nazi propaganda told them as to the dire fate in store for them if they surrendered. So it greatly helped the Nazis to keep the German troops and people to continue fighting—long after they were ready to give up."

[21] Kesselring, *A Soldier's Record*, p. 210.

[22] Kay, *From Cassino to Trieste*, pp. 138–39.

[23] Burdon, *24 thBattalion*, pp. 269–70.

[24] Pringle, *20th Battalion*, pp. 449–52.

[25] Kay, *From Cassino to Trieste*, p. 145.

[26] "Fanatical" is a pejorative adjective in English and in most Latin languages. For Hitler and his propagandists, however, it was a positive one—a view, it would seem, shared by the author of the Fourteenth Army report.

[27] Kay, *From Cassino to Trieste*, pp. 146–47.

[28] Ibid., p. 152.

[29] Pringle, *20th Battalion*, p. 457.

[30] Ibid., p. 459.

[31] Kay, *From Cassino to Trieste*, p. 164.

[32] Pringle, *20th Battalion*, p. 459.

[33] Kay, *From Cassino to Trieste*, p. 165.

[34] Kay, Ibid., p. 166.

[35] Kay, Ibid., p. 167.

[36] Kay, Ibid., p. 168.

[37] Kay, Ibid., p. 170.

[38] Puttick, *25th Battalion*, p. 468.

[39] Kay, *From Cassino to Trieste*, p. 175.

[40] Puttick, *25th Battalion*, p. 471.

[41] India, *The Tiger Triumphs*, p. 99.

42 Orpen, *Victory in Italy,* pp. 141–42.
43 Tutaev, *The Man Who Saved Florence,* p. 206.
44 Ibid., p. 214.
45 Ibid., p. 227.
46 Mariano, *Forty Years with Berenson,* p. 322.
47 Tutaev, *The Man Who Saved Florence,* p. 239.
48 Orpen, *Victory in Italy,* pp. 163–64.

IX

THE PARTISANS

North of Rome, Allied soldiers had reasons to be grateful to *I Partigiani*—the partisans—members of the Italian Resistance, who provided information about Wehrmacht defenses, disrupted enemy supply lines and harassed retreating German soldiers. Thousands of Allied soldiers also owed their lives to simple Italian folk who offered shelter, food and other aid as they made their way from prison camps to the Allied lines, or to Switzerland, or just hid until liberated by the advance of Allied arms. During Rommel's heyday, Italy had become, in fact, the repository for Allied soldiers captured during the Axis sweeps of North Africa. As the Allies drove the Germans back and invaded Sicily and Italy itself, prisoners of war were transferred to camps guarded by Italians in the Piedmont, Lombardy, Emilia Romagna, the Veneto and in Liguria—all in Italy's north. When Italy quit the Axis on September 8, 1943, many Italian prison guards simply deserted and the POWs walked away, while others found it a good deal easier to escape.

Diarist/historian Iris Origo makes the point that of the nearly 70,000 Allied POWs at large in Italy on September 8, 1943, the day of the Italian armistice, nearly half escaped, either over the northern frontiers or across the lines in the south to rejoin their own troops. Each escape, she remarks, "implie[d] the complicity of a long chain of humble, courageous helpers" whose lives were often at risk—"from the Garigliano to the Po, from the mountains of the Piemonte and the Abruzzi to the fishing villages of Liguria and Emilia." In the Orcia Valley, where the Origos farmed, escaped prisoners turned up daily in September 1943 "to ask their way. . . . They are a very mixed lot; not only British, Americans, Canadians, and South Africans, but also Tunisians with more than a touch of Arab, who can only speak Spanish, and Boers who can speak no European languages at all."[1]

Bernard Berenson, the noted Renaissance scholar, remarked in his diary in September1943: "The peasants are almost to a man on the side of the refugees and prisoners, including the British. They feed them and shelter them and help them to get away. Even shepherds driving their flocks to the Maremma, from our own hills, will dress British soldiers with their own clothes, and take them along. Persons of the upper classes, too, are said to be contributing a great deal with money and organization to feed, clothe and house 'these brigands and communists.' It is reported that they crawl, creep and drift towards the Allied forces, whom they hope to join."[2] The Marchese Paulucci de' Calboli and his wife, Pellegrina, friends of the Berensons, were denounced to the Germans and shot, "presumably [for] having sheltered in their country house [near Forli] a messenger sent from across the fighting lines to the partisans in northern Italy."[3]

"We made our way from one peasant family to another," Major Gordon Lett later recalled, "guided by their advice as to the safest paths to follow through the woods. Sometimes the youngest son would be deputed to take us part of the way; sometimes it would be the old grandfather who was our guide, leaning on his stick." Lett marveled at the friendliness and poverty of these samaritans. "Many of them had sons killed or taken prisoner."[4] It was dangerous to aid the escaping POWs. The Repubblichini, hard-line Fascists who rallied to Mussolini's new government based in Salo, on Lake Garda (Repubblica Sociale Italiana), hunted down partisans with a vengeance. A price of 1,800 lire was placed on the head of each POW. The Germans, too, offered prize money for recaptured escapees. Those Italians caught sheltering POWs were subject to martial law and risked the death penalty.

Origo avers that it would be a mistake to attribute this generous help to any political, or even patriotic, motive; the true inspiration was far simpler. As Major P. Gibson, an English officer who owed his life to such folk, put it: "Simple Christianity impelled them to befriend those complete strangers, feed them, clothe them, and help them on their way . . . All over Italy this miracle was to be seen, the simple dignity of a humble people who saw in the escaped prisoners not representatives of a power to be withstood or placated, but individuals in need of help."[5]

Inevitably, these gestures of human solidarity drew more and more Italians into the Resistance as the Fascists and Germans searched for escaped prisoners and arrested those offering shelter. Arrests were frequently capricious—well-known anti-Fascists were left at large while obscure citizens, innocent of political activity, remained imprisoned. But what tipped the scale against the Fascists was the *rastrellamento,* the "rake-up" or round-up of men between sixteen and fifty-five for work on the Gothic Line or for labor camps in Germany. Herded up by Fascist or SS troops, they were marched off without even being allowed to send a message home. Many were never seen again. Young men, therefore, took to the hills, ready recruits for the Resistance.

"There are sacrifices that redeem the failings and the blunders of an entire generation, that are not only a milestone on the long road traveled, but point to the way to follow in the future," Massimo Salvadori, a historian who worked with and in the Italian Resistance, observed. The Resistance, he adds, was also a way that Italians "redeemed themselves for Fascism."[6]

Redemption for many began when Marshall Pietro Badoglio, who replaced Mussolini, surrendered unconditionally to the Allies on September 8, 1943. Italian troops clashed against the Germans in Liguria, in Friuli, in the Three Venetias, in Tuscany, in central Italy and in Rome. In the first two days of the so-called Armistice, Italian army units counted 3,000 dead. When Italy declared war on October 13, it claimed to have an army of 400,000 men. Early in December 1943, the reborn Italian Army fielded the 1st Motorized Group, ten thousand strong, which fought creditably along the Winter Line against the Germans. In April 1944, it was replaced by the Corpo Italiano di Liberazione, 30,000 men, who took part in that summer's fighting up to the Arno and the Metauro; the Gruppi di Combattimento, six divisions, entered the line during winter 1944–1945 on the Adriatic flank. But many Italian soldiers simply deserted when the Armistice was declared, taking their rifles and whatever else they carried.

Many of the deserters became the nuclei of partisan *bande,* the Armed Resistance. In many instances they were joined by Allied POWs, who decided to remain where they were and fight. Initially, many of these youths—Italians and Allies alike—could be said, as Maria de Blasio Wilhelm puts it in her history of the Resistance, to be "camping out."[7] Soon, however, they were hunted and, often in self-defense, the hunted became hunters. In the months that followed Italy's surrender, some 25,000 were said to be active partisans in the northern parts of the country. By the summer of 1944, that number had increased to 80,000.

Though patriotism, hatred of the Fascists and of the German occupation motivated most of the youths joining the Resistance, the movement was politicized from the first. On the day following capitulation to the Allies, the Partito Communista Italiano (PCI), the Partito Socialista di Unità Proletaria (PSUP), the Partito d'Azione (Pd'A), the Partito Democrazia Cristiana (PDC) and the Partito Liberale Italiano (PLI) formed the Comitato di Liberazione Nazionale Alta Italia (CLNAI) to act as the high command of the partisan groups springing up within occupied Italy. But the Committee found it difficult to control the partisan groups from behind the Allied lines. So, a second command tier was organized on September 20: the Comitato di Liberazione Nazionale (CLN), headquartered in Milan.

Initially, the CLN, influenced by Ferruccio Parri, a founder of the Action Party, and Luigi Longo, a Communist apparatchnic, maintained that "the war of liberation . . . demands the sincere spiritual unity of the country" and that this was not possible under the government of the King and Badoglio. Alternative governments were to be formed not only in cities and villages but in factories and farmers' cooperatives. Then, Palmiro Togliatti, the Capo di Capo of the Italian Communist Party, returned from eighteen years in Moscow (where some 200 of his comrades were murdered by Stalin) with new orders. He issued them under the guise of a call for a nationally unified government. (The Soviets had recognized the Badoglio government a few weeks before Togliatti's arrival in Italy at the end of March, 1944.) The "institutional question"— that is, the nature of the state—was postponed until the end of the war. Togliatti became a minister without portfolio in a second Badoglio administration. The CLN decided to cooperate with the new government.

As in France, the Communists flourished within the Resistance. As a British War Office paper, August 30, 1944, put it, the Communists had numerous advantages: a leader with Russian cash, intelligence and diplomatic support behind him; an experienced organization with a clear program; even sympathy from the American Office of Strategic Services (OSS). The Communist Brigata (Brigade) Garibaldi, each unit with its political commissar, were the most numerous, with 38 percent of the total partisan membership. The nonpolitical Brigata Autonome, largely comprised of former members of the Italian Army and mostly located in the

Piedmont, were second with 30 percent. The Catholic Del Populo Brigade and the Giustizia e Libertà Brigades shared about 12 to 13 percent, while the Socialist Matteotti Brigades mustered a little over two percent of the partisan membership.

A partisan uprising in Naples harassed the Germans as they sought to destroy the city at the end of September, 1943. CLN strikes in March 1944 disrupted industry in Turin, Milan, Genoa, Florence and Bologna, bringing the giant Fiat Mirafiori plant in Turin to a complete standstill. In the months following the Armistice, partisans managed to form three Republics, or Free Zones, tucked up in the Apennines around Montefiorino, in the Ossola Valley north of Milan, and at Carnia, north of Udine. None managed to exist more than several months, but their suppression involved thousands of enemy troops that otherwise might have been fighting the Allies. Just before the fall of Rome, at the end of May, Alexander told *The Times* of London that the Resistance was holding down up to six of the 25 German divisions in Italy. Allied soldiers, however, only became aware of partisan activity after the fall of Rome. And the Germans, on their part, did not feel the pinch of guerrilla warfare until they began falling back to the Gothic Line.

"Partisan bands," Kesselring recalled in his memoirs, "began to be a nuisance in and on both sides of the Apennines for the first time in April 1944, being more active in the region of Florence, where, as their presence jeopardized our supplies, military counter-measures were required." However, he adds, the partisans "became more aggressive [after the fall of Rome], far more in fact than I had reckoned with, and this date may be called the birthday of the all-out guerrilla war. . . . From then on the Partisan war was an actual menace to our military operations."[8]

On July 22, the Fourteenth Army *War Diary*, notes: ". . . enmity of the Italian civilian population in the forward areas was observed to be greatly increased; it showed itself mainly in support given to the enemy— guiding patrols, giving away our positions, etc. In one divisional sector 26 Italians were shot as a reprisal."[9] Von Senger tells us, nevertheless, that by August, "in areas away from the front on the roads over the mountains life became increasingly insecure. . . . The routes we used for the withdrawal [from the Arno Valley] ran for 100 kilometers across bleak and coverless pass roads into the plain of the Po, which we were unable to dominate. Raids were a daily occurrence, and it was difficult to capture the guerrillas who roamed about the high mountains."[10] Though exact figures cannot be obtained, because, according to Kesselring, every kind of disappearance was simply listed as "missing," German casualties greatly exceeded total partisan losses. His estimate, based on oral reports, for June–August 1944 is: 5,000 killed, 7,000–8,000 more killed or kidnapped and another 8,000 wounded.[11]

"We were armed as well as possible," Luciano Gambassini, a partisan in the Arno Valley later recalled, "but were enthusiastic to be doing."[12] The Allied drive north of Rome provided the occasion, and General Alexander's proclamation, broadcast during the night of June 8–9, provided the call to action: "Patriots! As you know, the German divisions are withdrawing along all of the Italian front. . . . [They] intend to reorganize . . . [on the Gothic Line]: Do all you can to destroy, delay, deceive, the enemy. . . . Your work is of vital importance and the opportunity offered excellent. The soldiers of these divisions are discouraged, means of transportation are scarce and they are tired. . . . [M]olest the German troops . . . hinder . . . their transport. . . . It is equally essential . . . to prevent the Germans from blowing up bridges and destroying the roads. . . . Take careful note of German defensive measures, where they build their bases, where they prepare their minefields, which bridges they prepare to demolish, where they point their cannons, where they have their ammunition and oil dumps. Get all this information, note it down precisely and see that you get it through to us. This is not all: should the opportunity arise, those of you who have the means necessary go ahead and blow up from now on the ammunition and oil dumps. Instruction valid for all patriots: kill the Germans, destroy their equipment."[13]

"We were touched," Gambassini avers. "The order long awaited and desired was like the official consecration of our work."[14]

At the time of the proclamation, Allied commanders surely expected Churchill's "splendid advance" to be expeditious and rapid. In fact, after exhorting the civilian population to rise up, it became incumbent on the Allies to advance quickly. Delays would expose not only the partisans but noncombatant Italians—civilians-turning-spies in the expectation of liberation—to reprisals, hostage taking and execution. The CLN manifesto of June 15, which called for a "General Mobilization"—"Everyone has the duty to be in his fighting position"—also made sense only in the expectation of a rapid Allied advance. The manifesto, moreover, sowed seeds for a post-liberation purge: bloodshed flowing from political rivalry as well as from individual grudges, carried out on political pretexts.

All partisans, all "free citizens"—officials, too—were to follow the orders of the CLN. Committees of "workers, employees, technicians, and managers" were to take over public services, banks and "industries of relative importance." In addition, the manifesto stated that "[t]hose who, without just reason, refuse to obey the CLN and make available for the fight for liberation the means they have, will be put on a special list next to that of spies and collaborationists, for the necessary measures of civil purging."[15] The heady euphoria of liberation, as Iris Origo later remarked, would be followed by "the rise of party struggle and class hatred, the disappointments and resentments which follow upon excessive hopes."[16]

Liberation with all its trauma, however, lay ahead as Allied troops pushed north of Rome. When the 2nd Battalion of the 168th Infantry, 34th (Red Bulls) Division, on the morning of June 7 entered Civitavecchia, the seaport 44 miles above Rome already evacuated by the Germans, they were harassed by hidden riflemen. With the aid of partisans, the "Rattlesnakes" cleared out the snipers, who turned out to be chiefly Fascisti engaged in a fratricidal exchange with the partisans.

In Grosseto, partisans with rifles and machine guns attacked German reserve troops on the morning of June 15. Taken by surprise, the Germans resisted for half the day, then began to give way, a few at a time, "till that spring dusk began to fall that saw the first American jeep enter Grosseto," the 36th Division occupying it without opposition. Though the Texans repeatedly encountered strong pockets of German resistance north of the city, their progress along a fifteen-mile front gained momentum from partisan attacks upon the retreating Germans.

The partisan Bande del Gruppe Tirli, centered on a small village in the mountains some 15 miles northwest of Grosseto, numbered 600 men at the time—reinforced by 224 Russian deserters from the German Army. American air drops on June 8, 9 and 10 provided supplies that were put to good use above Grosseto, where a unit of some sixty SS lost 11 killed and 4 prisoners to the Tirli group. "Our losses," the group's diary noted: ". . . one woman, the mother of a patriot, whom we used as an informant." Over the next five days, the Tirli partisans killed 11 more Germans, wounded 5 and captured 12, with the loss of only one man taken prisoner. Soon, the diary concluded, "[t]he area was completely empty of Germans."[17]

Partisans were useful guides for the Red Bulls, working house by house through the rubble of Rosignano some weeks later, early in July. The village of Castiglioncello, the Oberdan Chiesa Brigade reported, was "controlled by two squads of the brigade. . . . Beyond the railway tunnel, at midnight today, there was a shooting match between our elements aided by an American tank and a squad of SS sappers. One of our partisans fell and two SS were eliminated from the battle."

Four squads, forty men, marched on Nibbiaia, a town perched on the ridges running north towards Leghorn, and "after an exchange of shots" the Germans withdrew, "leaving two dead on the ground, some guns and a machine gun." Another Oberdan squad, under the command of an American lieutenant, attacked Germans posted with machine guns and mortars in the castle of Sonnio on the coast in the vicinity of Quercianella, where they freed some American prisoners. One partisan fell, but as the Germans retreated another squad attacked. "The Nazis hit by our sub-machine-gun fire and by our hand-grenades end[ed] up in the sea."[18]

Partisans were useful to the 363rd Infantry on July 13 in "cleaning [Chianni] of many enemy," according to the regimental historian.[19] Partisans also accompanied Americans probing approaches to the Arno. One patrol from the 442nd Battalion entered the southern portion of Pisa with a partisan guide on the night of July 21. They had some bad moments, having had to hole up in a partisan house while a German patrol wandered around downstairs. But the patrol returned the next day with a sketch made by a partisan leader of the entire enemy dispositions, including minefields and river crossings used by the Germans.

The South Africans met partisans for the first time on June 7 on a minor road some twenty-five miles north of Rome, east of Viterbo. Ten Germans were handed over as prisoners. Partisans warned of catacombs and cellars in Chiusi, suggesting that clearing the town would be a tough proposition. Partisans were also active in the countryside as the South African tanks moved against the Trasimeno Line west of the lake and past Siena into the Chianti Hills. At the edge of Florence, the Witwatersrand Rifles/De la Rey Regiment engaged in street fighting "against both Germans and Fascists, who were being winkled out by Partisans." Orpen, the South Africans' historian, concludes, "Much help had been received from the activities of the Italian Partisans."[20]

Florence, across the Arno from the hesitant Allied forces, became a no-man's-land. On July 30, the Germans ordered the evacuation of a broad area surrounding the bridges over the Arno. Some 150,000 people were affected and given only a few hours to flee and find new quarters. Wheelbarrows were used to move the sick and infirm. Electricity and water were shut down. Food was in short supply. The Germans posted their last order on August 3, forbidding the Florentines their streets, and advising them to take to their cellars or churches or other large buildings—warning that German patrols had "orders to shoot against people who are found in the streets, or who show themselves at the windows."

On August 6, the German commander, Colonel Fuchs, permitted women and children to foray for food and water. Meanwhile, rats overran streets stinking of garbage and unburied bodies. Partisan courier Maria Luiga Guaita recalls hugging "the walls heated by sunshine, the closed doors. . . . Every now and then there appeared a German patrol or a small bivouac." The soldiers, by day, she noted, seemed indifferent, "too tired and discouraged." At night, "they did nothing else but fire here and there without reason, blindly, perhaps to make us keep still, quiet, to keep the city calm and dead, perhaps to give themselves courage."[21]

Many among the Allied soldiers south of the river and among those citizens taking a last look at their city before hiding from German patrols feared that they were looking at Brunelleschi's Cupola, Giotto's Campanile and Arnolfo's Tower for the last time. And, in the final days after the Germans withdrew to the northwest of the city along the Mugnone Canal, German shells intermittently struck the churches Santo Spirito and Santa Croce, one side of the Duomo, the center of the Uffizi Palace and the Loggia del Bigallo—knocking off the head of the Madonna by Arnoldi. The Allies had urged the Florentines "to prevent the destruction of their city" and, at the same time, warned that this "is not the time for public demonstrations . . . go about your daily business. . . . It is our job to destroy the enemy."[22]

The Florentines responded as best they could, given the circumstances and the contradiction inherent in "prevent . . . destruction . . . go about your daily business." In a fearless and imaginative stroke, Athos Albertoni, chief of the Tuscan Giustizia e Libertà partisans, occupied the Questura and seized ammunition stored in the police barracks. The partisans held the police chief's daughter and wife hostage as the chief went about town looking as if he was still in charge. Organized partisans within the city at the end of July numbered about 2,000, plus some 800 operating south of the Arno. They had available some 900 guns and rifles, 48 light machine guns, 1,300 hand grenades and ammunition for an hour's shooting.

Sporadic attempts by the Oltrarno partisans to save the bridges over the Arno were crushed by the enemy with little difficulty. Partisan youths, however, managed to save the aqueduct at Mantignano, just south of the river at the junction of the Greve, which was to prove so important in the revival of the city. Ascanio Taddei, an eighteen-year-old, and his five companions defused the mines at the aqueduct at dawn on August 4 just as the Germans were about to set explosives off there. Five lost their lives when some of the mines exploded. Gino Romoli lost a leg. Don Panerai, the parish priest of San Felice, among the first to scout the ruins on the south side of the Arno, remarked, "No one among those ruins asked for help, only the shots of the snipers began to hit their targets."

As the Germans left the city, the Fascist Black Militia remained active as Florence became a city of snipers. Gaetano Casoni, a Florentine merchant, noted in his diary on August 10: "The streets seem more deserted than usual, while from every side we could hear cannon which seemed closer today. I was told the usual sad news: always rapes, looting and killing."[23]

Earlier, on August 5, Enrico Fischer, a Partito d'Azione commander, had slipped into the Palazzo Vecchio (then German headquarters) with the help of a friendly civilian guard. He made his way to the adjoining Uffizi Gallery and scrambled through the Vasari Corridor above the Ponte Vecchio, a hallway built by Medici nobles who wanted to cross the river to the Pitti Palace without being observed. After conferring with an Allied officer in charge, it was decided that the ancient corridor was too weak and vulnerable for use. However, a telephone wire was threaded through to the Palazzo Vecchio, under German noses, to establish communication between the Allies and the Resistance within the city.

During the night of August 10–11, the Germans abandoned the area around the Stazione Centrale and withdrew to the Mugnone. The next day, courier Maria Luigia Guaitia reported the latest information gathered by partisan vedettes to the City Command. She was then sent to the Palazzo Vecchio with this message: "The bell of the Bargello must ring out immediately, and the tricolor must be raised immediately on Palazzo Vecchio." After delivering the message, she ran off to another partisan command center. "It was five o'clock," she recalls. "In front of the lowered blinds of the Bizzarri Chemists I stopped, lost; the bell of the

Bargello, silent for four years, had rung out once, and in that silence seemed magic; there it was a second time, I lifted my eyes up and another miracle happened: slowly on the tower of the Palazzo Vecchio the tricolor rose. I knelt down crying on the pavement while one by one the shutters in the square opened wide." A woman asked if the Germans were gone. Sobbing and opening her arms, Guaitia cried out, "We're free, free."[24]

The Germans blew the bridges over the Mugnone at six o'clock as the bells of the city rang out, calling for an uprising. "In a flash we were all in the open along the streets looking for the enemy," a partisan commander reported, "running, at times in groups, to where shots could be heard. It was in this first onrush of courage that we had the greatest losses."[25]

Two hundred and five were killed in partisan attacks on the German line along the Mugnone. German tanks fired down the streets leading to the center of the city. Slowly, the partisan command imposed order as the realization spread that the Germans were not in "retreat" but had formed a well-equipped line of defense. It arched across the northern edge of the city from the Arno to the Piazzale del Re, to the Cascine Park, along the Mugnone to the Piazza delle Cure, and from there along the Florence–Rome rail line as far as the Viale delle Cure. Fascist snipers and German sharpshooters were stationed along that front. Oltrarno partisans forded the river, single-file on the rib of the Santa Rosa fish weir. "Not a living soul was in the squares or streets to greet us on the other bank," the British liaison officer, Hubert Howard, later recalled. "A menacing silence had spread over the city and bit by bit, as they formed groups, the partisans advanced with the soft cautious tread of jungle beasts to take up their posts along the Mugnone front." Howard adds that a long, hushed applause came from behind the many shutters as the first patrol passed by.[26] The Germans, however, kept the partisans at bay along the Mugnane.

Florence was the first city in which the CLN had established itself before the arrival of the Allies. Indian troops entered Florence on August 13. "The Gurkhas advance warily," an observer recalled, "scanning the windows and roofs for snipers, treading carefully where mines were suspected. They darted from corner to corner; ahead was heard the clatter of machine guns. Italian partisans turned up, warning of booby-traps and bewailing the damage to their famous city. The Florentines began to appear at windows, cheering the Gurkhas. People thronged into the streets, picking their way between miles of rubble, to queue up for water, or to gaze angrily at the destruction."

German soldiers and even German tanks "bobbed up" from unsuspected hideouts. Outside the Palazzo Ricardi, eight Italian *carabinieri* were killed. An enemy raiding party backed by two tanks sallied among Mahratta billets on the Piazza Vasari and shot up a number of houses. German paratroopers who appeared on one of the main streets, however, were dispersed by the Royal West Kents. General Lemelsen on August 17 ordered his paratroopers to abandon the Mugnone Canal line. "Bit by bit," the Indian account concludes, "the great city was brought under control, the last enemies extirpated and the public services restored."[27]

Not all Allies were enamored of the partisans. Colonel Fry, commander of the Blue Devils' 350th Infantry, conceded that in the overall picture they were probably helpful: "Entire villages in the Apennine Mountains, razed to the ground in retaliation for their actions, is evidence of that fact." However, he adds, "my every dealing with them was a disappointment." One partisan band of some twenty-five men, "armed with every conceivable type of weapon, and with miscellaneous belts of ammunition draped across them in the fashion of Mexican bandits," turned up at Colonel Fry's hilltop headquarters at the Villa Barbiallo to report a violent firefight in which they had been engaged at the Blue Devils' right front. Colonel Fry dispatched combat patrols to the threatened sector only to discover that "the information given us had been mostly fiction."[28]

The notion that a popular uprising drove the Germans out of Florence has been disputed by some Italian participants in the Resistance. Carlo Francovich, director of the Istituto Storico della Resistenza (Historical Institute of the Resistance) in Toscana and a prominent figure in the Partito d'Azione, avers: "I would say that, as far as the citizen milieu is concerned in the early weeks, in the early months of the Nazi–Fascist occupation, not many engaged in clandestine fighting, and those few could not always count on the collaboration of all the citizens." It was with the impending German defeat, the advance of the Allied armies and the growing discomforts of the occupation that "the greater part of the people of the city participated in the fight for freedom," he explains. The clandestine struggle was led by "a politicized elite, coming from very different beliefs and ideologies," that formed the center of Resistance in the CLNs.

Francovich notes that the party that most controlled the masses in

Florence as well as in the rest of Italy was the Communist Party, which subsequently adopted the hagiography of popular uprisings. Guiseppe Rossi, a prominent Florentine Communist, acknowledged immediately after liberation, however, that the masses were not as the Communists wished. "It was thought possible [to call a strike] making the workers stay inside the workshops with the purpose of defending them arms in hand. . . . We realized, instead, late in the day that such a watchword was impossible." Rossi added: "One of the big deficiencies shown by our party in this period consists in not having managed to mobilize the popular masses of the districts of the city into a form of open struggle against the invader and against the Fascists."[29]

The partisan bands, too, attracted some odd types of men. Some were simply bent on revenge—something understandable, perhaps, for the Repubblichini, the new Republican Fascists, were increasingly vicious and, in their early stages, arrogant. As Iris Origo noted in her diary: "We are being governed by the dregs of the nation—and their brutality is so capricious that no one can feel certain that he will be safe tomorrow." Revenge shaded into summary executions with no foundation in law or morality, as in the case of the assassination of the head of the Fascists in Ferrara. Such killings, of course, increased the odds of reprisals against the innocent. Others appear to be the consequence of robbery, as at Mercale, where, Origo says, "a Fascist factor was shot by a group of partisans who came to fetch him in his house, stole his horse and some wheat, and left his corpse in a farmhouse with a bullet in his head."

One night in March 1944, Origo found her husband arguing with two strange men. It appeared that the day before an unknown man had handed her husband an illiterate intimidatory letter, ostensibly from a partisan group, requesting an immediate "gift" of 80,000 lire. He was told to get out. Now, these two, a day later, also "requested" money to help the partisans. The Marchese Origo said he would consider the request if the two men could prove that they really were partisans—"whereupon his guests turned upon each other with eloquent mutual accusations of dishonesty." Near Siena, Origo noted on April 4, 1944, another large farm was broken into by a band who removed 150,000 lire as well as twelve pairs of sheets and some food. "More and more," she adds, "the partisans are resorting to looting—a fact which is bitterly deplored both by the genuine patriots among them, and by the timid, but perfectly honest, peasant boys who have joined them merely to avoid their army service."[30]

No question but that the war that involved the Fascists and the Germans, on one side, and the partisans and much of the populace on the other became nastier and nastier as the Allies pressed hard on the heels of the retreating enemy. North of Arezzo, the historian of the Indian divisions remarks, ". . . the Germans had made war in the most detestable Nazi fashion." Three Allied prisoners of war were hanged at Talla on the Pratomagno. Near Arezzo, three partisans were shot and their bodies "bombed into senseless mutilation." An Indian Army observer saw in a nearby village the body of a girl who had been violated, murdered and mutilated. When an enemy garrison in Guilano was shot up by an Essex patrol, the Germans burned the village, "even though it cost them their billets."[31]

German reaction to the partisans is perhaps the best gauge of the effectiveness of the Resistance. The Germans became increasingly irritated at the daily raids mounted behind their lines by these loyalist Italians. A justifiable anger, Von Senger claims, generated by the raids and the failure to capture the raiders, led to reprisals. But the guerrillas evaded these counter-measures, too, he says, "which unfortunately fell too often on innocent people, thus producing the opposite effect to that intended. Consequently the Germans were hated by more and more people." It was wrong, Von Senger insists, to hold villagers responsible for the acts of terrorists. He tried, evidently, to keep his troops in line.

Von Senger was not happy over "the compulsory cooperation with the Fascist–Republican government-sponsored Black Shirt Brigades. They were probably more loathed, he said, by the populace than "the German occupiers, the Allied liberators, or the guerrillas of whatever political color." Cooperation with the Black Shirts, he adds, made the task of the Wehrmacht more difficult, "for it meant that the Germans were put in the same category with the most hated section of the population."[32] Still, the Germans were in no position to dispense with local spies who could keep an eye on guerrilla activity. Nor could the Germans simply ignore the partisan attacks. Von Senger was "compelled"—his choice of words—that autumn to move his headquarters from a country villa to the safety of a nearby village.

Kesselring shared the anger of his soldiers against that "motley collection of Allied, Italian and Balkan soldiers, German deserters and native civilians of both sexes and widely different callings and ages with varying ideas of morality, with the result that patriotism was often a cloak for the release of baser instincts." Kesslering held that "[t]he Partisan war was a complete violation of international law and contradicted every principle of clean soldierly fighting."

Under the Hague Conventions on the conduct of war, an occupying army in time of war was entitled to execute francs-tireurs (i.e., irregulars) unless they were organized in regular units under recognized commands and wore uniforms or other visible distinguishing signs and emblems. Clearly, many partisans and partisan units did not conform to these requirements, although, as Kesselring acknowledges, "later on . . . things were not so bad in this respect."[33] Partisans, Kesselring goes on to say: "almost always wore no emblems, hid their weapons or, again in violation of international war, went about dressed as Germans or Fascists, thus freeing themselves from the obligations a uniform carries." Small wonder, Kesselring argues, that the German soldier in a partisan area "could not help seeing in every civilian of either sex a fanatical assassin or expect to be fired at from every house." Nor would the partisan bands accept a fair fight, he complained; they would melt away after doing their mischief among the civilian population, much like "innocent country hikers."

In his summation of partisan characteristics, Kesselring acknowledges a grudging admiration for those he calls "reconnaissance troops"— professionally trained small groups, "gallant men who risked their necks." Excepting that they violated international law, he writes, "no objection could be taken to them." Saboteurs, who belonged to this group, however, increasingly "violated the laws of humanity," the criminal element being strongly represented among them. Then there were the riff-raff, "who robbed, murdered and pillaged . . . a national scourge." Last but not least were the main partisan groups, which increasingly took on a military character and enlisted more or less support "according to the attitude of the local inhabitants." In their areas were Partisan-occupied villages, even zones, "in which every man, woman and child was in some way connected with them, either as combatant, helper or sympathizer." Whether these supporters acted voluntarily or under "gentle pressure" made no difference. "When a bullet killed a German soldier it was not possible for us to discriminate."[34]

By June 1944, it was clear to Kesselring that the partisans "might critically affect the retirement of my armies." In the months that followed, German Army Intelligence reported on the "constant spread" of partisan activity, rising to five or six "special incidents" a day. Acts of sabotage on railways, depots and dumps were more or less localized and routine, but the frequency of surprise attacks changed constantly—governed by the situation at the front.

Orders issued by Kesselring reflected his growing alarm. On June 17: "The fight against the bands is to be prosecuted with the greatest severity. I will support any commander who in his choice and severity of means goes beyond our customary measure of restraint." The order, Kesselring insisted, had nothing to do with reprisals as such. His second order, issued on July 1 in response to Alexander's broadcast appeal for the intensification of partisan warfare and its call upon patriots to kill Germans, stated the terms of reprisal: "Every act of violence on the part of the bands is to be punished." Where the bands appear in considerable numbers "a percentage of the male population resident in the district, to be decided upon at the time, is to be arrested, and if acts of violence occur they are to be shot." Where soldiers are shot from a village, the village is to be burnt. "Culprits and ringleaders are to be publicly hanged." These, however, were not to be summary executions; courts-martial had to be convened. The order concluded: "All measures must be harsh but just. The good name of the German soldier requires this."[35]

Kesselring points out in his memoirs that in no proved case were band members executed after hostilities without a previous sentence by court-martial. In August he warned his troops against violence toward civilians that had no relation to retaliatory measures. Mussolini, according to Kesselring, complained of retaliatory measures that fell upon the population "instead of on the bandits." After the war, Kesselring acknowledged that "on the German side, too, abominable things were done. But the fact remains that only in a few exceptional instances has convincing proof been furnished of the guilt of German soldiers." Excesses or acts of barbarity, he insisted, "must be equally shared among partisan bands, neo-Fascist organizations and German deserter groups, whereas only the smallest fraction—if any—should be laid at the door of German military units. Perhaps also a good many incidents should be attributed to stragglers who overstepped the permissible limits of self-help."[36]

The partisan war exacted a bitter toll. "The local news is grim," Iris Origo notes in her diary on March 14, 1944. The deadline for "joining up"— with Mussolini's army—had passed and the recruits of the 1922–25 class faced savage penalties for evading what amounts to a draft. Three who failed to report "have been shot in Siena, in the presence of their comrades as 'an example.'"[37]

At Piancastagnaio, a village overlooking Monte Amiat from the southeast, two partisans, caught in the woods, were shot on the spot and their corpses hung at the town gates. . . . Florentines passing by a sedate, grayish marble and sandstone, five-story apartment house, Villa Triste, at the corner of Via Bolognese and Via del Pellegrino, could hear the screams and moans of the victims of Major Mario Carità, Fascist thug and chief of the Fascist Ufficio Politico Investigativo. . . . A young partisan, accused of shooting a German at Chiusi, was publicly hanged on a lamppost, though the mayor believed him innocent; a German soldier, however, had identified the youth and the alternative was the execution of ten hostages. (A guard was mounted to ensure that the body was not cut down in the night.)

"I remember one village above Arezzo," Origo says, "suspected of having helped the partisans, in which no male creature between the ages of seven and seventy had been left alive; they had all been lined up one Sunday morning in the little piazza after Sunday Mass and shot."[38] . . . Two German soldiers in an inn at Civitella della Chiana had been killed for their weapons; a third, wounded, had escaped to report to his unit. Two days later, German troops arrived to exact a reprisal, but the German commander—in response to a plea from the parish priest—sent everyone home. Four days later, June 29, however, SS troops accompanied by Fascists entered Civitella. "To be a man," writes Elda Morfini Paggi, whose husband and father were killed, "meant to be condemned to death." Even the old men in the workhouse. After the post-Mass massacre, the bodies were dragged into the houses and the whole village set on fire."[39]

Other villagers suffered a like fate. At Loro Ciuffenna, a village on the western slope of the Pratomagno, after an attack against a German vehicle by partisans in which four Germans were killed, thirty-one people were slaughtered on June 6. . . . At Chiusi della Verna, east of Bibbiena, a German was killed in a clash with partisans. Both groups fled. Fifteen armed Germans with sub-machine guns, pistols and grenades returned. "They seemed bedeviled," an eyewitness, a woodcutter, testified. At the first houses, "they killed the Pignatellis, father and son, and injured his wife and daughter, whom they left abandoned on the spot as dead."

Shooting blindly, they entered the village and dropped a sack of flour on the steps of the fountain. Father Raffaello came to help the injured and was ordered to go and fetch the sack. Forced forward, he was cut down. Oscar Minelli was told to approach the sack. "Minelli did not want to go near the sack, he implored mercy. They kicked him forward and shot him dead."[40]

Angelo Bigoni, "an old wreck of a man who could only just stand on his feet," got the same treatment. A doctor and a carter saved themselves by fleeing the scene. A Sister, who looked out the door of the kindergarten with an orphan girl at her side, was killed and the child injured. "Shooting and yelling like devils," the eyewitness continued, the Germans moved on to another group of houses. Feo Minelli and Guerrini were killed, as were, the next morning when the Germans returned, Pietro Lusini and Sisto Ridolfi. "There were no more Christians to kill," the woodcutter said. "In a field near the farmhouse, a donkey and goat grazed; they killed them too. They were thirsty for blood, those angry dogs."[41] There is an element of panic here—and more. . . . Outside Molino Nuovo, on June 24, ten peasants mowing a field were taken by the Germans. Their women asked for mercy, asserting their innocence. The unit commander through his interpreter replied: "I, too, am sure they are innocent, as I am sure that we have lost the war; however, I must have them shot no matter what."[42]

It would not be the last word in the grim partisan war.

NOTES

[1] Origo, *War in Val d'Orcia*, pp. 12–13.
[2] Berenson, *Rumour and Reflection*, pp. 130–31.
[3] Mariano, *Forty Years with Berenson*, p. 295.
[4] Lett: *Rossano*, pp. 19–20.
[5] Origo, *War in Val d'Orcia*, p. 13.
[6] Salvadori, *Storia della Resistenza*, p. 19.
[7] Wilhelm, *The Other Italy*, p. 33.
[8] Kesselring, *A Soldier's Record*, p. 225.
[9] Kay, *Italy: Volume II: From Cassino to Trieste*, p. 124.
[10] Von Senger, *Neither Fear Nor Hope*, pp. 269–70.
[11] Kesselring, *A Soldier's Record*, pp. 227–28.
[12] Casella, *The European War of Liberation*, p. 124.
[13] Casella, Ibid.

[14] Casella, Ibid.

[15] Ibid., pp. 125–26.

[16] Origo, *Images and Shadows,* p. 146.

[17] Casella, *The European War of Liberation,* p. 167.

[18] Ibid., p. 219.

[19] Strootman, *History of the 363rd Infantry,* p. 32.

[20] Orpen, *Victory in Italy,* pp. 164 and 170.

[21] Casella, *The European War of Liberation,* p. 248.

[22] Ibid., p. 235.

[23] Wilhelm, *The Other Italy,* p. 230.

[24] Casella, *The European War of Liberation,* p. 249.

[25] Ibid., p. 249.

[26] Ibid., p. 251.

[27] India, *The Tiger Triumphs.* p. 117.

[28] Fry, *Combat Soldier,* pp. 157–58.

[29] Casella, *The European War of Liberation,* p. 254.

[30] Origo, *War in Val d'Orcia,* pp. 118, 114, 155 and 160.

[31] India, *TheTiger Triumphs,* p. 110.

[32] Von Senger, *Neither Fear Nor Hope,* pp. 269–70.

[33] Kesselring, *A Soldier's Record,* p. 227.

[34] Ibid., p. 226.

[35] Ibid., pp. 301-302.

[36] Ibid., p. 232.

[37] Origo, *War in Val d"Orcia,* p. 152.

[38] Origo, *Images and Shadows,* p. 152.

[39] Casella, *The Europan War of Liberation,* p. 188.

[40] Ibid., p. 184.

[41] Ibid., p. 185.

[42] Ibid.

X

PAUSE ALONG THE ARNO

The Fifth Army reached the banks of the Arno on July 18 and by the 23rd it had cleared out most of the enemy's outposts and strong points south of the river. Sapped by exhaustion, and crippled by the loss of three divisions drawn off for the invasion of southern France, the Allies paused. Past experience had shown that an assault on prepared German positions must be well planned. Time, too, was needed to refit, replenish and retrain the weary troops. In fact, U.S. forces alone suffered 11,259 casualties between June 5 and August 15: 1,939 killed, 8,777 wounded, and 549 missing. And Leghorn was not yet open.[1] All this, as the *Fifth Army History* put it, "necessitated" a period of "relative inactivity."[2] Ironically, as Jack Delaney of the 88th Division noted, ". . . it was beautiful fighting weather—if any weather can be called that—with warm, clear days and crisp, cool nights."[3] Across the Arno, the Germans waited, while, in General Clark's words, "[t]he two weeks' rest that had seemed necessary before crossing the Arno stretched out through most of August."[4]

The German air force was all but gone by the time the Allies reached the Arno and anti-aircraft units were no longer needed. Since infantry was in short supply, Clark fashioned Task Force 45 out of redundant anti-aircraft units. Ack-ack gunners now carried M-1 rifles. Infantry equipment was borrowed from the 34th Division. The 45th Anti-Aircraft Artillery Brigade, which had provided ack-ack for most of the combat divisions and for the supply and communication routes in the IV Corps area, formed the nucleus of the new Task Force, joined by newborn foot soldiers from the 91st, 107th and the 434th Ack-Ack groups, the British Light AA Regiment less one battalion, the 751st Tank Battalion, and Company B of the 805th Tank Destroyers. After completing only one-half of their scheduled training, the new infantrymen went on line on July

24 to relieve the battle-weary 34th Division along a ten-mile sector west along the Arno from the Ligurian coast.

The hurried deployment of Task Force 45 was essential to the overall regrouping of the Fifth Army across a 30-mile front from the coast east to the Elsa River, near Empoli. Task Force 45 shared a 23-mile IV Corps sector with the revamped First Armored on its right. Five miles east of Pontedera, a regimental (362nd) combat team of the 91st Division covered II Corps' seven-mile front. This disposition enabled the bulk of the Fifth Army to rest, giving Clark five outfits—four infantry and one armored division—ready to resume the offensive by mid-August. (American strength was down to 147,036 from 231,306 on June 4; the British were down to 15,758 from 43,784; the Italians, 8,242 from 9,356. The French, who had been reduced to 88,460 from 95,142, left to join the fighting in France.) By now, two other outfits were on the way to Italy, however—the American all-black 92nd Division and the Brazilian Expeditionary Force, consisting of three regimental combat teams and auxiliary support. Even so, this gave the Fifth Army but seven divisions; as historian Ernest F. Fisher, Jr., remarks, "only half as many as in May along the Garigliano River at the beginning of the drive to Rome."[5]

An Army at rest is rarely an army at ease, as Shakespeare well knew: "From camp to camp. . . /The hum of either army stilly sounds,/ That the fix'd sentinels almost receive/The secret whispers of each other's watch:/ Fire answers fire, and through their pale flames/Each battle sees the other's umber'd face;/ . . . and from the tents/The armourers . . . closing rivets up,/Give dreadful note of preparation," he wrote, in *Henry V.* The dread notes heard on the eve of the battle of Agincourt were echoed along the Arno as August 1944 drew to a close.

Casualties were light, although troops were harassed by enemy artillery. Not much else happened during the day, but at night enemy patrols, often forty to fifty men strong, crossed the river to probe Fifth Army lines. Some enemy patrols holed up in houses south of the river during the day and resumed their forays in the dark. It was said that the Germans were offering a reward of a two-day furlough, twenty Reichsmarks (then about four dollars) and an Iron Cross Second Class for one Allied soldier brought back unharmed or slightly wounded. If so, one German patrol, "in strength," did well in mid-August when it caught out a 91st Division outpost on the San Miniato–Fucecchio road some 500 yards from the bank of the Arno. The Germans took ten men and two officers prisoner.

Fifth Army combat patrols of five to twenty men scouted the Arno for the "secret whispers" of this war, enemy strongpoints and possible river crossings. The 91st's History records laconically: "Their success varied greatly."[6] Powder River experiences during August suggest that the men had, indeed, to tread warily. More than one patrol had to return because the banks of the river—it was low and fordable that time of year, only two feet deep in places—were so heavily strewn with Schu mines (designed to blow off feet, legs, and, causing great trepidation among the infantry, sometimes other body parts). When the 3rd Battalion, 337th Regiment, of the 85th Division, relieved the 3rd Battalion, 363rd, of the 91st Division, along the Arno northwest of San Miniato, it found that "enemy patrolling had been very aggressive."[7]

The Arno loops north here, and it provided the Germans with a salient into the Allied sector. The Germans greeted the 337th's 3rd Battalion with a thirty-man raiding party that took one officer and fourteen men from L Company and four men from K Company prisoner at 0800 on August 17. The next night, the Battalion countered with ambush patrols. Lieutenant Tom F. Sneary's L Company 2nd Platoon patrol engaged in a firefight—three men wounded, casualties inflicted on the enemy "unknown." Several nights later, another L Company patrol ran into sniper fire from a house 800 yards south of the Arno. Lieutenant Ferris E. Ceccinelli was wounded and evacuated. Other patrols that night returned with nothing to report except Schu mines aplenty. Booby traps were also planted in the vineyards and drainage ditches. Eight-man teams were sent out to clean up the trails in the sector— with some success.

One night, an enemy SP gun drew up north of the river opposite I Company. It shelled the American lines intermittently for four hours, killing two and wounding three. Patrols kept prodding the enemy towards the river in an effort to clean out the salient. Booby traps and mines exacted most of a toll of five enlisted men killed, 21 and two officers wounded and 19 men and one officer "missing" in ten days on what was deemed a quiet front. Twenty Germans were reported killed, five wounded and three taken prisoner.[8]

For all the patrol activity along the Arno front, the pause allowed weary soldiers hot baths, a change of clothing, hot meals, and the opportunity to catch up on mail from home. Blue Devil Private Alvin J. Buckinger got a notice from his draft board telling him that they had voted to defer him from service! Folks back home in Texas wrote, saying that Lieutenant Herman Yezak, also of the 88th, had been nominated to the state legislature. Most mail, of course, brought family news, expressions of support and love, hope from home.

Now, too, there were passes to Rome, San Gimignano, Volterra, and Siena. Private Vincent Visco's Blue Devil pals organized "family-searching parties" to help the Philadelphian locate relatives in Florence; success was crowned with invitations to a wedding. In the vicinity of Leghorn, where the 88th was in reserve, Colonel Fry commandeered two partly destroyed buildings on the waterfront for the men of the 350th Infantry. "Under such conditions," Fry remarked, "young men are resourceful, and signorinas and Red Cross girls began to make their appearance."[9] There were even occasional dances in the enlisted men's clubs, as well as swimming and boating in the evening.

Fifth Army Special Services provided motion pictures, USO shows, including the popular "Stars and Gripes," games and sports. Cardinal Spellman of New York was among the many noted visitors who came to cheer the troops. Lily Pons and her husband, André Kostelanetz, entranced even the toughest G.I.s. When she began to sing at one concert, standing on a box in a forest where multitudinous crickets chirped in the hushed silence that greeted her appearance, it seemed to General Clark that "millions of crickets were singing with her in a fantastic but lovely duet under the pine trees."[10]

Rations of beer and cigarettes were boosted even as soldiers combed the countryside for *vino*, often getting the stock reply, "*Niente vino; i tedeschi hanno portato tutta via*" ("No wine; the Germans have carried all of it away"). Contests were organized. In the Blue Devils' 350th Regiment, companies vied—for a pool of $936—for the best scores in firing rifle, machine gun and pistol. Company B won, with a score of 1,006, and Company L, with a score of 1,005, won a day's free time and transportation to the beach for swimming.

Still, recreation was not without its grim reminders of war. A bulldozer leveling a field for sandlot baseball was blown up by a mine and its driver killed. And a "bouncing Betty"—a mine that sprang into the air when tripped—nearly killed Fry while he was following a company training exercise.

The three "Rs"—recreation, reorganization and retraining—waxed as the pause along the Arno lengthened throughout August. The 1st

Armored, withdrawn into reserve on July 18, lost its commander, Major General Ernest N. Harmon, who was sent to the States to command a corps. Old Ironsides' new commander, Major General Vernon E. Prichard, not only replaced a popular officer but also faced the task of reorganizing the division.

Prichard had commanded the 14th Armored Division in the States since its activation in 1943. A West Point graduate, he first saw service on the Texas–Mexico border and in the 1916 punitive expedition into Mexico. He served in France during World War I as an infantry officer and between wars taught at West Point, Yale and Maxwell Field, and attended service schools at Forts Sill and Leavenworth and the Army War College. The reorganization of the 1st Armored was long overdue—the "new" Table of Organization for armored divisions had been adopted by the Army in the fall of 1943, however major changes had been considered "inadvisable" for a division about to land at Salerno.

The new setup was based on lessons learned from the 1st Armored's combat experiences in North Africa. While reorganization was essential and inevitable, it came as somewhat of a shock to Old Ironsiders with a feel for its traditions. The new Table of Organization cut the strength of an armored division from 14,620 to 10,937 but since the 1st Armored was already undermanned their actual loss in the revamp was just under 1,000. Old-timers, nonetheless, were upset by the elimination of three regimental headquarters—each, as Division historian George F. Howe points out, with its own "lineage and traditions stemming from old and honored forebears." In their stead, Old Ironsides now had three separate tank battalions and three separate armored infantry battalions. These could be "mixed" with supporting units to form two combat commands. The engineer battalion was cut from 1,174 to 693 by disbanding two companies. Army became responsible for quartermaster supplies. The number of medium tanks was also cut, from 250 to 154. The old setup had been ponderous, of course, and streamlining did enhance control and maneuverability. Nevertheless, Old Ironsides was now, as Howe remarks, "in important respects a different unit."[11]

The 34th Division, too, lost a beloved commander to promotion. The Red Bulls had come a long way with few respites, from Tunisia in 1943 to the banks of the Arno. The men were weary and ready for relief. Major General Charles W. Ryder was a field soldier, and he fashioned a fighting outfit out of the inexperienced Red Bulls, making real the

Division slogan, "Attack! Attack! Attack!" But he was now close to mental and physical exhaustion.

General Clark decided to replace the 55-year-old Ryder, who became a Corps commander in the States, with a younger man, Major General Charles L. Bolte. Ryder turned over the Red Bulls to Bolte at a brief but moving ceremony on July 21, east of Leghorn and south of the Leaning Tower of Pisa. Ryder, a gaunt six-foot-three-inch figure, spoke briefly to his officers against the backdrop of a sunlit day and the rolling boom of artillery along the front. Division historian Lieutenant Colonel John H. Hougen reports that Ryder closed with simple words of appreciation, "God-speed." He then turned and "walked abruptly away with long, loose-jointed strides, determined not to trust a visibly faltering control of his emotions."[12]

Major General John E. Sloan of the Blue Devils became ill; "an annoying and puzzling skin condition," John Delaney reported in his history of the Devils.[13] Overexertion, Fry remarked, left Sloan "drawn and haggard."[14] After undergoing treatment in a field hospital near Leghorn, he was sent to the States to recuperate, and ended the war in the Pentagon. "The 88th without General Sloan was a prospect no doughboy liked to consider," Delaney wrote. His driving spirit had made the Division. Initially, it seemed that Brigadier General Guy Kurtz of the artillery—the surviving senior officer—would assume command. But General Clark decided that the outfit needed an infantryman as commander and jumped Major General Paul W. Kendall over Kurtz to take over the 88th. Kendall, nicknamed "The Bull" by the troops, had served as Assistant Division Commander and had won the respect of the men as he roamed the front lines from Minturno to the Arno. Delaney added that Kendall had "a taste for the dramatic and the flamboyant"—as well as the requisite guts.[15]

Reorganization, of course, was not simply a matter of shuffling top jobs or the replacement of commanders. Thirteen hundred men and officers had joined Fry's 350th Regiment over the last three months as replacements. Most were assigned to rifle and weapons companies. Changes were in order as the Blue Devils settled down to recuperate and reorganize. Men wounded earlier returned. Fry notes the kind of changes that took place throughout the Fifth Army.

Major Vincent M. Witter, wounded at Volterra, returned and was assigned to command Fry's Third Battalion; Mike Oreskevich was re-assigned from Regimental Supply to become Fry's Executive Officer. Captain James H. Ritts became Executive of the 1st Battalion and Lieutenant Roy E. Gray replaced him as D Company commander. "More intimately," Fry adds, George Ruppel . . . took over as my jeep driver, replacing Sergeant Kellerer, whom Rocky reported was anxious to get another job because he felt I was an unlucky man to be around." The 350th, as Fry remarks, "was a far different regiment from [that] which I assumed command only three months previously."[16] And much the same could be said for the others that had reached the Arno with like losses.

"We trained hard," Colonel Fry says of the lull along the Arno.[17] Blue Devil instructors emphasized combat in mountainous terrain, with battalion exercises on entering an assembly area, crossing a line of departure and driving the enemy from the high ground. Small-unit training stressed individual cover, physical training, extended-order drill and squad problems. Map work and compass reading were also reviewed in infantry classes.

The 85th Division practiced mountain warfare on the slopes of the ridge separating the Elsa and Pesa River. It was, after a fashion, an effort to make up for the loss of the French mountain troops to the invasion of southern France. Other outfits practiced embarking and debarking, in the expectation that the Germans would contest the crossing of the Arno. Powder River G.I.s crossed the Elsa near Certaldo in mock attacks on fortified river positions in training with the 316th Engineers. The 11th Italian Mule Group also taught troopers to pack mules and how best to use them in the mountains. Night problems were not neglected, nor marksmanship, as the 91st prepared for the next phase of the war.

The Fifth Army's G-4 grappled with the problem of rations acceptable to men of varying nationalities—the Brazilians, for example, demanded more sugar, lard and salt, as well as tomato juice, dried beans and rice, than did the Americans. Replacements, too, were hard to get. Artillery was in short supply, particularly for an army that depended on heavy barrages to pulverize enemy forces. Corps artillery battalions were down to 22 from 33, with additional battalions already committed to ANVIL. Clark had to borrow some sixty miscellaneous artillery pieces from the British as well as two battalions of Royal Engineers to make up for shortages caused by withdrawals for ANVIL. Florence became the major communications center for the Fifth Army. To protect historic and cultural monuments, supply facilities had to be located *outside* the city. Concealment, however, was facilitated by establishing a dump containing a million rations in an olive grove just south of the city. A million gallons of gas in containers were concealed in a vineyard a few miles down the road.

Morale among the divisions was good. Individual soldiers, Fry reports, "took on a degree of cockiness . . . and determination that boded ill for the enemy." The news from Europe was encouraging. ANVIL was going great guns. Paris was liberated on August 25 and the Allies were driving hard towards the Rhine. The Russians had taken Rumania and Bulgaria, and Russian troops were outside Warsaw. Rumors, too, abounded, including one embodied in the popular song, "*We'll* be home for Christmas." How much the good news from other fronts inflated morale is difficult to ascertain, although there is no doubt it had an effect then and later.

Still, the G.I.s along the Arno could see the mountain mass looming in the north. The hills and mountains of the Northern Apennines ranged from elevations of 300 feet to three and four thousand and higher. (Monte Cimone rose 7,095 and Monte Cusana 6,857 feet.) Some sixty miles of narrow defiles, canyon passes with sheer walls and uncertain roads lay between the Arno and the Po Valley. In these grim mountains the enemy was determined to make a last, desperate stand.

Although the Gothic Line and a fall-back line running along the high ridges that paralleled the Po Valley were not fully developed, the Germans had placed hull-down tanks at the base of hills, and they dug mortar and artillery emplacements in sheer rock or in solid cement-block houses. Enemy machine guns were ready to sweep all possible approaches. A huge antitank ditch wound over the lower hills for miles before Futa Pass. The Germans were clearly prepared to resist.

To break that resistance, the Allies planned a thrust north of Florence aimed at breaking through the center of the Gothic Line to Bologna. Kesselring was still worried about a flank landing in the Genoan Gulf even after ANVIL was well underway. As he points out in his memoirs, a landing would give the Allies a jumping-off position from the French–Italian frontier Alps for penetration of the upper Italian plain. Link-ups with partisan bands in the Turin–Milan area would unhinge German positions on the Ligurian coast and, he admitted, ultimately "lead to our being manoeuvred out of the Po plain."

The Allies, however, had long since given up the idea, largely because ANVIL's claim on resources precluded any such effort. Alexander decided to concentrate Allied efforts on a Gothic Line breakthrough to Bologna for essentially the same reason Kesselring was determined to hold on to the Apennines front: "If one or another sector in the Po plain between Bologna and the Adriatic were lost it might be of secondary importance, but if the front south of Bologna could not be held then all our positions in the Po plain east of Bologna were automatically gone."[18]

Timing, as it is so often in war, was crucial. As the lull along the Arno stretched out, the Fifth Army wasted good fighting weather. Unhappily, the gains secured by rest, refitting and retraining would not offset the coming of cold, rain and snow. The Germans knew that if they could hold the Allies in the Apennines, as Kesselring put it, ". . . the climate would do the rest." When British patrols in late August reported evidence of a deep German withdrawal above Florence, the Allies held back, although plans for continuing the offensive across the Arno were already well formulated. IV Corps on the left and II Corps on the right were to cross the Arno abreast, east of Florence. The British XIII Corps was to advance along the Florence–Firenzuola–Imola highway, assisting the advance of the Americans on the left. Then, as summer days slipped away, plans were suddenly changed.

NOTES

[1] United States Army, *Fifth Army History,* Vol. VI, p. 57. Leghorn had been thoroughly demolished. Moreover, engineers had to remove some 25,000 mines before operations became safe. The first "Liberty ships," with loads of engineering and stevedoring gear, arrived on August 20 but had to be unloaded by lighters. Vessels sunk alongside piers were bridged over and quays extended, and six days later two ships docked. Over September, tonnage rose from 4,242 to 45,328. Tankers entered the port at mid-month, filling the 275,000-barrel storage facilities. Eventually, this capacity was almost doubled. The Germans were not quite so thorough in the demolition of Ancona on the Adriatic. Five days after the fall of Ancona on July 23, a British supply convoy steamed into the port.
[3] Delaney, *The Blue Devils in Italy,* p. 119.
[4] Clark, *Calculated Risk,* p. 390.
[5] Fisher, *Cassino to the Alps,* p. 287.
[6] Robbins, *The 91st Infantry Division in World War II,* p. 84.
[7] Anon., *History of the Third Battalion, 337th Infantry Regiment,* pp. 18–21.

[8] Schultz, *The 85th Infantry Division,* p. 118.

[9] Fry, *Combat Soldier,* p. 164.

[10] Clark, *Calculated Risk,* p. 388.

[11] Howe, *First Armored Division,* p. 363.

[12] Hougen, *The Story of the Famous 34th Infantry Division,* p. 144.

[13] Delaney, *The Blue Devils in Italy,* p. 121.

[14] Fry, *Combat Soldier,* p. 163.

[15] Delaney, *The Blue Devils in Italy,* p. 123.

[16] Fry, *Combat Soldier,* pp. 161–62.

[17] Ibid., p. 164.

[18] Kesselring, *A Soldier's Record,* p. 213.

XI

ONE-TWO PUNCH

General Alexander had cause to be anxious—not so much about his Adriatic flank, where an attack in its second day was going well. Eighth Army troops had crossed the Metauro River against little resistance, while the Fifth Army was set to cross the Arno and head up into the Apennines north of Florence. The British general's distinguished guest, however, was worrisome. "Winston was always bothering me to take him to the front to see a battle," Alexander remarked in his memoirs. And here he was on August 27 in an old chateau overlooking a sharp declivity where, as Churchill put it, "one certainly could see all that was possible." The troops had pushed a mile or two beyond the Metauro. "Here Hasdrubal's defeat had sealed the fate of Carthage," Churchill, ever conscious of history, said. "So I suggested we should go across, too."

Stray bullets and bits of shrapnel were "whizzing around," Alexander recalled, but what really scared him was the approach. The general and his aide-de-camp had brought the prime minister and his personal assistant, Commander C.R. Thompson, to the chateau by jeep "over ground not swept for mines." To their front, the firing from the far side of the valley—about 500 yards away according to Churchill, more like 1,200 in Alexander's estimate—was, according to Churchill, "desultory and intermittent."[1] British tanks, says Alexander, seesawed up the ridge to fire, and then ducked back to avoid the response from German antitank guns. "[T]his was the nearest I got to the enemy and the time I heard the most bullets in the Second World War," said Churchill. "Winston," Alexander observed, "saw it all like a demonstration, and was as happy as the proverbial sand-hog."[2]

Churchill had flown early in August to Italy, ". . . where many questions could be more easily settled on the spot than by correspondence."[3] He had an appointment to see Tito, but Operation DRAGOON, the

American landing in the south of France, was still much on his mind. "He has got it into his head that Alex might be able to solve this problem by breaking into the Balkans," Lord Moran, Churchill's physician, noted in his diary a week before the prime minister's departure for Italy. Moran called the landings "sheer folly."[4] Alexander, who did not think much of DRAGOON either, says, "Churchill continued the argument until within five days of the landing."[5] Harold Macmillan, British Minister Resident at Allied Headquarter, noted in his diary, on August 7, "There is moreover a fresh problem. British Chiefs of Staff (impelled by Churchill) are now suggesting switching 'Anvil' from southern France (Marseilles, Toulon, etc., to Brest, St. Nazaire, etc.). U.S. Chiefs are strongly opposed and want to stick to the original plan. I have no doubt that (once again) British Chiefs will be overborne."[6]

Macmillan was right. The invasion went ahead as planned, on August 15, with Churchill aboard the British destroyer *Kimberly* to observe. He witnessed the long rows of boats filled with American troops moving continuously to the Bay of St. Tropez. As far as he could see or hear, "not a shot was fired either at the approaching flotillas or on the beaches." He was a bit put off at not being allowed closer than seven thousand yards, for fear of mines. "I had at least done the civil to 'Anvil,'" he avers, "and indeed I thought it was a good thing I was near the scene to show the interest I took in it."[7]

Macmillan may have shared this thought with General Mark Clark at lunch in Leghorn on August 19, where he found the Fifth Army commander "embittered that his army had been robbed of what he thought— and I could not disagree—was a good opportunity." Churchill was deeply affected by Clark's remarks. He was whisked off to a 240mm battery of the 697th Artillery, where the guns were sighted on a bridge north of Pisa. He was asked to yank the lanyard to fire the first round—which was done to good effect. The target was hit; Churchill left in high good humor.

Alexander, Clark and Churchill remained profoundly unhappy about DRAGOON, which, Churchill reported to the South African General Smuts, "quite delighted the Americans. . . . Their idea now, from which nothing will turn them, is to work in a whole army group through the captured ports instead of using the much easier ports on the Atlantic."[8] Clark felt that his own people—the Americans at AFHQ—were sapping his strength "in getting more and more of everything for ANVIL."[9] Even the Nisei, who had performed so well in the mountains of Italy, were shifted to France along with much of Clark's heavy artillery. Alexander termed DRAGOON "an operation that contributed nothing to the final victory."

On his return to General Leese's headquarters from his visit to the Metauro front, Churchill learned that the British had advanced since daybreak about seven thousand yards on a ten- or twelve-mile front, and that losses had not been at all heavy. "This was an encouraging beginning," Churchill felt. "My object now," he informed Smuts at the end of August, "is to keep what we have got in Italy, which should be sufficient since the enemy has withdrawn four of his best divisions. With this I hope to turn and break the Gothic Line, break into the Po Valley, and ultimately advance by Trieste and the Ljubljana Gap to Vienna. Even if the war came to an end at an early date I have told Alexander to be ready for a dash with armoured cars."[10]

Alexander had high hopes after the fall of Rome for a thrust into the Po Valley. "In the days when I still had my full forces," he said, "I expected to be able to reach the Apennines almost without stopping; in my present situation some slight pause would be necessary, but I was determined to reduce it to a minimum."[11] But circumstances would not have it so. The pause along the Arno stretched out—one, two, three weeks. Three out of four of the Fifth Army's divisions had experienced heavy fighting; the 1st Armored was being reorganized. The arrival of the 25,000-strong Brazilian Expeditionary Force in August and, later, of the all-black 92nd Division would boost the Fifth Army's strength. But they were green troops and could scarcely be expected to offset the loss of seven well-tried divisions to the invasion of southern France. As Clark told Alexander, "[W]e were using up every device to make up for our deficiencies, including . . . Italian troops and the use of tanks, tank destroyers and antiaircraft guns as supporting artillery, and antiaircraft artillerymen as 'doughboys.' " He believed the enemy's morale to be low. "We must take our chances and pound him from all directions." He told Alexander, however, that he would cross the Arno and go for Pistoia and Lucca—"after my troops [have] had a couple of weeks' rest."[12]

The South Africans, New Zealanders, Indian and other British troops engaged in the thrust for the Arno and Florence were weary, too. Nevertheless, to defeat Kesselring Alexander needed to bring the Germans to a decisive battle—soon. He proposed a thrust—Fifth and Eighth Armies as offensive backs—at the center of the Gothic Line. It was the shortest route to Bologna and the Po Valley, and both Armies were in their approximate assault positions. On the Adriatic side, opportunities for exploitation were poor: a spiderweb of small streams transversing the Adriatic corridor would enmesh troops in endless river crossings. (There was, in fact, a weakness at the center of the Gothic Line, at Firenzuola, though, unhappily, the Allies were unaware of it.)

To prevent Kesselring from receiving reinforcements and to cut his line of retreat, Alexander on July 12 launched an all-out air attack, code-name Mallory Major, at all nineteen Po Valley bridges between Piacenza and the Adriatic. Fifteen days later, the bridges were destroyed. The aircraft essential for keeping up the devastation, however, were needed for DRAGOON. Moreover, the pause along the Arno enabled the Germans to restore their damaged lines of communication. German engineers used pontoon bridges, ferries, pneumatic lines and overhead cables to get supplies going. Nineteen ferries, ten capable of carrying 24 tons, supplied Ferrara, the German hub behind the Wehrmacht's left wing. Rail lines were restored. By mid-August, the Germans were no worse off than before for supplies—a remarkable achievement.

The Allies, however, worked an elaborate deception designed to convince the Germans that the attack would be mounted on the Adriatic. Radio-signal traffic was increased in the coastal area. Soldiers wearing Canadian patches were seen in the right places, convincing enemy agents that an Adriatic offensive was in the making. Kesselring remarks in his memoirs that after the middle of August ". . . there was no longer any doubt the British Eighth Army was getting ready for a decisive out-flanking attack on the Adriatic."[13] General Oliver Leese, commander of the British Eighth Army, requested a meeting with Alexander and his Chief of Staff, General Sir John Harding.

August 4 was a hot day and the three officers took shelter under the wing of a Dakota at the Orvieto airfield. Leese was disturbed. He did not like the plan of attack. He had lost his most experienced mountain troops, the French Expeditionary Force, to DRAGOON. Tanks, which had worked effectively south of the Arno, would be immobilized by the Apennines. The Germans were well prepared, the element of surprise long since dissipated. Though the Gothic Line was, in fact, incomplete, the Todt Organization had built antitank defenses in depth along the approaches to La Spezia; antitank ditches, concrete casements and tank turrets fortified the Futa Pass; timber had been felled to open fields of fire on the southern side of the watershed, enhanced by pillboxes and minefields. Moreover, Leese was leery of what he felt would be an inevitable competition of the wrong sort and of the inevitable comparisons that would follow if the two Armies fought side by side. The Adriatic, where the mountains dwindled to ridges, was more appropriate for artillery/armor assaults such as those that had worked so well north of Rome and south of the Arno. He also argued—somewhat puzzling in the light of the deception plan well underway—that the attack would have the advantage of surprise.

Harding held to the center plunge, maintaining that a massive, jointly mounted American/British blow was the best and quickest way to defeat Kesselring. Leese assured Alexander that he would do his best whatever the choice; but it was clear that his heart would not be "in" a central assault on the Gothic Line. Alexander, after the war, said that he had had doubts about such an attack. "It was anything but certain that our heavy blow in the mountains of the centre would take us through to our objective," he wrote, "and if the first attack there fell short of our expectations, the advantage would be all with the defenders."[14] But what decided the Allied commander was Leese. As Eric Linklater put it: "Realizing how impolitic it would be to persuade an Army Commander to fight a battle against his inclination and judgement, General Alexander acceded to General Leese's new proposal."[15]

Alexander next informed Clark of the change in plans. "It is my idea," he said, "that the Eighth Army attack first and be followed at the proper moment by the Fifth Army in a boxer's 'one-two' punch."[16] To distract German attention from British preparations, Clark's troops were to show themselves as getting ready for a big attack along the Arno from Pontassieve to Pontedera. Though Leese was not happy with the decision, the British XIII Corps in the mountains left of the Fifth Army was assigned to Clark. "Thus," Clark notes in his wartime account, "I received into the polyglot Fifth Army still another group of nationalities: the 6th South African Armoured Division, the 6th British Armoured Division, the 8th Indian Division, and the 1st British Infantry Division."[17] Clark had also previously "borrowed" some sixty miscellaneous pieces of British artillery and two battalions of Royal Engineers to make up for Fifth Army shortages.

There now occurred one of those great bursts of energy that occur in wartime: a renewed confidence paradoxically fueled, in part, by General Truscott's stunning successes in the south of France. Toulon, Marseilles and Grenoble had all fallen to the Seventh Army and the Germans were in retreat up the valley of the Rhône.

It was clear to commanders in Italy that if the Gothic Line could be broken, the enemy would, of necessity, withdraw from northwest Italy. With its left flank safe, the Fifth Army would be free to wheel right, against Mantua and Verona, while the Eighth Army crossed the Po, the Adige and the Brent—on towards Austria and the Ljubljana Gap.

The Adriatic front had been a subordinate operation. Alexander had decided to ease attacks along the coast at the fall of Rome, in the hopes that the Germans, hard-pressed at the center and on the west coast, would fall back. The job of assisting them on the way was given to the Poles, a tough-minded lot hardened by their exile and by Cassino. Their commander, fifty-two-year-old General Wladyslaw Anders, matched his men in fighting spirit and toughness of mind and body, and with a fiery Polish patriotism.

Anders had been wounded five times in World War I while serving in the Russian Army (though a Pole by descent, he was technically a Russian subject). In Poland after the war, he agitated for Polish independence and commanded a cavalry squadron against the Bolsheviks through 1919–20. When Germany invaded Poland in 1939, Anders commanded a cavalry brigade, horses against tanks. He was wounded fighting his way out of a trap in East Prussia and again fighting the invading Soviets as his brigade sought to cross into Hungary. Anders was captured and, instead of being treated as a prisoner of war, he was imprisoned in dread Lubianka. Some million Poles were deported and scattered among prisons and concentration camps all over Russia. "God only knows how many were murdered," Anders says in his autobiography, "and how many died under the terrible conditions in the prisons and forced labor camps." One day he was escorted from his cell—"Nobody tripped me up or threw me down the steps"—to a study "full of carpets and soft armchairs." Beria, the notorious secret police chief, told him: "You are free." The Germans had attacked Russia; Poles were amnestied, and Anders was asked to form a Polish Army.

He did so from the remnants of the Polish Army released to him out of the camps. He never forgot his first visit to a camp where 17,000 of his countrymen became the 6th Infantry Division. "Most of them had no boots or shirts, and all were in rags, often tattered relics of old Polish uniforms. There was not a man who was not an emaciated skeleton . . . most . . . covered with ulcers. . . . For the first time in my life, and I hope the last, I took the salute of a march past of soldiers without boots. They had insisted on it. They wanted to show the Bolsheviks that even in their bare feet, and ill and wounded as many of them were, they could bear themselves like soldiers on their first march towards Poland."[18]

Stalin wanted the Poles to fight side by side with Soviet troops. But Anders was nobody's fool and he did not trust the Soviets. He seized an opportunity that developed during the negotiations over the fate and future of Poland to extricate an army 100,000-strong, getting his men across the border into Iran, and marched them through the Middle East and North Africa to arrive in time to capture Cassino. On June 17, General Anders took over command of the Adriatic sector where the line was drawn along the Pescara River. Under his wing were several British regiments, including the 7th Queen's Hussars; assorted engineer, signals, anti-aircraft and medical units; and the Corpo Italiano di Liberazione. The Italians, commanded by General Utili, were poorly equipped, but the thirteen infantry battalions, one heavy-artillery battery, one sapper battalion and a signals company were up to full strength.

Anders' orders called for a change of pace, "to pursue the enemy at the highest possible speed and capture Ancona harbour."[19] The pursuit of the Germans north of Rome had increased the distance from railhead to fighting infantry. The problems of supply would be eased with the capture of Leghorn on the west and Ancona on the east. Since the latter was strategically the more important, the change from a static stance to an operation full of movement was critical.

The 3rd Polish Division began its pursuit on June 17, crossing several rivers with considerable dash. The Germans checked the advance by retaking a bridgehead over the Chienti on June 22. Then the Germans withdrew to establish a stronger defense line on the heights above the Musone River, the last river obstacle before Ancona. The Poles resumed their pursuit, giving the Germans little time to organize their defenses. On July 6, Polish troops took Osino on the dominating heights above the Musone after stubborn fighting during which objectives changed hands several times. Anders' troops advanced on Ancona the morning of July 17, and after a long day's fighting the Carpathian Lancers entered the port at 1400 on the 18th, the day before the Americans entered Leghorn. With scarcely a breather, they pushed on to establish a major bridgehead across the Esino, taking Senigalla and moved towards the Cesano. The first phase of the Adriatic thrust cost the Poles 150 officers and 2,000 other ranks. German prisoners totaled 24 officers and 2,552 soldiers, with heavy losses in men killed as well as in captured arms and equipment.[20]

With the Italians on their left flank, the Poles pushed on up the coast, crossing the Cesano on August 10, the same night that the Germans in Florence withdrew from the city center to the Mugnone Canal. The enemy continued to fall back, but their rearguards, supported by self-propelled guns—with an assist from heavy rains—spoiled Polish plans for cutting off their main forces. The Poles, however, cleared the high ground between the Cesano and the Metauro, reaching the south bank of the latter along a 15-mile front early in the morning of August 22.

The Poles were on the starting line for Alexander's first punch at the Gothic Line, some twelve miles away. They were joined by the 1st Canadian and the British V Corps in one of the war's most remarkable shifts of manpower. The bulk of the British Eighth Army had to be moved east from central Italy around Foligno to behind the Polish Corps north of Ancona. The roads were barely adequate and had to be buttressed and reinforced by sorely tried engineers.

Donald Featherstone, a tanker man with the 51st Royal Tank Regiment, recalls the move beginning "on a note of comedy." To conceal their movement, the unit's tanks went by transporters at night, while the men were driven across in trucks, "their tell-tale black berets hidden in packs and each man wearing some form of wide-brimmed soft-felt hat from a hat factory captured at Montevarchi."[21] To speed up the movement of tanks and to preserve as far as possible other road surfaces, the engineers opened a one-way tank route 120 miles long from the central Italian province of Umbria to the Adriatic Marches. As it was, the mountain roads were thick with traffic. War correspondent Martha Gelhorn recalled: "Trucks and armored cars and tanks and weapons carriers and guns and jeeps and motorcycles and ambulances packed the roads, and it was not at all unusual to spend four hours going twenty miles. The roads were ground to powder by this traffic and the dust lay in drifts a foot thick . . . [W]henever you could get up a little speed the dust boiled like water under the wheels. Everyone's face was greenish white with dust, and it rose in a blinding fog around the moving army and lay high over the land in a brown solid haze."[22]

The wonder was—what with all the dust—that the Germans apparently did not catch on to what was afoot. Kesselring, it seems, had been deceived by Alexander's earlier plan: feint on the Adriatic, punch at the center. He reinforced the Tenth Army with the formidable 1st Parachute Division. It was now on the Adriatic coast ready to relieve the 278th Division. But Kesselring also hedged, possibly in response to the second deception, by keeping two divisions in reserve, near Bologna. Still, he had the excellent lateral Highway 9 at his disposal for the swift movement of troops east and west. Air reconnaissance, however, was next to impossible for the Germans, who were, in the end, reduced to guesswork when it came to intelligence. On the ground, Tenth Army Headquarters staff had noticed the dust and noise of British troop movements, but agreed with General Traugott Herr, commander of the 76th Panzer Corps, that the movement might be no more than the unloading of war materiel at the recently captured port of Ancona. The Germans were in for a surprise.

General Leese exuded confidence as he briefed senior officers in the theatre at Isei two days before the offensive began. The terrain ahead of the troops was not easy, he warned, but the Eighth Army was stronger than ever before. It had 1,200 tanks, 1,000 guns and ten divisions. Three corps would attack simultaneously along a thirty-mile front ranging inland from just below Fano on the Adriatic, west along the Metauro to the vicinity of Fermignano, four miles south of the ancient market town of Urbino. Leese remarked that this might well be the last battle in Eighth Army history. "Now," he said in his last message to his troops on the eve of battle, "we begin the last lap. Swiftly and secretly, once again, we have moved right across Italy an army of immense strength and striking power—to break the Gothic Line. Victory in the coming battles means the beginning of the end for the German armies in Italy. Let every man do his utmost and again success will be ours. Good luck to you all."[23]

Few combat soldiers welcome battle, but the men along the Metauro were certainly looking forward to the end. "Non-stop to the Po" was a spontaneous slogan. The troops of the British 56th Division were told, according to one soldier's recollection, that the timetable was: "Two days to reach Bologna, four days to reach Venice and a week to reach Vienna."[24] The men of the New Zealand Division, lying in reserve, were given lectures on Venice—as yet one hundred miles north of enemy lines. The fields were golden with ripe grain and the vines laden with dark grapes, auguries of an auspicious harvest. "Everyone was excited," wrote an officer of the King's Royal Rifle Corps, "and we were addressed by the army commander and the brigadier, and visited by our new corps and divisional commanders. We spent a very pleasant fortnight in this way, and then . . . we drove out of our easy life into the battle of the Gothic Line."[25]

The day, August 25, had been hot and sunny and the men along the narrow stream of the Metauro fell silent as the skies darkened above the hills. The air turned cool and the moon disappeared in the west before midnight. Stars in their innumerable number glittered in the heavens as the men gathered their strength and began to move forward. On the coast, the Polish Corps—the Kesowa and Carpathian Infantry Divisions with the 2nd Polish Armored Brigade—attacked along the first seven miles stretching inland from the sea. The Canadians—the 1st Canadian Infantry and the 5th Canadian Armoured divisions, bolstered by the 21st British Tank Brigade and the Household Cavalry Regiment—were concentrated on a narrow front of just over two miles.

The Poles were under-strength and lacked ready replacements, and were to be used only as openers on the coast, going for the high ground north of Pesaro, some fifteen miles distant. The Canadians were to segue across to the sea, take over from the Poles at Cattolica and then take Rimini. West of the Canadians, the British V Corps would attack, two divisions abreast—the British 46th on the right and the 4th Indian on the left—and would advance towards Bologna and Ferrara. The British 56th was in reserve, to be committed left or right, as the situation warranted. The British 1st Armoured, backed by the 4th British Infantry, were to exploit the anticipated breakthrough.

The Germans were caught off-base, though surely they, too, were confident—to a fault. Two days before the offensive, a German NCO wrote a letter: "At the moment it is fairly quiet, though Tommy is pushing forward with strong armed forces. We are in the hills near Pesaro. But we shall soon sort them out. The English have threatened every member of our regiment with twenty-five years' forced labour, and you can see how they hate us. But, then, we are acknowledged to be the best regiment in the southern theatre of operations. . . ."[26] The non-com had some reason for his confidence. General Herr, whose 76th Panzer Corps held the east wing of the Adriatic defenses, had five divisions—three in line, two in reserve. On his right, General Valentin Feurstein commanded the 51st Mountain Corps with five divisions. It was a respectable show of strength, although most of the German forces were behind the main fortifications of the Gothic Line some twelve miles north along the River Foglia.

The Gods of War are fickle. General von Vietinghoff, the Tenth Army commander, and General Heidrich of the 1st Paras were on leave. The Germans had chosen the moment for regrouping. The 278th Division, mauled by the Poles in their drive to the Metauro, was falling back through its relief, the 1st Paras, when the Eighth Army opened its attack. Caught off-guard, the Germans mistook the Polish attack for a normal follow-up after a withdrawal. It was a mistake that would cost them dearly, though they made a fast enough recovery along the Gothic Line above the Foglia.

The Poles, along with their comrades crossing the Metauro in the five-division-strong first wave, went in without a preliminary artillery barrage. Infantrymen waded through water almost three feet deep up into the olive groves on the far side. At midnight, shells rained down 400 yards ahead of the advancing troops moving forward at the anticipated rate of 100 yards every six minutes. The Poles inflicted heavy damage on a German Parachute Regiment caught out in the open in the act of withdrawing. By dawn, the five divisions were well across the river and into the hills before the Foglia. The first phase of the battle, as noted sailor and author Farley Mowat put it in his history of the Hastings & Prince Edwards Regiment, was over, and "it had been hardly worse than the training schemes at Piedmonte."[27]

The Hastings & Prince Edwards Regiment had been made up of 4,000 volunteers from the fishing hamlets of the Canadian Martitime Provinces and the hard-rock mines under the Laurentian shield. Grateful for the day's dispensation, the men of the Regiment, following the main attack in reserve, dropped down to rest on a ridge where an old church tower cast a long shadow on warm ground. But the moment of peace in shade and sunlight was rudely shattered when a salvo from some thirty guns obliterated the peaceful ridge, burying it "under a swirling curtain of grey dust and yellow smoke." Taking cover in hastily dug foxholes, in pigpens or in the nearest building, counting up their losses, the Canadians "understood that . . . war was with them once again."[28]

War for the soldier is made up of little things and major confusions. Hordes of dung beetles and lice-like creatures swarmed out of the ground at night. The Hastings & Prince Edwards' A Company dug in to face a counterattack. Enemy machine guns were so close that when artillery was called in, the shells dropped on the company. Heaping Pelion on Ossa,[29] friendly tanks joined in under the misapprehension that they were firing upon Germans. Two Spitfire fighter-bombers decided to join the fun, but veered off when an officer threw a canister of yellow air-recognition smoke. The tanks, too, recognized the significance of the smoke, and rumbled on to destroy two Tigers threatening to finish off Able Co. An officer, whose tank was attempting to cross the Arzilla, a steep-sided and bog-bottomed natural tank trap, opened his hatch to see better, only to have a mortar fall through and "brew-up" his tank.

Confusions multiplied in the night. Men of one outfit wound up among the men of another. One unit commander, in what Mowat says was a "matter-of-fact manner," inquired of another if he had "seen his battalion anywhere." Lieutenant Colonel Cameron set up his Battalion Headquarters in a farm outbuilding and the officers were sitting down to pitch into a bully-beef stew when they heard a deprecatory cough behind them. Mowat, who described what happened, calls the scene one of the most peculiar encounters of the war. If not, it surely comes close. The newcomer was a six-foot German paratrooper corporal.

"You," Cameron snapped, "are in the wrong camp. Go away." Startled, the German replied, "But I'm lost." "That's easily rectified," Cameron said, giving the corporal explicit directions to his own people on a hillside some four hundred yards to the front. The Colonel, however, remembering the duties of hospitality, asked the German if he had eaten. He had not for twenty-four hours and so was invited to join the dinner party. The bemused Canadian officers argued amicably about the possible social aspects of the Geneva Convention on prisoners. Replete with stew, the corporal, at the close of the meal, announced he was a bona fide prisoner of war. "Nonsense," Cameron said. The German had admitted he had wandered in by mistake. "And since we've already taken quite enough prisoners today, one more would simply be an administrative nuisance." The German pounded the table, "I am your prisoner." Cameron banged back, saying, "You are a soldier absent without leave. . . . You may even be charged with desertion. You go along, and when you get back, tell your C.O. that we're going to beat the hell out of him come dawn." The argument, Mowat says, might have lasted the night, but Cameron was called back to duty and reluctantly agreed to accept the corporal's surrender.[30] Much, it may be imagined, to the German's relief.

For the most part, despite confusions, the Canadians made good progress, as did the Eighth Army, along its entire front those first few days. The element of surprise favored the offensive, but success was also based on the kinds of action that Mowat, in one instance, describes as "a small masterpiece" of infantry and tank cooperation. Dog Company, supported by a troop of Churchill tanks, was to assault a German strongoint. "With consummate skill the Company, under command of Major Alan Ross, moved swiftly forward, covering the tanks and protecting them from the hidden-enemy armed with close-range Faustpatronen [bazooka-like antitank weapons]. The tanks, lumbering in the rear, engaged and silenced the machine guns on the crest. . . . When a German anti-tank gun was spotted, an infantry platoon rushed it, firing from the hip, and so protected the armoured friends behind." Within an hour, the strong-point was taken, along with a 75mm gun, two heavy trucks, a self-propelled 20mm cannon, an armored half-track, a motor cycle and twenty-six prisoners. Twelve of the enemy were killed or wounded. A minor action, almost faultlessly executed, Mowat remarks, yet it also enabled troops on the right, caught in a trap, to break out and it freed others on the left to move forward.[31]

On the left of the Eighth Army line, the British 46th Division, commanded by Major General Sir J. Hawkesworth, and the 4th Indian Division, commanded by Major General Arthur Holworthy, in tandem led the advance of V Corps. The Indians started first, in the early hours of August 25. They had miles to go before reaching the Line of Departure along the Metauro. By nightfall, the jeep-borne 1st/9th Gurkhas had reached the river, where the north–south Via Flaminia, Route 3, turns east towards the coast and Rimini. The 4th/11th Sikhs legged twenty miles on a hot day to arrive some ten miles south of the Metauro, good going for foot-sloggers.

Unhappily, a misunderstanding with the Italian irregular forces screening the Sikhs' advance resulted in a costly delay. At Acqualagna, the Italians, after a conversation with the adjutant of the San Marco Battalion, a unit of the Italian Liberation Corps, reported that the town was clear of Germans. When the unsuspecting 2nd Royal Sikhs approached the walls of the town, they were hit by fire from mortars and guns on the heights that overlook Acqualagna on three sides. Company commander Major J.L. Key and all three of his platoon commanders were killed; on the right flank, company commander Major D. Farr was wounded. When a third company went forward to clear the town, it was fired upon by confused Italian soldiers. The shelling of the Sikhs continued until nightfall, when the Germans withdrew. The misunderstanding had cost the Indians two company commanders and seventy men of other ranks.

When the Eighth Army opened its attack on the night of August 26, the Gurkhas crossed the Metauro on schedule. General Holworthy had opted for speed in order to achieve a surprise, a decision that gained the advantage over the battered 278th and 71st German Divisions replacing the 5th Mountain Division in that sector. The Gurkhas clambered up the southern end of a narrow-backed ridge some 1,500 feet above the Metauro. Passing through the Gurkhas the next day, August 27, the 4th/11th Sikhs consolidated their lines on the northeastern spur of Monte della Cesena, near Urbino, the birthplace of Raphael perched on a pinnacle above the surrounding ridges. To their left, the British 1st Royal Sussex Battalion passed through the 2nd Royal Sikhs to enter Urbino unopposed, to the cheers of the city's 20,000 inhabitants. The Folgia and the Gothic Line were six miles ahead. As the Indians and the British "squared up" to the Gothic Line, the Royal Sussex moving north of Urbino to seize the flanking heights came under heavy and accurate fire from across the Foglia and were engaged in brief, savage firefights in which supporting armor lost seven tanks.

Hawkesworth of the 46th, considered by his peers a master of infantry tactics and, in the words of General Sir Richard McCreery, ever "ready to encourage surprise, a silent night approach, and field craft," was in his element. "46th Division will BUST the Gothic Line," summed up his intentions in his brief orders for the battle.[32] And his men took him at his word (though they were delayed by craters and demolitions), pushing on two to three miles across the Metauro in the morning.

Ahead lay a chain of three forbidding peaks: Monte Bartolo, Monte Tomba and Monte Grosso, the latter rising 1,400 feet. Lieutenant J.F. Wallace, a platoon commander with the 5th Hampshires, recalls the attack: "Two platoons were going up the slope when I heard some firing from the flank, and someone shouted that the other platoon commander had been hit." Wallace ran forward over a small ridge with his men behind, when a Spandau opened fire. They all dropped to the ground, but Wallace was ahead and forward of the ridge. He thought, "I've had it." But he heard a corporal shout, "Come on, lads, after Mr. Wallace." His men charged. "They cheered as they came—it was one of the few times I'd ever heard them cheer." A German up above rose to throw a grenade but was shot. The rest of the Germans ran off. "We'd captured the peak, and so we dug in."[33]

At close of day on August 27, all three peaks were in British hands. Hawkesworth hustled his men forward twenty miles, to the Gothic Line. Casualties were light, although German rearguards put up a brisk fight here and there. By noon on the 29th, the 2nd Hampshires and the 5th Foresters with the tanks of the North Irish Horse were in line overlooking the Foglia. The Germans of the battered 71st Division had withdrawn to the Gothic Line, releasing a good many prisoners on the way.

The prospect ahead for the British and the Indians was foreboding. The enemy's positions followed the north bank of the river, which meanders back and forth along the base of a ridge running four miles eastward. The hamlet of Monte della Croce stands on a spur at the center of the ridge, looped on either side by the Foglia. Monte Calvo rises still higher a mile to the north, where a white ribbon of road wanders along a rising crest to the northwest for three miles to Tavoleto, where the spur merges into Monte San Giovanni, an east–west transverse ridge system and the enemy's main battle position from Tavoleto to Monte Gridolfo, five miles to the east.

On both sides of Tavoleto, antitank ditches, wire obstacles, machine-gun pits, forward snipers and trenches were well placed. Fields of fire were cleared and all approaches were thickly sown with mines. Left of Monte Calvo, forward positions were held by outposts protected by intricate defensive fire lines. German counterattackers waited in sheltered reserve areas to the rear. "When we looked down on, and across, the River Foglia to Monte Gridolfo," an officer of the North Irish Horse said, "it must be confessed the situation looked anything but pleasant. All houses had been razed . . . trees and vines felled, and avenues prepared between extensive minefields for a hail of machine-gun fire. . . . The assault across the River Foglia and up the bare slopes appeared suicidal."[34]

Still, the precipitous retirement of the 71st Division suggested that the Germans might be off-balance, not yet ready to fully maintain their defensive positions. Though the Allies did not know it, this seems to have been the case—at least in part. Kesselring believed the Adriatic attack to be a feint somehow connected to the French landings and to a possible landing in his rear on the west coast. German intelligence, however, had a copy of Leese's order—"We have moved right across Italy an army of immense strength"—and showed it to Kesselring. The German Command dithered over whether or not it was disinformation, but ultimately agreed with General Herr's conclusion that it was "now certain that the enemy intends to carry out a big push to the plains of the Po."[35]

The Tenth Army was ordered to concentrate on its Adriatic defenses. It was already late—August 28. German reserves—the 26th Panzer Division and the 29th Panzer Grenadiers—were at least a day away from the critical front. General Wilhelm Raapke's 71st, exhausted, badly mauled, under strength, had been forced back to the Gothic Line three days ahead of a planned withdrawal.

Time favored the British Eighth Army. Neither Hawkesworth nor Holworthy hesitated. Daylight patrols along the south bank of the Foglia on August 29 encountered no resistance. Brigadier Saunders-Jacobs ordered two companies of Queen Mary's Own Baluchis Regiment forward in a silent attack. Men from a barren province in the northwest of India, Kiplingesque country, forded the gravel-bottomed Foglia before dawn on the 30th. They climbed the spur to Monte della Croce and entered the hamlet. The first fortified outpost of the Gothic Line had been taken without a shot fired. However, when the Baluchis probed further the Germans retaliated. A light counterattack was rebuffed. Tanks and the 4th/11th Sikhs advanced in support on the Baluchis' right flank, as the latter advanced north gaining one thousand yards, taking a strong-point halfway to Monte Calvo.

At dawn on August 31, the 1st/9th Gurkhas moved up and were ordered to encircle Monte Calvo while the Sikhs and Baluchis attacked head-on. The assault began at 1115 with an artillery barrage. Fighter-bombers joined in, bombing and strafing enemy positions. The Baluchis took advantage of dead ground to work up the spur. The enemy contested the ground vigorously; supporting tanks were disabled by well-placed mines. The 1st/9th Gurkhas, circling right, seized key positions to the rear of Monte Calvo and threatened the enemy's line of withdrawal a good mile to the north. By nightfall, Monte Calvo was in Indian hands, forty prisoners had been taken and the Indians' west flank was secure.

"The village was a shambles," an eyewitness observed. "Wire obstacles had been crushed by the tanks. Broken shutters, window frames and drainpipes swung in the breeze. Tileless roofs allowed clouds of dust and smoke to rise above the village. A bell from the church tower lay in the rubble but the altar was still intact. Piles of barbed wire and rail dumps revealed that the Germans had not finished their defenses."[36]

Hawkesworth may have sensed this when he ordered his two leading brigades, the 128th, commanded by Brigadier Douglas Kenddrew, a celebrated prewar rugby player, and the 139th, under Brigadier Allen Block, to cross the Foglia on the right of the advancing 4th Indian Division. The 30th was a rough day for the British. Block's Leicester Regiment crossed the river and managed to hold a precarious bridgehead despite murderous fire and the loss of 40 men in a few short hours. Hawkesworth, who came forward to look over the battle, was almost killed by a shell that exploded in front of his jeep. He agreed that the Leicesters had best wait for nightfall before renewing their attack.

On their right, at the center of the 46th divisional front, the 5th Sherwood Foresters tackled Monte Vecchio, a fortified village 600 feet above the Foglia. German machine-gun posts in five houses on the Germans' forward slope were silenced by a gallant Forester platoon. But the Foresters, too, were held up. The Germans were well entrenched in the village above. The Hampshires of the 128th Brigade on the right were hit by mortar and machine-gun fire. And they, too, were forced to wait for the protecting envelope of night.

Under its cover, the three battalions attacked again. The Leicesters made their way through a minefield under machine-gun fire and worked towards Mondaino, a village on the spur that dominated the countryside. The Foresters took Monte Vecchio under cover of a heavy barrage, and after a hard fight. The day's honors, however, went to the Hampshires, who had cleared the ridge approach to Monte Gridolfo of machine guns and passed through burning haystacks and houses to attack the town itself.

Heavily fortified Monte Gridolfo was crucial to the German defenses. Enemy fire from concrete emplacements and from flanking Spandaus pinned down the hapless Hampshires. A victory here might well turn the tide, and gain time for German reinforcements needed to hold the Gothic Line in the sector. Lieutenant G.R. Norton, a platoon commander seconded from the South African Union Defence Force, ran forward and threw a grenade into the first machine-gun post, killing three Germans. He then worked his way to another enemy position to take out two Spandaus and fifteen riflemen with his Thompson. His own men joined him as he cleared another strongpoint. Wounded and weak from loss of blood, Norton led his platoon on to destroy the remaining enemy positions. As his citation for the Victoria Cross put it, Lieutenant Norton "assured the successful breach of the Gothic Line at this point."[37]

On September 1, the Gothic Line had been well and fully broken along a fifteen-mile front, inland from Pesaro. German reserves were being committed piece by piece as they arrived at the front. Kesselring was forced by the Adriatic breakthrough to deplete his mobile reserves and to draw troops—three divisions in all—from the central front above Florence, where he had five. It was time, now, for Alexander to deliver his second punch.

NOTES

[1] Churchill, *The Second World War,* Vol. VI, pp. 121–23.

[2] Alexander, *Memoirs,* p. 137.

[3] Churchill, *The Second World War,* Vol. VI, p. 86.

[4] Moran, *Diaries,* p. 173.

[5] Alexander, *Memoirs,* p. 139.

[6] Macmillan, *War Diaries,* p. 499.

[7] Churchill, *The Second World War,* Vol. VI, pp. 106–107.

[8] Ibid., p. 101.

[9] Clark, *Calculated Risk,* p. 397.

[10] Churchill, *The Second World War,* Vol. VI, p. 101.

[11] Alexander, *Memoirs,* p. 139.

[12] Clark, *Calculated Risk,* pp. 386–87.

[13] Kesselring, *A Soldier's Record,* p. 212.

[14] Alexander, *Memoirs,* p. 139.

[15] Linklater, *The Campaign in Italy,* p. 349.

[16] Clark, *Calculated Risk,* p. 390.

[17] Ibid.

[18] Anders, *An Army in Exile,* p. 64.

[19] Ibid., p. 187.

[20] Ibid., p. 189.

[21] Lucas, *The British Soldier,* p. 110.

[22] Gelhorn, *Faces of War,* p. 168.

[23] Orgill, *The Gothic Line,* pp. 39–40.

[24] Lucas, *The British Soldier,* p. 110.

[25] Orgill, *The Gothic Line,* p. 39.

[26] Ibid, p. 42.

[27] Mowat, *The Regiment,* p. 203.

[28] Ibid., pp. 208–209.

[29] Mt. Pelion is a mountain renowned in ancient Greece (Thessaly). According to a myth, the giants—in revolt against Zeus—set it atop Mt. Ossa in order to attack Mt. Olympus.

[30] Ibid., p. 204.

[31] Orgill, *The Gothic Line,* p. 43.
[32] Ibid., p. 44.
[33] Ibid., p. 46.
[34] Ibid., p. 47.
[35] Stevens, *Fourth Indian Division,* p. 346.
[36] Orgill, *The Gothic Line,* p. 58.

XII

THE SECOND PUNCH

General Alexander threw his second punch on September 1. Allied patrols along the Arno during the last week of August encountered enemy fire, suggesting that the Germans still entertained notions of fighting a slow delaying action north of the river. The First City/Cape Town Highlanders, on reconnaissance patrols, swam the river at various places between Montelupo and Empoli because the enemy had fordable points so well covered. "It is indeed fortunate for many a patrol," a Highlanders historian remarks, "that it was not detected when across the river—being captured 'in the nude' would not have been a pleasant experience."[1] As late as August 31, a South African night patrol crossed the river, suffered two men wounded and found no sign of withdrawal. But sounds of demolitions north of the river suggested otherwise.

Meanwhile, artillery observers reported signs that the Germans were pulling out heavy materiel and guns, leaving their mortars and remaining guns screened by infantry. Italian partisans also reported German withdrawals. Reinforced patrols from Task Force 45 on the left, the 1st Armored in the center and the South African 6th Armoured on the left were sent across the Arno on the night of August 31–September 1. Mines sown along the river banks, especially at fordable crossings, and scattered enemy snipers and rear guards caused some casualties. The reports of an enemy withdrawal, however, were confirmed. It was decided that the time for crossing the Arno would be pushed up to 1000 that morning.

Monte Pisano rises north of Pisa near the Serchio and extends southeast towards the Arno for some ten miles (and seven in depth) along two 3,000-foot heights; in Dante's phrase, it is "*il monte/per che I Pisan veder Lucca non ponno*" ("the mountain because of which the Pisans cannot see Lucca"). The peaks of Monte Albano rise 1,750 to 2,000 feet some twenty-five miles to the east, an extended Apennine finger thrusting down to the banks of the Arno between Empoli and Signa, six miles west of Florence—where II Corps waited, poised for the drive north along Highway 65. These two mountain masses dominate the Arno plain from the coast to Empoli, and were the major portion of the Fifth Army's IV Corps front. Pisano and Albano were formidable obstacles even if defended, as IV Corps Intelligence estimated, solely by a reinforced company liberally supplied with automatic weapons, self-propelled guns and some tanks in each battalion sector. Such rearguards had caused the Allies a good deal of trouble south of the Arno. These had to be cleared out, not only to open approaches to the Gothic Line but also as a feint to cover the main Fifth Army thrust north of Florence.

Monte Pisano was assigned to the 1st Armored, Monte Albano to the South African 6th Armoured. Old Ironsides, rested, refurbished and reorganized, crossed the Arno two combat commands abreast. Colonel Howze sent his infantry—the attached 370th Regiment (less Company C) of the all-black 92nd—forward in a classic pincer movement. The 1st and 2nd Battalions moved towards the eastern flank of Monte Pisano as the 3rd went to the west. At first, the inexperienced infantry were slow, but the attack built up speed on the second day. Engineers cleared away riverside mines, improved fords and built a treadway bridge near Pontedera to get tanks across in record time. Sniper fire and mines caused a few casualties along the river, but inland the troops, at first, met no opposition.

By 2200 on September 2, the infantry had skirted the west side of Monte Pisano and reached the Serchio River at Pappiana, five miles north of Pisa. At the Ripafratta Gap, where the Serchio passes through a smattering of small hills, Company K suffered 24 casualties from enemy machine guns, small-arms fire, mortars and artillery. The 1st Battalion's B Company infantry rode tanks in a six-mile sweep around the east end of Pisano. Men of the 2nd Battalion dropped their packs to head up mule trails into the hill mass. By the close of September 2, Monte Pisano was in American hands.

Combat Command B tanks were held up by a canal in the open country east of Pisano Bridge and north of the Arno. Enemy fire and tanks ahead held up the advance of the infantry until the tanks were across the canal and on the move. Progress was slow over the next day, but on the 4th, tanks, armored infantry and Company C of the 370th took Altopascio, a road center on the Autostrada some six miles east of Lucca.

To the east, a 1st Armored reconnaissance force—the 81st Cavalry Recce Squadron and a company of the 701st Tank Destroyer—skirted the edge of an extensive swamp, the Padule di Fucecchio, that marked the boundary between the 1st Armored and the South Africans. Old Ironsides was now in position to take Lucca, where the Germans were withdrawing under a heavy artillery cover.

The 370th's Second Battalion attacked out of Monte Pisano on September 3 towards Lucca, reaching the village of Vorno later that day. The next afternoon, heavy artillery, machine-gun and sniper fire from rearguards of the 65th Grenadiers slowed the advance, but by evening Companies E and G had crossed the Autostrada a mile south of the city. Working with the tankers, a platoon from Company F seized and held the west and south gates. Casualties, so far, were light. On the morning of the 5th, the 2nd Battalion entered Lucca and garrisoned the ancient walled city. A company promptly moved north to secure the road crossing the Serchio River. Meanwhile, the 3rd Battalion, in a day of running firefights punctuated by heavy artillery, cleared the Lucca–Pisa road west of the city. To the east, the 1st Battalion pushed north of the Autostrada, drawing abreast of the city.

Task Force 45 moved north out of Pisa in concert with the 1st Armored, on its right. Its Japanese-American 100th Infantry Battalion crossed the waist-high Arno, keeping pace with the 370th's attack on Monte Pisano. Its only opposition came from two machine guns out in the Arno plain, and the Nisei reached the banks of the Serchio about five miles north of Pisa. The 100th was then relieved for its transfer to southern France.

Elsewhere the Task Force was delayed by extensive minefields. The British 39th Light Antiaircraft Regiment crossed the Arno to clear the woods near the coast. By September 5, the ack-ack gunners-turned-infantry had worked through the minefields to clear the area south of the Serchio from Lucca to within two miles of the Ligurian Sea. The advance of the 370th north of Monte Pisano threatened to outflank the enemy facing Task Force 45. The Germans pulled back on September 8 to allow the occupation of Vecchiano on the Serchio, about ten miles southwest of Lucca. Over the next three days, the Task Force lined up along the Autostrada.

The South Africans' Royal Natal Carbineers, who crossed the Arno at San Vito on September 1, securing their Division's left flank, considered that the ten days that followed "must be numbered amongst the most pleasant spent in Italy."[2] The Regiment fanned out north of the river, clipping along the eastern edge of the Monte Albano Ridge through a countryside of ochre-colored villages, ripening grain fields, orchards and vineyards. On the 6th Armoured's left flank, the 24th Guards Brigade, driving north between Monte Albano and the Fucecchio Marshes, kept pace with the 81st Cavalry Reconnaissance Squadron to within five miles of Pistoia. Enemy interference was slight. Partisans reported that Monte Albano, to the right, was clear of the enemy and they contributed several of the 21 prisoners turned in by the Brigade.

The Witwatersrand Rifles, crossing the Arno to tackle the Monte Albano Ridge, were heavily shelled. Six men were killed, 20 others wounded. Two other South Africans were killed and another wounded investigating anti-personnel mines while crossing the river. Sergeant C.M. Edwards of the Royal Durban Light Infantry and Sergeant C.A.B. Webber of the First City/Cape Town Highlanders were among the first South Africans to win American decorations (the Bronze Star) for their conduct during the river crossings. Otherwise, enemy action was slight and the lower slopes of Monte Albano were soon occupied.

The First City/Cape Town Highlanders in successive bounds and enduring a soaking downpour occupied all three thickly wooded heights of the 2,000-foot Monte Albano Ridge. Heavy rains on the 6th washed out tactical bridges over the Arno. Nonetheless, by the 7th the northern slopes were in South African hands and contact made with II Corps troops near Highway 66. Forward observers from the 7th/64th Field Battery, Transvaal Horse Artillery, on the high ground overlooking Pistoia saw no enemy movement and for a week did no firing.

Meanwhile, the British XIII Corps had expanded its cross-Arno bridgehead. A mobile column from the 2nd Brigade, British 1st Division, moved along the road from Florence to Sesto against light opposition to meet patrols from II Corps on September 2. (II Corps had been assigned a narrow sector just west of Florence. Two companies of the 442nd Infantry—due to go to France shortly— and a company of tanks from the 760th Tank Battalion crossed the Arno on September 1. They reached Sesto the next day and were relieved by the Blue Devils' 349th Infantry.) The 2 Brigade now began clearing the area west of Highway 65, while the 66th Brigade prepared to drive north.

The 3rd Brigade followed up a German withdrawal above Fiesole, overlooking Florence, until stopped by German fire from Monte Calvana. The 8th Indian Division struck north out of Pontassieve. The 1st/5th Royal Gurkha Rifles caught the 1st Battalion of the enemy's 715th Grenadier Division by surprise and routed it at Tigliano, a mountain village five miles north of Pontassieve.

During the counterattack that followed, the Gurkhas ran out of ammunition, and drew out their knives to meet the enemy. Confronted with three adversaries, Lance Corporal Naik Raimansingh Rana struck down one, but his kukri blade stuck in the German's skull. He clobbered a second German with a spade snatched up from the ground. The third enemy fled with Rana in hot pursuit with the spade. The Gurkhas held their objective. Rains forced the Indians to consolidate their positions on the southern slopes of the three mountains—Giovi, Rotonda, Calvana—guarding the approach to the Upper Sieve Valley.

The British 6th Armoured was busy opening up Highway 70, the lateral tie to the Eighth Army front on the Adriatic. But enemy troops shelled vehicles using the road, so the 61st Motorized Unit was ordered to clear the hills to the north. Then the Division regrouped to operate on both sides of the Sieve, working north along Highway 67 some eight miles to Scopeti. By then, it was apparent that the Germans intended to hold a line from Monte Morello west of Highway 65 east to Monte Senario, Calvana and Monte Giovi. The XIII Corps' bridgehead now roughly paralleled IV Corps advances to the west, establishing together a continuous line from the Ligurian Sea to the Sieve River some five to ten miles north of the Arno.

Nevertheless partisans, the *Fifth Army History* tells us, were puzzled by the slowness of "the almost unopposed advance across the Arno Plain."[3] South African officers, too, were frustrated at not being allowed to follow up their infantry's advance with the Division's powerful armored and artillery forces. The Guards Brigade, Sixth Armoured historian Neil Orpen remarks, making what they described as "stately progress from one habitation of the aristocracy to the next," felt that "the operations resembled the leisurely evolutions of seventeenth-century armies behind their cavalry screens rather than the pursuit of a retreating enemy by a highly mobile armoured division."[4]

General Poole itched to get on with the job. Pistoia was a tempting target, and a good thrust into the mountains beyond seemed eminently feasible. But he was constrained by his orders, as were other front-line commanders, which held his troops to reconnaissance patrols "for security purposes only" beyond the Monte Albano and Monte Pisano massif.[5] On September 5, these orders were reinforced. General Crittenberger ordered a regrouping of his forces along a line from Task Force 45's positions on the Serchio through the 1st Armored/370th Infantry at Lucca and Altopascio to Monte Albano. The troops—British and American— on line above Florence provided a screen for II Corps' preparations for the main Fifth Army assault on the Gothic Line. The IV Corps line was to be held with a minimum of troops, although the Corps was to be ready to follow up should the enemy continue his withdrawal to the north.

As for the restless South Africans, the *Fifth Army History* states: "It was particularly important that the advance of the 6th South African Armoured Division should not jeopardize the element of surprise hoped for in the main Fifth Army attack north of Florence."[6] But the logic here reflects an Allied weakness during the Italian campaign: a certain inflexibility when it came to meeting changes on the battlefield. It was apiece with the overlong pause along the Arno when the Fifth Army failed to take advantage of good fighting weather. General-Leutnant Freiherr Smilo von Luttwitz, commander of the 26th Panzer Division, remarked after the war of Allied operations in Italy: "The unquestioning adherence to a plan with short-range objectives prevented the catastrophic development of situations such as often happened on the Eastern front, and allowed us time to restore the front before the next attack."[7] "To veterans of the fighting in East Africa, Abyssinia and the Western Desert," Orpen avers, "such a failure to exploit success smacked of a rigidity and lack of initiative which could only be to the advantage of an enemy battling against the clock to fortify yet another delaying position." He adds, in retrospect ". . . any forceful thrust on the Lucca–Pistoia front" could only have helped to draw German forces away from the sector north of Florence.[8]

Still, the Fifth Army was ready by September 7. That day, General Clark confided to his diary, "The fate of the Fifth Army was tied up with that of the Eighth Army" (then stalled before the Coriano Ridge). Alexander, Clark expected, would hold up the Fifth Army until the Adriatic front got going again. "We are all set," Clark noted, "for the thrust over the mountains towards Bologna. It is hard to wait, for we are ready and eager to go. General Alexander is holding the lanyard, and when he pulls it we will be able to jump off with less than 24 hours' notice."9

The Fifth Army, indeed, was set to deliver a well-formulated stroke against the enemy. To cope with supply problems in the high mountainous terrain, nine Italian pack-mule companies, each with 260 mules, were standing by. British Intelligence had informed Clark that through Ultra it had learned that Hitler had ordered Kesselring to concentrate his defense astride Highway 65 at the Futa Pass. From the same message it had also learned that the inter-army boundary between the German Tenth and Fourteenth Armies lay some six miles east of the Futa, at Il Giogo Pass. Such boundaries are often a weak point in a front line.

Attack plans were quickly adapted. II Corps commander Keyes planned an advance on the Gothic Line with the 34th and 91st Divisions on either side of Highway 65 in what, it was hoped, the Germans would perceive as a continuation of a follow-up of the Wehrmacht withdrawal. The main attack would appear to be directed at Futa Pass. Once, however, the 91st came in contact with the Gothic Line, the 85th Division was ready to pass through and head towards Il Gorgio, while the 88th, also in reserve, would be poised to exploit either a breakthrough by the 91st or the 85th.

German defenses at Futa would be outflanked by a breakthrough at Il Gorgio, forcing a withdrawal there. The Fifth Army, then, would be in a position at Firenzuola to move either along Highway 65 through the Radicosa Pass to Bologna or to the northeast along a secondary road to Imola.

General Alexander pulled the lanyard on September 9. He visited Leese's headquarters the day before and decided that the Adriatic troops would need several days more to get on the move. Kesselring had shifted as much strength as he could spare to the Adriatic. Perhaps the Fifth Army assault on the Gothic Line would ease the Eighth Army's position, enabling it to start up again. Clark was ordered to start his offensive on September 10; Leese was to renew his attack two days later.

Allied bombers and fighters joined preparations for the battle. Fighter-bombers harassed road and rail lines on both sides of the Po. Medium bombers destroyed bridges repaired since the intensive bombings in July. All four main railroad lines into Bologna were hit by medium bombers and cut by nightfall of the 10th. Fighter-bombers scoured the Gothic Line, and for three days, beginning on the 9th, medium bombers joined in, flying 339 sorties against barracks, supply points and gun positions between the front and Bologna. From September 9 to 20, when weather worsened, fighter-bombers flew an average of 240 sorties a day against bivouac areas, command posts and supply depots in the vicinity of the Futa and Il Giogo Passes.

Despite Allied air superiority, Kesselring had managed to secure his Ligurian front and bolster his defenses on the Adriatic coast. The 356th Division was drawn from the Fourteenth Army—which faced the American Fifth Army—and sent east. Kesselring also committed the 26th Panzer and the 29th Panzer Grenadier Divisions to the Adriatic, tying up two units from the Tenth Army that might have been used to fill in his Futa and Il Giogo defenses. Moreover, just before the Fifth opened its September 10 offensive, Lemelsen's Fourteenth Army lost the 16th SS Panzer Grenadier Division to France. Partisans behind the lines had, meantime, stepped up their activity, demolishing a railroad bridge, tracks and bits of highway essential to bringing up reserves and replacements.

One battalion from each division in the XIV Panzer Corps sector on the western end of the Gothic Line was deployed to secure the Wehrmacht's rear. German defenses were stretched. Lemelsen's Fourteenth Army had but one division, the 4th Parachute, to cover both the Futa and Il Giogo Passes: Vietinghoff's Tenth Army also had one, the 715th, to oppose the British XIII Corps. So, as Kesselring remarked in his memoirs, it was "with a quite remarkable precision the enemy managed to find the soft spots at the seam of the Tenth and Fourteenth Armies and to exploit German weaknesses."[10]

On September 10, there was a great stirring all along the Fifth Army front from the Ligurian coast to the Sieve River, northeast of Florence. Within II Corps' sector, bracketing Highway 65, long columns of infantry threaded through narrow valleys and along steep, parallel ridges. For the most part, the men were silent; the tread of feet, the creak and rubbing of packs, rifles, munition belts—these were the multitudinous sounds of an army on the march. Those who lifted their eyes saw a jagged massif shrouded in a blue haze, forbidding and ominous, where a watchful enemy waited. On the Fifth Army's western flank, Task Force 45 crossed the Serchio and followed up the enemy's withdrawal to reach the outskirts of the prewar beach resort Viareggio. The 1st Armored moved north of Lucca to the sound of enemy demolitions along a twenty-mile front, increasingly relying on its infantry as tanks became nearly useless in the Northern Apennines. The 370th Infantry cleared the west bank of the Serchio and the last few miles of plain on the east side of the river.

Opposition was light, but in a firefight at Del Giglio, Company E killed six Germans on September 10. Three days later, Company A, riding on tanks, approached Ponte a Moriana and engaged the enemy. One tank caught fire as the enemy scored a hit. The black troops fought their way into town and beyond, where the Serchio flowed through deep gorges and where hamlets huddled at the foot of sheer drops and clung to precipitous hillsides.

The 370th probed an arc from Ponte San Pietro to Segromigno, a village tucked up on the lower edge of Le Pizzone. To the northeast, the 1st Armored Infantry entered Villa Basilica while the 81st Cavalry Reconnaissance Squadron—in effect, a mountain infantry unit—worked up a gorge north of Pescia.

The South Africans occupied Pistoia and were ordered to speed up the retreat of the enemy's 362nd Grenadier Division. Three brigades went forward on line to exert pressure in an assist to the main attack of II Corps. The 24th Guards Brigade advanced on the left in the mountains north of Montecatini, where communications were poor and forward troops had to be supplied by mule. On September 11, the Guardsmen approached Femmina Morta, a cluster of houses on a ridge-running-road from Montecatini to the junction of Highways 12 and 66. They were blocked by a waist-high wire belt two meters wide.

The enemy no longer fell back when fired upon, and shelling increased in intensity. At the center, the 12th South African Motorized Brigade reached the "V"-shaped flats where Highway 64 branches off Highway 66, both highways twisting sharply into the mountains. On the Brigade's right flank, C Company, Imperial Light Horse/Kimberley Regiment, occupied Kesselring's former headquarters at Santomato on the Pistoia–Montale–Prato road. Farther east, above Prato, the South African Armoured Brigade pushed along Route 6620 (325 on today's maps), a secondary road to Bologna. Advance elements of the Brigade reached Migliana, a mountain village seven miles north of Prato, on September 12.

The South Africans were pushing up within a triangle formed by Highway 64 on the west and Route 6620 on the east with a short base, Pistoia to Prato, and its apex at Sasso Marconi, where the two roads meet some seven miles south of Bologna. Above Pistoia and Prato a line of

3,000-foot peaks—Pozzo del Bagno, Acuto, Alto and Moscoso—covered by scrub forests with dense underbrush, dominated the sector. Beyond, a series of streams—the Reno, the east and west branches of the Limentra, the Bisenzio—cut through rugged valley northward to the Po Valley.

One major railroad followed the Reno and Highway 64, while another paralleled Route 6620. At Vernio, on 6620, the railway plunged into the world's longest double-track tunnel for nearly 12 miles, to emerge just below Rioveggio. The Germans destroyed the channels and pipes that normally carried 45,000,000 liters of water a day to Prato and neighboring villages to flood the Apennine Tunnel. At the Prato end, the tunnel was blocked for some 115 feet with blown locomotives, trucks and miscellaneous rubbish. When the South Africans reached Vernio, in a driving rain on September 24, the South African Railway Construction Group, 10,000-strong, began to clear the tunnel. As for the fighting troopers, the South African Regiment, Orpen remarks, would "see its toughest fighting in the war" within the rugged terrain and heavily populated Apennine triangle.[11]

On the eastern flank of the Fifth Army, the British XIII Corps, by and large, managed to keep pace with the early advances of II Corps. The 1st Division pushed north along the east side of the Florence–Borgo San Lorenzo road, where the enemy fought a series of small rearguard delaying actions. At L'Olmo—about halfway up the road from Fiesole to Borgo San Lorenzo—the Dukes, held up by an anti-personnel minefield, came under heavy-machine gun and mortar fire, suffering some sixty casualties. The major problem, however, was getting supplies forward. Even four-wheel jeeps that could climb impossible slopes found it difficult going. A.M. Cheetham, a Royal Artillery forward observer, lost his jeep when it slid off a hillside, slithering down two hundred feet into a ravine. His driver and a passenger suffered concussions and another man was thrown clear. Transport problems were eased with the allocation of twelve mules for each battalion. The 1st Division, over the next two days, reached the Sieve on September 10 and pushed on until slowed by enemy outposts along the approaches to the Gothic Line.

On XIII Corps' left flank, the British 6th Armoured followed a German withdrawal up Highway 67 from Pontassieve to Dicomano on September 10. Elements of the 1st Guards Brigade swung slightly northeast to occupy Casaromana, a village at the edge of the mountains above the Sieve, the next day. In the center, the advance of the 8th Indian

Division was hampered by the lack of roads and the mountain fastness. Nevertheless, as the Germans fell back the Indians reached the Sieve near the village of Vicchio on September 10.

Three miles beyond the river on the next day, Indian patrols found wired and entrenched positions that had been abandoned. Endless streams of mules and jeeps bumbled along the innumerable small valleys feeding the Sieve, where farmers and their womenfolk paused in the fields and vineyards to watch the advancing troops. Cattle and sheep grazed in summer sunshine. The imperturbability of cows while fighting raged about them was a topic of endless controversy among the Indians. Some said cows had no hearing; all agreed that cows had no sense.

Just ahead was the great wall of the San Benedetto Alps, whose trackless crests rose to over 5,000 feet above the Arno. These heights were riddled with camouflaged trenches, elaborate bunkers and concrete machine-gun posts slotted to take maximum advantage of well-prepared fields of fire. This was the Gothic Line.

The XIII Corps was now in position to carry out its mission: support of the II Corps attack on Il Giogo pass.

NOTES

[1] Murray, *First City/Cape Town Highlanders,* p. 43.

[2] Orpen, *Victory in Italy,* p. 196.

[3] U.S. Army, *Fifth Army History,* Vol. VI, p. 36.

[4] Orpen, *Victory in Italy,* p. 196.

[5] Ibid., pp. 196–97.

[6] U.S. Army, *Fifth Army History,* Vol. VI, p. 36.

[7] Orpen, *Victory in Italy,* p. 196.

[8] Ibid.

[9] Fisher, *Cassino to the Alps,* pp. 320–21.

[10] Kesselring, *A Soldier's Recod,* p. 213.

[11] Orpen, *Victory in Italy,* p. 201.

XIII

JABBING A THICK CLOTH

General von Senger, watching the renewed Allied offensive from his Corps Headquarters,while tucked away at Albinea in a quiet sector on the right wing of Fourteenth Army, observed: "The incessant prodding against our front across the Futa Pass was like jabbing a thick cloth with a sharp spear. The cloth would give way like elastic, but under excessive strain it would be penetrated by the spear." He felt depressed, not because his corps was being thinned out to meet the needs of the other sectors; *that* he accepted as necessary. But having to stand aside, he felt "like a hunter chafing at the stable door when the other horses are led out and he has to remain behind." He wanted to apply the lessons he had learned at Cassino to the new situation. "I could see enough," he says in his memoirs, "to realize that we would not have to reckon with any new surprises." The Allies, he assumed, would maintain the direction of their attack against the left wing of the Fourteenth Army. Movements in the mountains were difficult and time-consuming because of the deployment of artillery. "And so we were the sorrowful witnesses of the enemy's almost daily successes against our neighbors."[1]

However, he was wrong about one matter: the Germans did have to reckon at least with one surprise. Kesselring and his field commanders continued to expect the Fifth Army to focus on Futa Pass, where the principal north–south road, the two-lane, macadamized Highway 65, crossed the Apennine divide. General Lemelsen, commander of the Fourteenth, deployed his forces in light of that expectation. Two regiments of the 4th Parachute Division manned the Futa Pass defenses while one, the 12th, guarded Il Giogo, its bracketing heights, Monticelli and Monte Altuzzo, as well as additional heights to the east. The Paras had suffered heavy losses in the fighting south of Rome. Its combat-hardened troops were fleshed out—600 replacements arrived just before the attack on Il Giogo, some who had yet to fire live ammunition. To complicate matters for the Germans, the boundary between the 12th Paras and the 715th Grenadier Division east of Mount Verruca was also the boundary between the Fourteenth and Tenth Armies. Thus, the enemy had a divided command in the critical sector where II Corps struck its main blow against the Gothic Line.

II Corps' initial approach—the 34th Division to the left of Highway 65 and the 91st to the right—conformed to German expectations of a concentrated attack on Futa Pass. The early movements of the British XIII Corps just east of Highway 65 screened II Corps preparations for its main attack. General Charles L. Bolte's 34th Division, meanwhile, pushed on towards the Futa defenses. The Red Bulls followed up the German withdrawal on II Corps' left flank along the Monte della Calvana ridge to clear the rolling hill country at the head of the Sieve River Valley on September 10. The next day, the 1st Battalion of the 133rd Infantry occupied the 3,000-foot Monte Maggiore without opposition and pushed on to the forward slopes of Monte Il Prataccio, a five-mile advance through rugged terrain. At the close of day, the regiment came under some artillery and machine-gun fire. The 168th Infantry on the Red Bulls' right flank, slowed by the need to take cover from artillery fire, made an advance of only three miles.

On the morning of September 11, the 168th's 1st Battalion took the hamlet Le Croci, with its stunning view to the north and down the Sieve Valley. A brisk firefight drove the enemy down the northern slopes and the Red Bulls passed gingerly through Cavalina, an unoccupied but heavily mined and booby-trapped village on the Sieve where the heavy weapons company suffered five casualties. Scattered artillery fire gave notice that the enemy was on the alert as the battalion passed through Barberino. An enemy patrol in an old castle north of the village held up the Red Bulls until dark, just two miles short of its objective, Monte Frassino. The 2nd and 3rd Battalions attacked but at dawn Colonel Hine called a halt to avoid any daylight assault over open ground. The 168th was relieved during the day by the 135th Infantry, which had fought forward through bypassed enemy rearguards. Meanwhile, the 133rd had renewed its drive to advance on La Dogana Hill, an outpost of the Gothic Line some two miles southwest of Monte Frassino. The 2nd Battalion worked its way around the east side of an extensive minefield covered by machine-guns to gain a mile in its approach to La Dogana, while the 3rd worked around to the west to reach positions on a ridge north of the hill. Enemy resistance had stiffened, and by nightfall on September 12 the Red Bulls' gains were down to hundreds of yards from miles the day before.

The 91st made comparable progress with the 362nd advancing astride Highway 65 and the 363rd bracketing the San Piero–Futa Pass–Firenzuola road. The Wild West infantrymen waded the Sieve on September 10 and two days later were positioned for an attack on the Gothic Line's strongpoints from Mount Calvi to Il Giogo. The 362nd, in effect, joined the Red Bulls in mounting pressure on Futa's defenses, fleshing out the deception of a frontal attack while striking at Il Giogo. Its 3rd Battalion was to continue up along Highway 65 while the other two opened a flanking attack to the east, designed to come behind Futa by taking a series of peaks: Calvi, Linari, Alto and Grazzaro. On September 12, the 1st Battalion—with the 2nd in reserve—jumped off for Calvi and gained its southern slopes by day's end. The 3rd Battalion along Highway 65 advanced less than a mile against increasing enemy resistance.

Meanwhile, the 363rd Infantry deployed its 1st and 3rd Battalions against the Il Giogo defenses, jumping off at 8 in the morning under a smoke screen laid down by chemical mortars. Both units attacked towards Mount Monticelli. The 1st moved northeast for nearly a mile until small-arms fire from the front and from Monte Calvi to the left held up the attack about a mile short of the objective. The 3rd Battalion attacked along the Il Giogo highway, Companies K and I out front. L Company followed, prepared to branch off to the right to seize Mount Altuzzo in order to facilitate the movement of the 85th Division. K Company was halted at L'Uomo Morto, a cluster of houses inside a horseshoe curve on the road to Il Giogo. Working up a deep gully on the left the night of September 12–13, I Company came within 400 yards of Monticelli's barbed-wired crest. Machine-gun crossfire and mortar fire forced the company back to the base of the ridge, with 25 casualties.

L Company tackled Monte Altuzzo that night, almost to the crest, before taking cover under an escarpment. Lieutenant Tisdale, the only officer left, radioed: "Friendly artillery barrages falling on hill—casualties—under hostile mortar and artillery fire—request permission to remove company from hill."[2] Permission was granted and L Company dug in on a small hill just south of Altuzzo. The 91st had opened the way and had narrowed its front; the 85th was now in position to join the assault on Il Giogo.

The Scylla and Charybdis of Il Giogo were Monticelli, to the west, and Monte Altuzzo, east of the Firenzuola road south of the pass. More was known about the Futa Pass defenses than those at Il Giogo, where the road, paved but inferior to Highway 65, twists in a series of horseshoe turns to cut through the Apennine roof ridge. Although aerial reconnaissance had spotted twenty huts for housing the Todt workforce, suggesting that defenses were in place, it found little else: one pillbox and a few machine-gun emplacements covering two stretches of knee-high barbed wire six to eight yards deep. Monticelli, a cone-shaped mass with a hog-back ridge running northwest, rises 2,857 feet to a bare summit. Two spurs connected to the main ridge by narrow saddles—Poggio al Pozzo to the west and Poggio di Castro to the east—winged southward. Three draws slashed the face of Monticelli: the easternmost cut to the peak; the other two, separated by a rocky nose, scarred the western ridge. Bare, rocky and steep, Monticelli afforded little cover save gullies worn into the forward slope by the rain. Scrub brush and a grove of chestnut trees near Borgo, a farmhouse at the foot of the western ridge, promised some concealment for advancing infantry.

Altuzzo is some 180 feet higher than Monticelli, at 3,038 feet. Its forbidding heights were reinforced by Monte Verruca, rising 3,050 feet to the east. Both Altuzzo and Verruca are chipped by sheer cliffs. Parts of the latter were heavily wooded with pine and chestnut trees that afforded some cover for advancing troops. The approach to Altuzzo was a sort of natural amphitheater formed by fields enclosed on three sides. Troops in the amphitheater, working through the fields or among the trees at their edge, could be seen from two and sometimes three sides. A series of knob-like hills on the ridges leading to the crests of Altuzzo and Verruca formed a heavily defended obstacle course.

To break the Gothic Line, the Fifth Army had to take the heights that arched across above the Mugello—the upper basin of the Sieve—from Sasseta past Futa and Il Giogo to San Godenzo on the east–west Highway 67. If Il Giogo were captured, Futa would fall and the broad front to the Po would be cracked. Understandably, then, General Clark was not about to take any chances. With the commitment of the 85th Division on September 13, II Corps had three divisions—the 34th, 91st and 85th—on line, with the 88th in reserve. Each of the forward divisions was reinforced: the 34th was assigned the 757th Tank Battalion; Company C and a recon platoon of the 804th Tank Destroyers; and the Red Bull artillery component was boosted by the British 10th Army Group Royal Artillery; the 91st gained the 755th Tank Battalion; the 804th Tank Destroyer Battalion (less units assigned to the 34th), Company D, the 84th Chemical Battalion and the 77th Field Artillery Group; the 85th was boosted by the 752nd Tank Battalion (less Company D), the 805th Tank Destroyer Battalion, the 84th Chemical Battalion (less Companies A and D) and three 105 mm howitzer battalions from the 88th Division. The 39th Engineer Combat Regiment provided engineer support for the 34th and 91st Divisions.

In the Il Giogo sector—less than one-third of the II Corps zone— General Keyes massed, roughly, 50 percent of his committed infantry strength and an equal proportion of his tank, tank destroyer and chemical units. This gave him, according to the *Fifth Army History,* "an estimated superiority of three-to-one over the defending enemy forces." He also had air superiority. Engineers had opened up Highway 65 and the road to Il Giogo to enable the long-range artillery to move into positions around Vaglia, a village on Highway 65. The bulk of medium-range guns were concentrated closer to the Sieve Valley, where air strips were set up for artillery observation planes. By September 12, corps and division artillery units were in firing positions and had begun to soften up the enemy's defenses. "The time had come," as General Clark noted in his memoirs, "for the Fifth Army to strike northward . . . and thus crack the Gothic Line wide open."[3]

On the morning of September 13, when II Corps launched its attack on the Il Giogo defenses, the situation on both the Altuzzo and Monticelli heights was muddled. Neither mountain had been taken in the attacks of the night before and the 363rd Infantry had only confused reports from its forward units. Preparatory and supporting artillery fire could not be laid down until the advance units of the 363rd could be located. On the lower slopes of Monticelli, in fact, the 3rd Battalion was falling back before an enemy counterattack and barely held on to its positions at L'Uomo Morto. To its left, 1st Battalion Companies A and C jumped off together. Company A worked up the draw towards Casacce but was driven back by mortar fire, which killed five men and wounded 17; Company C managed to reach the southwestern slopes of Al Pozzo. The 2nd Battalion was then committed at 1600. Screened by smoke, it was to move from Al Pozzo over Hill 763 to the eastern summit, Hill 871. Company F, passing through C Company southwest of Al Pozzo, was caught in a minefield in the saddle between Al Pozzo and Hill 763. Exploding mines alerted the Germans, who covered the field with fire. At dawn, the infantry had worked its way forward to resume its attack on Hill 763. But machine guns from eight pillboxes lashed the steep slope, reducing the 3rd Platoon to nine men and one commissioned officer. The company was forced to halt.

On the 91st's right, the 85th opened its attack on Monte Altuzzo and Verruca. But the first day was largely limited to feeling out the enemy and jockeying for ground from which new attacks could be launched. At the end of the day, the 2nd Battalion had reached positions near L'Uomo Morte while the 1st secured precarious positions on the west edge of Altuzzo. Company A, in the lead, passed Company L of the 363rd to reach a trail northwest of Hill 624, where barbed wire and enemy machine-gun fire halted the attack. Behind Company A, Company B came under enemy observation at the edge of an open field, where it held up short of the mountain. The 339th Infantry, meanwhile, crossed a line of departure two miles below the crest of Monte Verruca.

By seven in the morning Companies A and B were on the knob at the end of the western ridge where they were stopped by crossfire from Altuzzo and fire from a strongpoint on the ridge ahead. Companies F and G clambered up the right arm of Altuzzo. F Company was stopped in three houses below Hill 732 at the head of a draw below a strongpoint. Fire from positions on a nose covering the main draw to the right of 732 stopped Company G. East of Verruca, Company E moved along a ridge to the crest of Rotto Hill but was forced to take cover in a draw to the left by small-arms and mortar fire, suffering over 30 casualties. A night attack by the 2nd Battalion failed. Enemy crossfire from Hills 691 and 732, as well as flanking fire from Altuzzo and Rotto, was all too effective. By the end of September 13, II Corps learned the bitter truth of Clausewitz's maxim: "Defense is the stronger form with the negative object, and attack the weaker form with the positive object."

Meanwhile, General Bolte's Red Bulls came within striking distance of Futa Pass, fostering the illusion among German commanders that Futa was the focus of II Corps. Still, by September 14, the enemy sensed that something was up at Il Giogo. They held fast to their conviction that the big thrust would occur at Futa but recognized that the "jabs" at Il Giogo called for a response. The 11th and 12th Parachute Regiments had held a line from west of Monte Calvi to Monte Verruca from the start of II

Corps' offensive and were increasingly in need of reinforcements. Every available man was thrown into the line. Replacements came from the 4th Parachute Replacement Battalion, the 4th Antitank Battalion and miscellaneous headquarters and service personnel. But II Corps Artillery's harassing fire allowed only a trickle of supplies and ammunition to reach the front. The 10th Parachute Regiment was pulled out from Futa and deployed behind Monte Altuzzo and Montcelli. The 305th Fusilier Recon Battalion (305th Grenadier Division) was rushed over from Rimini to reinforce elements of the 715th Grenadiers below Monte Pratone. The 2nd Battalion, Lehr Brigade, attached to the 65th Grenadier Division, was ordered to relieve the 12 Paras' 3rd Battalion on Monte Verruca on the night of September 17–18. A Lithuanian labor battalion was sent up to replenish the Paras' 1st Battalion.

Many replacements could not get through or were too demoralized to be effective. As a 91st Division intelligence report on prisoner interrogations noted: ". . . the 4th Company left for their present position 24 September. They were repeatedly attacked by our bombers on the way and suffered heavy casualties. Company was committed night of 17 September. POWs state that the personnel of the company consists mostly of very young recruits and that morale is very low. Many men lost their weapons on the march to the main line of resistance because they were too exhausted to carry them."[4]

The Germans, nonetheless, fought a determined and skillful defensive action. Their defenses were more extensive than II Corps' intelligence had been able to discover. Hidden machine-gun emplacements were exposed only as troops came within range or when artillery barrages tore away protective camouflage. Though the steady pounding of the artillery knocked out pillboxes and reinforced dugouts, far too many were intact as infantrymen fought uphill against well-placed German troops. All rations and ammunition had to be brought up at night on mules and by backpackers. The troops received only a minimum of supplies, and losses were heavy and mounting. At the end of two days' fighting, over the 14 and 15th of September, the 91st and 85th Division had gained "but little ground."[5]

The 1st Battalion of the 363rd, as an instance, was ordered on the morning of September 14 to seize the long western slope of Monticelli. Company C was held up by small-arms fire on the lower, eastern slope of Hill 579. Company B followed a rolling barrage to good effect when an

English-speaking German radio operator called, complaining that "artillery was falling on the Company C troops." The barrage was lifted and B company had to contend with two mutually supporting machine-gun positions without artillery support. By dark, nonetheless, the company was above Borgo, halfway up the slope.

The next morning, Company B faced the Germans across a shallow, sandy draw rising some 220 yards to a five-foot embankment below the crest of the Monticelli western ridge. A grazing fire swept the barren draw from log-framed dugouts camouflaged by sod. Company B, backed by two platoons from A Company, pushed on, the men taking advantage of every fold and wrinkle in the ground. Sergeant Roger W. Blount carried his machine gun across the open draw to the left flank, where he buttoned up two machine-gun emplacements to his left and right for forty minutes, enabling riflemen to knock out the pillboxes at the cost of only one casualty. Pfc. Ralph J. Metheney provided invaluable support to the attacking infantrymen, firing his 60mm mortar without base plate or sight by holding the tube between his knees. When he ran out of ammo, he gathered his squad and joined the riflemen in their assault. When they reached the relative safety of the embankment at 1500, seventeen men were left of the two A Company platoons, eighty of Company B. Technical Sergeant Charles J. Murphy of the 1st Platoon and Lieutenant Ross A. Notaro of A Company ordered their men to fix bayonets. They charged the crest to the left and north of the embankment, where the rest of B Company kept on going.

Staff Sergeant Joseph D. Higdon's light machine gun was posted to protect the left flank. The Germans counterattacked, rushing despite casualties to within grenade-throwing distance. Higdon was hit, but he stood up, cradled his gun in his arms and charged into the enemy. Hit again by a grenade fragment, he staggered but kept on firing until the Germans fled. Hit again, Higdon attempted to return to his position but fell short by thirty yards and died. Three enemy counterattacks were beaten off the ridge. That night, the troops were pulled back off the exposed ridge, taking refuge along the embankment. The 363rd Regiment had a leg up Mount Monticelli. But its 2nd Battalion was still below Hill 763—and the enemy held the summit at 871.

Given the impressive superiority of II Corps, it is remarkable how much turned on the actions of a relative handful of men. One badly depleted

company aided by two additional depleted platoons takes a heavily fortified embankment, and in so doing makes possible the capture of a critical mountain massif. Those who close in with the enemy and bear the
brunt of the fighting at a critical juncture often comprise no more than a
platoon or, in greater strength, two rifle companies—anywhere, that is,
from 48 to 350 men. As Sidney T. Mathews puts it in his account of the
taking of Altuzzo: "When a prize fighter strikes a blow against his opponent, his fist alone makes contact. So it is with the main effort of a modern military force: a fraction of its bulk acts as the fist and delivers the
punch in the name of the entire army."[6]

On the second day of the 85th's attack on Monte Altuzzo, B Company secured a foothold on the western ridge. The Germans mounted a
series of counterattacks, which were repulsed at a high cost. The lead platoons—the 2nd and 3rd—were reduced to a fighting strength of twenty
men. All the officers and noncoms had been knocked out. Staff Sergeant
George D. Keathley, the 1st Platoon guide, moved up and took over.
Under sniper and mortar fire, he crawled about the ridge from one casualty to another, administering first-aid and collecting much-needed ammunition from the wounded and dead. This he distributed among the
remaining men.

Following a mortar barrage, the Germans attacked again, overrunning thirteen of the defenders. Keathley's forlorn hope, however, held the
center. An enemy grenade exploded, hitting the sergeant on his left side.
Holding his entrails in his left hand, he fought on. Then, letting go, he
rose to his feet and used his left hand to steady his rifle, killing an attacker. For fifteen minutes, he shouted commands while still firing at the
enemy. Artillery was then brought to bear on the enemy, regrouping some
fifty yards away. But the Germans withdrew, leaving their dead and seriously wounded behind. A few moments later, Keathley died. He was
awarded the Medal of Honor.

Sometimes, however, a solid punch fails to knock out the opponent.
When the 85th Division's 338th and 339th Infantry fell short of taking
Monte Altuzzo and Monte Verruca on September 15, General Keyes
committed his reserve, the 337th, to a flanking attack on Monte Pratone,
to the Custer men's right. The 2nd Royal Scots had scored a limited
advance, securing Hill 938 some 1500 yards short of Pratone. The 3rd
Battalion of the 337th passed through the Scots on September, 16 along
the ridge north to Pratone, but fire from Hills 973 and 885 to the north

and east halted the attack some 1,000 yards short of the objective. Attempts by the 339th Infantry to take Signorini Hill to the southwest of 938 also failed. This attempt to outflank the enemy, *Fifth Army History* observes, "succeeded only in broadening the division front and in stepping up the process of attrition."[7]

That night, the Custer men resumed their jabs at the enemy on Altuzzo. The Todt organization had built two well-timbered bunkers with four layers of ten-inch logs capped with soil just below the mountain crest to the rear, at point 926. Both bunkers could hold at least a platoon. Zigzag tunnels connected the bunkers to observation posts south of the crest. Concentrated artillery fire reduced the western OP to a gigantic crater and punched another crater on the northern edge of Point 926, directly in front of the right bunker. (The left bunker was farther north, down slope.) Three platoons of C Company and one of A Company of the 338th Infantry made a silent approach in the dark and dug in the rocky soil just below the south edge of the peak.

It was hard going, the lucky soldiers scratching out 18-inch-deep slits for cover. As his men dug in, C Company platoon leader Lieutenant Krasman, platoon Sergeant Fent and their German-speaking scout, Private Schwantke explored the trench on the east side of 926. At a bend, they startled a German soldier. Schwantke called on him to surrender and, when he dodged back, Krasman and Fent fired, knocking the soldier down. Two 55mm mortars, a machine gun and several packs of food in the trench convinced Krasman that there must be more Germans on the northern slope. The three men returned for help.

Men from the 1st Platoon, C Company, followed Schwantke into the right-flank zigzag trench, where they were stopped at the last bend by a machine gun firing from near the entrance to the right bunker. At the center, Sergeant Strosnider rushed forward to take shelter in the giant crater a yard short of the right bunker. Sergeant Fent with two men from his 3rd Platoon, Privates Lightner and Kubina, moved around on the left flank and discovered the second bunker, with a bespectacled German officer on top. Lightner moved along the trench towards the bunker entrance and Fent shot the German. For a while, the Custer men and the Germans tossed grenades at one another, firing guns whenever an opportunity opened up. Private Anthony W. Houston, in the crater with Strosnider, prepared to fire a rifle grenade, but before he could pull the trigger of his rifle, a machine-gun burst from a knob up ahead cut him down. Pfc

Kermit C. Fisher, also in the crater, spotted Schwantke trapped in the bend of the zigzag trench below him. He shouted, "There's Schwantke, let's go help him." As he raised himself to climb out of the crater, a bullet from an enemy machine gun struck him in the throat. The men in the crater crawled back to their old positions on the southern slope.

Something of a stalemate developed until Sergeant Fent climbed on top of the rear bunker. While Lightner covered the entrance, he called out to the Germans to surrender. A German rushed out, hurling hand grenades. As these sailed over his head, Lightner shot him in the stomach. Slumping to the ground, he went for his pistol. Lightner shot him in the stomach again and in the hand, knocking away the pistol, and, for good measure, shot him four more times. Fent kept up his calls for surrender and the Germans began to file out, fourteen in all, including a first sergeant. Leaving their prisoners with guards below Hill 926, Fent returned to the left bunker, where he accepted the surrender of ten more Germans led by a medic from some point on the north slope. Inside the bunker, the two men found a large store of arms and rations, including fresh bread and sardines. These they promptly ate, having had no food since the day before. While in the bunker, the telephone rang. Fent answered; the caller hung up.

The Germans, as expected from information gleaned from the prisoners, counterattacked. Kubina, 3rd platoon BAR man, was posted in the left zigzag trench and in the firefight that followed killed some eight of the enemy and wounded several more, disrupting the attackers. A second counterattack was broken by the effective defense mounted by the Custer men. Those in the right zigzag trench had run out of grenades, so they began throwing German grenades and the surviving enemy made a hasty withdrawal. The 1st Battalion now held Point 926 on Altuzzo. A night attack by the 3rd Battalion completed the job of clearing the mountain and the heights across the highway. By morning on September 18, as the *Fifth Army History* laconically put it, ". . . the 338th Infantry had achieved a clean break at the most important point in the Il Giogo defenses."[8]

The capture of the Altuzzo heights on the 17th accompanied a general collapse all along the 85th's front. The 339th Infantry took Signorini, Hill 918 above Rotto, and Hills 732 and 724 on the bitterly contested eastern ridge of Monte Verruca, and the summit. The Lehr Brigade's 2nd Battalion arrived on the night of 16–17 September to relieve the battered 3rd Battalion of the 12th Paras. Disorganized by artillery fire, it was caught by the 339th and almost entirely destroyed just as it took up its new positions. The 337th seized Monte Pratone and Hill 945 to the east on the afternoon of September 17. At the close of that day, the 85th held all the major heights on the great divide between the Sieve and Santerno Valleys on a four-mile front from Monte Altuzzo to beyond Pratone.

West of the Il Giogo road, on the morning of September 16, the five-foot embankment at the northwestern end of the Monticelli ridge was held by a remnant of Company B, 363rd Infantry—17 men of Sergeant Charles J. Murphy's 1st Platoon, plus seven co-opted mortar men. Throughout the day and well into the next, the Germans attacked. To get a better field of fire, ex-mortar man Pfc. Oscar G. Johnson stood in his slit trench and emptied his carbine into the attackers. Throwing his useless weapon aside, he grabbed guns from the wounded men around him and kept firing until the initial attack was repulsed. He then gathered, under fire, four M-1 rifles, a BAR and a Thompson sub-machine gun. Again and again, he swept a 180-degree arc with a deadly fire. During attack intervals, he cannibalized all the weapons he could find. By midday, he was the only one of his original group left. The others had been killed or wounded. Twice men from the depleted company were sent to help Johnson, but to no avail—they were either driven back or wounded by the intense fire. Relief arrived on the morning of the 17th. Private Johnson was awarded the Medal of Honor.

Company B was reduced to some fifty men. Four of its officers were knocked out; Lieutenant Bruno Rosellini took command when Captain Lloyd J. Inman was hit in the right shoulder and evacuated. At dawn, several Germans emerged from an emplacement on the crest with a white flag. Rosellini called out to his men to cease fire. A German captain requested a truce to enable both sides to evacuate their wounded. Rosellini radioed for instruction and, as he waited, a group of 24 enemy soldiers, apparently assuming that their commander had surrendered, came down the slope with their hands raised.

It was the beginning of the end of the battle for Monticelli—but, as yet, the barest of beginnings. A final assault was set for the 17th, but Company B would not participate. More than 150 German dead were counted in the company sector, at least 40 attributed to Private Johnson's steadfast efforts. The company also captured 40 prisoners. Lieutenant Rosellini was killed, leaving the company without any officers. Altogether, B Company lost 14 men killed, 126 wounded. The rest were absorbed into neighboring G Company.

Though the 363rd was about to close in on Monticelli, its situation was precarious. Colonel W.B. Fulton committed his reserve 3rd Battalion on the afternoon of the 16th. To cover its attack on the mountain from the southeast, the heavy machine guns of the 2nd and 3rd Battalions were combined. During the afternoon and night of September 16, the guns fired 130,000 rounds while the 81mm mortars laid down 3,700. Company L came up against four-strand barbed wire where Lieutenant Eyherabide lost his left foot to a mine, which also blew a gap in the wire. Eyherabide lay on a stretcher directing his men through the wire, but the alerted Germans brought down enough fire to force a retreat. Company K was also driven back just as it prepared to blow a way through the barbed wire with bangalore torpedoes. Three men were dead, twenty wounded. The first attack had failed.

General Livesay decided that a visit to the 3rd Battalion command post at Collini was called for, to restore morale. Exploitation of the 85th's breakthrough on Altuzzo depended on clearing Monticelli, where the Germans could still fire upon the Custer men. The 1st Battalion was occupied fighting off enemy counterattacks while the 2nd was still trying to knock out pillboxes blocking its attack. The 3rd remained the 91st's sole hope of securing Monticelli's crest. It was ordered to follow a rolling barrage laid down by the 347th Field Artillery at 1400, while Corps artillery blasted targets to the enemy's rear. "Take the ridge at any cost," Livesay commanded. "Go up, and don't stop until you get to the crest." Lieutenant Colonel Long replied, "I'll get them up there, but I don't expect to have many men left."[9]

Captain Fulton's Company K led off on the right, followed by Company L on the left and I, initially in reserve, to the right rear. All three companies ran into increasing artillery, mortar, and self-propelled gun fire. Fulton took the east branch of a draw within 300 yards of the crest, only to find himself with ten men under direct fire from a German observation post on the peak. The eleven made a dash for it through a prepared concentration of mortar fire along an exposed run to the top. They rushed the German emplacements and tumbled into the trenches. Pfc. Theodore R. Thompson got Battalion on his radio as his comrades set up defensive positions within the emplacements that the Germans had just abandoned. Captain Futlon reported that he was on Monticelli: "I've got ten men with me, we're played out and I'll be goddamned if I know what to do next."[10] At Battalion, the executive officer, Major Jacob B. Beal, noted the time: 1448, 17 September.

Major Beal called the supporting artillery and told Fulton to get busy directing fire on the retreating enemy. Fulton called for replacements—the Germans were forming for a counterattack behind Montecelli. Colonel Long overhead the messages. He gathered up a group of men and moved up from the tail of what was left of K Company. At a point, some 50 yards short of Fulton's position, he looked around and saw that twelve of his men had been knocked out by machine-gun fire. Fortunately, a smoke round provided the cover needed to join Fulton without further casualties. Long deployed his 30 men as the artillery liaison officer, who had accompanied Long, joined Fulton in directing artillery fire. Lieutenant Wessendorff led each of Company I's platoons through concentrations of machine-gun and artillery fire, sweeping up elements of K and L, to bring six platoons to the top of Monticelli at dusk, just as the balance of Company L came up on the left.

Meanwhile, a diversionary attack by the 2nd Battalion from the west was held up by a network of German fortifications. Riflemen fixed bayonets at 1530 and Companies E and G assaulted the crest of the ridge ahead. The enemy opened up with machine guns and mortars on the men advancing up the open slope. Company E lost 7 killed, 27 wounded; Company G, 25 killed, 32 wounded. The left wing had to fall back. Company E had no officers; Captain Conley was the only officer left in Company G, and he was hit in the arm. Then, he was knocked out while reporting to the 2nd Battalion commander. The radioman finished the call, noticed a counterattack forming up, and called for artillery, which broke up the attack.

When Captain Conley recovered consciousness, he reorganized Companies B, E and G. The German rebuff of the latter two marked the end of resistance on Montecelli. Artillery fire in support of the men on Monticelli had been intense. On September 17 alone, 4,000 rounds were fired in the breakup of enemy counterattacks. One target of the all-night, 17–18 September firing was a command post 30 feet wide and dug one hundred yards into the mountain. When 33 prisoners were taken out of the dugout, all were shaken-up and dazed. Small wonder, then, that those Germans who could withdrew to the north. The 361st Infantry, after a tough day sweeping the central ridge, pushed on to take Hill 844 on the 18th. Its loss crippled the enemy's defensive position in the sector.

The western defenses of Il Giogo Pass were now broken. II Corps, at a cost of 2,731 casualties, controlled a seven-mile stretch of the Gothic Line on each side of the passes. The 85th and 91st Divisions moved on into the Santerno River Valley as the German Futa Pass defenses became untenable. The 34th Division had exerted considerable pressure on its front—a two-regiment attack against that segment of the Gothic Line lying between Highway 65 west to the Prato–Bologna road. Though the Division's advance was measured in yards on the forward slope of the main divide—a range of knobs and ridges slashed by deep clefts formed by streams draining south and east to the Sieve River—the Red Bulls succeeded in protecting II Corps' left flank and pinned down enemy troops that otherwise might have been used in the Il Giogo defenses. The lack of roads prevented the use of tanks or tank destroyers until the engineers improved the dirt road north of Barberino, which enabled armored vehicles to move into positions where direct fire could knock out pillboxes that had withstood pounding by division artillery. After seven days of bitter fighting, the 34th captured Monte Citerna and Montepiano and the Red Bulls were through the Gothic Line.

The honor of taking Futa Pass fell to the 362nd Infantry. The 91st Division had committed its 361st and 363rd Regiments to the battle for Il Giogo. This left the 362nd with the responsibility for a four-mile front from Monte Calvi to Highway 65. West of Calvi, two broad north–south ridges rise to the northern crest. Highway 65 followed the spine of the westernmost ridge to Futa Pass; a secondary road followed the eastern ridge from Gagliano to Santa Lucia on Highway 65 just below the pass. Colonel Cotton decided to commit his 3rd Battalion as a holding force up along Highway 65 while the other two battalions attacked north of Gagliano to Calvi and on to Monte Gazzaro, the dominant peak overlooking the Futa Pass defenses to the west. From Gazzaro, they could hit the Futa defenses from the right flank.

The 2nd Battalion took Calvi in a frontal nighttime assault on September 14, the first rupture of the Gothic Line by a Fifth Army unit, which took a good deal of pressure off the regiments at Il Giogo. The attack was resumed on the 15th, the 3rd Battalion quickly moving up Highway 65 until, south of Santa Lucia, it reached an anti-tank ditch, 8,000 yards long, eight feet deep and fifteen feet across. The ditch was rimmed with barbed wire and minefields. The 3rd Battalion, however, took Hill 588, west of the highway, and Casa Sodi, on the east side, before digging in. The 2nd, meanwhile, was unable to get off round-top Calvi, 2,454 feet high, in the face of intense artillery, mortar and machine-gun fire. The north side of Calvi dropped precipitously to the foot of Hill 840, in places 500 feet in 200 yards. The gully between Calvi and 840 was so deep and narrow that even high-angled artillery fire could not reach the Germans dug in below. Getting through an area zeroed in by enemy fire—mortar, machine-gun, and snipers—required, in the words of 91st Division historian Robert A. Robbins, "the combined qualities of a mountain goat and Superman."[11]

The 1st Battalion was then committed at midday to a flanking attack from the west through Morcoiano towards Monte Gazzaro. The two battalions fought throughout the next day, but gains were slight and heavy losses were suffered, in particular, by the 2nd Battalion. Company G's commander was seriously wounded, and because all other officers were gone, Technical Sergeant John C. Brooks took over. It was slow going until the 19th, when Company I, under a rolling barrage a scant 300 yards ahead, assaulted Poggio, a tiny but well fortified village above Morcoiano. Artillery fire buttoned up the Germans, and before they could jump out to man their weapons the infantry was on them. Two hundred prisoners were taken and the town cleaned out as the 2nd Battalion claimed Hills 840 and 821. The 2nd went into reserve and spent the next two days cleaning out bypassed Germans.

Enemy defenses at Il Giogo to the east had been cracked, and the Germans hadn't a prayer of holding on to the Calvi Ridge. The 1st and 2nd Battalions reached the lower slopes of Gazzaro on the 20th and to their left the 3rd was ready to go for Futa Pass itself. During the attack on Gazzaro, Pfc. John Czinki, Company B, investigated enemy movements near a draw on the company's right flank. When a German emerged from a dugout, Czinki fired, wounded the man and took several prisoners. Driving his captives before him, he approached an adjacent pillbox and ordered its occupants to surrender. When they refused, he tossed in a grenade without pulling its pin. Fifteen Germans came out, hands high. Herding his prisoners on, he visited three other enemy positions and captured 43 prisoners altogether. To say the least, he facilitated the work of his comrades that day. Later, he volunteered as an observer in a building under heavy enemy fire to furnish his company with invaluable information on enemy dispositions. On a trip to the company command post with information about a self-propelled gun, he was mortally wounded by shell fragments.

The final attack on Futa Pass was a classic pincer movement, the 1st Battalion attacking northeast from Gazzaro while the 3rd attacked from the southwest. Again, a rolling barrage was of great help to the attacking infantry. It enabled Company L to cross the gigantic antitank ditch against medium resistance. At 0830, 21 September, Companies K and L were west of Santa Lucia. While K Company cleared the village, L Company moved through the pine-covered slopes west of the highway. I Company, attached to the 1st Battalion, moved along the Gazzaro Ridge to positions south of the pass. K Company then took up a position in a draw to the left of Company I, which had outposts in the pass itself. Early in the morning of the 22nd, the 3rd Battalion attacked and inched its way up Hill 952 under heavy enemy fire. By nightfall, it occupied the summit—and control of Futa Pass was in American hands. It was the culmination of the Division's twelve-day battle to crack the Gothic Line!

Futa Pass was the crown of the German defenses along the Gothic Line. Here the Todt Organization had constructed its most powerful defensive positions—antitank ditches, barbed-wire entanglements, reinforced pillboxes and antitank gun emplacements, including an embedded Tiger tank turret. The 362nd Infantry had won the honor of clearing the pass the hard way. Nonetheless, as the *Fifth Army History* points out, it was "a tribute to the tactical skill with which the attack on the Gothic Line was carried out that these positions [Futa Pass] to which the Germans had devoted months of hard labor were taken by the troops of one battalion in one of the least costly of the Gothic Line battles."[12]

NOTES

[1] Von Senger, *Neither Fear nor Hope*, pp. 276–77.
[2] Strootman, *History of the 363rd Infantry*, p. 69.
[3] Clark, *Calculated Risk*, p. 394.
[4] Robbins, *The 91st Infantry Division*, p. 116.
[5] United States Army, *Fifth Army History*, Vol. VI, p. 62.
[6] Forty, *Fifth Army at War*, p. 122.
[7] United States Army, *Fifth Army History*, Vol. VI, p. 64.
[8] Ibid.
[9] Strootman, *History of the 363rd Infantry*, p. 80.
[10] Ibid., p.82.
[11] Robbins, *The 91st Infantry Division*, p. 122.
[12] United States Army, *Fifth Army History*, Vol. VI, p. 70.

XIV

DASH AND DOGGEDNESS

On September 3, John Strawson, troop commander, 4th Hussars, riding the lead tank beneath a bright moon, approached Coriano, an agricultural center overlooking the hills and Adriatic coastal plain from Riccione north to Rimini. The Hussars were a proud outfit, whose cavalry record went back to the Charge of the Light Brigade at Balaclava, and before that to Wellington's campaign in the Peninsula. About a mile from the village, 1st Armoured Division Commander Major General Richard Hull ordered a halt. The next morning, Strawson discovered that had he "advanced a few hundred yards farther and [had I] turned a corner, my tank would have been directly in the sights of a dug-in and concealed 50mm antitank gun."

Strawson's good fortune, however, was not so good for the British Eighth Army. Had Hull, Strawson speculates, "sent up a company of the 60th Rifles we might have taken Coriano that night" and the British would have placed the Hussars on the vital Coriano Ridge, opening the way to Rimini and beyond into the Po River Valley.[1] As it was, Strawson's tanks that morning deployed on a ridge overlooking Coriano, where they were subjected to remorseless artillery, mortar and antitank fire. By the time the 4th Hussars were withdrawn—after 60 sleepless hours—they had lost five officers, thirty-five men and nine tanks.

The British Eighth Army on the Adriatic crossed the River Foglia to good effect on September 1, punching through the Gothic Line on a 15-mile front inland from Pesaro. Alexander set the Fifth Army in motion, chasing after the Germans as they withdrew into the Apennines above Lucca and Florence. But at the close of the first week in September, Eighth Army prospects were not encouraging. Artillery spotter aircraft reported a substantial number of enemy troops crossing the Conca some six miles to the north of the British lines. No question but that Kesselring was going to contest the Gemmano and Coriano ridges, which lay athwart the narrow coastal plain, as well as each of many river crossings. And reinforcements were on the way to beef up German defenses! The arrival of the 20th Luftwaffe Field Division from Lucca and a battle group of the 90th Panzer Grenadier Division from northwestern Italy by mid-September placed roughly the strength of ten divisions at the disposal of the German Tenth Army Commander, General von Vietinghoff. Six were deployed in the San Fortunato sector; three about Ceriano, a village some five miles to the west.

Leese counted on the Canadians taking Rimini to free the coastal flank so that V Corps could bust out into the Po and on to Bologna and Ferrara. But V Corps was stalemated by a stiffened German resistance on the inland heights. Indications of trouble ahead developed early, as the Eighth Army surged through the Gothic Line. The 4th Indian Division had secured Monte Calvo on the first day of the Eighth Army offensive. Fighting, however, intensified as the 1/9th Gurkhas and 2/7th Gurkhas battled beyond that key height towards Tavoleto, where the rising hill crest north of Calvo merged into a transverse east–west system. On both sides of the village, the divisional account goes, "the advantage of ground had been studiously exploited by the enemy with a variety of fortification devices—anti-tank ditches, wire obstacles, machine-gun pits, forward sniping guns and trench systems. The glacis had been cleared to provide an open field of fire. Thickly sown minefields covered all approaches. . . . German counterattack forces waited in sheltered reserve areas to the rear."[2]

General Holworthy decided on a night attack, using the 2nd Camerons while the 1/9th and 2/7th Gurkhas remained on the outskirts of Tavoleto. But the best-laid plans even of good generals "gang aft astray." A massive "deception shoot" away from the projected line of attack failed to distract the Germans, who counterattacked, heading for the 2/7th Gurkhas crouched in holes scratched out on the southern outskirts of the village. The enemy were beaten back by concentrated defensive fire; then Company C under Lieutenant Smith got up and chased the Germans back into the village. Throwing grenades and wielding kukris, the Gurkhas cleared out the houses one by one. Camerons and Sikhs waiting for the signal to attack were puzzled by the screams and thuds of grenades coming from behind the village walls. The battle raged for four hours. Then artillery observers went forward and reported that the town had been taken. The streets were strewn with the dead, dying and wounded. Two 88mm guns and a number of prisoners were captured. Fewer than 30 Gurkhas were still on their feet. Tavoleto was taken—although it was a portent of what lay ahead as the Eighth Army fought towards the Romagna plain.

The Canadians fought in a coastal corridor scarcely four miles wide and dominated by the ridge running north and south from Coriano. They, too, experienced a foretaste of what lay ahead. Upon crossing the Foglia River, the British Columbia Dragoons and the Perths mounted a joint attack on what appeared to be a modest height north of the Foglia, Point 204. The Perths were pinned down, losing men by the score, in a hellfire of mortars and artillery. The Dragoons' fifty gray Shermans pushed ahead alone up the slope swept by German 88mm guns, firing twice-as-hard-as-steel tungsten-carbide core shells that slammed into tank turrets, gas tanks and ammo bins at 3,400 feet a second. Twelve tanks flared up, two dozen more were disabled, leaving eighteen at the end of the day still able to fight.

Perths with tanks from Lord Strathcon's Horse managed to capture Point 204, clearing the way for the advance to the Conca. Though they crossed the Conca and on September 5 captured Besanigo five miles farther north, the Canadian attack was checked by heavy fire from the Coriano Ridge. They were then forced to wait for the outcome of the battle for the ridges.

In the two weeks since the British had crossed the Metauro, they lost nearly 8,000 men, killed, wounded or missing. Tank losses were bearable—one hundred destroyed—but the enemy's Panthers were superior in armor and gunpower and greatly feared. While 3,700 prisoners had been taken and a proportionate number of the enemy killed or wounded, the Germans retained an advantage in the terrain. The three-peak Gemmano Ridge was a mile long and 1,500 feet high; the Coriano, a ragged three- to five-hundred-foot-high spur, dominated the coastal approach to the Romagna plain. "It was clear to me," Alexander reported in his dispatches after a visit to the front on September 8, "that we could not continue our advance on to Rimini until we had driven the enemy off the Coriano Ridge."[3]

The battle, however, appeared to be going well despite the loss of tanks and men at such places as Point 204 and Tavoleto. Corps and divisional engineers had opened up the main road through Fossombrone to

Urbino, blasting away a hillside cliff, filling in countless craters and building several Bailey brides. Though the British 56th and the 4th Indian Divisions lagged on the left behind the Canadians on the coast—a somewhat alarming development—historian W.G.F. Jackson, then a member of Alexander's staff, avers that Eighth Army Headquarters anticipated an early breakthrough.[4] If Coriano Ridge, a two-mile, north–south finger ridge, could be captured quickly, nothing could stop the roll of British armor and troops into the Romagna . . . so long as the weather remained favorable. Hawkesworth's 46th Division bypassed the Gemmano Ridge, gained the north side of the Conca and tried for an advance along the ridge from San Clemente to Coriano, creating a "gap" for the tankers headed for the Po. Hawkesworth also hoped to seize the crossing of the Marono at Ospedaletto before his men were to be relieved by the 1st Armoured.

The Germans, however, halted Hawkesworth's battered troops well short of Coriano, in front of Croce, a village just below the southern tip of the ridge. Hopes of opening a gap for the armor to pass through on a run to the Po were fast fading. Hawkesworth later told 1st Armoured commander Major General Richard Amyatt Hull that he had felt like a man out hunting who had held the gate open for his friend and then let it slam in his face.[5]

The fault, however, was not Hawekesworth's nor his exhausted infantry's. The 1st Armoured had been briefed for pursuit with its armored brigade in the lead and ordered forward, in what Jackson terms an "overconfident move,"[6] with only its motor battalion and one infantry battalion in support. The tankers got off to a bad start on September 2. The approach march over ill-favored ground was a nightmare grind in low gear: tanks broke down, shed their tracks; twenty tanks out of 156 Shermans were "out of action"—approximately a 13 percent loss without going into action. Moreover, the tankers were exhausted and had little rest when the 10th Hussars and the Bays set out to attack Coriano Ridge. The tanks crossed the Conca in the morning, but traffic was horrendous on roads cluttered by Canadians and others. The 10th Hussars found their crossing at the Conca blocked by 1st Armoured headquarters vehicles halted for tea. By the time the tankers reached the start line for the attack on Coriano Ridge, the four o'clock sun was low and shining in the gunners' eyes.

One Bay squadron ran into trouble along an approach road with deep ditches on both sides. The tanks could do little but push on in the face of devastating fire from German antitank gunners on Gemmano Ridge to the left and at Croce to the front. The rear radio-link tank was knocked out and three more were soon lost. As the tanks climbed the winding road to Coriano, German bazookas knocked out yet another tank and killed its commander. Two others lost contact with the balance of the troop as it left-wheeled across the starting line. Proceeding cautiously along the road, Captain J.C. McVail later recalled, ". . . we machine-gunned everything—hedges, ditches, houses, haystacks—in fact, every possible place which might conceal the enemy." When the two tanks came upon a village, "we put H.-E. (high explosive) into the corner houses while our scatter gunners machine-gunned the doors and lower windows" and the tank commander tommy-gunned the upper windows. When a bazooka man jumped out of a ditch behind the second tank, Major J.W. Hibbert shot him with his pistol.[7]

These tactics proved successful, but north of San Savino, the village on the southern tip of the ridge, the two lead tanks passed a Mark IV. Fired on from all angles, the nervous tankers, edging north along the road, "could visualize the Mark IV creeping out . . . and startling us from the rear." Rounding a corner, McVail's tank confronted a Mark IV reversing as fast as it could. Before the German could reply, McVail's tank opened fire at a range of fifteen yards and "brewed up" the enemy tank, killing the crew. Then Major Hibbert's tank was hit, but the crew baled out. The road was blocked in both directions, and the two tank crews took cover as best they could, just as friendly fire capped the situation. "We think our tank received a direct hit," McVail reported. After several days behind enemy lines, the Bays managed to rejoin their regiment. McVail was killed two weeks later.

Elsewhere, there was little or no progress. Another tank squadron sent up to assist Hibbert's lost its tracks maneuvering in the loose, sliding earth on the hillside. Those who managed to keep going were halted by enemy fire. On the right, the 10th Hussars were also caught in intense mortar fire that wounded six tank commanders. When the 9th Lancers attempted to pass through the Bays and Hussars to take San Savino, two tanks overturned in a gully as several others bogged down on the hillside. By then, night had fallen and the infantry were called up to hold the ground; however, neither infantry brigade was in a position to assist. Delayed on crowded roads, they were too far back to be of much use.

The next morning, B Squadron, 9th Lancers, nine tanks strong, attacked San Savino, two other squads providing support. At first, they waited on the infantry but after an hour attacked. Leapfrogging forward—fire, then move—the tanks reached the edge of a cemetery, left of the village at the southern end of the ridge, though two tanks had bogged down on the way up. Corporal Moffat maneuvered his turret-less Honey tank so that he could sweep with his Browning a sunken road that offered protection to bothersome German snipers and bazooka men. A few minutes later, the Honey was hit and its crew killed. A 1st Kings' Royal Rifle Corps platoon arrived to give the tankers much-needed support. As enemy bazooka men stalked tanks, an artillery observer in an exposed Jeep directed fire, holding the Germans at bay for hours on end. And the armor held among the cemetery's graves.

The crack 71st Panzer Grenadier Regiment arrived on September 4 to reinforce the German defenses. More infantry was sorely needed by the British tankers. A battalion of the Buffs came up, its lead company having been caught in a British barrage and shot at by a 56th Division battalion en route. During the night of September 5, the balance of the Buffs tackled San Savino to little effect. The infantry then consolidated the position centered on the cemetery. Eight Lancer tanks had been destroyed or ditched; one officer was taken prisoner, another killed along with one NCO and several of other ranks. Two enemy tanks, however, were destroyed, 30 Germans killed and sixty taken prisoner.

The British tankers were stalled before Coriano; the 4 Indians, on the left flank of the Eighth Army effort, had worked forward of Tavoleto but were halted at Pian de Castello. The best bet at the moment appeared to be an attack on Croce, a village on the heights beyond the Conca between the Gemmano Ridge to the south and Coriano to the north. The 56th Division, Major General John Yelde Whitfield in command, already had two brigades—the 167th and 168th—across the Conca and was in position to make the thrust. It looked to be a classic move, outflanking Coriano while bypassing the Gemmano Ridge. On the ground, however, it was a bit dodgy. As C. Northcote Parkinson remarks in his history of the Royal Fusiliers, the 9th Battalion led the 167th Brigade across the starting line at midnight, 4–5 September, to begin "what seemed a crazy advance over ground no one had reconnoitered and against an enemy there was no time to locate."[8] General von Vietinghoff, however, had a good idea of where the British were and what they were up to. Units from the 26th Panzer, 29th Panzer Grenadier, 98th Infantry and 5th Mountain Divisions were rushed forward to block the British infantry. German artillery observers on Gemmano and Croce looked over the approaches as poachers might view sitting pheasants.

The lead companies of the 168th Brigade's 1st London Scottish Battalion, en route to Croce, had to pile out of their trucks and scurry for cover as surviving vehicles got off the road as best they could while the rest burned. The Scottish, however, escaped catastrophe despite heavy shellfire from the heights, because their truck drivers had maintained a strict life-saving interval. Fighting for Croce, to say the least, was chaotic. "After advancing some three thousand yards," a Fusilier officer wrote, "with the Commanding Officer leading, in blissful ignorance that he was at the head of the battalion, a noise of digging was heard by Jerry Burnett, a platoon commander, who asked whether he should investigate."[9] There was little need, for the diggers opened fire. The battle for Croce had begun at about 0400 hours.

A Company of the Fusiliers made a frontal attack while B Company moved around on the right flank. Dawn, on the 5th, found the infantrymen barely holding the outlying fringe of the hamlet. Little could be done but bear up under the shelling, which killed, among others, Major Rupert Legge, a descendant of the Regiment's first Colonel. An attack that evening succeeded in entering the village but running out of ammunition (the Company ammo carrier was blown up by a direct hit); the attackers withdrew, taking five prisoners with them. On the morning of the 6th, the Fusiliers were ordered to take Croce "at all costs." This time the infantry had the support of tanks from the 7th Hussars and managed to clear the village, taking fifty prisoners in the process. Still, as historian C. Northcote Parkinson later wryly put it, "the position was far from the staff college school situation."[10]

The battle for Croce, as Parkinson recalled, was "haunted" by the belief that the enemy was in retreat. The troops engaged had no illusions that this was so, but expectations overrode reality among the higher-ups. At midnight on the 5th–6th, the 8th Fusiliers came forward on orders to attack Travari, five miles beyond Croce; orders, Parkinson says, "based on an optimistic belief that Croce was in our hands. In point of fact it was not."[11] Nonetheless, despite erroneous orders, the 8th was now in position to assist the beleaguered 9th Fusiliers holding on in Croce. Enemy shelling intensified as two 8th Fusiliers companies moved into the area around the Croce church. A 7th Hussars Sherman was "brewed up," and two others seeking out snipers beyond the church were hit by bazookas, jamming up their turrets. On the move, Z Company was reduced to a strength of sixty men. These men were still digging in when the Germans mounted a counterattack led by the 129th Tank Battalion of the 29th Panzer Grenadiers.

"Soon after dark," according to an eyewitness, "the enemy counterattacked in strength, sending one tank straight down the main road." No antitank guns were forward and the PIAT was the only weapon available to Z Company. "Two platoons were overrun and the company headquarters surrounded. The Company Commander and a Platoon Commander . . . escaped from the church and joined up with the remaining platoon, which, although it had not been involved, numbered only eighteen men."[12] As American G.I.s might have said, "Situation Normal All Fouled Up." A recon patrol to size up the enemy's strength was "met with a hail of machine-gun fire and grenades" It managed to report the area strongly held and the need for a stronger force to retake the position. Z Company pulled back to rejoin X Company at the foot of the hill. The 9th Fusiliers were also under attack, and after a confused night of fighting they were withdrawn.

The Germans were now back. The 167 Brigade was ordered to recapture Croce with the 8th Fusiliers, supported by the 9th. The 8th Battalion was reformed on a line of departure as the artillery laid down a ten-minute "stonk." At zero hour—1500 hours on September 7—the German artillery was active and accurate. "The companies were in no state to advance," Parkinson says, "and in fact did not." A request for postponement of the attack, however, was denied and fifteen minutes later the Fusiliers went forward. To avoid the British barrage, the Germans pulled back. A patrol reported the village empty and the Fusiliers entered at 1620 hours. But the village was "not quite clear." A Tiger tank and a self-propelled gun were all too ready, and Company Y was cut down to three men. They joined Z Company, then all of twenty men strong.

Nevertheless, the twenty held on and were joined by troops from the 44th Reconnaissance Regiment, followed by the 1st Battalion of the Welch Regiment from the 168th Brigade. A squadron of Shermans arrived and knocked out a Panther. "It added to the sense of security to have the tanks," a Fusilier said, adding a reservation common to the infantry, "but they were always moving around looking for a better position and drew a lot of fire, and we were inclined to be rather rude about them."[13] Z Company's commanding officer cussed out a tank commander who had drawn up next to his CP in a house which had already had three direct hits, only to be embarrassed to find the tanker to be the Tank Regimental Commander, who tartly explained that he was only trying to get a good look at the enemy; everyone, he said, was telling him to "hop it." The depleted Fusilier battalions were relieved on the night of September 8–9, leaving Croce in the hands of the Welsh.

The 8th Battalion casualties numbered 193, including ten officers killed or wounded. The 9th's were on the same order, according to Parkinson, who gives no exact figures for the latter. As for Croce, an 8th Fusilier officer tells us, "[T]hat battlefield presented a terrible sight. Dead enemy and Fusiliers lay across each other where they had fallen fighting at close quarters, blackened hulls of burnt-out Sherman tanks, Bren carriers lying on their sides, not to mention the usual flotsam of battle. . . . The little Italian cottages smouldered; the church spire, decapitated by a medium shell, stood jagged and grotesque. It was a tired but spirited battalion which once more wound its way back down the road. . . ."[14]

Croce was a key position, as the intensity of German resistance clearly attests. This hilltop crossroad village changed hands five times. General Whitfield called it "the dirtiest battleground I saw during the war."[15] Artillery barrages pounded Croce into a landscape that recalled Flanders to those senior officers who had served in World War I. If its fall did not make for an immediate breakthrough, it did much to prepare for one, though the Germans still held the Gemmano and Coriano ridges. The London Scottish enlarged the Croce salient, holding a precarious perimeter around Il Palazzo. Whitfield was determined to exploit the advantage, slight as it was, by taking Montescudo, which would turn the German line and force the enemy to withdraw from the Gemmano Ridge. But as the Queen's Brigade started forward, the rains, in Eric Linklater's apt phrase, "fell on Kesselring's side."[16] Roads crumbled, rivers overflowed and riverbanks collapsed. The ground oozed; vehicles churned in muck. Exhausted troops crouched in water-soaked slit-trenches. Though an attack was called for, circumstances would not have it so.

Among the circumstances were the well-placed enemy troops on the Gemmano Ridge—the anchor point of the German defense line, running north through San Savino and down the Coriano Ridge to the Adriatic.

Kesselring posted one battalion of the crack Austrian 100th Mountain Regiment on each of the four peaks of the mile-long, 1,500-foot-high ridge—west to east: the Farneto Spur, Point 402 above the hamlet of Zollara, Point 449 (which was surmounted by a wooden cross) and finally Gemmano village.

Though the British were painfully aware of harassing fire from Gemmano, Eighth Army intelligence had little idea of German dispositions on the ridge. To protect his flank at Croce, Whitfield sent the 44th Reconnaissance Regiment to Villa, a small height east of Gemmano village taken under heavy fire. The action, however, convinced Whitfield that a stronger force was needed, though, lacking information, he foresaw no real difficulty. The 7th Oxfordshire and Buckinghamshire Light Infantry were ordered to attack Gemmano in battalion strength in the late afternoon of September 7. By dark, the infantry had scrambled up thorn-scrubbed steep slopes and over an ancient, twenty-foot-high wall to enter the village. During the night, however, the Germans who had fallen back counterattacked, driving the Oxford and Bucks out and back to Villa.

Whitfield then ordered the Queen's Brigade to take Gemmano. Delayed by the heavy rains, the Brigade's two attack battalions went forward when the rain slackened at two in the afternoon on September 8. The 2nd/6th Queen's, on the left, headed for Points 414 and 449; the 2nd/7th Queen's, on the right, went for Gemmano village; the 2nd/5th Queen's, in reserve, were scheduled to attack Zollara the next day. Two squadrons of the 8th Royal Tank Regiment joined the attack. Divisional artillery and 4.2-inch mortars pounded the ridge top as the attackers moved up the slope against deadly machine-gun, Spandau and sniper fire. The 2nd/6th commander, Major G.E. Smith, and two other officers were killed as the battalion gained ground, stopping to wait for the dark within 200 yards of Point 414 and its one house. Snipers used the red light of burning haystacks to good effect, picking off the men trying to reach the top of 414.

It took four hours. The battalion captured 40 prisoners and clung to Point 414 all the next day. Nearly surrounded, the 2nd/6th were then ordered to fight their way out. Reduced to two composite companies, the battalion regrouped on the slopes to the southeast.

On September 9, the reserve battalion, 2nd/5th Queen's, moved out in single file along the course of a tiny stream at the foot of the ridge towards Zollara. Two miles along, the two attacking companies branched off to follow separate gullies. At this point, the Germans had laid on an effective ambush. All efforts to succor the trapped infantry failed. Thirty men—the remnant of one company—attacked again the next morning but were finally withdrawn that afternoon. Meanwhile, the 2nd/7th Queen's had gained a toehold in two houses at the rear of Gemmano village. Captain David Rossiter gathered the survivors of the day's battle, some 40 men, and fought off the Germans until the exhausted enemy ceased their counterattacks.

On the morning of the 9th, another company joined Rossiter's band to clear the village and secure the eastern end of the Gemmano Ridge. The next day, Hawkesworth's 46th Division took over the sector. The 6th Lincolns were ordered to take Point 449, and, though badly cut up by shellfire, got one company up to the wooden cross that topped the hill. The Austrians of the 100th Mountain Regiment, however, were brave and brilliant in their defense of the knobbed Gemanno Ridge. Whenever British guns pounded it, the Mountaineers scrambled down the reverse slope for protection, then ran back up to their posts when the shelling stopped to spray the attacking British troops with their Spandaus. Three battalions were now crowded into Gemmano village, taking and retaking ground as best they could. The King's Own Yorkshire Light Infantry, which had relieved the Lincolns on Point 449, lost and regained the cross several times. Still, the crucial Gemmano height remained in German hands.

By then, Lieutenant General Sir Oliver Leese, Commander of the British Eighth Army, had decided that a "properly prepared"—the phrase is W.G.F. Jackson's—army attack had to be mounted against the German defenses blocking the advance to the Romagna.

One of the great strengths of the British Army was the thoroughly planned set-piece battle. V Corps and the Canadian I Corps, augmented by the 4th British Infantry Division and the New Zealander Division, were to attack, side by side, and in three stages capture Coriano Ridge, establish bridgeheads across the Marano, the next river to the north, and clear the high ground beyond, in particular the critical Fortunato Ridge. Then, the Eighth Army would break through, past Rimini, onto the plain of the Romagna and it would be "good tank going." Jackson characterized what happened as "one of the most costly [battles] ever fought by the British Army in Italy."[17] Each day for a week, the Eighth Army lost a hundred and fifty killed and some six hundred wounded.

Croce, now in the hands of the British, was the heart of a critical sector. From this hilltop crossroad above the Conca, the 56th Division Queen's Brigade, after a two-day rest, attacked to the northwest. Its objective, a little over a mile away, was a ridge capped by two villages, Casiccio and San Marco, and, farther to the north, the high ground around Casa Fabbri. Both positions overlooked the next river north, the Marano. Tanks from the Royal Tank Regiment and the 7th Hussars supported the Queen's Brigade infantrymen. A barrage of three thousand 25-pounders opened the attack in the early hours of September 13. Moving out on the left, the 2nd/6th Queen's seized Casa Menghino and held Il Palazoz, which enabled the 7th Hussars' tanks to reach San Marco and approach Casiccio, where German antitank hits fired up three tanks short of the objective.

The 2nd/7th Queens was badly hit as the battalion attacked Casa Fabbri at six in the morning. In the first ten minutes, all the officers of one company were wounded; two in another were killed. Casualties were so heavy that the reserve company had to be committed. Its Captain, David Rossiter, who had gallantly defended Gemmano five days before, was killed. The Shermans of the 2nd Royal Tank Regiment fared better as the attack unfolded. "We moved off just after first light," Captain S.R.F. Elmslie later recalled. A smokescreen laid down to shield the tanks from San Savino in the dawn's half-light limited vision to a few yards. "[W]e were worried . . . we had no infantry with us and [had] to maneuver amongst enemy positions without being able to see them until we were well within bazooka range."[18] Three tanks got stuck in the plowed fields but they were the only casualties at the start. Tanks on the right were hung up in rough country below the ridge, but the two remaining tanks of the lead troop made it to the top. They had passed through positions held by more than 300 enemy infantry and had to turn to fire backwards in order to help the remaining tanks surmount the ridge. All this was managed in about ten minutes.

Nine tanks were concentrated on the northern end of the Fabbri Ridge shortly after six o'clock. "As the light grew and the smoke cleared, we saw that we were splendidly placed; looking back at the whole of the enemy's reserve positions along the Coriano Ridge, and overlooking any movement that he made. . . ." Two hours later the infantry caught up. "We had a number of excellent shots. . . ." When a Mark IV appeared, the Shermans cut loose some 80 to 100 rounds, forcing the crew out. "We also brewed up a half-track near some haystacks, which caught fire, revealing two enemy 88mm antitank guns concealed in them." The 2nd/7th Queen's took over 300 prisoners that day at a cost of six officers and 100 men dead and wounded. The battalion was relieved during the night of the 13th by the 9th Royal Fusiliers, which was now in a position to cross the Marano. "Everyone was completely exhausted," one of the 7th Queen's remarked, and, though shelled all the way back to a reserve area, they "would have marched twice the distance to get out for a few hours."[19]

The 56th Division's exploitation of the Croce sector worried the German high command. "The depth of the penetration cannot be ascertained with accuracy as yet," Von Vietinghoff informed Kesselring. "The front has been greatly weakened."[20] Signs of disintegration were increasingly apparent. When the 9th Fusiliers relieved the 2nd/7th Queens, the Commanding Officer, the Battery Commander and the Intelligence Officer came across a solitary shivering German in a slit trench. Drawing pistols, they called on the young soldier to surrender. Much to their surprise, "the whole countryside came to life, and forty-seven very willing Germans came running forward to give themselves up. . . . German mortars," the Fusiliers' account goes, "each with a stack of ammunition, stood unattended in a hedgerow. A ration limber was standing with one dead horse while the other two grazed unconcernedly. . . ."[21]

That night, the 168th Brigade advanced some 6,000 yards to occupy the last ridge in the Croce sector. The 56th Division now overlooked the Marano and, as Fusilier Parkinson put it, "Pressure on the enemy was certainly being maintained."[22] The Fusiliers prepared to cross the river and tackle the high ground beyond.

On the Coriano Ridge, Germans gave way before the British 1st Armoured, the 9th Lancers, and the 43rd Ghurkas. In Coriano village, on September 13, the 11th Canadian Infantry Brigade fought hand-to-hand with 29th Panzer Grenadiers. The town was secured at the end of the day at a cost of 210 men. The German position on the Gemmano Ridge had become less and less tenable. Nonetheless, the German hold on Gemmano had not only caused difficulties at Croce but also had forced the 4th Indian Division to bear west into the mountainous country north of the flooded Ventano River. From the crest of the Pian di Castello Ridge, three miles due south of Gemmano and held in strength, the Germans could observe the advance of the Indians for some miles. German mortars found adequate cover on the reverse slope for continuous fire on the river crossings. Sniping guns zeroed the roads; minefields were as widely sown as Cadmus' legendary teeth. High, driving winds and pelting, cold rain contributed to the bitterness of the slow slogging match.

In the attack on the village Pian di Castello, on the western end of the ridge, B Company, Royal Sussex, lost nearly a score of men, including two officers killed. D Company was trapped in a Schu minefield. A German counterattack ended in a "hand-to-hand melee" with the Ghurkas victorious. When a C Company platoon, Royal Sussex, was cut off, Lieutenant R.A. Roach beat off all attacks with grenades. On the night of September 9–10, D Company, Royal Sussex, seized Cemetery Hill, a thousand yards north of Pian di Castello village. When B Squadron, 6th Royal Tank Regiment, moved forward to support the Royal Sussex, the lead tank struck a mine and blocked the advance. A second tank shed a track. The remainder cut across country only to miss the rendezvous with the infantry. A self-propelled gun destroyed a tank; the troop knocked it out. Then, the 4th Indian account continues, "50 Germans raced into the shelter of a near-by house. The tanks blew it to pieces killing most of the occupants. Advancing across a cornfield, weapon pits were discovered under the stooks. 20 Germans including 5 bazooka men were captured. A chaplain took 20 prisoners while attending the wounded. . . ."[23]

By September 13, the 4th Indian was about a mile south of Gemmano Ridge. The 46th and 56th Divisions had assaulted the ridge eleven times, but the key bastion, Point 449, with its stark wooden cross, was still in German hands. V Corps Commander Keightly decided to divert the 46th from Gemmano along the north bank of the Conca in order to assist the 56th in exploiting the Croce sector by taking Monte Columbo and Montescudo. The Indians' 2nd Camerons were picked to assault Zollara, the tiny hamlet on the left of Gemmano, and Point 449, just above it. Once cleared, the attacks above the Conca and towards the Marano could go forward.

Artillery preparation—260 guns ranging from Bofors to 7.2 howitzers—was impressive, underscoring the importance of the objective. Zollara was blasted by 2,000 shells an hour and a half before jump-off; an hour later, Bofors laid down deceptive tracers left of the main line of attack as crash shoots played along the front and other guns hit deception targets. At 0300, September 15, the Cameroons crossed the crest of the spur south of the German defenses as the field guns laid down a barrage.

The taking of Zollara and Point 449 was anticlimatic. The attack, the 4th Indian historian states, "won home with surprising ease."[24] Most of the Germans had cleared out, having decided that the position could no longer be held. So, Cameroon commander Lieutenant Colonel Alistair Noble later remarked, "we felt that we had been deprived of our pound of flesh and not fully avenged the losses of the 46th Division. However, we killed some Boche and took twenty-one prisoners of war, all at no cost whatever to ourselves, which was most gratifying." That success, as Noble quickly pointed out, "was very largely due to the hard fighting of our predecessors and to the excellent support which we were given."[25] Some 900 Germans died in defense of Gemmano Ridge. "A good show," General Holworthy of the 4th Indians jotted in his diary. "Gemmano full of dead and smells like another Cassino."[26] On Point 449, at the center of the khaki and field-gray dead, heaped around the wooden cross, one of the Lincolns—the first to try taking the hill—gripped the foot of the cross in his dead hands.

That week was a daunting maze of confused fighting over hodgepodge ridges and twisting steams. As Douglas Orgill aptly summed it up: "There were no great roads . . . no big communications centers; no railheads. Only the names of tiny and seemingly insignificant hamlets leap into the unit war diaries and regimental accounts—Travari, Mulazzano, Cerasolo, Ospedaletto. Sometimes they were not even hamlets, but the names of single houses which happened to crown some hill or knoll, commanding the head of some miniature valley. But all of them had one thing in common. Somewhere, dug in . . . would be a Spandau post, or a mortar section; an 88mm gun or a Tiger Tank."[27] The promised land—the low flats of the Romagna—was always just ahead. British infantry joked, "Jerry's retreating all right, but he's taking the last ridge back with him."

Kesselring was playing for time. Hitler had promised that a secret weapon would strike terror in the hearts of the British and bring an end to the war. The first V-1 "buzz bombs" hit London seven days after D-Day, and V-2 supersonic rockets bombarded England three months later, on September 8, 1944. Young German soldiers were dying in Italy—and elsewhere—in the hopes that their Führer could bomb a "victory" out of disaster. Kesselring's immediate task was to slow the Eighth Army down until the rains came that would make movement in the Romagna impossible. On October 13, Von Vietinghoff fed the 356th Division onto the Mulazzano Ridge in yet another attempt to delay the British advance. Though the Division was down to a company strength of forty to fifty men with only one mortar each, they were determined to give a good account of themselves. The British were, understandably, cautious in their approach. Orgill says a "quick push" might have yielded "surprising dividends." But Parkinson believes that such an attack—without proper observations—would have been "exceedingly rash." In the event, the Fusiliers spent the 14th in reconnaissance.

Mulazzano was a "naked" ridge with two spurs running down to the Marano River. On top, adds a Fusilier report, "was a small but strongly built village with a conspicuous church with a tall tower which could be seen for miles. On either spur were several farmsteads with a large cluster of farm buildings at the foot of each."[28] At midnight on the 16th, the 8th Fusiliers attacked on the right to take the village, while the 9th Fusiliers took the other spur.

All went "tolerably according to plan" on the right flank, where machine-gun fire held up the Fusiliers until tanks arrived. The Germans apparently exhausted their ammunition and the village was taken and held, though under heavy artillery fire. However, shelling reduced the Battalion to three companies with little prospect of replacements. On the left, D Company crossed the river and established a beachhead, but A Company, which was to pass through, went "up the wrong trouser leg," as Brigadier J. Scott-Elliot put it.[29] Battalion Headquarters took the right turn and found itself in a firefight. D Company commander Captain John Gordon, seeing that things were cock-a-hoop, swung his men to the right and scaled a steep scarp as supporting tanks went around the top to capture the objective from behind.

While the 56th Division's 8th and 9th Fusiliers coped with the Germans on the Mulazzano Ridge, the 4th Division's Royal Fusiliers and Black Watch Battalions attacked the last ridge before the Marano River south of Ospedaletto. One Tiger tank destroyed seven Churchills during the afternoon's fighting. The enemy, ensconced in well-prepared positions, were finally driven out, killed or captured in hand-to-hand fighting. When the Tigers counterattacked the Black Watch, one tank "ventured" near the Fusiliers. Its commander stood up in his turret and was killed by Captain D. Thomas, a keen-eyed Fusilier, with one rifle shot at a distance of 250 yards. Before midnight, September 15, the Royal West

Kents passed through to establish a bridgehead across the Marano at Ospedaletto.

Both Corps of the Eighth Army made good progress as the enemy regrouped its forces and carried out a slight withdrawal. The 3rd Greek Mountain Brigade made its debut repulsing a German reconnaissance in force, and then drove on to the south bank of the Marano, making way for the Canadians to cross the river. Canadian infantry took San Lorenzo and advanced to within three miles of Rimini. The 4th Division exploited the bridgehead at Ospedaletto. On the night of the 15th, by the light of burning haystacks and vehicles, the 2nd Somerset Light Infantry tackled the Frisoni Ridge, which overlooked the Ausa. But a German counterattack mounted in armored lorries drove the Somersets back. Before the advance on the Ausa could continue, Major General A.D. Ward decided that enemy guns and observation posts had to be cleared from Cerasolo, off to the southwest. This the 2nd/4th Hampshires did on the morning of the 17th, taking 50 prisoners.

That night, startled 29th Grenadiers reported a sea of light falling across the battlefield. Searchlight batteries on the Coriano Ridge were focused on the Frisoni Ridge as the Black Watch stormed the heights. "This new enemy trick," General Herr of the 76th Panzer Corps reported to von Vietinghoff, "has harassed our moves and blinded our people." It's "the weirdest thing I ever saw," the German commander said, as the enemy "turned on a display like Party Day in Nuremberg." Frustrated, he added, "I don't know what we're going to do about it. We may detail a few 88mm guns to deal with them. Couldn't we send a few aircraft over? . . . It's a great worry to the boys to be lighted up and blinded and not be able to do anything about it."[30]

"Artificial moonlight" worked. The 4th Division took Frisoni Ridge and placed three companies across the Ausa the next day. On the right, the 2nd Bedfords of the 19th Infantry Brigade crossed and advanced 500 yards to contest the next ridge. However, the Germans were still forward of the Ausa on either flank, entrenched on the Fortunato Ridge on the right, overlooking the coast near Rimini, and on the heights on the left before the oldest Republic in Europe.

For 700 years, San Marino, perched on 2,500-foot Monte Titano, overlooked the surrounding area for miles on all sides. It was jammed with people—14,000 of its own and over 120,000 Italian refugees. Both sides had respected San Marino's neutrality until Kesselring posted a strong force to "defend" the Republic and block the main road to it. Moreover, as the Allied troops approaching were painfully aware, the Germans had placed artillery observations posts on the San Marino heights. This "gave us a new role," Major General Holworthy of the 4th Indians noted in his diary on September 17. "It is a chancy business—if we surprise the Boche we will get there, otherwise we may get stuck under direct observation from . . . San Marino and its towers." Corps was optimistic, Holworthy wrote, "absurdly so, I think" to expect a breakthrough all along the front." The Boche, he added, had more reinforcements "than they think."[31]

Foul weather contributed to the congestion on the approach roads. The 3rd/10th Baluchis, nonetheless, crossed the Marano without opposition on the night of September 17–18. The 1st/9th Ghurkas moved through to tackle Points 343 and 366 just across the river—knolls held by two battalions of the 993rd Grenadiers, 278th Infantry Division. Ghurkas scrambled up the cliff-like sides of Point 343, gaining the top at 0515. Support tanks had bogged down and the Ghurkas who had pressed on to Point 366 ran out of ammunition and had to fall back. Rifleman Sherbahadur Thapa and his section commander charged a machine-gun post, killing the gunner and forcing the rest of the enemy to flee. The Germans then struck back, killing the section commander. Thapa drove the attackers back beyond the crest of the hill with his bren gun, and held off attacking Germans for two hours. As his platoon, out of ammo and virtually surrounded, withdrew, Thapa provided covering fire. He then dashed forward to rescue two wounded comrades, and was killed bringing back the second man. Rifleman Sherbahadur Thapa was awarded the second Victoria Cross of the Gothic Line campaign.

On Point 343, the Ghurkas, as an observer remarked, clung "to the sides of the gully like flies on the wall."[32] No doubt they felt as vulnerable as anyone else to the swats of German shells. They had lost 63 men but held on until a concentration of friendly fire dispersed the enemy and eased the situation. By evening, tanks had come forward. The 4th/11th Sikhs swung around the right flank to come up against the northern buttresses of San Marino. The 11th Brigade passed through to continue the encirclement of San Marino.

On the evening of the 19th, the 2nd Camerons sent patrols around the northern haunches of the mountain and into the lower streets of the city. The next morning at 0800, the Highlanders were checked by machine-gun nests at the northwestern corner of the mountain, where the road twists upward into town. Tanks shot up Borgio Maggiore, a lower suburb, while D Company worked up winding streets towards the palaces and castles on the summit. By two o'clock it was over, as the Camerons searched the city in a driving rain, picking up 20 dead and 54 bedraggled prisoners. San Marino cost the Camerons 4 killed, 32 wounded—all things considered, a cost well below the fears of the troopers who first glimpsed the forbidding heights four days earlier.

On the next day, the 21st, General Holworthy, in battle dress, met with the Captain Regent of San Marino, who wore a tailcoat, butterfly collar, pepper-and-salt trousers and elastic-sided boots. Refugees were to be kept off the roads; local labor was to mend the road. Holworthy informed the Captain Regent, "We had come to kick out the Boche and not to take over the Republic." Holworthy booked a room in the Albergo del Tritorno and had a first-class lunch—"wonderful muscat wine—some ham and olives—macaroni—superb steak (due to cattle killed by our artillery fire) and a sweet omelette." The hotel was crowded with well-to-do civilians. "It was strange in the middle of a battle to find ourselves seated at a nice meal among a civilian community of all ages and sexes." Outside, Holworthy says, "[T]here was a thick mist and some rain with visibility nil. The 3/12 (Royal Frontier Force Regiment) were getting their objectives beyond the town without trouble."[33]

Over the next ten days, as gales from the Adriatic whipped the front with torrential rains, the 4th Indian Division plowed on, as the Division history put it, "like a vehicle . . . in heavy going, gradually losing speed until it finally bogs down."[34] After the fall of San Marino, the dispirited 278 Division—the Royal Frontiersmen captured 20 prisoners asleep in the Marecchia Valley—was replaced by the 114 Jaeger Division, described by the Indians as "tough, surly and truculent." German artillery stitched the roads, at one forward conference driving General Holworthy and a clutch of Brigadiers into the ditches. (Brigadier Defonbianque was seriously injured.) The 2nd/7th Gurkhas lost 130 men, almost half of them killed, in an attempt to seize a shaggy piece of tableland beyond the Marecchia. The 2nd Camerons crossed the Uso (Caesar's Rubicon) to penetrate 4 miles into enemy territory. Assault troops slipped and slithered on greasy slopes and hoofed through ankle-deep freezing mud on low ground. Little streams became icy torrents, supply to the front was minimal, and the Indians came to a halt on the ridges above the Uso between San Martino (on the left) and Borghi (on the right of a transverse road), where they were finally relieved by the 10th Indian Division during the first week of October.

General Holworthy had taken command of the Fourth Indian Division after it had been badly shaken—destroyed, some said—at Cassino. In 32 days of battle on the Gothic Line the Division once again proved itself combat-worthy, advancing more than 60 miles over the "abominable terrain" of Apennine foothills and in foul weather. The three brigades lost 1,892 men of all ranks, including a high percentage of junior officers. Average company strength at the end was down to less than 30 rifles. Though the weary soldiers withdrawn for rest along three one-way rain-rotted roads did not know it, their Italian tour was over. Their next assignment was Greece.[35]

The Fifth Army was now at the portal to the Po Valley. Only one more ridge remained unconquered: San Fortunato, the key to Rimini and the plains beyond. The ridge thrust five miles northeast from Ceriano, a tiny village just north of San Marino, across the Eighth Army front above the River Ausa to the village of San Fortunato some 450 feet above the valley floor. Vineyards clung to its steep sides and groups of stone houses were strung along its crest, like ramparts of old battlements, to provide sturdy fortresses for its defenders. San Fortunato was well packed with Germans: a battalion of the 1st Parachute Regiment, two of the 71st Grenadiers, a rifle battalion from the 20th Luftwaffe Field Division, two from the 162nd Turcoman Division and two from the 314th Grenadiers. To reinforce the center, Von Vietinghoff sent in the 90th Light Panzer Grenadier Division, fresh from its summer in reserve near the French–Italian border. This division had been a pride of Rommel's Africa Corps and its commander, Leutenantgeneral Ernest Gunter Baade, a "Hero of Cassino."

Baade was an unconventional soldier by any army's standard, most certainly the Wehrmacht's. He was the son of a Brandenburg landowner, married well and was financially independent. He was a hands-on officer—in General von Senger's phrase, "a true fighting man." He wore a Scottish khaki kilt over his riding breeches with a large pistol suspended in a holster from his neck in place of the sporran. In battle, he was always up front. In his forward command posts he had the habit of leaving "bottle mail," containing his name, that of his adjutant, his dog and the date of the battle. "In the midst of his fighting men," Von Senger said of him, "he sees everything, and like an artist at the piano, masters the keyboard of the battle." In Africa, having driven well up front, he would radio the British, "Stop firing. On my way back, Baade." And at times his enemy did just that! He liked fine things, Von Senger said, ". . . sports clothes, good weapons, shiny mahogany-coloured leather in a smart saddle room, strong well-schooled hunters."[36] He often relaxed reading Aristotle and Seneca. One of the bravest and best, his soldiers loved him.

When Lieutenant Colonel Cameron, commander of the Hastings & Prince Edwards Regiment, briefed his officers on his plan of attack, a night attack across a swollen stream and up the heights of Fortunato, a new company commander blurted, "Sir, we'll never make it."[37]

The Canadians had a rough time approaching Fortunato, which makes the young officer's reaction understandable. First, they had been held up by British V Corps' slow going in the hills to the west, then, once again on the move, they bollixed up on a knoll just south of the Ausa. The Van Doos, the French-Canadian Royal 22nd Regiment, had occupied the knoll about a mile and a half south of Rimini on September 15. That night a screw-up in contact between the Van Doos and the relieving Seaforth Highlanders left the knoll briefly unoccupied. The 1st Paras wasted no time in taking advantage, and held up the Canadian advance with well-placed fire from the knoll and San Fortunato—a mile and a quarter or so northwest. Under heavy German artillery fire, the 48th Royal Tank Regiment lost six tanks out of twelve in support of a vain day-time attempt on the knoll by the Highlanders. Attacking Canadians were cut down by shrapnel as the Germans huddled in dugouts and cellars and called down fire on their own positions. On September 17, the Seaforths lost 90 men, the Royal Canadians 74 and the 46th Highlanders 86.

Two companies of Princess Patricia's Canadian Light Infantry managed to get within 200 yards of the embankment of the Rimini–San Marino Railway, the starting line for the attack on San Fortunato, though reduced to 60 men each. On the left, the Carleton and York Regiment crossed the embankment only to take what cover they could in the open ground between the rail line and the Ausa. To the right, the Greek Brigade, at a cost of 314 men, seized the Rimini airfield. Major General Voces decided to bypass San Martino, cross the Ausa at night and strike for Fortunato. Voces' push, which brought the Canadians to the foot of Fortunato by late afternoon of the 19th, compelled the Germans to yield San Martino, and the village knoll passed into Canadian hands without a

American brass pose with French General Juin on Rome's Capitoline Hill. To the curiosity of the British, Mark Clark announced a "great day for the Fifth Army." Truscott (center) commented that he was "anxious to get out of this posturing and on with the business of war."

Romans greet their liberators and soldiers enjoy a brief respite before going on to the war north of Rome.

"I didn't realize our artillery was so powerful." American soldiers tour the Roman Colosseum.

Black troops of the 370th Infantry, 92nd Division, moving up to the front.

Japanese-
American
"Nisei" of the
100th Bat-
talion, 34th
Division.

Field Marshall
Albert Kesselring,
shown here living
up to his nick-
name, began the
war in the
Luftwaffe, however
went on to com-
mand entire army
groups.

Above and left,
American vehicles
and troops fording the
Arno River in September
1944.

In December 1944, American 1st Armored guns pound Monterumic in support of advancing infantry.

Bombs falling on Leghorn are aimed at the oil tanks in the middle of the picture.

Winter in the Apennines near Loiana where a heavy weapons company, 91st Infantry, sandbag a foxhole.

Mountain troop reinforcements move up Mount Belvedere in February 1945 to bolster attacking infantrymen.

Soldiers move out over a ridge in the mountains south of Bologna-Modena. The German has been killed by preceding shellfire.

A soldier covers a house in which Germans are holed up on the Apennine front in March 1945. The effects of artillery blasts are everywhere.

Gordon Highlanders approach the Gothic Line through the ruins of Ronta,
above the valley of the Sieve.

More than one veteran of Italy has remarked on the resemblance of the battlefields to scenes of World War I. Here, troops of the 92nd Division are pinned down by a sniper.

Sometimes towns were so damaged it was difficult to tell where the streets had been. Here 10th Mountain troops with tanks attempt to negotiate Corona.

G.I.s of the 91st Infantry Division advance on Casalecchio along with tanks of the South African 6th Armoured.

April 15, 1945. As the offensive to the Po gains momentum, Germans begin to come in, here escorted by men of the 10th Mountain Division.

A British
artillery crew
"brews up"
before resum-
ing fire on
the enemy.

Winter in the Apennines. 10th Mountain men carrying snowshoes.

G.I.s of the 85th Division repair a supply trail in the mountains, rifles hanging at the ready.

Ski troops being towed by a Weasel. Once at the front they would be on their own for a patrol into enemy territory.

A 10th Mountain column on Mount Nuova. In this terrain, mules were an integral part of the supply effort on both sides of the front line.

91st infantrymen move towards the last hill before the Po Valley and Highway 9 between Imola and Bologna.

The beginning of the end. Germans surrender as the final offensive gains speed in the Apennine foothills west of Highway 64.

General von Senger surrenders to General Clark at the end of the war in Italy on May 2, 1945.

Scouting the Po River on the 23rd of April—first crossed by the 10th Mountain Division, once across the river it would be tank country.

Polish soldiers line up in liberated Bologna's Piazza Vittore Emmanuele, a long fight up the Italian boot from their victory at Monte Cassino nearly one year earlier.

further fight. San Fortunato soon followed suit, but not without a bitter hand-to-hand struggle among the mangled vineyards and orchards.

On the left, the 4th Division crossed the Ausa and reached Sant' Aquiline, where it was stopped by artillery fire from a high crest to its right. The 56th Division contested the ridge east of Ceriano, holding the crest, barely. The key role was assigned to the British 1st Armoured in the center, where the General Staff still hoped for a "breakthrough." The Germans were short of infantry, it was believed, and ready to crack. With a little luck, and weather permitting, the tanks were expected to cross the Marecchia, sweep out into the plains, and cut off Von Vietinghoff's Tenth Army as it raced for the Po. Speed was essential, and, on September 20, Sherman tanks filled the Ausa Valley on the Via Roveta, which led to the summit of the Ceriano–Fortunata Ridge. "The roar of their engines gave an impression of irresistible force," it was said.

There was, however, a hitch: a small spur running off the eastern tip of Ceriano, Point 153 on the map. Here Baade's crack Grenadiers waited. The 88s were positioned at San Paolo, Villa Gabriella, Balducci, Conti, as well as on Point 153. General Hull's 1st Armoured was to go all out for the breakthrough, its 2nd Armoured Brigade forcing the pace. The brigade's three regiments—10th Hussars, 9th Lancers and Queen's Bays—were down to 117 tanks from 156. Most were still south of the Marano and had to be brought forward at night over chancy country where bridges were blown and "every formation seem[ed] to be using the same road."[38] Brigadier Richard Goodbody issued his orders on the evening of September 18. The Bays' 27 tanks (as against 52 of three weeks' earlier) were to take Point 153 supported by the brigade infantry, the 1st King's Royal Rifles; the 9th Lancers were to move up behind and be ready to exploit any breakthrough.

Congestion fouled up the approach. The infantry suffered shellfire casualties on the way up. Tanks were delayed and were still jammed up on the road before the starting line on the evening of the 19th. Goodbody sent infantry patrols forward to Point 153 to seize it if possible. The patrols fell back, having lost lost several men, and reported the position as well defended. Weary tankers were roused in the early hours of the morning and ordered to attack at first light. A lead tank was knocked out by a bazooka as the squadrons jockeyed into position in the dark along the starting line. As it got lighter, a Bays officer later wrote, "[W]e could see our infantry, dug in the ploughed fields around us—rather thin on the ground . . . We had to avoid [their] slit trenches . . . and the men gesticulated wildly so that we should see them. They looked tired and did not like us being there and hoped we would move on quickly."[39]

Goodbody by then believed that he could not take Point 153 with the forces at his disposal. He was overruled; V Corps ordered the attack to take place forthwith. The Bays' 30-ton Shermans moved out at 1050 on September 20. "There wasn't a stitch of cover anywhere that a tank could get hull-down behind and fire," the Bays' officer reported. "We could see [our objective] plainly about 2,000 yards ahead with a few trees and farms scattered about on it."

The countryside dipped down a long slope, then climbed gradually to the Point. Officers who knew the history of their sister regiment, the 4th Hussars, at Balaclava could not but help feel the attack another "Charge of the Light Brigade." As for Baade's tough lot, even they may well have rubbed their eyes in astonishment. As the Shermans nosed over the crest, German gunners pointed their 88s like snipers in a shooting gallery. "Armor-piercing shot seemed to come from all directions," the Bays account continues. "Some, the bad shots, passed overhead, others hitting the ground with colossal force and kicking up earth and stones in front of the tanks." As tanks halted to fire or to locate targets, they were knocked out one by one. Most burst into flames; others were disabled by jammed turrets or thrown tracks. Those survivors fleeing for safety were machine-gunned. "The craftier men lay flat or dived into small hollows . . . and lay immobile, waiting until they could get back under cover of darkness. All but three tanks . . . were destroyed, and many gallant officers and men were killed in action that morning."[40]

Twenty-four out of 27 Shermans were destroyed, 64 men killed or wounded. The Lancers were now ordered to pass through the burning tanks. Appalled by his orders and fearful of a like fate, Colonel Price of the Lancers radioed Brigade Headquarters that an attack could achieve little or nothing. Bowing to fate, Headquarters replied: "Hold on to the ground already won." Divisional infantry came up to carry out that task while the tanks regrouped. It then began to rain, and in ten minutes not a Lancer Sherman could move.

The stalled tanks were an apt symbol of the plight of the 1st Armoured Brigade. Poor Goodbody was sacked though he cannot be blamed for the Point 153 fiasco. Why was it, John Strawson perceptively asks, "we did not deploy our soldiers in the way the Germans did, in teams of tanks, infantry, antitank guns, artillery and sappers, making use of every skill and every ounce of firepower in coordinated and carefully prepared attacks, rather than driving forward with tanks, virtually unsupported by anything else and simply writing them off as a result?"[41] The answer, surely, lies elsewhere than at Goodbody's level of command, back and beyond in Corps and Army, where an undiluted optimism sent tankers forward deployed unwisely and on unsuitable ground. Hull was given an infantry division to command and the 1st Armoured was disbanded. While the 2nd Armoured under its new commander, Brigadier John Combe, remained intact and available for use by other formations, its 18th Infantry Brigade was reduced to cadre and its men salted out as replacements in other outfits.

The Eighth Army as a whole was running out of replacements. The battered 56th Division had lost 3,000 men. The 168th Brigade was reduced to cadre and its soldiers were split up among the other infantry battalions in the division. All British battalions were reshuffled, reduced from four companies to three each. This, of course, squeezed the tactical strength available to the Army. Yet Macmillan, on a visit to General Alexander, reported that he seemed in good spirits. "Good progress is being made," he noted in his diary on September 21, "and there is a good hope that the slogging match is drawing to an end and that the enemy will not be able to take much more punishment."[42]

In fact, the Canadian breakthrough to the east made it clear to Kesselring that the Tenth Army could no longer hold south of the Marecchia. The Army's War Diary quotes Kesselring as saying, "I have the terrible feeling that the whole thing is beginning to slide."[43] The Germans blew their dumps and on the morning of the 21st the Greek Brigade entered Rimini through the ancient Arco di Augusto on the Via Flaminia. By midday, the Canadians were across the Marecchia, foot soldiers slogging over sodden ground where tanks could not follow.

The battle of the ridges was now over; the battle of the rivers lay ahead.

NOTES

[1] Strawson, *The Italian Campaign,* pp. 165–66.
[2] Stevens, *Fourth Indian Division,* pp. 343–45.

[3] Orgill, *The Gothic Line,* p. 113.

[4] Jackson, *The Battle for Italy,* p. 272.

[5] Orgill, *The Gothic Line,* p. 94.

[6] Jackson, *The Battle for Italy,* p. 272.

[7] Orgill, *The Gothic Line,* pp. 91–92.

[8] Parkinson. *Always a Fusilier,* p. 211.

[9] Ibid., p. 212.

[10] Ibid., p. 213.

[11] Ibid., p. 213.

[12] Ibid., p. 213–14.

[13] Ibid., p. 215.

[14] Ibid., 216.

[15] Orgill, op. cit., p. 120.

[16] Linklater, *The Campaign in Italy,* p. 367.

[17] Jackson, *The Battle for Italy,* p. 276.

[18] Orgill, *The Gothic Line,* p. 122.

[19] Ibid., p. 123.

[20] Ibid., p. 125.

[21] Parkinson, *Always a Fusilier,* p. 217.

[22] Ibid., p. 217.

[23] Stevens, *Fourth Indian Division,* p. 351.

[24] Ibid., p. 353.

[25] Orgill, *The Gothic Line,* pp.127-28.

[26] Ibid., 128.

[27] Ibid., pp. 130-31.

[28] Parkinson, *Always a Fusilier,* p. 218.

[29] Ibid., p. 219.

[30] Orgill, *The Gothic Line,* pp. 137–38.

[31] Ibid., p. 138.

[32] Stevens, *Fourth Indian Division,* p. 355.

[33] Ibid., pp. 356–57.

[34] Ibid., p. 359.

[35] Ibid.

[36] Von Senger, *Neither Fear nor Hope,* pp. 206–209.

[37] Mowat, *The Regiment,* p. 226.

[38] Orgill, *The Gothic Line, p. 147.*

[39] Ibid., p. 151.

[40] Ibid., pp. 155-56.

[41] Strawson, *The Italian Campaign,* p. 176.

[42] Macmillan, *War Diaries,* p. 527.

[43] Orgill, *The Gothic Line,* p. 138.

XV

DEAD SECTOR

A ll along the Fifth Army front that fall there was movement. From the Ligurian beaches through the multitudinous mountains and passes across the high arch of the Apennines above Lucca, Montecatini, Pistoia, and above the Mugello, to the heights bracketing Highway 67 at Il Passo del Muraglione, men advanced, fell back to advance again, gained a few hundred yards here, a thousand there. When the weather was good, British Spitfires and American P-47 Thunderbolts dive-bombed in thundering roars or screeched overhead in strafing runs. Artillery rumbled in remote valleys, and the crump of mortars punctuated rifle and machine-gun fire along ragged ridges. Farmhouses and villages were pounded into rubble. In German bunkers, soldiers huddled for safety, emerging to contest the ground with grim determination. Allied soldiers from four continents dug foxholes in the unyielding earth. On the slopes, wounded men cried out for succor as medics braved fire to come to their aid. Here, there, dug in or out in the open, men died.

General von Senger considered his section of the front—a line running from the Ligurian coast to the mountains above Pistoia—a "dead sector." Nonetheless, on September 29, he prudently moved his XIV Panzer Corps headquarters from Villa Collemandina on the Upper Serchio to Albinea, a small village at the northern edge of the Apennines just below Reggio nell'Emilia. It was harvest time and though the house he chose "seemed empty and inhospitable," he had an "unrestricted view over the extensive vineyards" of the Po Valley from a top floor window. His command was thinned out by the demands for troops from threatened sectors in front of Bologna and on the Aegean. Middays in early October, Von Senger wandered among vines heavy with ripening clusters of blue, velvety grapes. The vine leaves, he tells us, gradually changed their color under "the steel blue sky" from a faint yellow tint to ever-deep-ening shades of red. He noted that bucolic lads and lasses with bare legs stood on the ladders, "singing and cackling." Lambs grazed on the dark grass. White oxen with hides "the dull colour of parchment" and horns with a span of two metres hauled carts of sweet grapes. All the men, women and children of the farms joined in trampling the fruit with bare feet. "The sweet scent of the fresh grape juice filled the air, adding spice to the odour of the sun-baked earth." As for the front, Von Senger remarks, it "remained free from attack."[1]

Just twelve days before Von Senger moved his Corps Headquarters, the American 92nd Division's 370th Combat Team was engaged in a frontal assault on Monte Castellaccio, west of the Serchio River and north of Lucca. Concertina-wire barriers, minefields and heavy German machine-gun and mortar fire slowed the attack. On the morning of the second day, the Buffalo soldiers were within a few hundred yards of the rugged 1,800-foot ridge top. An enemy machine gun in the wall of a church opened up on a lead platoon. But it was a second gun on the right flank that pinned the men down. Private Charles J. Patterson crawled up the hill until he was in position to drop a grenade into the machine-gun nest, killing two gunners. Meanwhile, his squad leader had been killed by shrapnel. Patterson made his way back to the squad, took command and led the charge to the top of the ridge. His action enabled the Buffalo soldiers to clear Monte Castellaccio and he was awarded a Silver Star.

Within an overall view of the Fifth Army front on that day—the day II Corps assaulted Il Giogo Pass—it was a small action. In Von Senger's dead sector, however, it was that kind of war. Here, a short, bitter exchange; there, a withdrawal and follow-up; everywhere, an effort to pin down the enemy. IV Corps held the Fifth Army's weakest sector as II Corps mounted the main attack on the Gothic Line. Two green divisions—the Brazilian Expeditionary Force and the all-black 92nd Buffalo Division—and the hodge-podge Task Force 45 were strung out along Von Senger's attenuated front. Veteran First Armored tankers were salted in where needed; and the indomitable South Africans worked up along IV Corps' right boundary to protect II Corps' right flank.

On the coast, Task Force 45 patrols skirted the southern beaches of Viareggio, where the schooner *Ariel* foundered and Percy Bysshe Shelley drowned. On September 15, a task force of armor and infantry took the beach resort. On the same day, the Brazilian Expeditionary Force entered the line, relieving Task Force 45 troops in the mountains overlooking the coastal plain. As the Brazilian 6th Combat Team liberated Massarosa and moved north towards Camaiore, Task Force 45 regrouped on the narrowing coastal plain and resumed its attack. A platoon of tanks and tank destroyers rumbled north the next day in support of the 434th and 435th Antiaircraft Artillery Batallions and the 47th Light Antiaircraft Artillery regiment, now all infantry, until German resistance slowed the advance at Motrone, four miles up the coast. Over the next three days, the Task Force worked up to Forte dei Marmi, an elegant resort with a fortress on the main piazza built of Apuan marble some two hundred years ago by a grand duke of Tuscany. Three miles to the east at the edge of the Apuan Alps, on the 23rd, ex-antiaircraft artillerymen took Pietrasanta after a vigorous fight that battered the ancient marble center. Here the attack ground to a halt.

The Brazilian 6th Combat Team, commanded by Brigadier General Euclides Zenobio da Costa and reinforced by three tank companies, operated on a five-mile front that traversed the southern portion of the Apuans, a region of jagged peaks, overhanging cliffs, marble quarries and rushing torrents. On September 18 the Brazilians took Camaiore, at the head of a valley cutting down to the coast, without opposition. To secure the Camaiore–Lucca road, the Brazilians tackled the heights to the north, focusing on the 4,000-foot-peak, Monte Prana, which offered the Germans a superb observation post overlooking the coast and the southern edge of the Apuans.

Though the 8th and 9th Companies gained positions on Prana's southeastern slopes, 7th Company to the west was stopped a short mile from the summit. Intense mortar fire held up the advance of the 3rd Battalion on the ridges farther east. Tanks and artillery pounded German positions for six days, ultimately forcing a withdrawal of elements from the German 42nd Division. On the 26th, Brazilian patrols occupied the heights from Prana to Monsagrati, an advance of some eleven miles over a ten-day period, taking 31 prisoners, at a cost of five dead and seventeen wounded. As BEF Commander João Baptista Mascarenhas de Moraes said, it was "a happy conclusion to the first operation of the Brazilian Forces in the Italian Theater."[2]

On September 26–27, the Buffalo Soldiers, working with 1st Armored Division tanks (in Task Force 92), moved four to five miles up the Serchio to overlook the junction of that river and the Lima. Von Senger's then-Headquarters at Villa Collemandina were some twenty miles up the

Serchio. The next day a Buffalo patrol entered Bagni di Lucca, the famed spa where Montaigne in 1581, Shelley and Byron nearly three hundred years later, among others, partook of its warm and sulfurous springs. The bulk of the 1st Armored was assigned to II Corps for an expected break-out into the Po near Bologna, while some elements of Combat Command B remained on the Lima line with the Buffalos. In October, however, CCB was assigned a sector along Highway 64 near Porretta Terme.

On September 30, the 370th's 3rd Battalion crossed the Lima and entered La Lima. Over the next few days, the Buffalo soldiers pushed up Highway 12, now running north along the river, to Ponte di Sestaione. IV Corps then shifted forces, moving the 370th Combat Team to take over its sixteen-mile western flank from the coast to the Serchio Valley. The 107th Anti-aircraft Group, composed of the British 39th and 47th Light Anti-aircraft Regiments and the 74th Anti-aircraft Artillery, was assigned an extended line from Bagni di Luccca to Pontepetri on the Reno River, western boundary of the South African 6th Armoured. The advance units of the 92nd had passed through the Gothic Line defenses of the Serchio Valley and sealed off the east–west portion of Highway 12. In forty-two days of combat, the Buffalo soliders had suffered 263 casu-alties, including 19 killed, 225 wounded and 19 missing.[3]

During October, as II Corps tackled the Livergnano Escarpment, the Werhmacht's last natural defense line in the Apennines, IV Corps con-tinued its pursuit of limited objectives along its western flank. On Octo-ber 6, the 1st and 2nd Battalions of the 370th Infantry moved abreast against German defenses on Monte Caula, the first in a series of heights protecting Massa. The fall of Massa would open the way to the capture of the port La Spezia. To their left, the 434th and 435th Antiaircraft Artillery Batallions attacked up the coast. The Buffalos advanced a mile while slight gains were scored on the coast. Heavy rains and insufficient reconnaissance, however, hampered the troops. The next morning, tanks and tank destroyers from the 2nd Armored Group supported the troops on Highway 1 but were blocked by the lack of suitable stream crossings over the swollen creeks tumbling out of the mountains. When the 2nd Battalion of the 370th reached the upper slopes of Caula, it was driven back by mortar and artillery fire. After dark, the Buffalo soldiers re-grouped and scaled the steep rocks to the crest without opposition. But the next afternoon, mortar and artillery fire forced another withdrawal. Meanwhile, ack-ackers-turned-infantry, assisted by two platoons of Sherman tanks, seized the cemetery just north of Querceta.

Over the next two days, the Buffalo soldiers prepared for another assault of Monte Caula. Ladders were constructed to enable the infantry to scale the cliffs. Crossings were sought over the swollen Seravezza Creek. Again, the Buffalo soldiers reached the summit; again, mortar and artillery fire drove them back down. On the night of October 17–18, a patrol fought its way to the crest and held on. A Company's F squad was trapped in a house at Giustignana; five men were killed and three captured. The positions on Caula were reinforced the next day.

Attempts were made to expand the hold on Caula and to seize neighboring heights. Engineers used bangalore torpedoes to blast the wire before the German defenses of Monte Strettoia, opening the way for a night attack on October 22 by Company L. Enemy machine-gun and mortar fire created considerable confusion; the company was disorganized. Company Commander Lieutenant Cotheren pulled the men together and, by three in the morning, Company L reached its objective— which they held precariously under heavy enemy fire. Cotheren was among the many casualties. Support Company C was unable to get through the wire. Lieutenant Reuben L Horner's platoon held off eight counterattacks that night but was forced to withdraw when ammunition ran out. The offensive along the coast was called off.

As the 370th mounted its attack on Monte Caula, the BEF's 6th Regimental Combat Team attacked up the Serchio Valley The sector was held by elements of the German 42nd Division who would be relieved by the Italian (Fascist) Monte Rosa Alpini Division at the end of the month. The Brazilians advanced against little resistance, taking Fornaci and its munitions factory on October 6. The Germans infiltrated back into town, perhaps to sabotage the factory, but were driven back, leaving four dead and one wounded. After a brief halt, the Brazilians captured Barga, a characteristic hilltown with a fine Romanesque cathedral. For the rest of the month, the Brazilians sent out numerous patrols and improved their positions by occupying Sommocolonia above Barga, and Trassilico and Verni, heights west of the Serchio.

At the end of October, the Brazilians moved towards Castelnuovo di Garfganana, the picturesque center that marks the boundary of the Alta Garfagnana, some six miles south of Von Senger's former Corps Headquarters. Small gains were made in the rain and heavy fog. Then, on October 31, the enemy launched a diversionary attack during a downpour. To put it mildly, in General Moraes' words, "Our troops were surprised." He adds: "Tired from fatiguing days and certain that the enemy elements they were facing had no combative spirit, they relaxed certain security measures and did not even establish a reasonable fire plan, necessary measures for maintaining a conquered objective."[4] The Brazilians fell back on previously held positions in the hills above Barga. Their advance of nearly 13 miles up the Serchio from its junction with the Lima was stopped. Since entering the line on September 15, the BEF's 6th Regimental Combat Team had taken 208 prisoners and progressed 24 miles, at a cost of 290 casualties: 13 dead, 87 wounded, 183 accident victims and seven missing.[5]

IV Corps shifted its forces once again during the first week of November. The black 371st and 365th Regiments arrived in Leghorn (Livorno) in mid-October to join the 370th in a sector from the coast to the Serchio above Barga. Two battalions of the 370th held a four-mile front bracketing the river; the 365th/371st sector ran five miles inland from the coast. Buffalo foot patrols met roughly midway between Serravezza (371st) and Gallicano (370th) at the tiny villlage of Fornovolasco. The retread artillerymen of Task Force 45 held down a division-sized sector between the Serchio in the vicinity of Bagni di Lucca and the Reno Valley north of Pistoia. The Brazilian Expedionary Force, now at full divisional strength, moved into the Reno Valley, taking over the Bombiana hill-mass between the Silla and Marano Rivers from the 1st Armored's Combat Command B. Formerly attached to CCB, the 370th's Second Battalion was now attached to the BEF. Combat Command B, now centered along the Reno, reached Riola.

An attack on Castelnuovo, a hilltown above Riola, was halted short of the Command's final objective on October 29. Thereafter, the front bracketing the Reno became stabilized, though harassed by enemy artillery and mortar fire and enemy efforts aimed at interdicting supply lines, destroying tank units and demolishing bridges at Riola, Marano, Silla and Porretta Terme.

During October, IV Corps had edged up the left shoulder of the 5th Army front as II Corps pushed north, exploiting the breakthroughs at Il Giogo and Futa Passes. IV Corps, however, lacked the strength to keep pace with II Corps' drive for the Po. To eliminate the possibility of a gap developing between the two Corps, the South African 6th Armoured Division was to keep pace with II Corps on the right and to maintain contact with IV Corps on the left. To do this, the South Africans had to seize control of the mountain chain running north between the two river valleys at heights ranging from two to three thousand feet. In late September, the 6th Armoured advanced along two widely separated axes, the 12th SA Motorised Brigade pushing north along Route 64 and the 11th up Route 6620.

The First City/Cape Town Highlanders, who had crossed the Apennine watershed on the Passo della Porretta on September 26 without opposition, expected to fight "downhill" all the way along the Reno to Vergato. General Poole was then ordered to concentrate his efforts along Highway 6620 to give maximum support to II Corps. The U.S. First Armored's Combat Command B with the 74 Light Antiaircraft Regiment took over along Highway 64 and headed downriver. The 12th SA went into reserve for ten days. Meanwhile, the Germans withdrew in such haste that they left five 100mm guns behind in the vicinity of Montepiano on 6620. The cold and rain cramped South African troop movements, but winter battle dress issued on September 25 helped some. Imperial Light Horse/Kimberly Regiment carriers successfully reconnoitered to Castiglione dei Peopoli, a popular resort of the Bolognese Apennines in peacetime. Troopers of the Imperial Light Horse also occupied Camugnano, a modest hamlet roughly midway between Highways 64 and 6620 with stunning views of the sawtooth crags to the north, the *campanile* of Vigo and the heights of Monte Vigese.

As the South Africans consolidated their forces in the Camugnano and Castiglione zone, the 91st Cavalry Squadron of II Corps had reached Prediera some two and a half miles to the north and east of Highway 6620. Monte Catarelto loomed ahead east of the highway, shrouded in the mist and heavy rain. Its 2,590-foot summit capped a six-mile ridge running north belted by wooded slopes and farmers' fields. Despite the ghastly weather, morale was high among the tankers and foot soldiers. There was an air of expectancy, an eagerness to continue the chase. Some optimists, Neil Orpen remarks, visualized a breakthrough to the plains of Lombardy. Brigadier Archer Clive's 24th Guards Brigade bracketed Highway 6620 with the Coldstreams on the left and the Scots Guards advancing on the right. The British infantry were backed by Pretoria Regiment tanks. Visibility was limited to about 100 yards by rain as the troops moved out towards Prediera.

As usual, the advance went by fits and starts. Narrow, winding mountain roads, bad weather and heavy traffic created unavoidable delays and serious supply problems. The 136th Field Battery coming into position to support the assault on Catarelto had only 200 rounds per gun. Nonetheless, when the Germans opened up with machine guns and mortars from a position on the main road near Prediera, accurate artillery fire from the 136th drove them back. On September 29, the Scots Guards occupied Sparvo without opposition, placing them in position to tackle Point 678, an enemy outpost to the north. Moreover, the Guards occupied Palazzo, a ridge that offered first-class observation of Monte Catarelto and its approaches. Royal Durban Light Infantry medium machine guns were also posted to deliver direct fire to cover the attack on 678 and the mountain. Still, the Scots Guards had to cover a front of a thousand yards, going up against the tough, veteran 16th SS Panzer Grenadiers.

On the 30th, the Scots Guards attacking Point 678 ran into heavy machine-gun fire from the summit and near Creda. Artillery fire also slowed the infantry, but the Spandaus were soon neutralized and the enemy was slowly forced back. In two hours, the Scots were on the crest and consolidating. By 1500, the assault on Catarelto was underway. C Company met stiff opposition and dug in, with the enemy well entrenched behind a stone wall just over the crest. At 0200, a counterattack from the southeast was thrown back. A Scots Guard platoon, however, had to withdraw and dig in at the corner of a nearby wood. Tanks were called up, but the Pretorians found it difficult to build up a road in full view of the enemy. In the morning, the Germans attacked again from the west and southwest. Artillery broke up the assault from the west and small-arms fire pinned down the other.

On the left of Highway 6620, the Coldstream Guards worked up the west side of the Brasimone Valley towards Bucciagni, a hilltown overlooking the river and the highway. The entire SS Division was now committed against General Clive's 24th Guards Brigade. Tanks threw tracks in the mud but managed to work into positions from which they could fire acrosss the valley onto the summit of Catarelto. By late night on October 1 the Coldstreams had dug in on the southern slopes of Bucciagni Ridge under harassing machine-gun fire. Meanwhile, the Scots Guards' Left Flank Company 6, down to 45 men, on Catarello, had to withdraw. B, the reserve company, was committed but was hit heavily by defensive fire. Brigadier Clive brought up the Grenadier Guards and pulled the Scots Guards back slightly to give the Grenadiers room, backed by C Squadron Pretoria tanks for an attack on Catarelto at dawn on October 2. Swirling mists and driving rain soaked the infantrymen as they moved out. By eight o'clock, one company was on the eastern shoulder of Catarelto though little headway was made on the western slope. That night the Germans withdrew, having suffered 250 casualties among their 400 defenders of Catarelto Ridge.

To the west, the Royal Natal Carbineers maintained contact with Combat Comand B of the 1st Armored, working up Highway 64. Snow dusted the highest Apennine peaks while rain turned valley roads into mud. To clinch progress along Highway 6620, the South Africans had to clear Monte Vigese, where the Germans overlooked from outposts at some 3,575 feet the advancing 24th Guards Brigade. Patrols from the Imperial Light Horse, Kimberley Regiment, had worked up to the road north of the mountain, and flushed out Germans who had crossed the Reno to pillage houses east of the river.

On October 3, the South Africans occupied Cardeda, a hilltown on the southeast tip of Monte Vigese, a mile and a half east of the ridge just taken by the Coldstream Guards. Kimberley Regiment's D Company kept going until counterattacked just before midnight near Torlai, another hamlet on the eastern side of Vigese. Fighting was so close that Private J.W. Latsky was able to beat back several attacks with a tommygun and grenades. Still, one section was driven back with its ammunition gone; then two others were forced to follow suit.

The next day, Torlai was the scene of bitter fighting. A tank that moved up on the village became bogged down and went out of action. The infantry gained ground, coming within three hundred yards of the summit. But one platoon was forced back down a gully by heavy mortar fire. Spandaus firing on stretcher-bearers had to be silenced by artillery fire. II Company of the 36 SS Panzer Grenadiers mounted an atttack from the saddle between Monte Vigese and Montovolo on the two South African platoons. Haystacks burned brightly as surviving South Africans withdrew, taking cover beneath a ridge some hundred yards south. Spandau fire from the slopes of Vigese drove them back again. Lieutenent C. G Solomon alerted the Kimberley companies in Cardeda, speaking in Zulu over a tank radio. When D Company pulled out, it had suffered 23 casualties plus 19 missing. To relieve the hard-pressed Kimberley troopers, the Royal Natal Carbineers were ordered to attack up the western side of Vigese. The area taken back by the Germans was heavily shelled.

The Germans paid a stiff price for their success—going in with 120 men, coming out with only 40 to 50. The Carbineers occupied Vigo, on the west side of Vigese, and one platoon, moving up in a thick mist, surprised the enemy near the summit. The Germans on the heights were shot or dispersed. Nine prisoners were taken, including the captain in charge of the mountain's defenses. Another Carbineer platoon drove back 40 machine-gunners and mortar men, who had been so helpful in the attack on the Kimberley Regiment. All this, accomplished without casualties. Though it poured all day on October 6, the South Africans pushed on, occupying Torlai and Montovolo north on the road to Collina. The rain lifted the next day, only to fall again later. The Kimberleys reached Collina, pounded to rubble by South African artillery, and the way seemed clear to 2,350-foot Monte Stanco, some three miles to the north, and 2,700-foot Monte Salvaro, six miles beyond. From these heights, the Germans were in a position to dominate Highway 64 and Route 6620.

When the Grenadiers cleared Catarelto, II Corps was able to advance another five or so miles without much opposition. It seemed that the South Africans were carrying out their mission of keeping pace with II Corps while maintaining contact with IV. Still, General Clark was worried lest a gap develop between the two corps. Control of the 6th South African Division, therefore, was passed from IV Corps to the Fifth Army on October 5. Under direct Army control, it was felt, the actions of the South Africans could be coordinated more closely with the advance of II Corps. To beef up General Poole's command, 6th Armoured divisional artillery was enhanced by the 178th Medium Regiment, Royal Artillery, 76th Heavy AA Regiment, Battery C of the 697th Field Artillery Battalion (with two 240mm howitzers towed by track vehicles with tank chassis), an 8-inch gun from Battery A, 575th Field Artillery Battalion and four observation aircraft. Combat Command B—U.S. 1st Armored 11th Infantry Battalion, the 13th Tank Battalion, a field artillery battalion, a recon troop and an engineer company—were also attached to the South Africans' command.

General Poole was now in command of what amounted to almost a small Corps. To fulfill his mission, it was essential that the South Africans take Monte Stanco and Monte Salvaro. Divisional G-2 warned Brigadier Furstenburg of the 11th South African Brigade that Monte Stanco was held by two German battalions. When the Brigadier briefed the Carbineers, historian Neil Orpen remarks, they were left with the impression that it "all sounded like a cake-walk." The Kimberlies were pulled out for a much-needed rest and the Frontier Force Rifles were to pass through the Carbineers and head north towards Grizzana (on the shoulder of Stanco) and, ultimately, Monte Salvaro. The Rifles did gain a foothold on Stanco after a stiff fight with units of the 16th SS Division. But on the morning of October 8 they were driven off with heavy casualties. Brigadier Palmer's 12th SA Motorised Brigade was then ordered to take over the sector while the Carbineers took over the attack on Stanco from the Rifles.

The South African Armoured Division was deployed in a region totally unsuited to tank warfare. The Natal Mounted Rifles were converted to infantry. To protect the armored brigade's left flank, tankers from the A Squadrons of the Special Service Battalion and Prince Albert's Guard dismounted and fanned out like veteran foot-sloggers. Matters were not improved by the lack of adequate roads. Supplies and ammunition for four battalions had to be brought forward over one muddy jeep track. At 0530 on October 10, Carbineer B and D Companies opened the South Africans' second attack on Monte Stanco from Stanco di Sopra on the left and Casa Forlino on the right, south of the mountain. At first, the South Africans were lucky, hitting the German lines while a relief was in progress. The Fusilier Battalion and III/Grenadier Regiment of the 94th Division came in under the command of the 16th SS Division. By 0640, the South Africans were on Stanco, despite their losses, and a platoon from A Company was sent up to reinforce the line on the summit.

Oberst Grassau, the Fusilier/Grenadier commander, however made a good recovery, his men crossing the open ground along the ridge from Grizzana into cover on the northeastern slope of Stanco. More of the enemy pounded in from the northwest. By mid-morning, the South Africans' lines of communications were shot away. Lieutenant V.C.J. Chapman's platoon was overrun and he was killed. Lieutenant H. Fraser, an Ack-ack officer just turned infantryman, took charge but was killed in a valiant effort to hold the line. B and D Companies were forced back, withdrawing in good order under cover provided by C Company. Captain H.T Going of the Cape Field Artilllery set up an impromptu observation post and ordered a heavy concentration on his own position, getting away just as it pounded the advancing Germans. He was awarded the American Silver Star. C Company's rearguard platoon suffered eleven casualties out of the 56 sustained by the Battalion that morning. A new line was established on three heights—688, 643 and 683—running south of Monte Stanco.

Since two battalions in succession had failed to take Monte Stanco, the South Africans decided to launch a two-battalion attack to take Stanco, Campiaro, Monte Pezza and Monte Salvaro—one after the other. It would to be the largest set-piece attack launched by the South Africans in Italy, according to Neil Orpen.[7] The Witwatersrand Rifles/De la Rey Regiment was assigned Monte Stanco, while the First City/Cape Town Highlanders tackled Point 602, east of the summit a short mile, on the track to Grizzana. The two battalions churned forward along a rutted jeep track, mucky after the rains, to starting lines along the southern approaches to the two objectives. A dummy barrage on the morning of October 13 hocused the enemy as to South African intentions. To overcome crest clearance problems, which allowed Germans cover on the reverse slope of Stanco, Royal Durban Light Infantry 4.2 mortars were sited to hit enemy concentrations on all sides of the mountain. The lead companies of both battalions crossed their starting lines at 0445; divisional artillery and the mortars opened fire fifteen minutes later, laying down a forty-five-minute barrage to excellent effect.

That night, Lieutnant Tinz and his men, 9th Company, 274th Grenadiers, had climbed the steep slopes of Monte Stanco to relieve an SS Company. They were in position with orders to hold the heights to the last man, when the South Africans launched their attack. As it happened, the German 94th Infantry Division was in the midst of taking over the western sector of the 16th SS Division front. Often such relief operations made for a certain amount of confusion. However, in this instance, it also meant that elements of both divisions were in place to oppose the South African attackers. German shellfire exacted its grim toll from the start. One WR/De la Rey platoon lost four killed and eight wounded as the attack opened. Later, Corporal J.H. Thompson recalled, ". . . bushes and undergrowth caught and tugged at equipment and boots slipped on grass and pebbles. The ground was pitted and scarred by numerous craters and grew more so higher up. Broken branches leaned sharply."[8]

It was a cold, wet morning. Instead of taking the obvious route up a watercourse—which afforded protection from guns sited on the heights of Stanco—Major W.N.A. Barends' A Company, WR/DLR, went straight up the steep-pitched forward slope and crossed the summit ridge by 0600, despite murderous mortar and machine-gun fire. West of the ridge, C Company worked up slopes so steep that at times the men had to scramble on all fours. On reaching the beacon on Stanco, they were hard hit by German mortar fire. B Company provided left-flank protection but came under heavy machine-gun fire from Germans forted up in Casa Forlino, a farmhouse sitting on the ridge to the right of the summit. A Company had outflanked Forlino but, unfortunately, was badly hit. Major Barends felt that his men might be cut off. He called on the Cape Town Highlanders for help.

The Highlanders already had a platoon on Point 602, their chief objective that morning, but were severely harrassed by Germans on Point 650, a rise situated between the two attacking South African battalions. The troublesome Casa Forlino, just south of Point 650, fell when an enterprising Highlander, Corporal W.A. Betts, blew a hole in the wall of the house with a PIAT mortar round, enabling D Company to move forward. The intrepid Lieutenant Tinz, however, still held Point 650. D Company attacked the point three times, to no avail, even though a mortar round blew a bothersome German machine-gunner and his gun into the branches of a nearby tree. The company was then ordered to take 650 frontally, at all costs. Yelling, as Orpen puts it, "in approved battle-course manner,"[9] the Highlanders charged the steep slopes, laying into the enemy with bayonets and tommy-guns. Prisoners were taken and the rest driven toward the Witwatersrand Rifles, who killed 12 and captured 13. The taking of 650 won the Military Cross for D Company commander Major E.R. Bartlett and Lieutenant C.T. Macfarlane.

With Point 650 secured, Monte Stanco was in good hands by 1355, and by 1600 the heavy fighting was over. Though some areas were heavily shelled during the night of October 13–14, the mountain was well and truly held. The South Africans counted their losses for the day: 24 Rifles killed, two dying of wounds and 63 wounded; 19 Highlanders died, two of wounds and 38 were wounded. German losses were greater—128 prisoners and some 60 killed, apart from artillery and mortar fire casualties. Total 94th Infantry and 16th SS casualties were estimated at 500. Of Lieutnant Tinz's forlorn hope, only 18 survived the day.

As is often the case, the taking of a key point—in this instance, Monte Stanco—opened possibilities for the attacking forces. South African patrols the next day found Grizzana, Poggio and Grizzana east all clear, as well as Campiano on the northwest road to Vergato. On the 15th, the engineers opened the road from Route 6620 at Pian di Setta westward to jeeps. This proved to be a useful alternative to the hazardous one-way track through Collina and north to Grizzana, the last mile of which was dubbed the "Mad Mile" by drivers who dashed as best they could through momentary lulls in harassing shellfire. Work on the roads procceded over the next five days, enabling South African tanks to move up in support positions for the advancing infantry.

Before taking on Germans entrenched on Monte Salvaro—considered by them a "key" to holding Bologna—the South Africans had to clear the enemy off Monte Pezza and Monte Alcino. Two troops of the Prince Albert Guards made "an effective demonstration" down the road to Vergato in the Reno Valley as the Royal Natal Carbineers and the Cape Town Highlanders cleared up enemy pockets, machine-gun posts and snipers on Monte Pezza and its ridges. The Highlanders routed a German counterattack at Casa la Fame beyond the crest and took 27 prisoners. The Carbineers lost 6 killed, 13 wounded; the Highlanders, one killed, seven wounded, before consolidating their positions during the night of October 17–18.

The Witwatersrand Rifles then passed through the Carbineers to advance along the ridge line a half-mile to Point 806, a rugged 2,600-odd-foot rise about halfway to Monte Salvaro. Again the advance along the ridges was confined to a single path—here, past two good defensive positions, Casa Ruzzone and Point 752, on the route to Point 806. In such situations, intelligence on enemy positions is crucial to attack plans. Royal Sergeant Major Bert Wheeler volunteered to lead a Rifles patrol of four that found Casa Ruzzone and Point 752 clear, but ran into a German 8-man patrol a bit farther on. The Rifles killed two, wounded another and drove the rest off. But in the exchange, RSM Wheeler was gutshot. His men carried him back some 300 yards before he ordered two to report forward as quickly as posssible. Wheeler subsequently died at the regimental aid post. The Rifles decided, on the basis of the Wheeler patrol's findings, to attack in silence on the morning of October 19.

The attack went as well as could be expected. The two Rifles companies got a good start before the South African mortars chimed in at 0600, firing along an east–west line through Point 805. Two guns, however, fired short, delaying one company. Still, one company was "secure" on Point 806 by 0740. But the men holding the point were soon subjected to heavy German shell fire, much of it from Monte Alcino, across the valley to their right rear. The Scots Guards were already engaged in tackling the 1,700-foot peak, but were badly hit by small-arms fire when caught in a ravine. The company had to be withdrawn, leaving the Germans in a position to pound the Rifles with mortars, particulary during the following night.

No Rifles company by then had more than 55 men left; 44 replacements barely filled in—the Rifles had lost another 28 during the day. On the following day, October 20, the Rifles threw back eleven counterattacks between 0900 and noon. That afternoon, nonetheless, the Rifles managed to clear the immediate approaches to Monte Salvaro in 40 minues of "wildly confused" fighting. Then, for some two hours, they were bombarded in an ordeal, Orpen remarks, "such as they had never before experienced in all their months of hard fighting." The battalion had suffered 223 casulaties since the battle for Monte Stanco had opened, and the men were exhausted. General Poole wisely called off the Rifles' projected next-day attack on Salvaro. Then, as Sergeant R.A. Goldberg observed, ". . . the weary, unshaven and nervewracked infantrymen stumbled from their positions, acting only only upon instinct, as human feeling had been sapped from their bodies."[10]

While the Witwatersrand Rifles were being pounded, two Scots Guards companies mounted an attack on Monte Alcino and a neighboring height, Point 580. The Germans on 580 on the approach to Salvaro were suprised, and withdrew in disorder. But only a handful of Scots managed to reach the summit of Alcino on the 20th and had to be withdrawn. The movement of supplies became impossible and the Scots on line had to subsist on nuts. Patrols after dark on the 21st, however, found Alcino empty. The Scots moved forward to occupy the height the next day. An attack on Monte Salvaro by the Kimberly Regiment at dawn on October 23 was put into motion. The Regiment, in Orpen's words, was "very much under establishment" and the men were "all but tired out" after seven weeks' fighting in the rain and the cold.[11] The weary men on foot made their way from Collina and were on line by nightfall on the 21st, huddling in foxholes swamped by rain. It was not an auspicious beginning.

Visibility was limited to a few yards; Monte Salavaro, a 2,700-foot crag, beetle-browed with thick brush and rocky cornices, was a felt presence. The German 94th Division held good defensive positions with five-foot-deep trenches on the mountain's eastern slope where the Grenadiers had almost as many Spandaus as rifles. A battle group of some 150 men was on the mountain crest. II/274th Regiment spread out to the west from Salvaro's shoulder down to the Reno. A battalion was posted in the saddle between Salvaro and Monte Termine to the east and another battalion, at least, on Termine itself—in position to deliver destructive fire on South Africans attacking from the south. The valley of the Rio Sabbioni, plunging northward to the Reno, provided the enemy with valuable dead ground. The South Africans' room for maneuver was limited to an assault from the south along a track that dipped into a saddle beyond Point 806, rising to Points 778 and 793, then to the crest of Salvaro.

On the afternoon of October 22, in a swirling mist, two Carbineer patrols cleared enemy-occupied houses on 778, taking 45 prisoners in a brisk firefight. The Germans counterattacked, killing platoon leader Lieutenant J. Adamson, two of his men and wounding two others. But the South Africans held their ground, providing the Kimberly Regiment with a more favorable starting line on the following morning at daybreak. Moving forward under the divisional barrage, the two lead companies forced the enemy back until the South Africans came under fire from houses on 793.

Casualties mounted as the South Africans moved grimly forward to within hand-grenade range of German positions on the southern slope of Monte Salvaro. The Kimberlies had to pull back for cover as the Germans countered with deadly machine-gun and mortar fire. As the troopers held on, mortars and all the divisional artillery that could be brought to bear smothered enemy positions for ten minutes. Then, at 1330, the South Africans attacked into the mist and the settling dust, one platoon going for the crest and another going beyond to a track junction. When the 3rd Platoon of A Company was held up by Spandau fire, Private R. Greenway on the razor-back ridge opened up with his bren to cover Private Private R.H.F. Nicolson, who crawled forward to silence the machine gun with grenades. Greenway continued forward along the mist-covered ridge, silencing seven more German machine guns. Sergeant E.G. Timms led his section around to the left, where it secured a German strongpoint and captured 20 prisoners.

As the mist began to lift, the South African advance along slopes dewooded by shellfire was clearly in view of enemy observers. When the advance was halted by intense German fire, Captain G.R.L. Canning lost his two machine guns and five of his men. Undeterred by a mortar bomb blast, he collected abandoned enemy guns and led his 12 remaining men in an attack on three enemy machine-gun nests, killing six and capturing seven. That night, hearing coughing out in front of his position, he darted forward, surprised and captured six infiltrators. Captain J.H. Smallwood's men were pinned down in front of an enemy strongpoint. Canning crawled forward, tossed hand grenades, then rushed forward, firing his tommy-gun from the hip. When the enemy counterattacked, his men charged and accounted for all 18 attackers.

That night, the Kimberlies could only muster 160 riflemen. But they had secured the crest of Salvaro. The South African position was consolidated the next day despite continuous artillery and mortar fire. The enemy's main forces withdrew across the Reno, abandoning outposts on the southern bank and a battalion bridgehead east of Vergato at Carviano. General Poole considered the battles for Monte Stanco and Monte Salvaro the hardest fighting in which the South Africans had engaged in World War II. The Kimberlies had lost 15 killed and 81 wounded in overcoming five companies—some 650 men—from the 276th and 274th Grenadier Regiments. All but 100 were casualties, including 92 known killed and 112 captured. The South African divisional artillery had fired some 7,369 rounds: 4.2 mortars, 1,753 and the 3-inchers, 883 rounds.

On the 24th, the Scots Guards occupied Monte Termine, deserted by the Germans, about a mile east–northeast of Salvaro. On the South African left flank, the American 1st Armored's CCB gained the high ground northwest of Highway 64 and the Reno, capturing the hill towns of Palazzo, Castellaccio and, later, Riola. General Poole's "small corps" had consolidated the left flank of II Corps.

NOTES

[1] Von Senger, *Neither Fear nor Hope,* pp. 270–71.
[2] Moraes, *The Brazilian Expeditionary Force,* p. 54.
[3] Hargrove, *Buffalo Soldiers in Italy,* p. 24.
[4] Moraes, *The Brazilian Expeditionary Force,* p. 64.
[5] Ibid.
[6] Scots Guards companies were: HQ, Right Flank, B, C and Left Flank companies.
[7] Orpen, *Victory in Italy,* p. 223.
[8] Ibid., p. 225.
[9] Ibid., p. 227.
[10] Ibid., p. 239.
[11] Ibid., p. 240.

XVI

ONE MORE MOUNTAIN

The breakthroughs at Il Giogo and Futa Passes on September 20–22 offered opportunities too good to be missed. By funneling II Corps through Futa Pass down Highway 65 to capture Bologna, the Fifth Army could gain a first-class supply route across the mountains. In addition, the Allies just might trap the German Tenth Army south of the Po. But the rapid advance of the 85th and 91st Divisions into the Santerno Valley offered II Corps the shortest route (though over the less attractive Highway 6528) to the valley of the Po. A breakout at Imola also would give more immediate help to the Eighth Army, bogged down in the Romagna. German defenses, too, were less developed in the mountains bracketing the Santerno. Moreover, as the *Fifth Army History* put it, "There was a possibility of catching Kesselring's forces off balance in their troop disposition."[1]

Instead of choosing one or the other, General Clark decided to exploit both the Futa and Il Giogo breakthroughs. II Corps was ordered to continue its attack along Highway 65 towards Radicosa Pass, while mounting a major attack down the Santerno Valley in conjunction with the British XIII Corps attack towards Faenza. Combat Command A of the 1st Armored was to provide II Corps with a mobile armored force. The 88th Division, until then in reserve, was to pass through the right flank of the 85th on the September 21 to spearhead the thrust towards Imola.

The passthrough took place the next day, September 21, in the vicinity of Firenzuola, a 14th-century Florentine colony on the Santerno cradled within the Northern Apennines seven miles north of Il Giogo. The 85th Division occupied the town just before the arrival of the Blue Devils. The Custer men found the town in ruins; midway between Florence and Bologna on the only half-decent supply road in the 85th's sector, it had been bombed and shelled into rubble so deep that the infantrymen could hardly tell where the streets had run. The 85th's immediate task was to ease the way for the commitment of the 88th. To do the job, it was essential to clear Monte Coloreta, looming 3,300 feet east of Firenzuola and north of the Santerno. Heavy machine-gun fire from a hill west of Coloreta held up Company E, 338th Infantry, and posed a serious threat to the Custer advance.

Lieutenant Orville E. Bloch, a lad from Streeter, North Dakota, and three volunteers wriggled forward to a large rock in front of a group of five buildings where the Germans had posted machine-gun nests. Leaving the volunteers, Bloch charged into enemy fire, kicked over a machine gun and captured its five-man crew. He turned the prisoners over to his men, pulled the pin of a grenade and charged again towards another building some fifteen yards away. When he was within twenty feet, he threw the grenade, wounding a machine-gunner. Two Germans took refuge in the house. Bloch and one of his men advanced to the opposite end of the building and spotted a five-man machine-gun crew running forward. The two Custer men fired, forcing the crew to abandon its gun for cover inside the building. Bloch rushed the door, firing his carbine from the hip. He wounded four and the rest promptly surrendered. Then, Bloch and his man moved on to the next house, where they discovered an abandoned machine gun and spotted another nest at the corner of the building. Again Bloch rushed the enemy, who vanished within the house with the Custer man hard on their heels. Firing his carbine from the hip, he wounded two and captured six Germans. Single-handed, Bloch captured nineteen prisoners, wounded six, and eliminated five machine-gun nests. His company renewed its attack with success. Bloch won his Division's third Medal of Honor.

As the Custer men occupied the Coloreta massive and struck north into the mountains towards the Sillaro, the Blue Devils entered the Santerno sector. The river and black-topped Highway 6528 twisted and turned through a narrow gorge flanked by high mountains for over half the 30 miles separating Firenzuola from Imola. It is rugged country with high-peaked ridges on both sides of the stream slashed by deep ravines. General Paul W. Kendall had little choice but to send most of his men along the ridges—the 349th on the left, branching out to sweep in Monte La Fine and Monte Pratalungo; the 351st in reserve in the center, poised to take Castel del Rio on the Santerno; and the 350th on the left along the heights stretching northeast from Monte della Croce to Monte Battaglia that form the divide between the Santerno and the Senio. Pratolungo, west of the Santerno, and Carnevale and Battaglia, east of the river, were the last commanding peaks in the Blue Devils' zone. This chain of mountains offered the Germans their strongest defensive positions between Castel del Rio and the Po Valley.

The Blue Devils moved forward on a rainy, disagreeable night. "Mud to the top of combat boots tugged at the spirits of the weary column that hugged the edge of the road," Colonel James Fry recalled. His regiment had "the doubtful honor" of "the right of the line"; his mission was to "protect the right of II Corps and maintain contact with the British XIII Corps on the right" and "to capture the high ground to the front."[2]

The importance of Fry's mission was underscored by the visitors to his command post that first morning. Fog blanketed the sodden Stygian landscape. Shattered ten-inch pines dangled at weird angles on shell-slashed slopes. Water dripped on hapless G.I.s beneath improvised shelters. Mud gripped at Fry's boots as he made the rounds of his battalions. "Grim, young, ageless boys," Fry observed, "munched their cold K-Rations." Their cheerfulness, as always, was a source of amazement to their commander. The fog lifted as Fry returned to his command post, a knocked-about woodshed close to the road leading to Firenzuola. He gulped a Benzedrine tablet to put off badly needed sleep. An aide popped in to announce, "Four stars just drove up." Fry clapped on his helmet and hurried out of the hut, where he was greeted by General Clark. The general introduced him to the only man rating four stars in the Italian theater at the time, Field Marshall Alexander, whose handclasp was firm and comforting.[3]

The three officers trudged up to the top of a barren knob above the CP where they could view the fortresses—a broken sea of ravine-scarred peaks with their barren and shrubbed slopes—provided by nature to the enemy. At the top they discovered three dead Germans lying almost at their feet. "For a moment we all looked down," Fry says. "Their field-green uniforms proclaimed their nationality, but the rain had washed the dust from their slightly bloated faces, leaving only relaxed peace. Except for their clothing, they might have been our own dead. There was a brief silence." Then the three soldiers talked of troop dispositions and plans for the future.[4]

Blue Devils commander General Paul W. Kendall also dropped by that day to check on Fry's plans, and left with a word of cheer. Moving his troops along the ridge that formed the 350th's main line of attack, Colonel Fry was hopeful despite his soggy surroundings. A straggle of twenty prisoners, who had surrendered without a fight, passed by in the fog. He sensed "Victory . . . in the air. The enemy was withdrawing in front of us so fast that some of us felt that the Germans would endeavor to salvage what they could of their army and withdraw from all of Italy."[5] Fry's regiment made good progress on the 22nd, and the headquarters group occupied a peasant *casa* for the night. An outbreak of heavy firing on the slopes of Del Fabbro above them interrupted their evening meal of K-Rations heated in an ancient fireplace. On the radio, the First Battalion S2, Lieutenant John May, reported that his Battalion CP was surrounded, that he had escaped (jumping from a second- story window) and was trying to organize a rescue.

He hadn't a prayer, as it turned out.

A Captain Knoll, 2nd Battalion, 132nd Grenadiers, had been moving his men to a new position when he spotted a dim light from a building in the area. He investigated to discover that he had stumbled upon the First Battalion CP in Vallibona, a house on the slope of Monte del Fabbro.[6] Lieutenant Colonel Walter Bare had made his troop disposal, but only Companies A, in the northeast sector, and C, northwest, were organized for the night with adequate security posted. Heavy Weapons Company D and Headquarters Company were responsible for the Command Post security, B Company covering the trail to the south. But B Company had yet to close in and D Company, burdened by heavy equipment and with a "green" officer in command, lagged behind on the steep mountain trail leading up to Vallibona. Company A's commander, Captain Albert Romano, had stopped in to confer with Colonel Bare.

Captain Knoll seized the initiative, catching the Americans unaware and far from prepared. The supposedly safe inner-left was for all intents and purposes left open. A lone figure carrying a lantern approached Vallibona and called out in Italian. The two guards posted outside the CP told him to put his light out. Immediately a machine pistol burst killed one guard and seriously wounded the other, and the Germans quickly surrounded the building. Knoll ordered his men to take up "a porcupine position," which enabled them to fire in all directions. A grenade tossed into the CP caught the Battalion commander and his staff by surprise. They dashed upstairs for their weapons, leaving the Germans in command of the first floor. The firefight between the trapped Americans and the Germans went on for about an hour.

The rifle companies were slow to realize what was going on. An officer in the vicinity—who might have saved the situation, Fry later concluded—chickened out when an enemy machine gun opened up across the trail between his troops and the command post.[7] His second in command, "an able officer," according to Fry, was at the rear of the company and had no way of knowing the situation. Radios had been shut down to conserve batteries, and platoon runners had yet to report in at the time of the attack. Nevertheless, D Company's First Platoon managed to get in position to fire its machine-guns on the invaded CP, and six Germans were wounded. Company A, too, opened fire with rifles and 60mm mortars. Grenades blew down the door to the room where Colonel Bare and his Operations Officer, Captain Sterling Borquest, had taken shelter behind mattresses. Both officers were wounded.

Captain Knoll informed Colonel Bare that he could fight his way out but in that event the Germans would take no prisoners. Bare surrendered. The remainder of the command post, including Executive Officer Captain James Ritts, Artillery Liaison Officer Captain Murphy, Captain Romano, Lieutenants Ashcroft and McCabe, and twenty enlisted men soon followed suit. Bare was given two minutes to decide whether to order a battalion cease-fire.

Colonel Bare decided he had no alternative but to comply. Once outside, he told his men that it was too late to help Battalion Headquarters and requested them to cease fire. When they did so, the German Captain Knoll ordered his prisoners to line up, single file, each holding the belt of the man in front of him; gingerly, they made their way down a narrow ridge line. Captain Romano told Colonel Fry after the war that the Germans had marched their prisoners through Bologna, where civilians lined up to jeer and spit. The audacious Captain Knoll also captured top-secret operations maps, battle plans and journals.

At dawn, the Blue Devils continued their advance. There was no time to change plans, although the Germans were now presumably well informed. Regimental commanders were urged to press on: "Fifth Army plans require the capture of Carnevale and Battaglia. Take them as soon as possible."[8] Oddly enough, the loss of battle plans made no apparent difference. The Germans, too, were hard-pressed, possibly even in some disarray as they dropped back before the Americans. II Corps had opened a gap between the weakened 4th Parachute and 715th Grenadier Divisions. The Blue Devils' thrust enlarged the gap; the Germans hurried to head off an American breakthrough. Italian Bersaglieri, elements of the 1028th Grenadier Regiment, and three regiments of the 44th Grenadier Division were rushed forward to fill the gap. Rear-echelon personnel from the 715th Grenadiers were already in line, reinforced by the 305th Fusilier battalion and elements of the 132nd Grenadier Regiment—altogether, a formidable lot boosting German resistance.

Colonel Fry now reorganized his 1st Battalion; he placed Major Mike Oreskovitch in command and put the battalion in reserve for a breather. His 2nd Battalion moved slowly but steadily along the ridge line towards Monte Faggiola with the Third "generally abreast." On the Blue Devils' right flank, the 349th had enveloped the Germans from behind, on impassable Monte Frena after the engineers blasted and bulldozed a trail into a jeep and supply route. This freed the 349th to tackle Monte la Fine, a high ridge northwest of Monte Pratalungo on the Division's left boundary. On La Fine, the Regiment beat off three German counterattacks. Two hours later, at 1900 on September 23, the 351st was committed at the center of the Blue Devils' sector. By nightfall the three regiments were moving abreast on a line extending from Monte la Fine to Monte della Croce.

What followed was a simple story of mountain warfare. As Colonel Fry described it: "Men moving with determination from one bit of terrain to another, each success being achieved at a price; captured ground marked by bodies; mule pack trains moving up the hills carrying rations and ammunition; the same pack trains returning down the hills carrying the bodies of our dead."[9] At one point, worried about the fate of Major Vincent M. Witter's Second Battalion, Fry went forward, arriving at Della Croce just as a platoon of Company I was driven off the hill by a counterattack. Crouched behind a rock, Fry and I Company commander First Lieutenant George Carpenter discussed the situation. His last words to Fry were a promise that his men would be on top by morning.

They were. The next day Fry saw Carpenter's body on the side of the trail on the rocky and barren crest of Monte della Croce. He had paid the price for success—leading a countercharge against the enemy about to overcome his position.

By September 25, Fry's 350th Regiment was well on its way to

Monte Battaglia, drawing ahead of the 351st, down in the valley on its left, and the British, some 8,000 yards back on the right. To protect his right flank, Fry sent his 1st Battalion to take Puntale, a jutting 2,475-foot peak overlooking the 350th's approach to Battaglia. Major Mike Ores- kovitch moved across the battlefield with a heavy walking stick in his hand. His soldiers moved up the slopes, Fry later recalled, "as if on parade." The sun shone on red clay slopes. White puffs of smoke revealed enemy gun positions at the base of some haycocks up ahead. "Occasion- ally one of our soldiers fell, but the line moved on steadily."[10]

It was a confusing time. Prisoners were taken, as Fry put it, from "a multitude of different German units;"[11] Here and there, advancing units were held up by well-placed German guns. Herbert G. Goldman, a young soldier from Brooklyn, tackled one such fortified house. He was wound- ed but continued to crawl forward until he was in a position to fire his submachine gun at the enemy. Hit again, Goldman kept going until he arrived at the house. He stuck his gun in an opening and emptied its mag- azine. Then, mortally wounded by German machine-gun fire, he crept to a window and tossed in several hand grenades, killing several of the enemy. His action freed up his pinned-down comrades. Goldman was posthumously awarded the Distinguished Service Cross.

Puntale was taken at a heavy cost, but the 350th was now in position to take Monte Battaglia. Its right flank, however, was exposed, its supply lines endangered, and the Wehrmacht artillery continued to pound the Blue Devils from three sides. General Kendall ordered the dismounted 760th Tank Battalion, under Major Andrew R. Cheek, to guard Fry's right flank. But as the gap had opened up to some 8,000 yards it was clear that this would not do the job. The 14th and the 6th Armored Infantry Battalions were drawn from the CAA in Army reserve and, under General Daniel, committed to the exposed flank. The British, though still five miles to the rear, were attacking Palazzuolo, drawing German artillery fire away from the Blue Devils' right rear. Daniel's armored infantry helped, too. Most important, touch-and-go supply lines that threaded up on the 350th's right edge would now remain open. Supplies were brought up over a single-lane secondary road from Highway 6524 to regimental dumps in the mountain village of Moschetta. From the dumps, all sup- plies were carried by mules or pack boards over a ridge trail for ten miles to troops on Monte della Croce. The 12th Mule Pack Group did yeo- man's work bringing supplies up to the Blue Devils over slippery, mud-sodden trails. Engineers strove to keep open the all-too-few barely usable roads and hacked out new ones wherever possible. Enemy artillery, machine-gun and mortar fire drove off engineers building a bypass over the Santerno River. T/4 Raymond L. Ashe, however, ignored these distractions. Although he could not hear the warning whistle of incoming shells over the roar of his motor, he worked his angle-dozer—hit several times as the construction crew ducked the shells—until the job was done.

Fry wanted to halt his advance to give his men a chance to rest. But Division Headquarters ordered otherwise. Fry studied his map, fretting with good reason. Monte Battaglia was the last major height on the long ridge running northeast from Monte della Croce in the hands of Fry's 350th. A battered stone castle sits on the top of the 2,345-foot pyramid-like peak, the steep slopes of its knife-edged ridges scarred as if some angry giant had gouged the sides with his fingernails. To the 350th's front, in Fry's words, "to the right, and to the left, there was no one but the enemy."[12] To cover terrain that the enemy might exploit as the attack unfolded, Fry directed Major Cheek to take over Puntale with his dismounted 760th Tank Battalion. As soon as his relief arrived, Major Mike was to move his 1st Battalion from Puntale to the vicinity of Battaglia. Major Vincent M. Witter's 3rd Battalion moved through the hills south of Valmaggiore in reserve. The 2nd Battalion, under Lieutenant Colonel Corbett Williamson, had grabbed a day's rest in the crevices of Monte Alto. It was now ready to pass through the 1st Battalion on point to take Battaglia.

On the morning of the 27th, Williamson's men surprised the enemy digging in on Monte Carnevale, the 2,332-foot hump on the approach to Battaglia. In a brief skirmish, twenty prisoners were taken and the rest of the enemy cleared off. Meanwhile, Fry moved his command post on to Carnevale, where he kept in touch with the attacking 2nd Battalion by radio. Though the Germans recognized the importance of Monte Battaglia, they were slow in getting there. Moreover, they may have been inhibited by the presence of 36th Garibaldi Brigade on the mountain, although the partisans, armed only with sten guns and German machine pistols, had not set up an organized defense. Roberto Battaglia, a Communist partisan leader and historian of the Resistance, wrote that when the Germans attempted to dislodge the Garibaldi the night before the Americans arrived, "the patriots . . . hurled grenades at them from the heights, forced them to retreat, and pursued them down the slopes."[13]

The next day, the partisans guided the Blue Devils to the peak, reaching the crest at 1530. There was no opposition and an exultant Williamson broke radio silence: "Hell, Colonel, I can see the Po."[14]

Those who fought in the Northern Apennines and survived will remember how much we longed for the Po. "Cruel mountains," General Alexander called them, and everyone wanted out—an end to endless slogging up steep and pitiless slopes. Once out of the mountains, tanks would be brought into play; a war of motion would succeed that of seemingly interminable "small action" mountain warfare. A breakout of the Apennines into the Po Valley meant, if not the end of the war, at least the beginning of the end. Combat soldiers sensed that the Wehrmacht would fall apart, once driven out into the plains. Until that happened, however, the Germans would fight. And so the first enemy appeared on Monte Battaglia within an hour of the Blue Devils' occupation of the height. "Jerry," as Fry observed, "had not failed to appreciate the importance of this dominating height" though he had "never quite learned to estimate how fast we could move on occasion."[15] G Company Lieutenant Charles Lesnick was amazed when the unsuspecting Germans came on in a double column. They were killed to the last man.

Those unwitting Germans, nevertheless, were only the first wave of attackers. Rain and fog soon enveloped the mountain, nullifying Allied superiority in artillery. On most of the days that followed, air observation planes were grounded and the ground observers were, as in the words of English poet John Milton, "Presented with a universal blank." Colonel Williamson set up his defensive perimeter, and G Company dug in around the ruins of the ancient castle on the summit. Captain Stoner set up his aid station on the bottom floor. At first, the Command Post occupied the third floor, but it was soon moved to the bottom because German artillery pounded down the castle—the Germans having the advantage of being able to fire on fixed points despite the fog and rain. Before E Company on the left and F Company on the right and slightly to the rear in reserve were in position, elements of the German 44th and 715th Grenadier Divisions launched a counterattack in company strength.

G Company fought in the driving rain under the inspired leadership of its commander, Captain Robert C. Roeder, who seemed to be everywhere at once, encouraging his men to stand fast. Every man with a rifle in the battalion's Headquarters Company was sent to defend the left flank, where they remained for three days. At dawn, after a night of shell-fire, G Company was still on the mountain. The Regiment, however, was stretched beyond the breaking point. The 2nd Battalion was under heavy attack and nothing was available for reinforcement. Colonel Fry endured "the torments of the damned" that first night, but finally decided on an additional gamble: he ordered forward Company K of the exhausted 3rd Battalion. Fry joined them. A partisan guided them along a muddy trail in drizzling rain. After an hour or so, Fry became puzzled by the direction taken by the Italian guide. "I have always thought," he said later, "the man deliberately led us into the enemy lines."[16]

Fry called a halt. The company retraced its steps until he ordered it to dig in on the high ground framing a farmhouse in a small horseshoe-shaped valley. In setting up outposts, two men were killed by a German patrol. Their bodies had to be placed in a farm cart to keep them out of reach of two famished hogs.

The windows of the house were covered with blankets and a fire started to warm soldiers as they were relieved of guard duty. Out of contact and out of control of his regiment, Fry was furious at himself for what he called "an inexcusable blunder." Furthemore, no doctor was on hand, although a crack Medical Corpsman, Owen L. Sanderlin, improvised an aid station in the house: a litter on the table, a few bottles of plasma and first-aid packets nearby. When a soldier, hit in the thigh and bleeding profusely, was brought in and placed on the stretcher, Sanderlin deftly cut away the trouser leg and applied a tourniquet. Plasma ready, he inserted the needle but a faulty connection broke. The plasma poured out on the floor. Sanderlin grabbed another plasma container, but it was too late. The medic collapsed across the dead man's legs, sobbing, "The goddamn thing. I could have saved him. I could have saved him."[17] That terrible moment was an all too apt summation of that wasted night.

Morning dawned, the sun appearing long enough to restore warmth and morale. K Company went forward, accompanying a mule train with badly needed supplies. Fry returned to the Regimental CP at Valmaggiore. On the mountain, G Company drove back a dawn counterattack that came within a few yards of the crest. Captain Roeder was wounded by shrapnel and knocked out by a shell burst. He was carried to the company CP, where he regained consciousness. Refusing medical treatment, Roeder dragged himself to the doorway, picked up a dead man's rifle and began firing at the attackers. He shouted orders, encouraging his men. He accounted for at least two Germans before he himself was killed by a mortar burst. For his intrepid leadership, Roeder was awarded the Congressional Medal of Honor.

That afternoon, the Germans shelled Battaglia for three hours, then followed through at 1700 with a four-battalion attack, one coming in from the right flank as the rest headed for the castle and the crest. The enemy carried pole charges and flame throwers to dust off the defenders.

Out on the forward slope, Pfc. Felix B. Mestas ". . . mowed the enemy down like grass" with his BAR. He would be in his lonely post for three days. On the last, he ordered his assistant to leave, then killed 24 Germans before he was overrun and downed. When Staff Sergeant Rocco Cotoia's machine-gun section was cut down to four men, he went a thousand yards to the rear along a trail exposed to enemy fire, rounded up 19 men and brought them up to reform his group. Meanwhile, Lieutenant Edmund B. Maher knocked out a German mortar crew with his rifle, a bazooka and his bayonet. He rallied his platoon as the German attack mounted in intensity; then he dashed to the castle, bayoneting four enemy paratroopers as they reached the doorway. G Company had repulsed the attack but was nearly out of ammunition when K Company arrived with the mule train and much-needed supplies.

Back at his Command Post, Fry learned that the 351st had reached the vicinity of Castel del Rio, securing his right flank sufficiently to warrant committing his entire regiment to Battaglia. The 3rd Battalion was on its way, and the 1st was coming up as fast as the terrain would allow. Major Mike Oreskovitch joined Fry on the morning of the 29th in the command post for instructions. Fry told him that he and a small party would accompany 1st Battalion to Battaglia to set up an advance CP. Major Mike reported that he had about one hundred fighting men left in each company. "We really caught hell on Puntale."[18]

On their way to the next circle of Hell, Fry and Major Mike passed by the dribbling stream of walking wounded and stretcher-bearers with their burdens. Among the wounded was Lieutenant Charles Lesnick, who, tears streaming down his begrimed face, told Fry and Major Mike about Captain Roeder's death. Lesnick did not want to leave the mountain, but the doctors considered the shrapnel in his neck "too dangerous to fool around with."[19] Major Mike put his arm about Lesnick and said something in Polish, an apparent comfort to the wounded soldier.

On the eerie crest—swaddled in dust, smoke from mortar fire and drifting smog—men poked their heads out of their foxholes to greet their commander, whom they soon fondly dubbed "Fearless Fosdick." German and American bodies were strewn everywhere. Men killed on the steep slopes rolled down until caught by some obstacle, grotesque testaments to the nature of war.

While Fry scouted his defenses, the sun came out and an artillery liaison plane flew overhead. Friendly artillery silenced the enemy and suddenly, Fry says, "we felt strangely safe and secure." It was not a feeling that would last, for the enemy had a way of hitting Battaglia with mortar fire and then, when the shelling ceased as suddenly as it started, they would again attack the crest. Fry recalls his first night on Battaglia as "passed in relative quiet," punctuated by the occasional call of the artillery observer at the field telephone—"Fire Becky" or "Fire Daisy" or "Fire Mary," designated reference points for enemy concentrations. Restless, Fry stepped outside the command post and chatted briefly with a sentry posted nearby. He was standing in a foxhole half-full of water with a shelter half over his head. To reassure the soldier, who looked up at the castle on the crest, silhouetted against black clouds, through chattering teeth Fry said, "It is a lot better here than on top of that hill."[20]

Aroused by the sounds of battle at daybreak, Fry rushed out to get a look at the crest. A German flame thrower lit up the sky beyond the castle and the rattle of machine guns and rifles suggested that a full-scale attack was underway. This time, indeed, the Germans made it into the castle. A flame thrower burned the face of Staff Sergeant Lewis R. Hamm. In agony, the feisty Texan killed the German and his assistant. Though his hand took a bullet, Hamm stuck it out long enough to kill three more of the enemy before he was evacuated. Finally, the Germans were driven out of the castle and back downhill.

Fry sprinted across the top of the hill and joined Lieutenant Nicolas Vergot, an artillery observer huddled with his radio operator behind the forward stone wall. A mortar round hit close by, and the radioman dropped the transmitter and sagged across his radio. Expressionless, Vergot, himself wounded in the leg, said, "He's dead," pulling the radio free to call in a concentration of artillery fire. Fry walked back up the hill, met Lieutenant Walter Scott of A Company and told him to relieve exhausted G Company, which was now down to 50 men.

As Fry and Scott scouted the hill to plan the relief, Fry, standing, was surprised by a mortar round and hit in the right arm. On the way back to the aid station, he was asked by an A Company sergeant what he was to do about rifles so clogged with mud that he was afraid they would not fire. Fry told him that ground taken must not be relinquished. "You have undershirts," he told him, unbuttoning his shirt to tear off his own. Wrapping it in a scarf he wore about his neck, he gave it to the sergeant. "Undershirts make good rags," he said. "See that your rifles are cleaned."[21] At the aid station, Colonel Fry told the 2nd Battalion surgeon, Captain Willard Stoner: "The Germans must be worse off than we are. We are certainly killing enough of them."[22]

When the enemy all but overwhelmed the castle on the crest, T/Sgt Ben Mazzarella picked up a handful of grenades and charged the old fortress, tossing grenades. He killed six and wounded more. Out of grenades, he emerged from the fog firing a machine gun to drive off the enemy. Pfc. Jose D. Sandoval fired his BAR until it overheated and jammed. He then ran to a neaby machine gun whose crew had been killed, unhooked the gun from its tripod and fired it from the hip—to the consternation of the attackers. When Pfc. Cleo Peek's gun jammed, he, too, threw grenades; this was nothing unusual, except that when he ran out of grenades he started throwing rocks. Whether the enemy was surprised or stunned, they stopped less than 25 yards from Peek's position.

S/Sgt. Raymond O. Gregory ran out of ammo and grenades on the crest, but then, undaunted, he rolled huge boulders down the steep slope into the enemy ranks. Sergeant Manuel V. Mendoza earned the Distinguished Service Cross when he cut loose with a tommy-gun on two hundred Germans who were following their barrage up the forward slope. Before Mendoza was through, after using another gun and grenades, the surviving enemy withdrew. Then, while leading his platoon to beat the remaining Germans to the crest, after the enemy barrage had lifted, Mendoza spotted a G.I. cowering in a shell hole. "C'mon," he said, "the Jerries are coming." "I can't, I'm just a replacement," said the G.I. Mendoza grimaced. "I know you can't shoot, but come on up and watch me."[23]

Slowly but surely, the enemy attacks waned. Gazing out over six dead German paratroopers killed during the second and last time the Germans actually reached the castle, Fry noticed that their clothing was relatively fresh and clean. He was puzzled at the time, but later learned from captured prisoners that fresh battalions had repeatedly been brought forward from far to the rear, with orders to take Battaglia at all costs. "From the way they performed," Fry concluded, "they must have been drunk or doped."[24] Some twenty enemy attacks were made over the very same ground—poor sods carrying heavy weapons or equipment, all of them doomed. The enemy side of the mountain was clotted with its dead. Neither side could remove them. Those who died at the aid station were laid out in rows outside along the trail that threaded the mountain's ridge. Litter hauls stretched five to fifteen miles. Much of the way was under enemy observation and frequently subjected to fire. To ease evacuation, emergency relay posts were set up at intervals along the track to the rear.

The daily morning counterattack on October 1 was driven back in less than an hour. Clear skies that afternoon enabled the 338th Field Artillery Battalion to fire 3,398 rounds, effectively dampening German shellfire. The capture of Monte Capello by the 351st Infantry two days before, and the arrival of British units on the right, cut off enemy attacks from both flanks. One morning, Fry said, ". . . suddenly it was all over for me."

Brigadier General Rufus Ramey, Assistant Divisional Commander, had called to tell Fry that the British were going to relieve the 350th; an advance party of the Coldstream Guards would be up that afternoon. Colonel Avery Cochran would take over until Fry recovered from his wound. "I had begun to wonder if I was entirely rational at all times," Fry said. His departure from Battaglia remained hazy in his memory. He recalls briefing Cocheran, talking with the British commander, not much else. "As we left, we passed the row of neatly racked up bodies, ready to be tied across the mules' back for their trip to the rear that night." And, once on the trail back, he "note[d] that nearly every rock was marked by blood."[25]

On the night of October 2, the first of the 2nd Battalion's weary men came down from Battaglia. Just before they left, however, they had to fend off yet another enemy counterattack. The 3rd Battalion, still on the mountain, was hit by another German assault. Sergeant Lee H. Beddow of Company L moved quickly to the defense of Regimental Headquarters (then housed in the castle), killing every German who had managed to gain entry with bursts from his sub-machine gun. He then positioned himself in the doorway and fired at attackers seeking to enter the ruins. Beddow held out until grievously wounded and blinded by a shell burst.

Over the next few nights, the British replaced the Blue Devils on

Monte Battaglia—forever known as Battle Mountain to the men of the Regiment. After seven days of continuous action, the 2nd Battalion was off the mountain on the night of October 3–4; the remainder of the Regiment followed the next night. The Regiment suffered 50 percent casualties, and every company commander but one was either killed or wounded. The bulk of the 1,420 casualties that the 350th Infantry suffered during the drive that extended from September 21 to October 3 occurred on Battaglia. Of these, 235 men were killed in action, 277 missing and 908 wounded.[26]

The Blue Devils had held Battle Mountain with grim determination. Yet the Germans would not give up. After the Blue Devils were relieved, the enemy kept on trying to knock off the 1st Guards Brigade. Guardsman George Webb recalled life in the slit trenches of Battaglia, "half-filled with water and lashed by driving rain," as a "virtual hell on earth," with its "incessant shell and mortar fire, day and night, filth, excrement and the stench of unburied corpses of German and American dead." Then came the attack in force, and confusion as the first Germans fell over the tripwire. "For men who for six days or more had been pinned in their slit trenches there was no need to cry, 'Up Guards and at 'em!' " When the fight was over, the Guardsmen had taken nearly one hundred prisoners and the rest of the enemy were dead on the slope. "They did not attack the position again."[27]

Though the Germans never retook Battaglia, they did force Clark to reconsider his two-pronged drive to the Po Valley, simultaneous thrusts along Highway 65 to Bologna and down the Santerno valley to Imola. Clark's tactics worried Field Marshal Kesselring, for the Fifth Army "with a quite remarkable precision . . . managed to find the soft spots at the seam of the Tenth and Fourteenth Armies and to exploit German weaknesses." His Chief of Staff remarked that it was "a miracle" that the Northern spurs of the Apennines were held as they were. "The fighting was very costly," Kesselring concluded, "supplies insufficient and sometimes difficult to bring up, and our resistance for the most part stubborn. Where the attack came up against good divisions the enemy's efforts and losses were all out of proportion to the results."[28]

In front of Battaglia, the Germans had effectively blocked the road to Imola. Elements of the 334th Grenadiers were brought over from the 34th Division front (west of Radicosa Pass on Highway 65), the 44th Grenadier Division from opposite X Corps, elements of the 715th and

305th Grenadier Divisions from before XIII Corps and a regiment of the 98th Grenadier Division from the Adriatic Coast. While these troops could not retake Battaglia, they did block the road to Imola. The "balance of logistics" was now in the enemy's favor, the Fifth Army historian avers.[29] The initiative had been lost; the corridor of the Santerno was unsuitable for a larger force than that of the 88th Division.

The boundary between II Corps and the British XIII Corps side-stepped westward as the axis of the attack northeast towards Imola now swung almost due north. Clark had shifted the emphasis of the II Corps offensive back to Highway 65.

Although the heights were dropping as the Fifth Army pushed on in October towards Bologna and the Po Valley, the terrain remained rugged, a wild place made to the liking of its defenders, where each clump of bushes more often than not could camouflage a sniper or machine-gun nest. Precipitous mountain walls flanked stony river valleys. A constant drizzle soaked hapless G.I.s. Drifting fog grounded artillery liaison planes, though an intermittent sun allowed for effective fire from heavy weapons, artillery, mortars and 50-caliber machine guns. "If the hills ahead of us," Fry has remarked, "had been persistently machine-gunned from the air I am sure that the enemy would have been forced to withdraw faster." Such assistance, however, was rarely available. "In those bitter days," Fry adds, "I have always felt that this lack of coordination, coupled with the leth-argy of the British, prevented the Fifth Army from reaching the valley of the Po, the results of which will never be known, but might well have ended the war."[30]

Fry's opinion of the British was widely shared among Americans. Neither Clark nor McCreery, Commander of the British Eighth Army, quite trusted one another. "I had a continuous problem with him," McCreery said of Clark. "Not that we did not get along well together, but I had to be on my guard the whole time to prevent him from giving orders or mis-interpreting events which would inadvertently undermine Alexander's expressed objectives and overall strategy." Clark believed McCreery "a damn fine General," who, once disagreements were resolved, "never let me down." But the Americans and British had opposing philosophies of combat. As Clark once put it, "We Americans tend to be what I would call 'broad front' men." In crossing a river, Americans preferred to attack all along the line more or less at once, seeking to confuse the enemy about where the big punch would come and allowing that to develop during the battle, then bringing up reserves to exploit any opening. "The British tend to concentrate a jab at one point or two alone [which, incidentally, is what Clark did to punch through the Gothic Line], and then only after a big buildup of preparations beforehand with all the supporting arms and firepower they can muster. This could and did lead to excessive delays." McCreery felt that the "broad front" called for too many risks, too much waste of resources, and above all unnecessary casualties.[31]

Conflicts over opposing philosophies were reinforced, or, so it often seemed, by experience. The British 78th Division now moving up on the Blue Devils' right, taking up positions on Battaglia, had earlier taken over or recaptured positions American troops had failed to hold at Kasserine Pass in Tunisia and at Salerno. British soldiers, too, were amazed, put off by, and perhaps a bit envious of, American prodigality.

A British sergeant who had considerable experience following up behind both American and British troops (he was in an intelligence unit that worked up behind the lines, maintaining radio contact with partisans) told this author that one could always tell the difference between an American and British battlefield. The U.S. ones were dirty, strewn with discarded weapons, ammunition, cigarettes and rations; the British were clean of such debris. Once his unit had a radio go out and dropped into an American supply depot for a needed set of tubes. The supply sergeant told them to chuck their radio on a pile of damaged units, and handed over a brand-new set. "As individuals," another British soldier said, "[Americans] certainly had greater freedom to move about than we had. They were a highly mobile army; all of them could drive and they had access to transport to a degree which would have been impossible for an ordinary soldier in the British Army. They were also very well equipped and it seemed they could lose equipment without a court-martial."[32]

Of course, the British had considerable experience on their side, having centuries worth of practice in military operations. G.I.s often cursed the army for sometimes going strictly "by the numbers," but compared to the British the U.S. Army was lax. Prescribed drill has the advantage of ensuring all possible best reflexes for the widest variety of probable situations. In giving orders, for example, it makes for clarity and lack of ambiguity which, as Brian Harpur puts it, "enable even generals to comprehend what they think they should be doing." Harpur, who served in Italy as a machine-gun officer, witnessed a dramatic confirmation of the different ways Americans and British do things. He had arrived at a battalion CP just as its American commanding officer gave orders to a soldier to take a rock-tipped mountain, Point 508 on the map. He anticipated SOP British-type battle orders: Information (disposition of friendly and enemy troops); Intention (explanation of objective that X unit "will attack"); Method (planning details sufficient to avoid misunderstandings); Administration (arrangements for food, supplies, etc.); Intercommunication (location of headquarters, unit boundaries, and so on); Any Questions?; and Synchronize Watches.

Harpur relates the conversation as follows: "Listen, Joe, I've gotta special assignment for you," the Colonel shouted at his exhausted subordinate while managing to intimate that Joe was the luckiest guy in the world. "How many men ya got?" Joe reckoned that he had "about seventeen." The Colonel pointed to the massive height looming above them, and asked if Joe could take it. "We gotta have that knob, Joe." Joe nodded, "Ah reckon so, Colonel, ah reckon so." The Colonel asked if Joe could go in at 1930 hours and promised artillery support: "I'll . . . give you as easy a ride as I can." Joe turned on his heels, in Harpur's words, "a pathetic but proud silhouette of the eternal soldier." He adds, "I had never heard orders before which so flouted the conventions yet went so quickly to the heart of the matter."

The next morning at dawn, Harpur crawled, under heavy shellfire, over the same ground with the relieving British brigade. Everywhere bodies of men like Joe and the Colonel ". . . lay like grotesque stepping stones" on the way to the knob taken the evening before. Later, Harpur wondered if the British way of doing things would have succeeded with fewer casualties. But he acknowledged that a pause for reinforcements— arranging "a proper set piece"—would have enabled the enemy to reinforce the height, causing even greater carnage. "It is impossible to say," he concluded, "but my instinct tells me that in this instance the Americans were right."[33]

However, some of what Americans thought of as a British reluctance to attack was rooted in the realities of war. Not only was XIII Corps having a hard time of it on the Americans' right flank, but its drive on Faenza, as the Fifth Army historian observed, was overshadowed by the need to assist the thrust to the north. With each mile that II Corps' salient extended into the mountains, more troops were needed to protect the flanks. Even with the addition of the 78th Division, XIII Corps was forced to devote most of its energy to taking over the 88th Division's zone. This was further complicated by the fall rains that bogged down the four-wheeled British trucks much more quickly than American transport. The British 6th Armoured, astride Highway 67, made only minor advances in mid-October. With the 1st Guards Brigade on Battaglia and the 26 Armoured Brigade guarding the exposed flank with X Corps, the offensive strength of the 6th was greatly reduced. General Kirkman of XIII Corps had to draw heavily on units holding his less vital right flank and, as the Fifth Army historian observed, "there was little value gained from expending lives to win minor objectives."[34]

Meanwhile, exhaustion was taking its toll within II Corps. Supplies were brought up by mule, long columns slogging forward up slippery slopes during the dark nights. Each animal carried three heavy boxes of K-rations or similar loads of mortar, rifle or machine-gun ammunition. Mule ears were pierced so that the animals, each led by an Italian mule-teer, would not shy at the sounds of shellfire. On their return, the mules carried back the dead. The seemingly endless movement of the mules lent force to the remark of an officer of the Grenadier Guards to Brian Harpur, "Don't let on, dear boy, but the war will be won by mules, not by men."[35]

Steadfast mules, however, could not make up for the fall-off in the number and quality of replacements for II Corps. All divisions were committed. On October 6, when II Corps was twenty miles from Bologna, Clark sent a message to General Wilson: "Infantry replacement situation is so critical that current operations may be endangered. . . . Losses in my four infantry divisions during the past five days have averaged 550 per day per division over and above returns to units." The supply of replacements were "only sufficient to maintain divisions at authorized strengths through 9th or 10th of October."[36]

Lieutenant George Fumich joined the Blue Devils' 350th Regiment "at a hectic time. There were dead G.I.s and Germans all over the landscape." His platoon had only four experienced men, one a Pfc. After trying to find his squad leaders, Fumich had to appoint the Pfc. his platoon sergeant. Afterward, Colonel Fry told the platoon leader to "infiltrate" his men out to the edge of a valley, where "there won't be any chance of your being surprised during darkness." An hour later, Fry returned to find the lieutenant's body on the ground not ten yards away. The platoon sergeant explained, "Colonel, the Lieutenant was a replacement from Antiaircraft.

I don't think he ever understood what you meant by infiltrating the line forward." Lt. Fumich had walked out from a covered position behind a building, blew his whistle and ordered the platoon to follow; he was then killed by a sniper. The sergeant explained to the men what was wanted and got the platoon forward in short rushes without any losses. It was, as Fry observed, "a forcible and violent indication of the lack of training of the men who were now being sent forward to replace our losses."[37]

It was also an ominous sign of what lay ahead for II Corps in its last push that fall.

NOTES

[1] United States Army, *Fifth Army History*, Vol. VII, pp. 89–90.

[2] Fry, *Combat Soldier*, p. 172.

[3] Ibid., p. 173.

[4] Ibid.

[5] Ibid., p. 175.

[6] Initially, Colonel Fry had claimed the house for his command post; then he changed his mind, telling Colonel Bare to take it as "this shack right in front us . . . will put me between you and Witter [his two lead battalion commanders]."

[7] Fry, at first, gave him the benefit of the doubt. "After all, it was his first command. . . . Against my better judgment, I left him in command . . . [A] week later . . . he deserted his company under fire."

[8] Delaney, *The Blue Devils in Italy*, p. 135.

[9] Fry, *Combat Soldier*, p. 178.

[10] Ibid., p. 180.

[11] Ibid., p. 179.

[12] Ibid.

[13] Battaglia, *The Story of the Italian Resistance*, p. 201.

[14] Fry, *Combat Soldier*, p. 181.

[15] Ibid., p. 181.

[16] Ibid., p. 182.

[17] Ibid., p. 183.

[18] Ibid., p. 184.

[19] Ibid., p. 185.

[20] Ibid., p. 188.

[21] Ibid., p. 191.

[22] Ibid.

[23] Wallace, *Blue Devil "Battle Mountain Regiment,"* pp. 121–22.

[24] Fry, *Combat Soldier*, p. 194.

[25] Ibid., p. 196.

[26] Wallace, *Battle Mountain Regiment,"* pp. 129–30.

[27] Lucas, *Experiences of War*, p. 114.

[28] Kesslering, *Memoirs,* p. 213.
[29] United States Army, *Fifth Army History,* Vol. VII, p. 97.
[30] Fry, *Combat Soldier,* p. 204.
[31] Harpur, *The Impossible Victory* , pp. 107–108.
[32] Lucas, *The British Soldier,* p. 48.
[33] Harpur, *The Impoassible Victory,* pp. 17–19.
[34] United States Army, *Fifth Army History,* Vol, VII , pp. 143 and 146.
[35] Harpur, *The Impossible Victory,* p. 82.
[36] Clark, *Calculated Risk,* p. 396.
[37] Fry, *Combat Soldier,* pp. 206–207.

XVII

ONE MORE RIVER

On the Adriatic, the British Eighth Army had breached the Gothic Line and reached the promised land: the vast delta of the Po River Valley. On September 21, the Greek Brigade entered Rimini and the Canadians crossed the Marecchia. The stream was a little more than ankle deep. Highway 9—the ancient Via Emilia—ran straight from Rimini to Bologna, like an arrow aimed at the heart of the Valley. It formed one leg of a triangle flaring out from its apex at Rimini. The other leg—Route 16—ran northwest along the coast to Ravenna, then inland to Ferrara, well out in the Po Valley. The rivers south of Highway 9 were not considered major obstacles and the two highway flanks of the Ro- magna triangle were on embankments, safe from flooding. There was much optimistic talk of "good tank going" among the New Zealanders moving up from reserve to take over the coastal drive from the Canadians.

And the Italian front was given a boost of sorts when Churchill, Roosevelt and their Combined Chiefs of Staff met at the Second Quebec Conference to coordinate plans for the quick defeat of Germany and the redeployment of forces to the Pacific. The Italian theater ceased to be a source of controversy. It was agreed that no more troops would be taken from Italy to reinforce forces in northwestern Europe until the Germans were defeated south of the Po. An advance on Ljubljana might as well go ahead, since there was no point, post-DRAGOON (the invasion of southern France), in turning northwestward from Italy to France.

The price of breaking out of the mountains into the flat country had been heavy. While the Eighth Army had advanced thirty miles in twenty-six days, it lost 14,000 killed, wounded and missing. In September, 250 tanks had been destroyed and almost as many were bogged down or rendered useless from mechanical failure. Yet, as Alexander said, ". . . no one in the Eighth Army doubted that a real victory had been gained, for it was confidently expected that, after breaking into the flat country of the Romagna, we should be able to exploit rapidly into the Po."[1] The Germans pulled back from the Marecchia in the pouring rain, adding to the general euphoria among the pursuers and feeding rumors of an enemy withdrawal from Italy.

Kesselring had again requested permission to withdraw behind the Po. Hitler, however, held that such a withdrawal would be "too much of a shock for the German people." Moreover, the wartime production of the industrial Po could not be sacrificed, while "the loss of the Po plains would have a most deleterious effect on the food situation, as it would mean that the food supplies for the forces committed in Italy would have to come from Germany."[2] Vietinghoff, Commander of the Tenth Army, ordered his corps and divisional commanders "not to relinquish one foot of soil to the enemy without inflicting heavy casualties. . . . The enemy's reserves are not inexhaustible."[3] To win time, the enemy dug in along the River Uso,[4] the fateful Rubicon of the ancient Romans. But they gave way grudgingly, then turned to hold firm on the line of the Fiumicino, three miles north of the Uso.

Alexander had high hopes for his *corps de chasse*, the 2nd New Zealand Division and its armored cavalry. The New Zealanders, in reserve, were rested, refitted, and retrained. Special attention had been given to river crossings, cooperation with the engineers, the use of assault boats and bridge-laying tanks. Snipers practiced on the rifle range as the troops brushed up on weapons, mine recognition and mine lifting. On September 22, the New Zealanders, assigned to I Canadian Corps, passed through the Canadians on the Marecchia and headed northwest up the coast along Highway 16 towards Ravenna, right leg of the fateful flatland triangle.

Operation CAVALCADE, the code name for the run on to Ravenna, in the words of Lance Corporal L.B. Crews of the New Zealand 21st Battalion, "appeared a piece of cake at the start." Several companies of the 24th and 25th Battalions reported "the rather startling experience" of having an enemy tank pass across to the rear. Around midnight of the 25th, the New Zealanders captured a German private strolling along a hedge of grapevines and occupied a two-story house just off a crossroad. Pickets were posted, then footsteps were heard running across the cobbled yard. "Up to the door rushed a German," Section Commander Corporal J. Wooten later reported, "who immediately had a tommy-gun thrust into his stomach and was invited inside." By dawn, the section had taken some 17 prisoners, including a doctor, in this fashion. The house, it turned out, was a German Company Headquarters.

Along some segments of the New Zealand front the enemy seemed to have been taken by surprise. Close to Highway 16, a New Zealand section captured a German ration truck with hot boxes of rabbit and poultry and a ration of black bread—and the section did not eat bully beef for breakfast that morning. Initially, the Kiwis took quite a few prisoners, 123, mostly Turkomen—"Just like Japs" said Crews—in the mopping up beyond the Marecchia.[5] The Turkoman troops of the German 162nd Division came from Turkestan, east of the Caspian Sea, and were recruited from captured Russian forces. The Canadians had broken their ranks and spirit at San Fortunato. Had they been the main element in the German rearguard, as Douglas Orgill remarks pointedly, the New Zealanders "would have been swinging out towards the Po by evening." But, as Orgill adds, the main body of the enemy were of "a different caliber."

CAVALCADE was scarcely two days old when the Paras, Heidrich's proud 1st Parachute Division, reported: "During the last thirty-six hours the division has beaten off twenty-seven attacks in battalion strength. It is still holding a continuous line. . . ."[6] The 2nd New Zealand Division lost five tanks and more than 50 men on September 24. Two days later, the Staghound armored cars of the Cavalry at last reached the south bank of the Uso, a scarce six miles north of Rimini. It was hardly the exhilarating pursuit earlier envisaged. To their left, the Canadian Armoured Division had lost 350 men since the fall of Rimini. As for the Germans, Heidrich complained that his new reinforcements were "not like his old people." His casualties over the two days dedicated to holding back the New Zealand advance on the Uso—35 killed, 83 wounded and 156 missing— were "at least" twice as heavy as the New Zealanders'.[7]

General Burns of I Canadian Corps wanted to keep the pressure up so that the Germans could not stabilize their front. Canadian tanks crossed the Uso, a narrow, high-banked stream which the Germans did not intend to hold, north of San Vito; the 1st British Armoured crossed the river on Highway 9 near Santarcangelo. The New Zealanders crossed the river overnight and by dawn on the 27th had gained a thousand yards towards the Fiumicino.

That morning, Vietinghoff told Kesselring that "the rear units in the main defense zone will hold."[8] To help do the job, 100 tons of high explosives were on the way for demolition. Meanwhile, bridges, culverts and roadways would be blown by aerial bombs and shells as improvised demolition charges. Having blown culverts, bridges or anything else of transit use, the Germans would surprise troops as they came forward to inspect the damage with mortar or small-arms fire. It was an effective ploy, as two companies of the Greek Brigade discovered on the coast before they were stopped by a German obstacle course: a concrete pillbox, "dragon's teeth," and anti-tank rails and wire from the mouth of the river to the coastal railway. The Greeks came within 700 yards of the Fiumicino at a cost of 23 casualties.

Machine-gun posts in the houses and snipers firing from the tops of haystacks contested the New Zealand advance towards the Fiumicino. Smoke shells from supporting tanks sent the snipers hopping for cover but the machine-gun nests were not so easily displaced. More often than not, the German Paras slipped away to fall back on prearranged positions where ample supplies of ammo were cached. The presence of civilians complicated tank and infantry operations, especially at night when it was difficult to distinguish civilians from the Germans. Any movement drew instant fire. In one house, the New Zealanders had to cope with a hundred hysterical civilians; in another, however, working with two tanks, the infantry captured nine Germans.

Mines were a constant threat. Lance Sergeant Alex Cunningham, 20th Armoured Regiment, was sent by an infantry commander to shoot up a couple of houses near a crossroad. "Like a fathead," Cunningham later said, he decided to cross a plowed field, ran over a box mine "and bang went a track and one bogey. . . . [So] there was nothing for it but for us to bale out and slink back . . ." to the crossroad.[9] A sweep before the attack could be resumed found nearly 30 mines in the field. Mortar and shellfire also exacted a toll among tanks. On one occasion, the enemy's accuracy was explained when an observer was spotted on a power pylon. A Squadron, 20th Armoured Regiment, had four tanks "brewed up" and one knocked out in the five-day approach to the Fiumicino River. One officer and seven men were killed, nine wounded. Five tanks survived the action.

On the night of 27–28 September, a company of the Canadian Irish Brigade waded the Fiumicino but was surprised by a superior force of German infantry and tanks. Nine men were killed and fifty taken prisoner, the consequence of sending a company to tackle a battalion objective.

The advantage of the crossing was lost as the Canadians and the New Zealanders fought all the way up to the Fiumicino.

Then, as the Germans had counted on, the weather broke. As one New Zealander put it, a stream "you could wade across in gumboots . . . [became] capable of drowning a tall man."[10] It came out of the Yugoslavian mountains, crossing the Adriatic—a 40-mile-an-hour gale and torrential rain that turned plowed fields into gumbo in which men sank to their boottops and wheels to their axles, that swelled countless irrigation ditches and steep-sided canals into full-fledged rivers and turned roads greasy. There were floods from the south of Cesenatico north to Ravenna. Slit trenches filled with water as they were dug. Tanks mired down in muck. Artillery gunpits were knee-deep in water. Telephones failed. New Zealand and Canadian attacks across the river scheduled that night were canceled.

The rains intensified, and rarely stopped as October opened. Transport of supplies and reinforcements became exceedingly difficult in what Alexander called "the richest mud known to the Italian theatre." Bridges were washed away. The ankle-deep Marecchia was now a raging torrent twelve feet deep. Every ford over that river and the Uso was well-nigh impassable. The Fiumicino was a raging torrent thirty to forty feet wide. "Water was now the main obstacle," Alexander later remarked.[11] The promised land became a nightmare.

On October 1, as the rains fell, Lieutenant General Sir Richard L. McCreery replaced General Leese as Commander of the Eighth Army. (Leese was appointed Commander-in-Chief of the Allied Land Forces in South-East Asia.) Educated at Eton and Sandhurst, McCreery served in France during World War I with the 12th Lancers. His regiment was among the first to be mechanized, so a crack cavalry officer became a top-notch tank commander. He was at Dunkirk, served as Alexander's Chief of Staff in North Africa and as commander of the British X Corps in Italy. Alexander considered him "a scientific soldier with a gift for the offensive." McCreery, Harold Macmillan remarked in his diary, "is the most charming man—and a very clever one in addition. He has always struck me as one of the ablest of the military officers whom I have seen out here."[12]

McCreery would need his considerable gift for the offensive in the months to come. Not only were the rains falling on Kesselring's side—but the wily German managed to come up with reinforcements for de-

pleted divisions, and the line of the Fiumicino, above the Uso, was fortified. Meanwhile, south of Route 9 in the Apennine foothills, the battered
278th Division was reinforced by the Austrian defenders of Gemmano,
the 100th Mountain Regiment; across the highway, the 20th Luftwaffe
Field Division, with the 1st Parachute Division and the 114th Jaeger Division, was ranged towards the coast; while the 90th Grenadier
Division, to the rear, was set to cover Route 9. Kesselring, too, was prepared to take advantage of the natural fall-back lines provided by the nine
rivers—the Fiumcino, Savio, Ronco, Montone, Lamone, Senio, Santerno, Sillaro and Indice—between Bologna and the Italian east coast that
ran out of the Apennines northeastward across the plain into the River
Reno or into the Adriatic between Rimini and Lake Comacchio. These
streams ran in dredged and embanked channels with banks rising up to
forty feet to form effective defensive barriers. The precipitous spurs of the
Apennines that flanked Highway 9 to the south—still in German
hands—afforded the enemy good observation over the highway and the
surrounding country.

Eighth Army plans called for a three-corps attack across the broadening Romagna plain with the Polish Corps on the coast—relieving the
New Zealanders, the Canadian Corps in the center and V Corps on the
left along the edge of the Apennines. Taking stock, McCreery decided to
cancel the Polish Corps' relief of the New Zealanders. The Poles instead
would shift into X Corps' sector, where, it was thought, they could outflank the Germans on the axis of Highway 71, which followed the west
bank of the Savio out of the mountains to Cesena, some ten miles up
Highway 9 from Savignano where it crossed the Fiumicino.

The Poles, who experienced considerable transportation difficulties,
were not in position, however, in time to carry out that task. Plans for
forcing the Fumicino were postponed from day to day as the weather
worsened. In the foothills south of Highway 9, the 10th Indian Division
relieved the exhausted 4th Indian Division, which had been fighting continuously in rugged country since August 25. Though rain and mud-soup
roads hampered the forward movement of the Indians, it was soon apparent that the terrain, rugged as it was, offered opportunities unavailable in
the sodden plain.

The 10th Indian Division had been trained to fight in rugged terrain
and its hill-fighting qualities had been tested in the mountains glowering
over the Upper Tiber and Arno Rivers. The countryside that edged the Po

Valley, says the Tenth's historian, "lacked the substance of the Tiber land-scape." Its hills were "little more" than bare, razor-back ridges slashed by precipitous ravines.[13] It was also more heavily populated, with sturdy farmhouses and villages providing ready-made pillboxes. Each village had a high-towered church overlooking the countryside—a boon for artillery forward observers. Thick, high-walled village cemeteries were nodal points for the German defenders.

The 10th Indians were in place on October 3, holding a line from Borghi, a village perched on the edge of the Fiumicino Valley, south to Montebello Ridge, just north of the Marecchia. Near Borghi, the Indians killed two German scouts on patrol in civilian clothes and established the presence of the 114th Jaeger Division, old opponents from the Tiber basin, along the Fiumicino. On the morning of October 5, the Indians mounted a two-brigade attack: one, striking from Montebello for So-gliano, a hilltown on the edge of the upper valley; the other, south from Borghi to San Martino. The attack was a squeeze play to set up an attack along the foothills parallel to Highway 9. The King's Own moved out under artificial moonlight; the lead company entered San Martino but was thrown back by a counterattack surging out of the darkness, losing 50 men. But the support company held its ground during the day until a troop of North Irish Horse tanks arrived to turn the tide of battle. By 2100, San Martino was in their hands.

The 2nd/3rd Gurkhas, with North Irish Horse tanks in support, made their way towards Sogliano with little difficulty, excep for a stub-born clash at a crucial crossroad. Meanwhile, the Punjabs' attack on neighboring Strigara to the south was frustrated by its German defenders. The Punjabs then turned north, occupied Sogliano, and exploited a northwest road that descends seven hundred feet with seventeen hairpin curves in less than a mile. By doing so, the Punjabs secured intact two bridges across the swollen Fiumicino. The Germans in Strigara fended off the Punjabs, who attacked in thick fog and pouring rain the next day. After dark, the Punjabs, reinforced by two companies of 4th/10th Baluchis, captured Strigara after a ninety-minute fight. In two days, the Indians had cleared the Fiumicino line on a five-mile front. The axis of attack now turned northwest towards Monte Farneto, a key position for the German defense of Cesena.

Farneto rises 1,600 feet above the plain; its slopes are a maze of deep-cut watercourses. Some 2,000 yards to the west a 1,300-foot buttress,

Montecodruzzo, marks the start of a long ridge dotted by hamlets that curves to the north and dribbles into a series of hillocks along the Savio as it runs towards Highway 9. Ridges with steep-pitched slopes and ragged ravines seemingly run amok among lesser crests north of Farneto—Monte Spaccato, Monte Leone, Monte Reale—with the last, Aquarola, looking down several hundred feet upon Cesena. "A mountaineer's battlefield," says the 10th's Indian historian, with cause.[14] Two German divisions held the battlefield. Lady Luck favored the Indians as they closed on Monte Farneto after a long night's march. The weather was awesome, lulling the enemy, who must have decided that no one would attack in the pelting rain and impenetrable dark. In the event, the Germans failed to man their forward positions, and two battalions—the 2nd/3rd Gurkhas and the 3rd/5th Mahrattas—seized Farneto with few losses. At dawn, October 7, North Irish Horse tanks arrived, an hour behind the infantry.

The enemy was slow to respond, mounting a battalion-strength counterattack at noon. By then, the German troops had orders to retake Farneto or perish in the attempt. The Indians rebuffed the first counterattack with the aid of effective artillery fire. Fighter-bombers joined in breaking up the second German attempt. In the evening, Northumberland Fusilier machine-gunners backed the infantry to drive off the enemy. And so it went, all night and the next day.

A mortar barrage destroyed a forward section of Mahrattas. Another went under as the Germans swept over them, but emerged under Lance Corporal Naik Keshav to clear out the Germans with grenades and bayonet. That evening, the Indians resumed the offensive. The 3rd/18th Garhwalis cleared a ridge running north of Farneto, killing 38 and taking 14 prisoners at a cost of fewer than a dozen casualties. The 2nd/4th Gurkhas fought house by house in San Paolo, a road-junction hamlet flanking Roncofreddo, a key German position. Fierce fighting flared up among the tombstones of the village cemetery as the Germans infiltrated replacements into San Paolo. Daylight brought a series of quick and deadly clashes that forced the enemy to withdraw the following night.

On October 7, as the Indians battled Germans in the Apennine foothills, McCreery decided to concentrate his forces there and abreast Highway 9. The Canadian Corps was ordered to extend its front a thousand yards to the south of Highway 9 to relieve the 56th Division, whose two brigades aimed at Cesana were in bad shape and had to be withdrawn. The Canadian infantry division was to thrust towards Cesena with the 2nd New Zealand Division on its right flank. The Canadian Armoured Division was assigned to a watching brief on the sodden coastal plain. The Indians and the 46th Division were to continue the attack along the raking ridges, outflanking the Germans who were defending river lines astride Highway 9. As they crossed the ravines and upper waters of the "mountaineers' battlefield," turning the river lines in the foothills, the Germans would be forced to withdraw before the pressure of the Canadians and New Zealanders in the Romagna.

"No rest was vouchsafed the enemy," the 10th Indian Division historian wrote later. The Punjabis swept through Roncofreddo on the night of 9–10 October. The Durhams of the 10th Brigade passed through the Gurkhas holding San Paolo to tackle the next ridge to the north, Monte Spaccato. Under the cover of a heavy ground mist, the North Country Durhams filtered through the German lines to the surprise of enemy soldiers going about their morning chores. In the hand-to-hand fighting that followed, all the company officers became casualties, but the Durhams forced the Germans back. On the left flank, however, the 4th/10th Baluchis, en route to Montecodruzzo, encountered heavy going along slopes slashed by innumerable ravines. On October 11, the 43rd Brigade was committed to the attack. One company of the 2nd/6th Gurkhas clambered up the greasy, rain-soaked hillside, killing three enemy sentries and capturing six others without alarming the enemy, and then seized the hamlet.

The 2nd/10th Gurkhas, after an arduous march, passed through Montecodruzzo hamlet the afternoon of the 12th, towards Monte del Erta. Again the German outposts were caught sleeping. Fifteen prisoners were taken. The Montecodruzzo feature ran at right angles to the 10th Division's main line of advance. If held, it would have been a serious threat on the division's flank.

By now Allied commanders were becoming curious. Were the sleeping Germans merely exhausted infantrymen, simply careless, or did they reflect a growing malaise among German troops in Italy? Or, was there a consensus among German commanders that losses in the Romagna would be more than offset by gains in strength from a shortened front before Bologna? A shortened line is far easier to defend than a long, exposed front. Supplies and shifting troops would move shorter distances more quickly. The attackers' supplies, reinforcements and replacements would have longer distances to cover coming up to the front. Although the Germans subsequently fought tenaciously, contesting each house along the Montecodruzzo Ridge until the Gurkhas secured Del Erta, the failure of outposts to alert the defenders on Farneto, Montecodruzzo and Del Erta surely helped to speed the 10th Indians' attack on the flank of Highway 9 at a critical point. The 2nd/6th Battalion was now free to leapfrog the 2nd/10th in an attack on Monte Chicco, the last high knoll above the Savio as it roiled north to Cesena.

To set the stage for the attack on Monte Cicco, the Durhams crossed the Soara Valley to the east on October 12 to take the next ridge to the north after a sharp fight in which 23 prisoners were taken. On the left spur of Monte Chicco, the 2nd/4th Gurkhas went up against Monte Bora. Major Scott's company was caught in the open by enemy tanks and the major was wounded but remained with his men. At dawn the next morning, the Gurkhas rushed Bora, Major Scott's company going against the center of the German defenses—a thick-walled farmhouse with outbuildings. The company was pinned down, but Major Scott picked up a bren gun from a dead man and raced in, firing as he ran. Though struck again, he was on his feet at the head of the Gurkhas when he fell, within ten yards of the enemy. The German garrison was indeed wiped out, but an enemy "shoot"—concentrated artillery fire—compelled a withdrawal until others moved up to take the position.

Now the attack on Monte Cicco could go forward with 2nd/6th Gurkhas' flanks protected by the gains scored the day before. Though the Germans were swept from the crown of the hill early in the morning of the 13th, they rallied, infiltrated along the slopes, and the struggle for control continued all day long. The weather had cleared and fighter-bombers dived on enemy mortar positions. The artillery laid down a box barrage that protected the immediate flanks and front of the beleaguered hillmen. As night fell, heavy fire from German machine guns and mortars presaged another counterattack but turned out to be a deception. The Germans withdrew and, by dawn, as the 10ths' historian puts it, "the Gurkhas walked freely along the high ground above the deep valley of the Savio."[15]

The 4th/10th Baluchis and the 3rd/1st Punjabis cleared the ridges and hilltops to the north. The Baluchis cleared Monte Reale and could see the spires and turrets of Cesena. The Punjabis passed through to take

Aquarola, a mile closer to the city. On a lower ridge, in San Demetrio, the Germans held out for fourteen hours as the battle waxed and waned around the church and town square. A German tank shelled Punjabis at point-blank range but the Grenadiers could not dislodge the Indians, and withdrew the morning of the 17th. Meanwhile, Central India Horse explored the upper Savio for fords. On October 20, three regiments of the 20th Brigade crossed the Savio at Cella, south of Montecodruzzo, and moved towards Monte Cavallo, the first of the fortified German positions west of the Savio. Other units crossed downriver within five miles of Cesena. By the following evening, the Division was posed to attack Cavallo and Tessello, two miles to the north.

Once across the Savio, squelching through the mud in the dark of October 21, the 10th Division infantry was almost clobbered by the enemy. The King's Own and the Garhwalis were thrown back in the hills above San Carlo on the way to Tessello. At one point, the Garhwalis ran out of ammunition. Section leader Naik Trilok Singh told his men to sit tight; he would see what he could do. Naik crept forward, stalked a German machine-gun crew as they crept into position, killed them in hand-to-hand fighting and brought back the gun with its ammunition in time to drive off the next counterattack. He was killed later covering the withdrawal of his section.

On the evening of the 22nd, the 20th Brigade mounted a set-piece attack. A general assault followed a heavy barrage—10,000 shells on enemy positions defending Cavallo. The 2nd/3rd Gurkhas crept forward, then rushed the slopes of the mountain. The 3rd/5th Mahrattas then passed through to close up on the crest in bitter and confused combat, the Mahrattas holding their fire until counterattacking Germans were silhouetted on the skyline. Monte Cavallo was theirs at first light on October 23. The Indians began mop-up operations along the high ground west of the Savio. Cesena had been well and truly flanked.

The Germans yielded ground along Highway 9, folding back as each line was turned on the upper river by the Indians and the British 46th Division. Still, German rearguards forced the attackers to pay a stiff price for their gains. On October 10, the day after the Indians secured Monte Spaccato north of Farneto and the day the 46th Division captured Longiano, the Germans fell back four to five miles from Savignano to the Scolo Rigossa canal. The Canadians abreast Highway 9 and the New

Zealanders on their right followed up with sensible caution. Some of the Canadians coming up to the front, Farley Mowat reports, sang a sardonic song to the tune of "Lili Marlene": "We shall 'debouch' into the Valley of the Po,/Jump off from the Gothic Line and smash the cringing foe,/ . . . /And this we know/Cause Corps says so!" The Hastings Prince Edward Regiment's 1st Battalion spearheaded the attack of the First Canadian Division: A Company north of Highway 9; B Company in the center; D Company left of the highway.

The Battalion crossed the Fiumicino on October 11 and went forward with little resistance, except a strongpoint at a blown culvert, which cost the Germans four prisoners and as many killed before they were driven off. Beyond the blown culvert, massive concrete tank obstacles well protected by mines and booby traps stopped a squadron of Lord Strathcona tanks. The infantry went ahead. By dusk, the Battalion had developed a salient a mile deep and a mile wide. One battalion was now ahead of the troops in the foothills to the south and the New Zealanders out on the plain to their left. As they came within a few hundred yards of the Rigossa, the Germans had the Canadians under observation from the hills to the south and the fortified town of Gambettola, north of Highway 9. The fall of shells and mortar rounds that drove the Canadians to cover testified to the keenness of their observers.

Major Cameron, the battalion commander, decided, despite the intensity of artillery fire, that his men had the advantage even though supporting tanks were still held up in the rear behind the blown culvert. Hot food and drink was brought up as plans were made for crossing the canal. At 0900, October 12, the Canadians attacked. On the right, D Company tackled enemy-held houses along a lateral road, one by one. It took most of the morning to do the job, but, when it was finished, D Company had taken four enemy strongpoints and twenty-three prisoners. On the left, A Company silenced two German posts on the back of the Rigossa, then waded the canal to establish a small beachhead. B Company, at the Rigossa, bided its time—tanks were essential to further progress. Under heavy artillery fire, the engineers built diversions at the culvert and demolished the roadblocks. The tanks closed up on the Rigossa by dawn on October 15.

Again, the tanks halted. To open up room for a crossing, Cameron called up his reserve company. At 0500, C Company crossed the canal to the right of Highway 9 and drove ahead almost a thousand yards before it was halted by intense fire from a straggle of houses to the north, named Bulgaria. These rose above the surrounding olive groves and were strongly fortified with at least one machine gun to a house. Bulgaria controlled German supply routes to Gambettola, a fair-sized town across the railroad embankment to the east and the enemy's central strongpoint on the line of the Rigossa. Cameron realized that the battalion was vulnerable to a counterattack where the base of the salient brushed up against the rail embankment; he needed to keep the enemy on the defensive until the tanks were across the canal. Luckily, the weather was favorable, and a squadron of fighter-bombers was available to strafe and rocket-bomb enemy positions. The Germans countered with a rolling barrage but remained on the defensive.

Before dawn on October 14, the Rigossa crossing prepared for the tanks by the engineers collapsed. Undismayed, Lord Strathcona's Horse eased their tanks across a partially demolished bridge. The first phase of the attack got underway in good time—B Company and supporting tanks were along the highway to clear a crossroads hamlet by 1100. Taking a half-hour "break," the tankers replenished their ammunition and joined C Company for the main attack on Bulgaria. Tanks and infantry, says historian Farley Mowat, "moved and fought almost as one unit."[16] For seven hours, in a deadly duo, the tankers protected the infantry with covering fire and the foot soldiers protected the tanks from the German killer Faustpatronen. Tankers fired armor-piercing shells through thick-walled houses, followed by high explosive shells that sent surviving defenders dashing to their dugouts. When the infantry crawled the last few yards to reach the enemy, the tanks provided the final bursts of covering fire.

It was murderous. Huron Brant, a Mohawk who had won the Military Medal in Sicily, was killed with his six-man section when caught by machine-gun fire ripping along a narrow ditch. Bulgaria was secured by 1630 hours; fifty-five Germans were taken prisoner and a larger number killed. Of eighty foot-sloggers and two troops of tanks, no tanks were lost and C Company suffered less than thirty casualties. An hour later, five Panther tanks with supporting infantry moved against C Company from Gambettola, but the attack faltered when a Sherman—a good deal lighter than the monster Panthers—destroyed the lead German tank from an ambush. The remaining Panthers left the field; the Germans withdrew from the town that night. C Company patrols went forward a good mile before finding German rearguards. B Company moved a half-mile up Highway 9 towards Cesena the next morning, where tanks and supporting artillery drove off a threatened counterattack. The Battalion was then relieved by the Royal Canadian Regiment.

Meanwhile, the New Zealanders engaged the Germans at San Angelo in Salute. The New Zealanders had crossed the Fiumicino, taken Gatteo and moved beyond to the Rigossa on the Canadian right. It was hoped the enemy would withdraw from San Angelo because they were bypassed by advances on October 12 towards Gambettola and the Rigossa (on the New Zealand right flank). But the Germans chose to remain. The hamlet on the Rio Baldona, a small stream running parallel to the Rigossa some five hundred yards distant, commanded a network of roads and was an effective strongpoint from which the Germans could harass attempts to cross the Rigossa Canal as well as cover withdrawals. At 1430 on the 13th—a Friday, the superstitious remarked—a company of Maoris went in to dislodge the Germans but were badly knocked about. At 1700, the Maoris, reinforced by a platoon, resumed the offensive. Under machine-gun and mortar fire, they gained a house at the edge of the hamlet but were then forced back 500 yards.

It was a so-so day for the New Zealanders in this sector. The Maoris took five prisoners, lost one man killed, had seven wounded and two missing. The 23rd Battalion sent a platoon backed by two tanks to the Rigossa. One tank was knocked out on the road, the other bogged down; the platoon withdrew, two men killed, five wounded. A patrol then sent to take a bridge over the Rigossa at Gambettola was caught by machine-gun fire; its leader was killed and three men were wounded and captured.

A restless night under mortar fire and Nebelwerfer concentrations was followed by a day of savage artillery exchanges. Improved weather, however, gave an edge to the New Zealanders. "Rover Paddy" called in effective air strikes against the Germans. One silenced two out of three 88s, much to the relief of the Kiwis. Otherwise there was little activity on the 14th, except that the success of the Canadians at Bulgaria relieved some of the pressure on the New Zealand Division.

That night, two Maori companies with a good deal more artillery support attacked San Angelo under "artificial moonlight," taking the town at a cost of one man killed and eight wounded. The Maoris then went into reserve. Engineers immediately started work on a bridge over the Baldona at San Angelo, and before noon the next day the tanks were across. Gambettola was cleared early in the morning, and a bridge over the Rigossa soon in place enabled tanks to go forward.

Indian and 46th Division successes in the Apennine foothills began to pay off as the New Zealanders and the Canadians resumed their advance. Intelligence intercepted a German radio message: the enemy was going to pull back to the line of the Pisciatello, a narrow stream some two and a half miles distant from Gambettola/San Angelo. Typically, Vietinghoff had authorized a fighting withdrawal. On the afternoon of the 15th, two 21st Battalion companies with a squadron of tanks moved along a road running northeast out of Gambettola. Before long, they were stopped by machine-gun and mortar fire from a group of houses to the north. One tank was set afire by a bazooka. The forward companies called it a day after gains of up to a thousand yards.

A quiet night and up and away at first light, the Canadians and the New Zealanders made slow but sure progress. The ground dried under the intermittent sun. Advancing vehicles churned up rolling yellowish-white clouds that limned roads for miles behind the lines. German outposts, however, prevented the New Zealanders from reaching the Pisciatello the evening of the 16th, as they had expected. During the day 21st and 23rd Battalions had taken over 70 prisoners at a cost of two men killed and ten wounded.

To the New Zealand left, the Canadians were up to the Pisciatello between its junction with the Rio Matalardo and Ponte della Pietra. Germans forming up for a counterattack in Ruffio's one street were caught by surprise on the morning of the 17th. A sapper saved a bridge north of the town from demolition by withdrawing an already burning fuse. The Germans reacted to the advance with shell, mortar and small-arms fire. Friendly aircraft now took advantage of the weather to engage machine-guns, mortar posts and occupied houses. The artillery, too, fired on similar targets. But the Germans drove back a patrol at a possible Pisciatello crossing. The Royal Canadian Dragoons to the south were forced back, but, reinforced, regained their position. Fifty enemy paras tried to dislodge two New Zealand platoons in a house close to the river but were dispersed at last by tanks and another infantry unit. Eight Germans were killed; many were wounded and six captured. Seven New Zealanders were wounded.

By the close of the 18th, the New Zealanders were ready to cross the Pisciatello. The Canadians had a bridgehead over the river by the railway crossing just north of Highway 9 and another over the Donegaglia, a tributary south of the highway. At 1100, three New Zealand and two Canadian field regiments laid down a creeping barrage, lifting 100 yards every five minutes for two hours. Though the enemy was withdrawing, the 26 Panzer Regiment was caught by the bombardment "and casualties were very heavy."[17] By eleven o'clock in the morning, two New Zealand battalions—the 24th and 25th—held an expanding bridgehead nearly a mile deep. They captured fifty prisoners at a cost of forty-four casualties, mostly from mines and shellfire. Two tank regiments were also crossed despite soft ground and collapsing, hastily built bridges.

The Pisciatello had been well and truly crossed. Beyond the Pisciatello, the land looked especially attractive for tanks. The road from Cesena to Cervia on the coastline, with tall trees and house clusters at its many crossroads, could be seen across the flat farmland crisscrossed with narrow lanes. On the morning of the 19th, the 18th and 20th Regiments of the 4th Armoured Brigade formed up within the bridgehead for "a swift advance at tank speed"—a right hook over five miles on a front of 2,000 yards aimed at the line of the Savio River. Success would cut roads north out of Cesena to the coast. In conjunction with a Canadian attack along Highway 9, it would also bring about the fall of Cesena. Each regiment was to be protected from enemy infantry by a company of the 22nd Battalion. The Divisional motorized cavalry would ride the right flank.

Brigadier Pleasants gave the order to go at 0950. The "Gambettola-Savio gallop" started out well, but it was soon dogged by German resistance and field conditions. Tanks "bellied in the mud . . . [and] some of them were running out of ammunition at awkward moments."[18] A self-propelled gun firing from a building at a crossroads caught three tanks in the open and set them on fire. Paras with bazookas fired up another that was stuck in the mud. Altogether, on the first day, fifteen tanks were "bogged" and seven knocked out. Still, the tanks shot up machine-gun and bazooka posts in ditches and farmyards to sufficient effect that the advance of nearly three miles was considered promising.

On the New Zealanders' left flank, Princess Patricia's Light Infantry crossed the Pisciatello at Ponte della Pietra and headed for the Cesana–Cervia road, while two other battalions worked along the railway and Highway 9 towards the city. By evening, the Germans withdrew from Cesena, which was then occupied by the Canadians from the east and the

46th British Division from the south. On the New Zealand right flank, Cumberland Force pushed through the mud from the Rigossa–Fiumicino to the Pisciatello. On the coast, the Germans still held out at the mouth of the Fiumicino.

The initial New Zealand penetration went according to plan. During the night, the 26th Panzers withdrew to the Savio, covering the withdrawal with shell and mortar fire and demolitions. The next morning, the armored regiments swung west towards the Savio, making slow progress. "Jerry had made a horrible mess of the roads, with mines and huge craters,"[19] it was noted. Engineers were busy extricating tanks from mucked up roadsides and fields. A mile was gained that morning, then a wait until the engineers bridged the Rio Granarolo.

Coming up to the Savio, two squadrons came under fire from German rearguards. They enjoyed, it was reported, "some good shooting" and took twenty prisoners while most of the enemy "just melted away."[20] By evening, the lead tanks were short of the Savio and, before the sun set, tankers were firing on enemy strongpoints across the river. Divisional cavalry roamed at will on the right flank but found the countryside not quite what was expected for the armored cars. As R. Pinney put it in his diary, "How different proved the reality. We hacked down trees to fill ditches. Axle deep we just got up the very slight inclines beyond, and ahead was another ditch to cross. . . . The lanes were very muddy, and with a wheel touching a ditch on either side it was a strenuous day."[21]

And so it was. But the New Zealand advance was achieved without the loss of a single tank. On the coast, where the Greek Brigade had been withdrawn to return home, the Governor General's Horse crossed the Fiumicino and occupied the seaside resort Cesenatico, three miles up the road. Inland, the 27th Lancers and 8th Royal Canadian Dragoons were on their way to the Cesena–Cervia road, which the Dragoons crossed later in the day. The New Zealanders closed the gap on the left flank and closed on the Savio as two companies of the Princess Patricia's Canadian Light Infantry attacked across the river about a mile south of Cesena. The Canadians were greeted by "a hail of mortar bombs and machine-gun bullets."[22] Only one and a half platoons of one company made it across, but they had to withdraw after dark. Seventeen men from the other company managed, with the help of a dozen stragglers, to cling to a narrow strip on the far bank all the next day.

October 21 was a clean-up day for the New Zealanders, who dealt with German pockets bypassed during the armored advance. That night New Zealand machine-gunners, mortar squads, tanks and artillery fired all along their four-and-a-half-mile front. Seventy-one tanks fired some 9,000 rounds in 75 minutes; field artillery fired more than 13,000 rounds of high explosives. All this was a deception in aid of a Canadian assault across the Savio south of Cesena. The leading Canadian troops were across within an hour, and shortly after midnight the reserve of the two assaulting battalions of the 2nd Canadian Infantry Brigade were also over the river. A company of Seaforth Highlanders, without supporting tanks, rebuffed a counterattack knocking out two Panthers, a half-track, a scout car and two self-propelled guns. They also captured another Panther bogged in a ditch. By mid-morning, the Canadians had a bridgehead nearly a mile wide.

During the night of October 22–23, the New Zealanders occupied Pisignano, Borga Pipa and La Rosetta, across the Savio. After seven weeks with the 1st Canadian Corps, the New Zealand Division was relieved by the Canadian 5th Armoured Division and withdrew into Eighth Army reserve. The Division suffered 1,108 casualties: 228 killed, 857 wounded and 23 captured. In addition, there were 1,079 cases of infective hepatitis or jaundice. Historian Robin L. Kay summed up the month that followed the crossing of the Marecchia River as one of "wastage and fatigue," in which the Division "had penetrated less than 20 miles in the southeast corner of the great plains of the Po Valley."[23]

Seven rivers and fifty miles remained to Bologna—and seemingly endless bad weather. Surely, however, as the days stretched out many a weary combat soldier would agree with the nameless British infantryman who said: "It weren't rain or bloody mountains held up advance. It were bloody Jerry sitting down behind Spandaus going blurp-blurp."[24] On October 24, the Germans withdrew from the Savio to the Ronco.

NOTES

[1] Orgill, *The Gothic Line*, p. 189.
[2] Kay, *Italy: From Cassino to Trieste*, p. 227.
[3] Ibid.
[4] There is some dispute about the Rubicon. The classicists among the Eighth Army believe Caesar crossed what is now the Uso. Present-day Italian maps label the Fiumicino *F. Rubicone.*
[5] Orgill, *The Gothic Line*, p. 189.

6 Puttick, *25 Battalion,* p. 496.

7 Kay, *Italy: From Cassino to Trieste,* p. 243.

8 Ibid., p. 246.

9 Pringle, *20 Battalion and Armoured Regiment,* p. 503.

10 Llewellyn, *Journey Towards Christmas,* p. 375.

11 Orgill, *The Gothic Line,* p. 161.

12 Macmillan, *War Diaries,* p. 739.

13 India, *Tiger Triumphs,* p. 142.

14 Ibid., p. 144.

15 Ibid., p. 147.

16 Mowat, *The Regiment,* p. 242.

17 Kay, *Italy: Cassino to Trieste,* p. 271.

18 Ibid., p. 273.

19 Ibid., p. 274.

20 Ibid., p. 275.

21 Ibid.

22 Ibid., p. 276.

23 Ibid., p. 279.

24 Llewellyn, *Journey Towards Christmas,* p. 373.

XVIII

JUST ANOTHER MILE

On October 3, General Mark Clark flew north to a field near San Piero a Sieve and drove up along Highway 65 through Futa Pass to Monghidoro, captured the day before by the 91st Division. From a height of some 2,750 feet, he saw the Po Valley for the first time. Bologna, across the mountains, was 25 miles away. "It seemed to me then that our goal was very close."[1]

If Clark sounds wistful, he had cause, because the Fifth Army was feeling the strains of extended combat. Three days later, Clark notified General "Jumbo" Wilson, commander-in-chief in the Mediterranean: "Supply of infantry replacements and infantry over strength in divisions only sufficient to maintain divisions at authorized strength through 9th or 10th of October. Losses in my four infantry divisions during past five days have averaged 550 per day per division over and above returns to units. . . . All divisions have been in heavy fighting twenty-three to twenty-six days under adverse weather conditions."[2]

One sign of exhaustion among the troops was the increase in psychiatric disorders. Non-battle casualties—respiratory diseases, trench foot and psychiatric disorders—exacted a toll almost as great as that from enemy fire. (Battle casualties for the four divisions totaled 1,734 for the first four days in October.[3]) Each division was ordered to hold out one regiment for rest and reserve, rotating the regiments in line approximately every five days—which helped to ease the situation somewhat. But it also limited the strength that could be committed in any given attack. The lack of significant progress on the Eighth Army front, where artillery rounds now had to be rationed—25 rounds per gun per day for field artillery, as against 65—enabled Kesselring to move the German 29th Division from the Adriatic front to that of the Fifth Army in mid-October. By then, the Germans had some seventy-two battalions opposing the

Fifth Army.

It was difficult, Clark said after the war, ". . . to explain the agonizing hope we then felt that 'just another mile' or 'just a few miles' would do the job." Every day, Clark said, they told themselves, "Now if we can just push on a little farther today, then we'll make it [into the Po]. We are right at the edge of success."[4]

The signs were encouraging after II Corps' breakthroughs at the Il Giogo and Futa passes on October 22. Two days later, though hampered by enemy shellfire and mud brought on by heavy rains, the 85th, 91st and 34th Divisions were in position for attacks on the three mountains protecting Radicosa Pass, some twelve miles north of the Futa Pass, on Highway 65. The 85th was to take 3,798-foot Mount Canda, east of the pass; the 91st, 4,231-foot Mount Poggioli, to the west; and the 34th, 3,903-foot Mount Bastione, farther to the west on II Corps' right flank. It was, potentially, a strong defensive position, though it lacked the prepared emplacements of the Gothic Line. Lemelsen managed to patch up the weakened 4th Parachute and 334th Grendadier Divisions with rear-echelon replacements. But the Blue Devils on Battle Mountain had forced the Germans to move elements of the 362d and 334th Grenadier Divisions from the Radicosa sector to that of the Sillaro. So, for the Wehrmacht, the battle for Radicosa Pass became a series of delaying actions.

The southwest face of Canda pitched forward at a disconcerting angle. General Coulter, therefore, decided to outflank the mountain by taking Torre Poggioli, a smooth-sloped 3,168-foot height to the northeast. The Germans, however, had spotted—and were quick to develop—the defensive potential of Sambuco, a small village nestled in a crown of craggy hills south of the Poggioli–Ravignana ridges. Machine guns were posted in the thick-walled houses and machine-gun positions were dug in around the town's perimeter. The enemy also reinforced its positions on the heights to the north, where observers overlooked the Custer Division's approaches.

By 0800 on September 25, the lead company, 3rd Battalion, 338th Infantry, outflanking Sambuco, was on the southern slope of Torre Poggioli. During the rest of the day, the 106th Grenadiers launched fruitless counterattacks. With the help of tanks, the Germans managed to force back one platoon on the right. Elements of the Lehr Brigade dug in on the Grenadiers' left blocked assistance from the 3rd Battalion, 339th Infantry. The 338th held on until it ran low on ammunition, withdrawing cautiously that night.

More troops, clearly, were needed to dislodge the Germans. General Coulter committed four battalions to the next day's attack—two at the center tackled Torre Poggioli, while another went for Sambuco and the fourth moved to protect the Custer Division's right flank. The day was marginally better for the attackers. Despite intense mortar and artillery fire, the two center battalions reached Highway 6529 just below the crest of Torre Poggioli. On the right, the flanking battalion moved north on the high ground to the east. A BAR man climbing a steep slope came upon an enemy machine-gun nest, a hastily camouflaged slit trench below the crest. The foes fired their guns almost simultaneously. And just as suddenly, the guns fell silent, leaving one American dead, along with three Germans. In Sambuco, the Germans held on that long day.

On the 27th, tanks that had been hampered by antitank mines managed to gain the highway and use their machine guns as well as high-explosive shells on enemy positions along the crest of Torre Poggioli. The infantry then drove the enemy off, though the crest remained under fire from enemy self-propelled guns and long-range automatic weapons. In Sambuco, Custermen fought from house to house and the town was finally reduced to rubble by supporting tanks. Mount Canda had been well and truly flanked. After dark, the 3rd Battalion, 338th Infantry, began a long night march over muddy and rough ground to the south and west towards Canda. During this time, the 362nd Grenadiers took advantage of the heavy rains and slipped away to the north. The Custermen arrived on the mountain's crest at noon on the 28th and found it unoccupied. The 85th consolidated its gains. Dry clothes, blankets and hot food were sent forward to the exhausted troops.

On II Corps' left flank, the 34th Division had all three regiments on line following up the withdrawal of the 334th Grenadier Division from the Gothic Line. The Corps' plan of attack on Radicosa Pass called on the Red Bulls to seize 3,903-foot Monte Bastione, which looms over the valley of the Setta to the west and the valley of the Savena to the east. But first the Germans had to be pushed off Monte Coroncina, to the Division's immediate north. Elements of the 2nd Battalion, 168th Infantry, taking advantage of the fog, scaled Coroncina's summit the morning of September 24. Service personnel from the 755th and 756th Grenadiers hastily mounted a series of counterattacks, promptly thrown back by the Red Bulls.

To protect the men on Coroncina, the 168th's First Battalion swung west to Highway 6620 and the 34th Cavalry Reconnaissance maintained contact with the 91st Division on the right. Meanwhile, the 133rd Infantry passed into Division reserve as the 168th swung northeast to assist the 135th in its attack on Monte Bastione. The enemy, apparently expecting the main attack to come down Highway 6620 along the Setta, pounded Montepiano with a thousand heavy-caliber rounds—"a volume of fire heavier than any received during the Gothic Line fighting," according to Fifth Army historians.[5]

As the 2nd and 3rd Battalions of the 135th crossed Torrente Bambellate, the Germans counterattacked from the heights above. The enemy also used the village of Bruscoli to good advantage, holding up the Red Bulls for another day. Harassed by the enemy at isolated points all along the approach to Bastione, the 135th and 168th foot-sloggers negotiated swollen streams, muddy valleys and steep slopes, Monte Bastione was occupied before noon on the 28th by the 135th as the Germans withdrew. The next day, the 2nd Battalion reached Fornelli, a road junction hamlet three miles to the north. On the 29th, the 1st Battalion, 168th Infantry, fought off a counterattack at Montefredente, three miles southwest of Fornelli on the ridges above the Setta. The 135th was withdrawn into reserve; the 133rd was recommitted, taking its place alongside the 168th. Pack mules brought up supplies in preparation for the next attack. The 168th had advanced some six airline miles in three days. Regimental wire crews, however, had laid 55 miles of wire over the same period, perhaps a better indication of the ground covered by the weary troops.

At II Corps' center, two rocky peaks over 4,000 feet high, Monte Freddi and Monte Beni, glowered like twin gargoyles over the 91st Division's narrowing two-mile front. The two guardians of Monte Poggioli, to their north, offered little cover and no concealment from enemy observers to the left on Monte Bastione and to the right on Monte Canda. Even if lightly held, the twin peaks were a ready-made delaying line for the 4th Parachute Division. Highway 65 turned eastward along the foot of Sasso di Castro, another 4,000-foot monster ridge south of Monte Freddi, and swung around below Monte Beni north to the Radicosa Pass. General Livesay opened the attack at 0530 on September 24 with two regiments abreast, the 362nd skirting the west side of Sasso di Castro and the 361st moving east of Highway 65 to clear the village of Covigliaio for an assault on Monte Beni.

Company K reached Covigliaio two hours later. But it took a day of house-to-house combat with grenades and rifle fire under constant mortar fire to clear the town. Elsewhere progress was "excellent," according to the 91st's historian Robert A. Robbins.[6] A 362nd patrol cleared out an artillery observation post on Sasso di Castro and the two regiments were roughly aligned and ready to take on the twin giants, Freddi and Beni, the next day.

"Opposition was surprisingly light," the *Fifth Army History* says of the attack on Monte Beni.[7] Scattered enemy pockets, however, fought to the bitter end. One tank-backed platoon knocked out five machine-gun positions on the slope of the mountain. Few prisoners were taken. Monte Freddi proved to be a more difficult undertaking. Intelligence estimates placed two German battalions on the mountain. A touch-and-go rain-drenched battle. which lasted through the afternoon and night of September 25, opened the way for a mop up of Monte Freddi. While Companies A and B, 363rd Infantry, killed or captured 80 Germans, Company B moved through the saddle between Freddi and Hill 1035, a western spur of the mountain. A German runner carrying withdrawal instructions to his company was captured; intimidated by the sodden riflemen, he led his captors to his unit, which was surrounded and captured. The twin peaks were in American hands at the end of the day on September 26.

Enemy resistance continued the next day and progress was slow in nasty weather. By nightfall, the eastern base of Poggioli was secured. The next morning, the 361st and 363rd approached Monte Poggioli in a driving rain. Both regiments used the one available trail, often intermingling, and simultaneously taking their objective in the early afternoon. The 4th Paras had taken advantage of the rain to slip away to the next defensive line at Monghidoro. After a brief halt—a wet and cold night on the mountain—the 91st swept through Radicosa Pass, occupying the hilltowns of Piamaggio and La Posta, some two miles to the north, on September 29. The Corps had advanced some twelve miles up Highway 65 from its breakthrough at Futa Pass on September 22. Rain washed out roads and bridges all along its front. Thick fog swirled around sodden soldiers, reducing visibility to a matter of yards. Ahead some two miles on a line running west to east through Monghidoro on Highway 65, the Germans waited.

II Corps confronted the enemy on a broad front from, roughly, the

Val di Sambroetta to the left, where the 34th Division was fighting up the approaches to Monte Venere, to Battle Mountain—occupied by the Blue Devils' 350th Infantry Regiment. Of the twenty-odd road miles ahead to Bologna, fifteen passed through the gradually descending northern slope of the Apennines, made hellish by rough spurs and streams running generally north and south with massive hills dominating the ravines and draws. The Monghidoro line was to be held briefly by the Germans, because Italian civilians were at work improving a natural line of defense east and west of the village of Loiano on Highway 65. Four miles beyond, another such line passed through Livergnano and yet another at Pianoro.

The day after the 91st moved through Radicosa Pass, II Corps ordered a resumption of its offensive along a 16-mile front with D Day set for October 1. Attacks were to be coordinated to take advantage of the regimental rotation, which placed "fresh" troops on line every five days. (According to the *Fifth Army History*, this system "corresponded closely with the rate at which each enemy defense line was developed."[8]) The 91st Division, astride Highway 65, and the 85th Division to its right, between Zena Creek and the Sillaro River, spearheaded the attack. The 88th Division protected II Corps' right flank in the ridges running between the Sillaro and Santerno Valleys, while the 34th did the same as it attacked north between the Sambro and the Savena. The idea was that the Fifth Army would debouch into the Po Valley on a broad front just west of Bologna.

The opening attack was auspicious. Low clouds and the morning mist concealed troop movements. Then the sun broke through, providing the kind of visibility that delights artillery observers. "Rover Joe," grounded by bad weather, was now airborne, directing effective close air support. A cold, blustery wind, however, swept the mountains with rain the next day. Low-hanging clouds, fog and showers followed, recreating the mud that had hampered troops and tanks over the preceeding week. Though the 4th Parachute and 362 Grenadier Divisions sustained heavy losses in defense of the Gothic Line, they fought a stubborn delaying action. "There was no decisive battle fought," the *Fifth Army History* observes, "no spectacular gain made during the first two days of the attack."[9]

On the ridge sloping up towards Monghidoro, however, Private Howard E. Weaver scored what must have seemed to his fellow G.I.s a rather spectacular gain. A replacement with four days on line, he was a first scout at the head of the 2nd Platoon, Company F, 363rd Infantry. A machine-gun burst missed him but killed his squad leader and demoralized the platoon, mostly replacements. Weaver rallied his squad, leading it uphill until the machine gun cut loose again.

To locate the gun, Weaver exposed himself, then crawled to within 35 yards of it. A well-thrown grenade killed one German gunner and wounded the second gunner, who was taken prisoner. Up another hundred yards, Weaver repeated his performance, using his last two grenades, and captured the two Germans still alive there. He found cover for his men beneath a steep bank, climbed over the top, and killed a sniper hiding in a tree. Again the squad moved forward, taking cover from sniper fire in a house up ahead. Weaver entered the building, capturing two snipers. His actions freed up the company, enabling it to take its objective. Shortly after, Weaver was given a well-deserved field commission as a second lieutenant.

Monghidoro was cleared the next day, October 2nd, house-by-house. Five hundred yards northeast of town, a Company I platoon captured two tanks and two self-propelled guns. Armored cars shot up a long house, bringing out 29 Germans with hands raised. Two hundred determined Germans launched a counterattack along the lateral road from Monghidoro. A break in the fog exposed the attackers, however, and a prompt artillery response killed over half of them. By day's end, the enemy's Monghidoro–Montepiano defense line had been overrun.

The men of the Wild West Division got their first look at the Po Valley. Not that they dallied over the view as the enemy withdrew to the Loiano line, the 91st in pursuit, gaining three miles in a day. After a night's pause, the 362nd and 363rd Infantry resumed the attack in the morning. Tanks were sent into Loiano but were withdrawn when the two leading machines were destroyed. The 11th and 12th Parachute Regiments on the west side of Highway 65 and the 106th Grenadier Regiment on the other were putting up a good fight. During the day, 1,018 rounds were fired into Loiano and on Monte Bastia, the height dominating the town from the north. At 1920, Artillery Colonel Cotton reported, "Seems to be a lot of stuff in Loiano. Have put artillery on houses and knocked them down, but Jerry still comes out."

And so he did. After each withdrawal, the enemy yielded ground to stand fast on the next ridge or forbidding height until ordered to drop back yet again. Whether it was on II Corps' right flank, where the Blue Devils contested the Germans for control of the ridges converging on

Sassoleone above the Sillaro, or on the left flank, where the Red Bulls battled for Monte Venere, the Germans came out when called to do so. East of Loiano, rocky, sprawling Monte Bibele rose 2,000 feet to dominate the Indice Valley. General Coulter of the 85th Division ordered the 339th Infantry to attack north from Canda and take Bibele, while the 337th Infantry cleared the ridge east of the Indice Valley.

Both regiments made good progress despite stiff opposition during the first two days, reaching Spedaletto on the eastern ridge and clearing La Martina and the fortified villages blocking the approach to Bibele. When Captain Clayton N. Little's I Company was stopped by heavy fire from hill positions overlooking the Indice River, he led his men in an attack across seven hundred yards of open terrain.

On his hilltop, Captain Little discovered that the enemy's main defense was on the reverse slope of two adjacent ridges. He then led thirty of his men across another fifty yards of open ground, personally killing fifteen Germans to force the enemy back. After an uneasy night under enemy fire, Little was ordered to take Colle de Tattini, a tiny hilltown in the Indice Valley dominating his segment of the front. His men managed to surprise the enemy, who nonetheless fought back. In the firefight, about fifty Germans were killed and sixty captured. When five enemy tanks counterattacked, Little directed artillery fire from an exposed position. The tanks were forced to withdraw.

The 106th Grenadier Regiment had fallen back on Monte Bibele, digging in to hold off the Custermen. On October 4 at 0700, the 1st Battalion of the 339th Infantry advanced east of the mountain while the 2nd headed straight for Bibele. While the 1st made some gains, taking its first object, Hill 504, early in the morning, the 2nd ran up against a fortified village, Quizano. Tanks broke down enemy resistance by direct fire on the stone houses. But other strongholds held out as the battle continued on into the night. The next morning, the Battalion resumed its attack. By late afternoon, one company was on top of the mountain.

On the ridge to the east, the 337th attacked beyond Spedaletto, inching forward under heavy artillery, mortar and machine-gun fire. Doggedly, the Custermen pushed ahead until they were south of the village of Palmona. From all sides, the Germans pounded the Americans. Sergeant Robert F. Hixon of Company L spotted a tank to the rear of his company's position. Ignoring enemy sniper fire, Hixon managed to get in position to fire antitank grenades, capturing the tank and its crew. On the way back to his company CP with his prisoners, he came across another tank. Working his way through the trees, he captured it and its occupants. After leaving his prisoners at the CP, Hixon returned through shell and sniper fire to render the two German tanks useless. The 337th had forced a salient well ahead of all other units of II Corps.

On the left flank, the 34th Division was southwest of the 91st. Working down the Sambro Valley the morning of October 2, the 1st and 3rd Battalions of the 168th Infantry met with such heavy opposition from SS Panzer Grenadiers in a church on Hill 789 that Colonel Hines ordered the two battalions to bypass the position. The enemy then withdrew that night as the position was no longer tenable. Colonel Hines' Regiment moved on to take the villages of Campiano and San Benedetto. At midnight, October 3, the 133rd Infantry's 1st Battalion attacked Monte Venere.

Supported by seven tanks, slogging up a muddy trail, the infantry gained the summit on the afternoon of the 4th. Pressing his advantage, Colonel Braun ordered his reserve battalion to mount one company on tanks to seize Monzuno, one and one-half miles north. Only three of the eleven tanks reached the line of departure; the rest bogged down in mud or threw their tracks. The lead tank was struck and set afire by a German bazooka a thousand yards short of the town; the remaining two bogged down as they tried to bypass the burning vehicle. The infantry were forced to dig in for the night. However, Monzuno was taken the next day, cutting the lateral road that led east to Loiano. II Corps' left flank was now anchored on a line that swept southwest down from Venere to the Sambro Valley, a thousand yards north of Campiano, where a blown bridge blocked the road.

The first phase of the October drive for Bologna netted four miles— and at two points, five miles—an average gain of slightly more than one mile a day. Bologna was only twenty-two miles away, lending hope for an anticipated breakout into the Po Valley "before the October rains turned to snow."[10] II Corps had taken 858 prisoners and enemy casualties were thought to be high. Ominously, Allied losses were heavy: 88th Division, 726 casualties (most on Battle Mountain); 85th, 443; 91st, 331; 34th, 234. There were also an equal number of non-battle casualties.

Rain and fog aided and abetted the enemy. Allied planes were grounded and few planned missions were flown. Tanks chewed up mud instead of the enemy. Rain-soaked trails and rutted roads bedeviled the movement of supplies. Water seeped into foxholes; fortunate troopers slept on damp stone floors in bombed-out farm buildings. Diarrhea cramped the gut and sent far too many men back to the hospital. Above all, the Germans were entrenched in the numerous farm buildings scattered throughout terrain that offered little cover for attackers.

West of the Indice–Sillaro Ridge, where the 337th Infantry held its exposed salient, the 338th's 3rd Battalion moved forward to straighten out the Custer line. Enemy riflemen and gunners in a house on a key ridge near Castelnuovo di Bisano halted an attacking Custer platoon. Pfc. Gordon R. True dashed across fifty yards of open ground, firing his submachine gun to kill two of the enemy. At the side of the house, his platoon's objective, he spotted three Germans in a stealthy approach over a small mound. A burst from his gun brought them down, but then he spotted forty others grouping for a counterattack. True took off again, running 35 yards through enemy fire to a better position. There he opened up again, killing or wounding six. The rest of the enemy, unnerved by True's bursts, withdrew and his platoon secured its objective. True was awarded the Distinguished Service Cross and Custer historian Paul L. Schultz credits him as "largely responsible" for the capture of Bisano.

The capture of that town on the morning of October 7 brought the left flank of the 85th parallel to the 337th's precarious position on the Indice–Sillaro Ridge. Meanwhile, the 338th Infantry's 1st Battalion had worked northward for two days along a series of deep ravines formed by streams running west to the Indice to within 1,000 yards of La Villa. Within the valley, the 2nd Battalion patrolled the river road, keeping open the Division's main supply route.

To strengthen the Indice–Sillaro Ridge position, Colonel Hughes ordered the 337th's 3rd Battalion to clear the ridge to the east. L Company did so, seizing a knob on a key eastern spur; but the company was driven off on the afternoon of the 7th. K Company retook the knob the next day. The enemy fell back on Monte delle Formiche to the northwest. Elements of the 362nd and 65th Grenadier Divisions were astride the Indice Valley. The 117th Grenadier Regiment (9th Grenadier Division) held the Monterenzio massif directly north of the 337th. The 91st, however, was in position for the next phase of II Corps' operations.

On its flanks II Corps ran the risk of exposure. On the left, the situation was eased considerably when General Alexander committed his "last remaining fully fresh division," the British 78th, in the British XIII Corps sector.[11] The 1st Guards Brigade (normally assigned to the British 1st Division) relieved the battered Blue Devils on Battle Mountain on October 5 and the 78th's Irish Brigade relieved the 351st Infantry astride the Imola road north of Castel del Rio. Up until then, General Paul W. Kendall had only the 349th Infantry and the 3rd Battalion, 351st Infantry, available to keep pace with the 85th. Freed of responsibility for the Santerno Valley, the 88th moved northeast into the mountains towards Poggio del Falchetto and Monte dellle Tombe alongside the 85th on the Indice–Sillaro Ridge. The 78th followed a week later to relieve the Blue Devils at Gesso and to attack Monte Spaduro.

After trying to storm Point 587 from the south on the ridge dominated by Falchetto, the 2nd Battalion, 349th Infantry, managed to dig in on the slope on October 6. Company A, coming up from the west, came to within 100 yards of the crest, but mud fouled their rifles and the Blue Devils had all they could do to cling to their positions. Then Colonel Crawford sent Companies I and L around to the left to cut the ridge short of Falchetto. And the fog and rain helped for once.

The Germans frequently sought refuge in farmhouses, which, if not properly outposted, became death traps. In one such farmhouse below the ridge, I Company captured 60 prisoners without firing a shot. L Company surprised its opposition and gained the crest, but then had to fight through the night to hold on. Company F passed through Company A to find the summit unoccupied.

The 3rd Battalion took Falchetto, a mile to the northwest—as well as 73 prisoners—in a daylight attack on October 8. A mile of ridge remained to Monte delle Tombe. To the southeast, the 351st Infantry moved north towards a lateral ridge that extended east and west through Gesso. Late in the afternoon of the 9th, the 1st Battalion attacked the town, but they were driven back by Germans armed with flame-throwers. The Blue Devils, however, were now roughly abreast of the 85th.

On II Corps' left flank, the 34th Division had taken Monzuno, but its position would not be secure until the enemy had been driven from the area lying between the Monte Venere–Monzuno Ridge and the Setta River Valley. The 168th Infantry and 91st Cavalry were assigned the job. An enemy shell landed on the 1st Battalion CP, killing several key officers. Company A lost three, its first sergeant and a platoon sergeant. The Battalion was so short of officers that its companies had to be reorganized.

Fortunately, the 2nd Battalion was able to pass through, and it advanced four miles northwest of Venere. Under cover of the ubiquitous fog, the two battalions held the high ground across the Setta. A roadblock was established at Gardeletta, a village on Highway 6620. By October 9, the Germans had been forced back to a defense line between the Savena and Setta Valleys, a thousand yards south of the Monterumici Hill mass.

On October 5, the 346th Field Artillery Battalion, 91st Infantry Division, laid down a rolling barrage on the German defenses at Loiano. By 0630, Company L, 362nd Infantry, fought its way into the town, beat off an enemy counterattack in the afternoon and joined Company K to drive the enemy off Monte Bastia. They succeeded by 2100.

To the west, the 363rd Infantry met stubborn opposition in its effort to clear the ridge along the Loiano–Monzuno road, but a second attempt the next morning did the job. To the right, the 1st Battalion, 361st Infantry, seized the high ground east of Bastia. Though the Loiano line collapsed in a little over 24 hours, the Germans held on to Monte Castellari, a long-fingered hump two miles north of Loiano—fresh troops from the 65th Grenadier Division had reinforced the sector.

In an attempt to surprise the enemy, the 1st and 3rd Battalions, 362nd Infantry, jumped off in the fog without artillery support at 0800, the morning of October 7, to storm Castellari, but with little success. A second attack was mounted the next day, and it was rough going: in places, infantrymen had to crawl on hands and knees up the steep slopes of muddy ravines. Company C lost all but one of its officers in a mortar barrage. Company B was halted by small-arms and machine-gun fire from concrete emplacements at the foot of the mountain. After fighting all morning on the 8th, elements of the 1st Battalion came within 75 yards of the crest. A halt was called for regrouping. B Company beat off a counterattack. A patrol overheard plans for another, which was forestalled by over 600 rounds from 60mm mortars. This enabled Company B to move over the crest after midnight. Ladders and ropes were sent up to aid in searching out the cliffs. The objective was occupied by 0215, October 9.

East of the Highway the 361st Infantry was ensnared for two days in a series of muddy ravines cutting east, down to the Zena. On the 8th the Regiment captured Barbarolo, just off Highway 65, and cleared several small villages. Freed up, Companies K and L moved over a mile north through the fog-haunted night and swung west to cut Highway 65, some

2,000 yards behind enemy lines. The two companies clashed in the darkness with enemy troops drifting back from Monte Castelli. First Sergeant Myers of I Company lured a goodly number into a trap by barking orders with the authority of a German Oberleutnant. On October 9, the two companies held off a fierce counterattack from the north mounted by German infantry backed by tanks. Elsewhere, the 91st cleaned out bypassed pockets and moved into position for its next attack.

In its second phase, II Corps had advanced slightly over three miles, with gains of only one to two miles on its flanks. Casualties were slightly less than in the first push, 1,474 as against 1,734. The 88th suffered 681 losses; the 91st, 382; the 85th, 224; and the 34th, 187. A total of 1,119 prisoners were taken.

NOTES

[1] Clark, *Calculated Risk*, p. 396.
[2] Ibid.
[3] United States Army, *Fifth Army History*, Vol. VII, p. 122.
[4] Clark, *Calculated Risk*, p. 398.
[5] United States Army, *Fifth Army History*, Vol. VII, p. 102.
[6] Robbins, *The 91st Infantry Division*, p. 139.
[7] United States Army, *Fifth Army History*, Vol. VII, p. 101.
[8] Ibid., p. 112.
[9] Ibid., p. 114.
[10] Ibid., p. 122.
[11] Ray, *Algiers to Austria*, p. 160.

XIX

ONE LONG STRIDE

The weather had been nasty, and it did not look as if it would improve. With each mile gained over mucky roads and trails, the difficulties of moving supplies forward multiplied. The possibility of a swift thrust to the Po faded. Ahead, the Germans held the most formidable line of defense north of the Gothic Line—in particular, in front of the 91st Division, a sheer rock wall three miles long and in places nearly 1,500 feet high. There are only two breaks in the escarpment, one at Livergnano—"Liver'n Onions" to the G.I.s—where Highway 65 cuts through, and another, a footpath, one and a half miles to the east, above the village of Bigallo. Though lower than the mountains to the south, the escarpment rim commanded every approach; and above the rim on a series of hills automatic weapons could place fire on any troops who should reach the plateau.

To the west, the enemy defenses were linked to the Monterumici mass in the 34th Division sector. To the east, across a narrow gorge formed by the Zena Torrent rose Monte delle Formiche in the 85th zone, Monte delle Tombe in the 88th sector and Monte Spaduro on the left flank of British XIII Corps. Yet, another mile . . . or two . . . and Bologna would be within 14 miles.

The 361st Regiment came up against the Livergnano escarpment well ahead of the other units of the 91st Division. It was exposed on its right to fire directed from Santa Maria di Zena, a church perched on 2,000-foot Monte delle Formiche. The 362nd was moving down the northern spur of Castellori and had reached La Guarda, a mile or so back on the 361st's left. The 65th Grenadier Division on the escarpment was not only well positioned but was relatively fresh, having suffered comparatively few casualties compared to most of the German units facing II Corps. The tactical situation did not allow for many choices. Lateral communications were almost nil, given the terrain—north to south ridges blocked most radio transmissions. General Livesay ordered the 361st's 2nd battalion to move eastward, up the rimrock north of Bigallo, then to swing west to take hills 392, 504 and 481 on the way to Highway 65. Meanwhile, the 1st Battalion was to take Livergnano, then shift west to pinch out the 362nd on the 91st's left flank. It was a classic pincers movement.

Before the 1st Battalion got underway on the morning of the 9th, German infantry backed by tanks hit K and I companies in holding positions below Livergnano. After a desperate firefight, the enemy was driven off. K Company, assigned to the 1st Battalion, followed up the Germans, reaching Livergnano at 1500.

When the lead platoon came under heavy fire, it took cover in a large building at the edge of the town. Held up by deadly snipers, the remaining platoons waited until dark before moving into Livergnano. Intentionally or not, they were "herded" into the same building where the lead platoon had taken cover. As the last soldiers dodged into the house, Sergeant Luke Owens and his men dashed for another. A machine gun zeroed on the door fired and killed the man in the lead. Owens and the rest dashed around the side of the house and ducked into the nearest hole—a pigsty.

Just before dawn on October 10, the enemy attacked the house. K Company withstood rifle and machine-gun fire, even grenades. Two tanks and mortars methodically pounded the building until it began to fall apart. Then, mid-morning, Captain Chetlain Sigmen informed Battalion headquarters that he had been asked to surrender. But suddenly his voice stopped. Helpless observers watched K Company survivors—81 men— file out of the shattered building. The rest had been killed or wounded. Sergeant Owens and his men sweated out the day in the pigsty. Under the cover of darkness, they escaped.

Meanwhile, the 2nd Battalion tackled the escarpment. Since the cut just west of Bigallo appeared to be a trap, foot-sloggers slung their rifles over their shoulders and scaled the cliffs, instant mountain climbers. Machine guns were broken down, squad members carrying the parts in their packs or pockets. Soldiers grabbed whatever handholds and toeholds they could find. Up a ways, the Jerries had zeroed in on a narrow ledge. By running a few men across at a time, the two companies made their way forward.

The fog lifted. Two scouts gained the rim and crossed over. A machine-gun blast from Hill 592 to their right killed the next four men over the rim, as well as the two scouts. Gingerly, E and G Companies gained the top of the escarpment by dusk. Daylight found them at the bottom of a "tilted saucer," rimmed by the enemy. It took twelve to sixteen hours to hand-carry a wounded man down over the escarpment to an aid station. Litters were too bulky for the width of the trail. It took a runner four hours to make a one-way trip to the battalion command post; supply was equally difficult. Despite all that and a decimating fire, the two companies held on.

General Livesay committed the 363rd Infantry on the right flank to add weight to the attack on the escarpment and to assist the 85th Division's assault on Monte delle Formiche and its troublesome church tower. Enemy troops secure in their caves on the twin hills 603 and 554, bracketing Livergnano, held off the 361st. It was touch-and-go for the 91st as the 85th deployed two battalions against the bald heights of Formiche.

On the 10th, the skies were clear, allowing for concentrations of artillery on enemy positions. In the afternoon, Company E, 338th Infantry, entered Casa de Monte, a hamlet on the west side of the mountain. But the enemy's response was prompt and effective, an attack that cut off two squads. The company was forced out of the village. At 0200, Company G passed through to work up to the crest by mid-afternoon of the 11th. In the assault on enemy positions around Santa Maria di Zena, 53 prisoners were taken. Artillery "disorganized" enemy efforts to bring up reserves. Enemy artillery, unfortunately, was also effective, causing heavy losses within the 2nd Battalion. Nevertheless, the Custermen had taken the troublesome church-topped mountain.

The capture of Santa Maria di Zena eased the situation of the 91st. The weather helped, too. Nine bombing missions were flown on the 11th, some of the targets only 350 yards ahead of the infantry. The weather held, enabling the 91st Division's artillery alone to fire 24,000 rounds during the three days, 12–14. After nightfall, the 363rd launched a night attack, coming up the Livergnano escarpment east of the 361st's second battalion. Advance elements reached Hill 504 before dawn of the 12th.

At the end of the day, eight rifle companies had climbed the escarpment. As for Livergnano, it was just about outflanked from the west, where the 3rd Battalion of the 361st had reached Casaino, 1,200 yards northwest of Livergnano on the 13th. Above Bigallo, to the east, the 2nd Battalion knocked out enemy strongholds, taking 73 prisoners on the way to Highway 65 on the 14th. To the right, the 363rd moved more than a mile north of the escarpment.

Though the situation on the Division's right flank improved by the 13th, the fate of Livergnano remained uncertain. One platoon of Company C reached the crest of Hill 554, the western guardian of the town, shortly after midnight on October 12. Two machine-gun nests were flushed out, a German officer captured and ten of his men killed. But the platoon was driven to take cover in a building, then driven out and downhill by a tank and a 120mm mortar barrage. Company B tackled Hill 603, the eastern guardian, and one squad managed to close in on caves at the foot of the hill under cover from tank destroyers. Fourteen prisoners were taken as the platoon tossed grenades into the caves. But the enemy held them off the crest by dropping potato-mashers down on their heads.

At six in the morning on the 13th, Company B resumed its attack. Sergeant Sumpter's first squad led the way. "Every German in Italy poured shells on the hillside," Associated Press correspondent Jack Bell reported. "Machine guns cracked. Tank guns thundered. The sergeant and his platoon went on, shooting with tommy-guns, throwing grenades, evading enemy shell holes. On and on they walked—and the Germans up there threw up their hands in despair."[1] The company crossed the crest by 1145, and held the position in the face of concentrated artillery and mortar fire.

Company A, in its attack on Hill 554, repeated the experience of Company C the day before. Advancing through mortar and machine-gun fire, the company knocked out with rocket launchers a machine gun that swept the only approach. On the ridge, the men were forced to take cover in the same building occupied by Company C. Two self-propelled guns pounded the building, and the infantry withdrew to the reverse slope. Enemy casualties were heavy, 225 prisoners being taken on the 12th and 13th. Company B then worked forward on a spur north of 603; observers scanned the sector to discover that the enemy, threatened by a cut-off, had left town. Hill 554 was clear. Livergnano was in American hands.

The next day—October 15—the 91st consolidated its gains along an east–west line a mile or so to the north. On its right, the 85th cleared the eastern slope of Monte delle Formiche. Across the Indice Valley, twenty Custermen managed to get into the church on the crest of Hill 578, the high point of the Monterenzio Hill mass. But they were trapped by machine-gun fire and the rest of the company couldn't move. During the night of October 12–13, the 1st Battalion, 338th Infantry, flanked and surrounded the hill. By noon, it was taken, along with 23 prisoners. Two days later, the 339th Infantry pushed ahead another mile. The 85th now held an integrated line across the Indice Valley.

On II Corps' right flank, the 88th Division segued to the northwest, tightening up the overall front, as the British 78th Division took over the Blue Devils' sector northwest of Castel del Rio on the Santerno. "Our operations," John Horsfall of the Irish Brigade remarked, "began badly." The rain, of course, did not help, but differences in command also confused matters. The Americans fighting technique, Horsfall observed, was "unusual." "One scarcely saw [British infantry] in the course of an assault," while G.I.s "merely advanced en masse spurning the usual precautions which our infantry thought necessary."

Indeed, there appeared to be no planning, aside from the assignment of objectives. Casualties were "colossal" in British eyes. One radio exchange fascinated Horsfall: "Gee why ain't your boys going up that hill?" "Aw, colonel, how can I attack the God-damn hill unless I have artillery?" "Hell, you can't have the guns all the time, can he Porky?"

And there were the inevitable clashes. When an American signal unit collided with an Irish Brigade outpost in the dark, it was shot down and killed, to a man. American helmets, alas, resembled the enemy's in the darkness. When Horsfall went around to express his regrets, the American regimental commander patted him on the shoulder. "Think nothing of it—it happens every night," the man said, and poured Horsfall a stiff gin. Horsfall prefers to remember the generosity rather than the possible truth of the comment. The Yanks, he adds, fought gallantly; the system somehow worked. "They were a joy to be with all right, and the elan of their youthful company commanders was most refreshing."[2]

Despite all difficulties, the British presence enabled the Blue Devils to firm up II Corps' right flank. To the west, the 34th Division was engaged in a deadly dance—the Red Bulls were expected to take the Monterumici Hill mass and to assemble two regiments for use east of Highway 65. General Bolte already had the 168th Infantry in reserve; for the second regiment he had to simultaneously relieve the 133rd, replace it with the 1st Armored's Combat Command A and keep attacking. He had a few days' grace, so he launched the 133rd down Highway 6620 at night, October 9–10, towards Vado, a village in the Setta Valley. At the same time, the 135th attacked along the ridge between the Setta and Savena Valleys. The idea was to take Monterumici before the 34th had to move east.

Supporting tanks were held up by craters in Highway 6620, however; and the infantry was stopped by fire from enemy positions below Monterumici. Machine guns and minefields did their work. Repeated attacks along the ridge made little headway. Reluctantly, General Bolte decided he had no options. On October 11, the 6th and 14 Armored Infantry moved to replace the 133rd—a shuffle of forces that consumed energies that might have been directed on the objective. To compensate, General Bolte shifted the 135th to the right, pressing the attack along the ridge with one battalion while another flanked Monterumici from the east. The enemy, however, held the advantage. To effect the relief, the 34th had to relinquish some of the high ground it had gained. Control of Combat Command A and, temporarily, of the 135th passed to the 1st Armored on October 14. The next day, the 34th started its move east of Highway 65.

Mid-month, at the close of the third phase of the October offensive, it was clear that the rate of attack was slowing down. While the Blue Devils' 350th Infantry advanced three miles on II Corps' right flank, the average gain was one to two miles, the front remaining virtually stationary before the Monterumici hill mass. It was not only a matter of the weather, actually vastly improved these last few days, but that German resistance had remained constant and unyielding. Prisoners commented on the demoralizing effect of the massive Allied artillery fire. And the enemy was having difficulties in recuperating recent losses—1,689 prisoners and untold dead and wounded. Yet, as the *Fifth Army History* puts it, the enemy "exhibited an amazing resourcefulness in putting together odds and ends to maintain a front."[3]

American losses were becoming huge. Over the six days 10–15 October, the 88th Division suffered 872 casualties; the 91st, 769; the 85th, 611; and the 34th, 239. Altogether, the four divisions lost 5,695 in October and had lost 12,210 since the beginning of II Corps' offensive on September 10. Mid-month, according to Clark, "We had replacements for one more day." Though the bulk of the losses was made up by returnees and replacements, there was a clear decline in effectiveness.

Battlefield commissions, especially for junior officers, where the casualty rate was disproportionately high, only partially alleviated the situation as the supply of experienced non-coms was also depleted. Of nine 88th Division battalions only four were commanded by lieutenant colonels on October 15. Yet, hopes die hard. Bologna was now only ten miles distant and the month had 16 days to go.

On October 14, General Clark received an ominous report. Army G-4 informed him that the supply of ammunition available in the theater soon would be critical. At the current daily expenditure, the Army would be forced to adopt a defensive role by November 10. II Corps girded itself for a final assault. Not quite Bologna or bust, but near enough.

General Kirkman's 13th Corps adjusted its lines to provide the best possible flank protection on the Fifth Army's right. With 1st Guards Brigade holding Monte Battaglia, the 61st Brigade took over a portion of the 78th Division's zone, enabling it to assume a bit more of the 88th's sector to tighten up II Corps' front. On the left, the South African 6th Armoured Division was spread out over 15 miles, bridging the Reno and Setta Valleys. However, it was securely anchored to the American 1st Armored, providing ample protection for II Corps' western flank. Its four divisions bunched like a fist, II Corps was poised for a punch towards a 22-mile stretch of Highway 9 in the Po Valley between Bologna and Castel San Pietro.

Three miles north of Livergnano, Highway 65 drops into the valley of the Savenna to run alongside the river to the Po. Roughly a mile east of where the highway drops down onto the valley floor, a formidable mass of ridges rises to 1,546 feet at its highest. Monte Belmonte—the watchdog height east of Highway 65—was in what Staff considered the enemy's weakest sector, centered on the Indice Valley. This was an evaluation based on reports of confusion in German battle orders and the fall of Monte Formiche to the south.

To take advantage of this weakness, the 34th Division was inserted on a narrow front between the 91st Division, bracketing Highway 65, and the 85th Division, on the ridge east of Indice torrent. A breakthrough here followed by a turn down the Indice would enable the 34th to cut Highway 9 some three miles southeast of Bologna. Corps artillery massed its guns in support of the 34th. General Bolte deployed the 133rd Infantry on the left ridge running to Belmonte and the 168th astride to the right, on the ridge between Zena Creek and the Indice River.

The 168th jumped off at 0500, October 16, going for Monte della Vigna, a 1,512-foot knob one and a half miles north of Formiche. All three battalions were committed. Germans in Crocetta, a cluster of stone-and-mortar houses on the ridge, stopped the 1st Battalion cold. When the attack resumed at 0900, a German antitank gun knocked out a tank—which effectively blocked the trail. Another attack failed, though one company managed to outflank the hamlet. On the right, the 3rd Battalion was blocked by a steep escarpment and deadly enemy fire. On the left, the 2nd Battalion broke through enemy outposts and reached the edge of Tazzola, a village northwest of Crocetta.

Over the next two days, the 168th contested the Germans' control of the knobs and stone houses of Monte della Vigna. Some 8,000 rounds of division artillery supplemented by corps, tanks and tank destroyers encouraged the Germans to quit their outposts. Both Tazzola and Crocetta were abandoned. Before noon of the 17th, the 168th seized the summit of Monte della Vigna. Two hamlets on the forward slope were taken the following day, but the 168th was unable to continue its advance.

At ten o'clock on the night of the 16th, the 133rd Infantry attacked Monte Belmonte. Fighter-bombers flew 137 sorties, dropping 72 tons of bombs and 94 fuel-tank incendiary bombs on gun emplacements, wooded areas and bivouacs. Artificial moonlight—the diffused glow from aircraft searchlights near Monghidoro—aided the cross-country approach on a dark and cloudy night. Enemy troops, however, supported by tanks, greeted the Red Bulls as they approached Belmonte's crest at dawn. Antitank guns and armor were bogged down far to the rear. A sudden sweep of heavy fog concealed the enemy, who surrounded one company and cut off part of another. After the loss of a better part of two platoons, the 2nd Battalion fell back to reorganize.

The Red Bulls clung tenaciously to bits and pieces of the Belmonte mass, but they were subjected to devastating fire from Castel di Zena, an ancient castle high above the village of Zena to their right rear. On the night of October 18–19, the 2nd and 3rd Battalions resumed the attack on Belmonte and the 1st took on the castle. The fighting dragged on through the next day. Every assault on Castel di Zena was repulsed. When the attack was renewed on the morning of the 21st, "friendly fire" broke it up, causing serious casualties. Another attack was thrown back, but some troops managed to dig in on the castle hillside. The main attack on

Belmonte was painfully slow. Finally, in the late evening of the 23rd, after a heavy artillery bombardment, Company I gained the crest of Hill 401, Belmonte's highest point. The enemy withdrew from Castel di Zena.

Unhappily, the Germans retained most of the remaining ridge mass. The enemy's "weakest point" turned out to be one of his strongest. The 34th had gone up against the tanks and infantry of the 29th Panzer Grenadier Division, "one of the best German divisions in Italy."[4]

The 91st Division, too, invested heavily in II Corps' offensive. All three regiments were committed on October 16 on a narrower front, a thrust down Highway 65 in the shadows of Monte Belmonte to the east and Monte Adone to the west. Assigned to assist the 34th Division's assault on Belmonte, the 363rd Infantry jumped off at 0500 on the 16th without artillery preparation. The two lead battalions—the 1st and 2nd—surprised the enemy as intended, and advanced a thousand yards well ahead of troops on either side.

Artificial moonlight on the night of the 16–17th, apparently, was not as much help for the 91st as the 34th, for it proved difficult to locate the Red Bulls' exact positions. For fear of firing on friendly troops, the 363rd held back. During the next day, however, the two Powder River battalions gained 500 yards. But little progress was made the next day under fire from Belmonte, although the 1st Battalion advanced towards Ca' Trieste on the lateral road from Zula on Highway 65 to Zena. The 363rd was ordered to consolidate its position until lateral units came abreast.

Bracketing Highway 65, the 361st came up against "the heaviest artillery and mortar fire concentrations yet encountered."[5] One company probing ahead through heavy fog found itself surrounded by the enemy west of the highway. Hit front, back and center by enemy fire, the company was forced to withdraw. Meanwhile, the 362rd Infantry passed through the 361st left, aimed at Lucca, a hamlet a thousand yards to the north along narrow ridge. I Company, squeezed on the ridge, suffered 37 casualties the first day, taking the town the next at 1400. Company E had to fight for its line of departure during the early hours of the 16th, killing 13 Germans in hand-to-hand combat. Two self-propelled guns and four tanks then attacked, one gun coming within 75 yards of the Company OP to blow the house down. Artillery came to the rescue, dropping high-explosive shells within a hundred yards of the beleaguered troops without a casualty, frustrating the enemy's attempt at driving a wedge through the 361st's lines.

The 91st made little progress over the 16–19th, a gain of a mile north of Livergnano. It was in no position to assault Monte Adone, the western watchdog of Highway 65. The 362nd gained the high ground southwest of Canovetta, a key German position on the east side of the highway. Over the next three days, the 91st jockeyed for positions along its front.

After a bitter seesaw, a patrol entered Canovetta. The next day, October 22, General Livesay ordered the Division to organize for defense. II Corps had decided to shift its emphasis to its left, where the 88th had scored some significant gains. In truth, II Corps had little choice. The enemy's hold on the Monterumici mass and Monte Adone remained firm. The Germans had assembled in front of II Corps elements of eleven divisions with an estimated strength of 13,000. The 29th Panzer and 90th Panzer Grenadier Divisions were moved in from the Adriatic sector and a 94th Panzer battalion had been brought in from the west. A counterattack in force, aimed at regaining Belmonte and Castelari, seemed imminent. Moreover, on October 19, the 91st's ammunition allotment was curtailed.

In the last week of the month, light artillery battalions were allowed an average of 363 rounds per day per battalion, which did not even match the fires of one 8-hour period on the second day of the month. In contrast, on October 20, 4,700 enemy rounds (artillery and mortar) fell on the 91st—900 rounds alone in two hours, in the area between Disorta and Canovetta along Highway 65. Understandably, the Powder River division settled down to build its defenses along a line that ran from Monte Belmonte west across Highway 65, some two hundred yards south of Canovetta, dropping southwest along the Savena River to the hills west of Livergnano at the edge of the Monterumici hill mass. Faced with a possible counterattack in force, and unable to breech the enemy lines, the 91st and 1st Armored were shifted gradually from the offensive to what the Fifth Army History calls "an aggressive defense."

Frustrated by the strength of the Werhmacht at II Corps' center, General Clark decided to step up attacks on the flanks, first on the right then on the left. This, he believed, would force the Germans to spread troops over a wider front as well as reduce their concentrations opposite the 34th and 91st Divisions—the nose of the II Corps salient. As he examined his options, General Clark was encouraged by developments on II Corps' right flank, where the 85th fought north of the Monterenzio hill mass on the ridge between the Indice and Sillaro rivers. After two days of fighting, the 338th Infantry reached the lower slopes of Monte Fano and cleared the Indice Valley north to Baccanello while the 339th swung east on a ridge branching off towards Monte Grande in the 88th Division's zone. By the 19th, the Custer Division was ahead of the 34th to its left and in position to assist the Blue Devils in an attack to the northeast: Monte Grande and beyond, towards Castel San Pietro in the Po Valley.

Although the British XIII Corps was escheloned sharply back on II Corps' right flank to Highway 67, the 78th Division was in position to join the 88th and 85th Divisions in a coordinated attack to open the way to Highway 9. While the Americans went for Monte Grande, the 78th was to take Monte Spaduro, a two-mile, horseshoe-shaped massif running north and south that shut off all progress towards the Po Valley and Castel San Pietro. It was, says John Horsfall of the Irish Fusiliers, "bare of cover, repellent and sinister—black as the pit in the morning light, with dark grey caps on the high parts and deep fissures slashed across . . ." its gut.

On the night of October 19–20, two 36 Brigade companies attacked from Monte Pieve a thousand yards along a narrow causeway—300 feet below and not more than ten yards wide in several places—to capture a group of farm buildings at the end of Monte Acqua Salata, an ugly outcropping that overlooked the ridge approach to Spaduro. The causeway was mined; there was little room between two slippery clay slopes for maneuver. When dawn broke, the attackers had to withdraw back to Monte Pieve.

On the same night, 38th Brigade sent forward two companies of 1st Royal Irish Fusiliers to take Monte Spaduro. The attack went well, at first, despite one company's difficulties in scaling an almost unsurmountable cliff. At dawn the two companies held the high ground. During the night attack, however, the Fusiliers had bypassed Casa Spinello, a house now to their rear and strongly fortified by the enemy—a mistake for which they paid dearly. As the mist lifted, German machine guns opened up, and "a long line of German infantry lying up on the eastern side . . . rose to their feet and surged forward." Horsfall adds, "Our defensive artillery fire was too little, too late, and too far out. . . ." The Irish Fusiliers were surrounded, outnumbered and soon out of ammunition. They flung rocks at the advancing Germans, used rifle butts, even bare hands. A smokescreen was laid down at midday so that the reserve company, trying to help their comrades, could be withdrawn.

During the following week, the 78th made good its losses. First, Acqua Salata was taken on the night of October 20–21, though friendly fire on the causeway caused some casualties. The Argylls charged with tommy-guns, bayonets, and in some instances hurled the Germans down the hillside in the darkness with their hands. The attack succeeded, in large part, according to 78th Division historian Cyril Ray, because of "the coordination of the infantry and artillery." The Argylls fell upon the enemy as soon as the 138th Field Regiment artillery barrage was lifted and before the enemy realized that it was over.

Spaduro proved a tougher nut to crack. As soon as the Argylls captured Acqua Salata, the London Irish swung left of Casa Spinello in a night attack on Monte Spaduro. But they were trapped in the gulleys, digging in at daybreak to hold whatever they could. After twelve hours and several attempts to scramble up the steep ravines to get at the enemy, the weary troops were withdrawn.

On the night of October 23, the London Irish concentrated on Casa di Spinello and took it and twenty prisoners after a room-to-room battle—one German posted in the cellar shot at them through the floor boards—that lasted until 6:30 in the morning. In their main attack, launched at 2230 after a pinpoint barrage, the Inniskillings (Irish Brigade) cleared the Casa Salara Ridge on the right and Point 387 while the Lancaster Fusiliers of the 11th Brigade attacked 396, Spaduro's high point, from the left. By one in the morning of October 24, Spaduro belonged to the 78th Division.

On October 19, fighter-bombers at fifteen-minute intervals in 158 sorties saturated enemy defenses in the Monte Grande area with high explosives and fuel-tank incendiary bombs. At 1700, 88th Division and II Corps artillery at five-minute intervals pounded the area from Monte Cuccoli to Monte Cerere for one hour. Twenty-three tanks and tank destroyers joined in with a harassing mission on targets north and east of Monte Grande. A total of 8,100 rounds were fired in the hour. For all that, the Germans on Monte Cerere and Monte Grande were caught napping when the Blue Devils' 349th Infantry attacked at 2200 hours. (The *Fifth Army History* speculates that a partial explanation for the surprise was that most of the fighting earlier occurred along the ridge west from Grande, where the 339th and 350th Blue Devils were heavily engaged.) Cuccoli, the major height, was not taken until the afternoon of the 20th, and it was dark before Farneto, a village 500 yards to the east towards Grande, fell. Lieutenant John Ernser's A Company climbed the rocky slope of Cerere in the dark and a driving rain to take the height and eleven Germans prisoners without firing a shot. Before dawn, the 1st Battalion was on the eastern edge of the Monte Grande massif. To their left, the 2nd Battalion fended off a counterattack on the lower slopes. On the ridge they contended only with mud, rain and artillery fire. Company F reached the summit 24 hours earlier than anticipated, at dawn of the 20th. Within a half-hour, the company drove off a counterattack and the mountain was theirs.

Though General Clark, on a visit to the 349th Command Post on that day, warned Colonel Crawford to expect a counterattack in force, he was surely encouraged by the Blue Devils' capture of Monte Grande to concentrate on exploiting the bulge. Fighter-bombers were called up on the 20th and 21st to bomb and strafe all German approaches to the area while the artillery laid down harassing fire to discourage possible enemy counterattacks. Clark decided that II Corps would move on its right flank to Poggio Ribano and Monte Castelazzo, the last possible defensible heights, some three miles to the northeast of Monte Grande and just short of that distance from Highway 9 in the Po Valley.

While II Corps troops at the center and on the left flank maintained an "aggressive defense," two 91st regiments—the 362nd and 363rd—were placed in reserve, ready to repel any counterattack on the left but also ready to join a breakthrough to cut Highway 9. XIII Corps was to clear the chain of hills south of the Sillaro beyond Monte Spaduro to assist II Corps in opening up Highway 937 to Castel San Pietro.

On the night of October 22–23, the 3rd Battalion of the Blue Devils' 351st Regiment attacked north of Grande to take Hill 568 before dawn. Though the Germans were caught off balance, they soon mounted respectable counterattacks—one involving 220 troops—which were beaten off. A mile west, the 2nd Battalion of the Custer 337th Infantry reached the crest of Monte Castellaro and dug in. The next morning, the 1st Battalion, due to pass through to attack towards Ribano, was held up, clearing enemy pockets. Farther west, Company B, 339th Infantry, took Hill 459, the last knob on the ridge north of Monterenzio, but did not fare so well. Enemy troops on the reverse slope attacked at dawn and killed or captured most of two B Company platoons, regaining the knob. The 85th and the 88th now held a line a mile north of Monte Grande. That night, the 23rd–24th, G Company, spearheading the 2nd Battalion,

351st infantry, exploited a gap in the enemy lines and pushed on to Vedriano, at dawn taking the village on a flat-topped hill a mile and a half east of Hill 568, along with 40 Germans.

Companies E and F were held up by German strong points 1,200 yards west of Vedriano. As they fought to catch up to G Company, they could hear the rattle of guns coming through the mist from Vedriano. G Company reported a radio intercept from the 1st Parachute Regiment to the 1st Battalion, 4th Paras with the order: "Attack Vedriano. Vedriano is decisive!" Three enemy battalions were ready to counterattack. The Germans offered to permit the company to retire, in exchange for captured troops, but Colonel Champeny ordered the village held at all costs. Artillery was called in north and east of the church, where most of G Company held on, but as the afternoon lengthened the sounds of firing died out. Another intercepted German radio message declared: "Vedriano retaken and 80 Americans captured." G Company had come closer to the Po Valley than any other unit in the Fifth Army—less than 9,000 yards from Highway 9.

The attack was renewed on the night of October 24–25. The 337th's 1st Battalion reached the first height north of Hill 568 and the Custermen secured the position. Elsewhere, the news was not so good. The 351st's 1st Battalion managed to gain a cluster of houses at the foot of Vedriano hill, but the Blue Devils were stopped by enemy mortars and self-propelled guns. Tanks and tank destroyers on Hill 568 did their best to soften up the enemy lodged in Vedriano, but they were unable to get through the mud to within support range. South of the 351st, the 349th gained Hills 309 and 339, but one platoon of I Company was cut off while trying to drive the enemy out of a cluster of houses and the rest were driven back as day broke. Company L on nearby Hill 309 lost all its officers and withdrew.

After dark on October 25, the Blue Devils' 351st again attacked Vedriano. Companies E and F moved northeast to protect the left flank while Company B struck at Vedriano from the northwest as Company A attacked along the road. Company C provided a base of fire. It was a good battle plan and Company B got partway up the hill to the town, when enemy machine guns opened fire. Most of the company were replacements; they were confused by the rain, fog, the dark and the deadly guns. Only a few managed to get back to the Allied lines. Rain poured down at dawn on the 26th; fog reduced visibility to only 200 to 300 yards. The

Germans, however, counterattacked, and almost all of Company F and the remnants of B were killed or captured. Company E rushed forward, but all efforts to retrieve the captured troops failed. "With three companies now virtually destroyed and others at less than half their normal strength," the *Fifth Army History* states, "the 351st Infantry had no choice but to give up the attack."

Conditions were not much better elsewhere around the Monte Grande salient. Other units of the 88th and 85th clung to their positions. Two units of Company A, 337th Infantry, bore the brunt of a counterattack on the 26th that resulted in heavy casualties. On Monte Spaduro, the 78th Division improved its position. At midnight of October 24–25, the Northhamptons attacked to take Point 362, the peak of the next mountain to the north.

The night was lit by reflections of searchlights on the clouds, and an artillery and mortar concentration opened the way. Company D reached Casa Maletto, the first objective, which was ablaze. But heavy machine-gun fire slowed the attack and at 0430 it was decided that the ground gained was untenable. The Northhamptons withdrew. Torrential rains on the 26th—ten inches in twenty-four hours—put an end to resumption of the offensive. A flash flood took out all the bridges across the Sillaro, cutting off the 362nd Infantry and supplies from the rest of the Blue Devils. "Both the strength and the will of the troops to go on were fast slipping towards a complete breakdown," says historian John P. Delaney. "One fresh division," he laments, "might have been enough punch to get the Fifth Army through to the Po—one fresh regiment assigned to the 88th might have taken the Division through Vedriano and on to Highway 9."

But there *were* no fresh troops; 3,000 flown to Italy from France arrived too late for the attack on Monte Grande. Bad weather accounted for the delay, but it was, clearly, a case of too few too late. From the start of the offensive on September 10 through October 26, the 34th, 85th, 88th and 91st Divisions suffered 15,716 casualties. The 88th alone had 5,026. At the end of the month, companies attacked with as few as two or three officers; platoons were half-strength, and much of that was replacements. General Kendall reported that he was short 115 infantry officers as of October 26 and that his Blue Devils were under-strength by 1,243 officers and men. There were not enough replacements to make up for these losses. By the last week of October, in contrast to the Werhmacht, II Corps imposed drastic restrictions on ammunition for medium-caliber weapons and had no heavy artillery available after the 17th, when the 697th and 698th Field Artillery Battalions were detached and sent to France.

The Fifth Army's offensive, General Clark later said, ". . . did not stop with any definite setback or on any specific date. It merely ground to a halt because men could not fight any longer against the steadily increasing enemy reinforcements on our front. In other words, our drive died out, slowly and painfully, and only one long stride from success, like a runner who collapses reaching out for but not quite touching the tape at the finishing line." This writer believes one can see from the above that Clark has not got it quite right. But there's no gainsaying Cyril Ray's observation: "It was tantalizing to see, in the brief interludes of good weather, the towns and villages of the Lombardy Plain only a few miles ahead, and the flat country dotted with farms. To the troops huddled on the bare hillsides in rain and wind it was like a mirage."

NOTES

[1] Robbins, *The 91st Infantry Division*, pp. 179–80.
[2] Horsfall, *Fling Our Banner to the Wind*, pp. 195–200.
[3] United States Army, *Fifth Army History*, Vol. VII, p. 140.
[4] Ibid., p. 153.
[5] Robbins, *The 91st Infantry Division*, p. 183.

XX

CHRISTMAS SURPRISE

"I'll be home for Christmas" was a pop refrain sung that fall by a good many G.I.s with remarkable restraint—"You can count on that"—and with no little irony. It was, of course, a Tin Pan Alley response to what seemed to civilians a rapid advance across France. There was a respite of sorts in November for weary American troops on the Italian front. General Clark shifted XIII Corps to encompass Monte Grande and Monte Cerrere; the 88th Division was withdrawn for rest and recuperation. Later, the other divisions were relieved in turn. On November 4, IV Corps resumed command of the South African 6th Armoured Division. The Brazilian Expeditionary Force was brought up to full strength and the 92nd Division beefed up by a fourth regiment: the 366th Infantry and the 758th Light Tank Battalion. Five thousand replacements arrived and were absorbed in the infantry divisions, which, however, remained understrength by 7,000. Artillery ammunition was rationed in an attempt to build up stock. The loss of big guns to the Seventh Army in France was made up by equipping several antiaircraft units with self-propelled 105mm howitzers, forming the 1125th Armored Field Artillery Battalion. Fifth Army artillery was further boosted by the attachment of the British 54th Super-Heavy (8-inch) Gun Regiment. II Corps' front was narrowed, focusing its impact for the expected resumption of a joint British–American offensive in early December.

Ever since 1st Armored's Combat Command B reached Porretta Terme and pushed north along Highway 64 and the Reno River, the Germans on the Monte Belvedere–Monte Castello–Monte della Torraccia Ridge threatened the consolidation of II Corps' left flank by CCB and the South African 6th Armoured. From 3,000-foot heights, the Germans directed deadly artillery fire on Highway 64 and on advances north in the Reno Valley. In early November IV Corps inserted a Brazilian combat team to relieve CCB. The Brazilians were to press forward and narrow the South African front. This would reinforce the thrust of IV Corps down Highway 64 when the offensive was resumed in December. But first the Germans had to be cleared off the Belvedere high ground west of the Highway.

Task Force 45 was assigned the job with assists from the 2nd Battalion, 370th Infantry (92nd Division), the 6th Infantry and Reconnaissance Troop (1st Brazilian Division) and the 751st Tank Battalion less two companies. Two hundred Partisans under "General Armando" also participated. The 68th Armored Field Battalion and the 1106th Engineer Group were in support. Units from the 804th Tank Destroyer Battalion and the 13th Tank Battalion were added a few days before the attack on November 24. The Belvedere–Torraccia massif, with its nine peaks, runs three and three-quarter miles (as the crow flies) northeast from the village of Querciola. Monte Castello knuckles out southeast of Monte della Torraccia towards the Reno River far below.

Cloudy weather canceled anticipated air support as the troops moved out on a misty morning. Task Force 45's 435th Antiaircraft Battalion (converted to infantry) attacked on the left from Vidiciatico, a hilltown perched above the upper reaches of the Silla River, and by noon had taken Querciola, a village on the long rise to Belvedere. Despite German machine-gun, mortar and small-arms fire, the ex-ack-ackers captured Corona on the crest of the rise by dark, and Battery B was on Belvedere.

Elsewhere, the attack did not go as well. The 370th's 2nd Battalion made good progress in the morning, attacking north from west of Gaggio Montana at the center of the Belvedere massif to reach Morandella well up on the ridge, but were driven back a short distance by a fierce counterattack. The Brazilians, in open terrain on the right flank, ran into heavy artillery and mortar fire as they moved towards the high ground in the vicinity of Monte Castello. The command tank of the supporting armor was disabled by mines almost at the start. By noon, the Brazilian 6th Infantry's 3rd Battalion was forced back to its line of departure.

At midnight, the Germans struck in company strength at Corona. A Captain Straube, it was reported, urged his men on from behind with a pistol in one hand and a grenade in the other. They screamed as they charged, curdling the blood of the G.I.s defending Corona. However frightened, they broke up the German attack with artillery backup and support from the tankers. Fourteen Germans were taken prisoner, six killed and ten wounded. Captain Straube withdrew his men, who were from the 1st Battalion, 1043rd Infantry, 232nd Division.

The next morning at 0800, November 25, the Buffalo soldiers and the Brazilians made another attempt to gain the heights. Disrupted by friendly tank fire and enemy mortar shells, the 2nd Battalion, 370th, reorganized and before the day ended formed a defensive perimeter around the 751st's Tanks in the vicinity of Morandella. The Brazilians advanced to La Ca, a cluster of houses just above the Gaggio–Abetaia road, while the 3rd Platoon of Company A, 804th Tank Destroyer Battalion, edged northeast to Casa di Bombiana. At days' end, however, because of casualties from intense mortar fire, all but one company had to fall back to a ridge line south of Guanella. Artillery dropped over 2,000 rounds on German positions during the day despite the mists shrouding the mountain mass.

German mortars opened the day of November 26 with devastating effect. The Brazilians were forced back to their original positions, yielding the gains of the day before. Buffalo soldiers withdrew a few hundred yards to safer ground. Battery C managed to mount an attack on the east side of Belvedere but made no progress in the face of German opposition. Little happened the next day, except that the Brazilian sector was beefed up. For an attack on Monte Castello, the 6th Infantry's 2nd Battalion joined the 1st along with the 1st Battalion of the 1st Regiment. Before the Brazilians could mount their attack, however, the Germans shelled Corona on the evening of November 28, wiping out a strongpoint and knocking out some 30 Americans. Two enemy companies followed up the artillery concentration, attacking across the Valpiana Ridge against the town while another two struck at Battery B on Belvedere.

Battery B held on for a while, but a lack of ammunition forced a fallback to Querciola. In Corona, the Germans infiltrated with Faust-Patrones (bazookas) and destroyed three of Battery D's supporting tanks. This and severe losses of seventy killed and missing compelled Allied withdrawal to Vidiciatico. Battery C held on until the next morning, when it withdrew to Querciola for fear of being outflanked. Partisan volunteers fought well alongside the Americans and shared their fate. Fifteen minutes after the attack on Belvedere, the Germans also went for the Brazilian 2nd and 3rd Battalions and were repulsed. An enemy sixteen-man patrol also attempted to penetrate along the Brazilian/South African boundary but the patrol was driven across the Reno into the hands of the

South Africans.

After a thirty-minute artillery barrage on the morning of November 29, the Brazilians moved out at 0800 for Monte Castello, three battalions abreast. The troops, some still adjusting to the cold of Apennine Italy, crossed a gentle rise and open fields with little difficulty under light mortar fire. They reached Abetaia at 1045, a village on the road at the foot of Monte Castello, but German resistance increased as they mounted the forward slope of the mountain. Mortar fire intensified. By late afternoon, however, they were midway to the crest, where the enemy hit them hard from fixed concrete emplacements. Suffering heavy casualties, the Brazilians withdrew to the relative safety of the lower slopes.

The Brazilians interested the Germans, who constantly probed and prodded their sector. Most of the Brazilian soldiers were black, came from a distant, warm country, and spoke a language that few then in Italy understood. Though some had gained combat experience in the Serchio in early autumn, most were green troops. The last elements of the 11th Infantry arrived in the Porretta area on December 1. As soon as they relieved the 1st Infantry, a patrol attempted to infiltrate their lines and an attack followed during the same night, forcing a slight fall-back, recouped in the morning when the Germans withdrew. While General Mascarenhas rearranged his forces for an attack on the Monte Castello–Monte della Torraccia Ridge, the Germans stepped up their patrol activity.

POWs said that furloughs were awarded for bringing back prisoners, while patrols who came back empty-handed were punished. An SS Propaganda unit turned up and the Brazilians were inundated by leaflets showing Stalin with a big stick herding Roosevelt and Churchill, dressed as children, as well as leaflets charging that the Brazilians were dying far from home for American capitalists.

At 0600, December 12, the Brazilians attacked following a thirty-minute artillery barrage. Task Force 45 mounted a diversion on the southern slopes of Monte Belvedere to the left of the Brazilians, while Task Force Nelson—a mix of infantry and tanks—did the same on the right in the Castelnuovo area. Initially, the attack went as well as expected. By noon, the Brazilians were midway on the slopes of Della Torraccia, and on the right flank the 1st Battalion, 11th Infantry, the "new guys on the block," were not far from the crest. But, as POWs and partisans had reported, the Germans were well prepared: trenches, mines and barbed wire had been added to their defenses since the last attack. There also had been a buildup of enemy artillery in the sector. The Germans were determined to hold the heights that overlooked the Reno Valley and Highway 64.

During the afternoon, intensified small-arms and mortar fire drove the 2nd and 3rd Battalions, 1st Infantry, back to their original positions. "It not being wise to remain out in front alone," as Colonel Peter S. Wondolowski put it in his *History of the IV Corps*, "the 11th Infantry pulled back also."[1] Task Force Nelson, which made a ten-mile finger thrust down Highway 64 from Silla to Malpasso, also withdrew. The next day, the 11th Infantry relieved the two 1st Infantry battalions and the attempts to clear the Belvedere–Della Torraccia massif came to a close.

General Alexander on November 27 declared: "Our primary task is to ensure that the enemy is afforded no opportunity to withdraw divisions . . . to reinforce his armies on either Western or Eastern Fronts. This object cannot be achieved by a purely defensive attitude. . . . [The] Allied Armies are to mount a major offensive on a wide front."[2] But one with limited objectives—Bologna and Ravenna—for, as Alexander understood, his resources were severely crimped. It was too late to drive the enemy back deep into the Po Valley as far as the Adige, where the Germans had erected a major defense line—the so-called Venetian Line—running from the Adriatic at Chioggia to Lake Garda in the Alps to defend northeastern Italy.

There was a need for a pause—to refit and refresh troops of both armies—if the Allies were to undertake a strong offensive in the spring. Allied forces in Italy, too, were feeling the pinch of a worldwide shortage of ammunition. Oddly enough, perhaps reflecting the optimism that followed the Normandy Invasion, production had been cut during the summer. It had since been increased but, as Alexander noted, it would be some time before results would show on the battlefield. Alexander's staff calculated that enough ammunition was on hand for a fifteen-day "large-scale" Eighth Army offensive in December whereas the American Fifth's stock sufficed for "about ten days' intensive fighting before the end of the year."[3]

Furthermore, the Eighth Army lost troops to Greece to forestall a Communist takeover. The Greek Mountain Brigade went home in October, and the Indian Fourth and the British Fourth Infantry Divisions were sent to Greece shortly after. The 46th Division would follow in January. To compensate for these losses, the number of light antiaircraft regiments was reduced, to provide added infantry. The Cremona Battle Group, the first of several organized by the Italian Government and armed by the British, arrived but not in time for the December offensive. General McCreery later remarked, "They had little equipment and even less will to fight. . . . [T]here was one Italian General who looked so dour and unhappy . . . that I gave orders for him to be excluded from conferences and my 'Order Group' sessions because he so depressed everybody."[4, 5]

"We wanted Bologna," Alexander said, "as a road-and-railhead to serve as an administrative center for the Spring offensive; Ravenna would, we hoped, be useful as a port for the same purpose."[6] The Germans, too, wanted Bologna. A glance at the map, as General von Senger suggests shows why: ". . . all the reserves that had been assembled in the Bologna area were [centrally] placed for operating either on the Adriatic front or at Bologna itself or with the army in Liguria."

Here—the sector came under Von Senger's XIV Panzer Corps at the end of October—the Germans had all the advantages of interior lines. An effective series of defenses had been developed on the west banks of the rivers that flanked the city to the east. The north–south running ridges between the rivers were dominated by positions arranged, as Von Senger put it, in "chessboard fashion." From these positions, infantry flanking fire flayed valley roads. Antitank guns were concealed on the roads while tanks and assault guns were held ready at a moment's notice to engage any Allied tanks that managed to break through. Von Senger also maintained a powerful concentration of artillery in his sector. "All I had to do," he says of his assuming the Bologna command, "was to arrange for an adequate position in depth of the front line divisions and for corresponding protection with armour"[7] The city, in Alexander's view, was "as strong a fortress as any in Europe at the time."[8]

Immediately ahead of the British forces, moreover, were the rivers with their gigantic flood banks built over the years to contain spring freshets and flash floods. The Germans were quick to take advantage of these ready-made obstacles. Belts of wire and aprons of mines were laid out in front; dikes were breached to allow flooding of the approaches. Oddly enough, the northern flood bank was slightly higher than the southern, a gain, however slight, that improved observation. Bridges were destroyed and replaced by footbridges that swung back when not needed. Tanks and wheeled armored vehicles could not mount the steep banks without approaching ramps. Therefore, bridges could only be built at former sites—yet another advantage for the German defenses. Todt labor teams scooped out and reveted tunnels with stout timbers. Gun muzzles protruded as if from portholes of buccaneer warships. The killing ground was so flat that a weapon situated a few feet above commanded hundreds of yards, while the winding river banks afforded converging and enfilading fire on a wide front.

Earlier crossings had taught the Eighth Army some lessons. Massed assaults incurred too many casualties; approaches in small numbers often gained the near bank. But the artillery was unable to deliver the covering fire needed to enable the buildup of sufficient troops to force a crossing. Experiments, however, showed that artillery could be deployed so as to bombard the inner slopes of a flood bank without undue risk to troops dug in ten yards away on the outer bank. "Littlejohns"—high-velocity, two-pound antitank guns, that could be manhandled forward—replaced the heavier, awkward six-pounders for "sniping" into gun portholes and for reducing enemy posts on the near bank. "Crocodiles" and "Wasps," large and small fire-throwing vehicles, were modified along with Lifebuoys, manual flame-throwers, to burn out the defensive warrens squirreled into the flood banks.

Further, the Americans sent over a lightweight wide-tracked carrier, the "Weasel," developed and tested in the deep snows of the Rocky Mountains, and the "Mud-hens" proved effective on swampy ground. Bridge-laying "Ark" tanks were deployed with an ingenious variation: Instead of being a full span, the "bridge" was just a little longer than a tank and could be raised hydraulically while the tank "rested" on the riverbed. Should the river be deep and the bottom tank be submerged, a second "Ark" could drive on top to construct a crossing two tanks deep. Sapper assault companies also moved forward with the infantry to throw up a new lightweight bridge invented by Captain E.A. Olafson of the Royal Canadian Electrical and Mechanical Engineers. Fifteen-foot lengths of half-inch pipe were welded into sections 18 inches wide, each weighing 200 pounds; by connecting these, a gap of 45 feet could be spanned by engineers, often working under fire.

"While we were ecstatic finally to receive all this modern equipment [long used in northwest Europe]," C.S. Frost, who served as a junior officer with the Canadian Patricias, recalled "we were under no illusion that our job would be made any easier."[9] Moreover, it seems, not everyone got what was needed. Farley Mowat tells us that his regiment was not issued any of the new Littlejohns. Planning for the offensive also appears flawed in retrospect, although the plans were readily approved at a commanders' conference on November 26. The Eighth Army was to move first, driving the enemy west of the Santerno River between Highways 9 and 16, ten miles above Faenza and fifteen above Ravenna; then it was to push on in a northerly direction, outflanking Bologna from the east. It was anticipated that the Eighth would reach the Santerno in a week; the Fifth Army was to stand by and attack at the appropriate moment, preferably as the Eighth crossed the Santerno. Both Armies, then, would go for Bologna.

The stage for the December offensive was set by the 10th Indian Division at the end of November. All three Eighth Army Corps were committed by General McCreery: the Polish Corps on the left in the Apennine foothills; V Corps (56th British, 10th Indian, 2nd New Zealand and, in the opening phase, the 46th) bracketing Highway 9; and the Canadian Corps on the right. The Canadian sector—roughly in front of Russi, some 15 miles above Faenza (and then along the lateral road to Ravenna)—was considered the enemy's weakest. The Germans faced the Eighth Army from behind a water barrier that began on the Lamone and ended just south of Ravenna. The only break was a five-mile defense line between Scaldino on the Lamone, six miles above Faenza, and Casa Bettini, on the Montone.

Before the Canadians could mount the "sudden and swift" assault expected to surprise the enemy for a breakthrough essential to the offensive, the 10th Indian Division was ordered to take the bridge site at Casa Bettini. That would enable the Canadians—in Operation CHUCKLE—to move up in position on the right of V Corps.

Eighth Army preparations were going well as the 4th and 46th Divisions seized crossings over the Cosina, a stream about midway between Forli and Faenza, where it went under Route 9. The ground inside a loop of the Cosina south of the highway was cleared during the night of November 21–22. By nightfall of the 23rd, the left wing of V Corps was across the Cosina on a three-mile front south of Route 9. The Polish Corps made comparable progress in the foothills to the south.

The German 26 Panzer Division pulled back to the shelter of the Lamone River, leaving the 278th Division to protect its three-mile exposed flank between the Montone and the Lamone. General Keightley ordered the 10th Indian Division to cross the Cosina on Route 9 and to move north on the right flank of the 4th Division to capture the bridge over the Montone at Casa Bettini. The Indians and combat group Porterforce were to screen the movement of the Canadians, who had been at rest, to the front.

It was slow, muddy going for the Indians because the enemy had flooded the countryside for a thousand yards east of the river. The only approaches along built-up roads were covered by machine guns and artillery. German strongpoints in houses near Casa Bettini thwarted the capture of the bridge. The Indian brigades, however, "by nibbling tactics"[10] edged towards Alberto, a village that was the crux of the German switch line between the Lamone, a mile to the west, and Casa Bettini, a mile to the east on the Montone. The weather improved on the 30th, freeing up supporting tanks, and the Indians closed in from opposite sides. A "free-for-all" raged at close quarters, until the enemy "slowly and sullenly" withdrew, leaving forty dead among the ruins at the end of the day. Casa Bettini was secured the following day and the Canadians began to cross the river.

Though rested, the Canadians were not in the best of shape, largely because events in Canada had badly shaken morale. That fall, the Canadian Government announced a home leave plan that promised long-service men would be repatriated by Christmas. Canadian forces had been overseas since 1939. But the plan, based on *points*, affected only a bare handful. Moreover, though Canada had a draft, only volunteers from among the conscripts were sent overseas. "Zombies"—the combat soldiers' name for the draftees—went on strike in British Columbia and burnt the Union Jack to protest a suggestion that they be sent overseas. As a letter quoted by Farley Mowat, put it: "We hear that the flag-burners were fined $11.00 each and that the incident can't be called a mutiny—just a little high feeling. This is great stuff for our morale as we go up the line."

"Disheartened and disgusted," according to Farley Mowat, the troops "approached the new battles in a state of resignation. . . . They had only one valid reason . . . for entering battle now, and it was not hatred of the enemy. It was because they were a part of their Regiment . . . the one intact structure remaining in their lives, and so it must be preserved even if the cost was death,"[11] And they would pay that cost gallantly. Once across the Montone, the 1st Canadian Division's Third Brigade, after heavy fighting on the Scolo Via Cupa canal, encircled Russi, a key enemy strongpoint on the Faenza–Ravenna road. In forty-eight hours its infantry battalions suffered 106 casualties. The Canadians then forced back the left flank of the German 356th Division and reached the Lamone, west of the town.

The neighboring 114th Jaeger Division was placed in an awkward position. The Jaegers fought their best for San Pancrazio, but could not hold it against the Canadian Armoured, which drove through the resulting gap between the two German divisions to capture Godo on the road to Ravenna. Highway 16 was cut at Mezzano. With an assist from several hundred partisans, the Canadians secured Ravenna on December 5. Meanwhile, for the 1st Division, as Charles S. Frost, of the Patricias put it, "carefully laid plans started to unravel."[12]

The Lamone, on the far side of a thirty-foot bank, was in full spate, cold—and so swift that a swimmer had little chance of survival. The Germans had withdrawn across its dikes, but the Canadian 1st Division's Third Brigade was unable to follow as planned. Acting Divisional Commander Brigadier D. Smith ordered the 1st Brigade to take over immediately, on the morning of December 4. There was little time— three hours to be exact—for preparation. The tank support had not yet been able to catch up to the infantry.

The Hastings and Prince Edward Regiment led the assault in full daylight without proper reconnaissance, without the new antitank Littlejohns assigned to the Division—and without an experienced commander. Brigade Commander Calder decided it was time that Major Stan Ketcheson took over the Regiment from Lieutenant Colonel Cameron, "to gain experience." For the same reason, a staff officer was given Dog Company. Another officer who had recently arrived from Canada was in charge of another company, while a third company commander had experience in only three previous engagements. As Mowat points out, "even in a minor action this combination of untried commanders would have been risky." Moreover, the Regiment was ordered "to do a job that the entire Third Brigade did not feel competent to attempt."[13]

Ketcheson, a good soldier, recognized the difficulties his men faced. He begged for more time for adequate preparation, but was told to get on with the job. He decided to test enemy strength with A Company, which would attempt a crossing if possible. With an hour's notice, marching three miles at top speed, the company reached the Lamone banks at 1430.

"Everything was frighteningly quiet," Captain Max Porritt said afterwards. Assault boats were supposed to be on hand but were nowhere to be seen. Able Company had arrived too late to gain advantage from the preparatory barrage. As his men waited for orders, Captain Porritt scouted the crest; one quick glimpse was all the enemy allowed. Bullets kicked up dirt around Porritt and his second-in-command, Captain Christiansen. "I saw his body go rolling down the slope, his beret flying past my head." He had been killed by a shot through his skull. Porritt tried to raise the artillery, but his radio went out. "There was nothing for it but to take the company back a hundred yards to the shelter of some buildings" where a messenger found him to say that the attack had been postponed.[14]

This time, attack plans were more realistic. Under cover of an artillery barrage, two regiments—the Hastings on the left and the Royal Canadian on the right—were to cross the river at 0100 hours on December 5. Olafson portable bridges and assault boats were to be on hand. Time, however, did not allow ground reconnaissance, nor did company commanders get to see the starting line beforehand. (One wants to have a starting line as close to the artillery targets as one can safely get.) All Ketcheson had to go on was an Italian topographical map. It showed a ditch parallel to, and about three hundred yards in front of, the Lamone south dike. It seemed an obvious landmark offering shelter to troops waiting to jump off.

Assault companies B and C moved forward in the awesome silence of the dark night. There were no challenges until the Lamone dike loomed some thirty feet over their heads. There was no ditch, though it had been shown on the map. (The actual ditch stopped short of their position.) As the men huddled against the bank and bridge crew wrestled on the crest with the unfamiliar Olafson, lights flickered in the blackness to the south, as guns rumbled. In C Company a sergeant cried out, "Get down, for Christ's sake, boys! They're falling short." In fact, the artillery was all too accurate, right on target. There was no place to hide; men wheeled about like poor sinners in Dante's innermost hell. On their belts phosphorus grenades hit by shrapnel spewed burning fragments over the living and the dead. Suddenly, it was over. Half of B Company were dead or wounded; C Company, which had gone in at two-platoon strength, was hit just as bad. Mowatt, tells us that one tardy gunner fired one more round—"the period that marked the end."[15]

When the news filtered back to Brigade—and registered—Brigadier

Calder asked Division to postpone the assault and relieve the battered Hastings. He was told in no uncertain terms to continue: A and D Companies were to move up. On the left, the Royal Canadians had got two companies across the river, drawing the attention of the 114th Jaegers away from the Hastings. As a result, the two Hastings companies crossed a half-completed Olafson bridge without a shot fired. They established themselves in a group of houses. The remnant of B Company crossed the river and moved to close the left flank gap between the Hastings and the Royals. Dawn came—and with it, the Germans.

A Canadian sniper in an upstairs window spotted them first—several German vehicles coming down the road, Machine guns and rifles opened up on three sides, followed by a sustained bombardment. A and B company commanders called for artillery—but their radios were blocked by the high dike walls. D Company attempted to expand the bridgehead but was beaten back by the Germans. A Company held on in the houses, though they were battling the enemy hand to hand. No one expected relief, for the Hastings had no reserves. There were no antitank guns within the bridgehead. As German tanks rumbled towards the besieged Canadians, a rumor that the Royals had abandoned their beachhead grew and spread. (The Royal Canadians had not, as yet, but they were badly battered. Of the 205 who had crossed the Lamone that night, three officers and 26 men were killed, three officers and 43 men were wounded, and two officers and 29 men were missing—slightly over a fifty percent loss.) Men gave way to panic, retreated, briefly rallied between the dikes, then retreated again.

Major Broad's B Company remnant advanced four hundred yards before it went to ground in an open wheat field under intense small-arms fire. Broad ran under fire back to the Lamone, where he found an RCR group of officers preparing to withdraw. It was fruitless to ask them for help, so he sent for his company—now reduced to less than a platoon—and occupied a group of stone houses at the abandoned RCR flank position. There he hoped to maintain a toehold. With the RCR bridgehead broken, the German tanks were free to concentrate on Broad's gallant band; they remained outside the range of the Canadians' one short-ranged PIAT to pound away at the sheltering stone walls. German mortar and artillery fire joined in. Broad and his men held out for an hour. Finally, unable to get any artillery support, Broad gave the order to withdraw. Men crossing the river were swept away and some survived only by jettisoning their equipment.

Sixty-seven Hastings had been killed, seriously wounded or captured. This was the least of it. As Mowat pointed out: "For the first time the unit had been severely beaten in the field and for the first time its spirit had broken." Incidently, Mowat tells us, the men did not blame the artillery. Nor, did they, so far as one can tell, fault the execution of orders from above by their officers. The commanders of the 1st Brigade, the RCRs and the Hastings were dismissed, in the Montgomery tradition of tolerating no failures—unfairly, many felt, because they were "singled out . . . for a failure which had been theirs only in its enforced enactment, and not in its design."[16]

The fault, as military historian Lieutenant Colonel Stevens, who served in Italy, put it, surely "lay not in the fighting men but in their management." Planners were overly optimistic. The new tools of battle, the harassed enemy, the surety of his defeat raised their expectations. They forgot, in Stevens' phrase, "that the trapped animal often fights to the death." There was little or no recognizance of the proposed crossing site. The failure lay in the structure of the operation. "After Canadian experience on the Pisciatello, the Savio and the Montone," Stevens concluded, "any plan of battle designed to capture three successive flood banked river lines in a single gallop was ludicrous."[17]

It had been anticipated that the Eighth Army would reach the Santerno by December 7, with troops in position to pivot above Faenza towards Bologna from the northeast. Plans to renew the attack on the Lamone defenses were washed away as the rains fell and the river rose to new heights. Fifth Army's II Corps' seventy-two-hour alert was canceled. It would stand by for a possible resumption of the drive to Bologna sometime around the 15th, when the Eighth Army would be ready to turn on Bologna.

While the Canadians contested the Germans for the Lamone, the New Zealanders and the British 46th Infantry Division moved to outflank Faenza, a city on Highway 9 that had known many a siege and sacking since it was established at the junction of the Marzeno and Lamone rivers some 2,400 years earlier. "*La mia bella Faenza*," an elderly woman cried, as an ancient tower collapsed on December 1 under pounding from a squadron of the New Zealand 18th Armoured Regiment. Visibility was so poor three afternoons later that the Regiment had to cease shooting.

Nonetheless, this did not prevent the New Zealanders, with help from the 10th Indian Gurkhas and a brigade from the British 56th Division, from mounting feints towards the city. Divisional cavalry even tossed large stones into the Lamone at one point to give the impression that assault boats were being launched.

While the Germans were distracted, the 46th Division, four miles south, established a bridgehead across the Lamone at Quartolo. Efforts to expand the bridgehead, however, were fiercely contested by the German 19th Panzer Grenadier Division. Another feint appeared appropriate, and the New Zealanders obliged. It helped some, delaying the Germans' concentration of reserves on the bridgehead salient where British infantry advanced through the roadless and broken country. Pideura, a village on the approach ridge to Faenza, was cleared of German troops on December 7. The Poles had crossed the upper reaches of the Lamone two days earlier, pushing on two miles to capture Montecchio and the high ground west of the river some eight miles south of Faenza; they had secured the Eighth Army's flank.

Worried lest Faenza should fall and endanger Bologna, Hitler personally ordered General Vietinghoff, Acting Army Group C Commander, to stand fast and yield no ground at Faenza. As backup, 2,600 replacements were promised, and the 90th Panzer Grenadier and the 98th Infantry Divisions were moved to the LXXVI Panzer Corps front. On December 9, the Germans attacked along the entire 46th Division front, the 200th Regiment of the 90th Panzer Grenadiers serving as spearhead. "After hand-to-hand fighting fiercer than any yet seen," a report to the German High Command stated, "we succeeded in reoccupying a considerable tract of ground . . . Our losses were considerable, The enemy . . . had enormous casualties."[18] But the Germans counted their gains before they were fully secured. Weather favored the defenders, enabling the artillery to lay down an effective curtain of defensive fire and Allied aircraft to bomb and strafe German concentrations. The German counteroffensive failed.

Now that the 46th Division had to be relieved and sent on to Greece, the Indians and the New Zealanders were shuffled into the bridgehead sector, the former fanning out to the left and the latter straddling the Lamone southwest of Faenza. Relief was completed on the morning of the 12th. The bridgehead was scarcely two miles deep, with Pideura at its center. Supplying the troops across the Lamone was well-nigh impossible along the one-way road from Route 9 to the crossing at Quartolo.

To improve transportation, the New Zealand sappers built a "circuit" with an "up" road over one bridge across the Marzeno and a "down" road across a second bridge—a hundred-foot Bailey bridge thrown up in one night under harassing Nebelwerfers. The road was "hacked . . . out of cattle tracks, fields and river marshes." To cope with mud, road builders at one point used a dozen "Itie haystacks," covered them with reinforced mesh, then topped them off with rubble from demolished houses. Sappers "put down hundreds of tree trunks . . . shored up the ditches."[19]

Enemy fire was troubling, but nothing compared with the condition of the road. It took up to twelve hours to bring rations by jeep from Forli to New Zealand 5th Brigade Headquarters. Out of a 26-jeep convoy with trailers on the night of December 12–13, two jeeps crashed over a bank and six trailers had to be temporarily abandoned; only 16 got through.

"At zero hour [2300 hours, December 14] to a second," New Zealander B.C.H. Moss noted in his diary, "the horizon behind us blazed with the flashes of the artillery. . . . The shells . . . cracking in the air like whiplashes as they hurtle up towards the top of their trajectories. . . . [Where they burst one sees] myriads of winking pin pricks of light, looking small and insignificant, but in reality . . . an expanding shower of deadly splinters. . . . [T]he explosions all blend into an insistent rumbling. When the barrage lifts and creeps forward, lesser signs and sounds begin. Wavering yellow flares hover briefly . . . necklaces of tracers curve through the blackness . . . haystacks here and there become lit and blaze brightly for an hour or so . . . then smoulder. . . . Pauses . . . are filled by the insistent chattering of the Vickers guns . . . the burrrr of the spandau . . . a short stutter of bren. Grenades pop, tank engines are roaring, Jerry mortar and shellfire crunches down, and now and then the giant-retching of the nebelwerfer is heard, followed by the moaning of rockets before they explode in rapid succession."[20]

Five 10th Indian battalions went forward to give the New Zealanders a firm left flank for their drive to the Senio, the next river to be crossed on the way to Bologna. Faenza was to be bypassed, then picked off by a Task Force of the 43rd Gurkhas with supporting tanks, artillery and engineers. The Durhams of the 10th Brigade attacked Pergola, a village at the junction of the Indian and Kiwi sectors. Uncharted schu-minefields broke up the assault and Pergola remained in German hands at the next day's end. To the left of the Durhams, the 3rd/1st Punjabs gained a low but sharp-crested ridge. Haystacks fired by enemy tracers silhouetted charging Punjabis, who might have held their own nonetheless if the 4th/11th Sikhs to their left had held their ground in the face of German infantry backed by self-propelled guns.

North of Pideura, beyond the Sikhs, the King's Own fought along a hilltop towards Camillo. At dusk, they captured the town and 24 Germans. At the end of twenty-four hours' fighting, Company C had one officer and 26 men left. On the 10th Indian left flank, the 3rd Garhwalis fared a bit better, encircling enemy positions at Casa Zula and Monte Coralli to win through in bitter hand-to-hand fighting. One rifleman mounted a haystack to get at a sniper with his bayonet, only to have his quarry pop out and pull away the ladder. When the enemy finally gave up their positions, sixty were dead and twelve made prisoner.

The 10th Indian Division, in the words of its historian, had "failed for the first time to make its principal objectives." But the fighting was not in vain, for the Indians "had pinned down the enemy's reserves and had given the New Zealanders a clear run to the Senio."[21] Perhaps not so clear as all that. Still, as the New Zealanders pulled ahead, the 4th/10th Baluchis passed through the New Zealand lines to swing south on the flank and rear of Pergola. The perspicacious Germans were one jump ahead and had pulled out.

The way was open, and on the evening of December 15 Indian patrols were on the twisting banks of the Senio between Renazzi and Tobano. The New Zealand attack opened with an advance to Celle by the 5th Brigade's 23rd Battalion. The town, north and west of Faenza, was occupied by 0400 on the 15th. Over 80 enemy were killed—100 taken prisoner by the 23rd Battalion alone, which itself lost 12 killed and 48 wounded.

On the left, the 22nd Battalion had to contend with a landscape cut up by steep ridges with Germans posted in well-placed farmhouses. Sergeant L.F. Seaman led his men uphill and around one house before making a charge. About 20 Germans were captured and 15 killed. Although seriously wounded, he refused aid until his men were posted against counterattack. At night's end, the 22nd Battalion was abreast of the 23rd, having taken over a hundred prisoners at a cost of seven dead and 30 wounded. On the right, the 28th Battalion fought in fallow fields lined by rows of mulberry and poplar trees. Despite muddy going and German opposition, the 28th pushed ahead until it was turned back by German tanks, losing 24 killed, 57 wounded and two men captured.

All three battalions were approximately abreast on a line pegged on Celle, outflanking Faenza, where they were effectively blocked by German tanks and infantry. To assist the Eighth Army, the Fifth had committed XIII Corps in the Santerno Valley with some success. But the 6th Armoured was unable to break through Tossignano because the Germans loomed over them from the Vena del Gesso escarpment to the east.

The drive down the Santerno towards Imola came to a halt on December 15. The night before, New Zealand tanks moved up to help their infantry break out of the Celle line towards the Senio. Many foot-sloggers were angry, feeling that the tankers were laggard, never on hand when needed. Initially, everything seemed to go badly for the tankers. One troop of tanks was caught "in a torrent of shells, apparently ours." An officer was killed, a tank damaged. Another squadron took a wrong turn and had to back up along a narrow road. Fields were bogs and mined, so that tanks nudged ahead in single file along obscure lanes, while their commanders walked ahead, despite shellfire, to show the way.

At last, on the straight run to Celle, blazing haystacks limned the road to deadly effect for German guns, "pumping shells . . . just clearing the Shermans." Fearing that the lead tank would be "potted like a sitting duck" and finding the surrounding ground unsuitable for maneuver, the tank commander waited out the Germans until dawn. Once in the hamlet, the tanks "knocked big chunks off a house" at the far end; the enemy infantry "left smartly." An artillery "stonk" in the right place drove off two Mark IV tanks.[22] By this time, the air force was all over the sky, swooping down on the slightest enemy movement. Other tanks reached the New Zealand line along a ridge that gave them a commanding view beyond the enemy line to the Senio. Nonetheless, it was clear on the morning of the 15th that the tanks would not be able to burst through to gain the river.

The next day the picture changed. Shortly after 0700, the New Zealanders heard an explosion from the Route 9 crossing of the Senio. The Germans now felt that holding Faenza—clearly outflanked—was no longer feasible. Cautiously, the Kiwis advanced towards the river. Mines had to be cleared from the roads. New Zealand patrols reached the river southwest of Castel Bolognese later that day. White flags fluttered in Faenza and the Kiwi Divisional Cavalry crossed the Lamone and entered the small city without opposition, except from one house that was soon demolished. Most of the population had fled earlier; most of the remaining 4,000 (out of 40,000) huddled in cellars, and suffered few casualties. The Germans had looted the city, then left. There was no fighting in the streets though there was some sniping and mortar fire at the northern edge of the town, where the Gurkha Task Force swinging down from the north ran into some roadblocks. On December 17, General Freyberg moved his divisional headquarters from Forli into Faenza.

Mid-month there were changes in the high command of the Mediterranean Theater. Field Marshal Alexander became Supreme Allied Commander of the Theater, General Clark took command of the Allied Armies in Italy and Lieutenant General Truscott returned to Italy from France to assume command of the Fifth Army on December 16. Alexander's November 27 order, calling for the capture of Bologna, remained in effect. Clark reiterated it when he instructed General McCreery to "proceed with current [Eighth Army] operations with the object of launching an attack to force the crossing of the Senio in conjunction with the Fifth Army's attack."[23] Now, however, the projected Fifth Army attack was to take place sometime before Christmas.

Kiwis patrolled the near banks of the Senio; the Indians attempted crossings farther upstream but were driven back by counterattacks. The enemy showed no indication of falling back, downriver, where he forestalled the 56th Division and contested all attempts to cross the Lamone northeast of Faenza. If the Fifth Army was to join in a drive to take Bologna, the Canadians had to get across the Lamone. At last, after five days, the weather improved enough to allow another attempt at the Lamone. With ample reconnaisance, antitank guns and an intense barrage, the Canadians crossed the Lamone the night of December 10. The enemy retreated. The Canadians expanded their bridgehead, successfully crossing their next hazard, the Vecchio Canal, the following night.

However, when the Canadians gained the north side of another canal, the Naviglio, the Germans struck with a vengeance. "We can't hold out," Hastings' B Company, a thousand yards in and under Mark IV tank fire, called back. "You must remain," the beleaguered troops were told. They had to buy time until tanks could come up. D Company, in reserve, was sent forward and driven back by enemy guns three times. On the left, a handful of Littlejohns held enemy tanks at bay.

The two-battalion bridgehead, a thousand yards broad and a thousand deep at its point, was now a narrow strip along the north dike. At any moment, it seemed that the German tanks would cross the canal and drive the Canadians back. In the crowded Hastings Headquarters building, when tanks were heard on the road alongside, men thought, "This is it." Someone, however, looking out the window, gave a triumphant yell. "Coming up the road," Q.M.S. Basil Smith later recalled, "was a squadron of British Columbia Dragoon tanks swinging their 17-pounder guns from side to side as if they meant business."[24]

And so they did, firing their guns as they crossed the Naviglio accompanied by the Loyal Edmontons' infantry. Confronted by the tanks and fresh troops, the Germans yielded ground, leaving smoldering tanks behind to fall back to the Senio.

Fourteen counterattacks were mounted against the Carleton and York and Hastings Regiments. The bridgehead sliver was held by a handful of surviving infantry and effective artillery fire. The Hastings lost over 100 men. A, D and C companies were hardly above the strength of platoons. B company was a remnant, patched up by a handful culled from the others. Still, their work was not done: the Germans still held positions on the Vecchio and the Naviglio, to the west of the Hastings/Carleton beachhead near Bagnicavallo.

On the 16th, the 1st Brigade, 48th Regiment, launched a new assault to dislodge the enemy. It failed. The Royal Canadian and Hastings Regiments then sent forward two battalions at 0400 on December 18. The attack companies, Farley Mowat avers, "were hardly more than straggling little mobs of somnambulists." The Hastings' D Company was down to 18 men. The Royals were forced back to the south banks. Others plugged on, occupied Bagnocavallo, and pushed the Germans in the sector towards the Senio. The Hastings continued on, as their commander, Colonel Cameron put it, "with only enough strength left to lean against the Hun as he withdrew."[25] The exhausted Canadians closed on the Germans along the Senio from a mile south of Alfonsine to a point just north of Cotignola. In twenty days, starting from the Montone on December 2, to the Senio, the Canadian Corps (1st and 5th Armoured) suffered losses of 548 killed, 1,796 wounded and 212 taken prisoner.

The Eighth Army front now arced 40 miles, from about ten miles southwest of Faenza, to the Adriatic, some six miles northeast of Ravenna. The Eighth, in fact, was nearly abreast of the Fifth. On December 20, Clark reiterated Alexander's still-standing order of November 27, telling his two Army Commanders that ". . . the time is rapidly approaching when I shall give the signal for a combined all-out attack of the Fifth and Eighth Armies."[26]

There was a light fall of snow in the Senio sector on December 23. Up in the mountains where the Germans waited, it was already a white Christmas. In her nightly broadcasts, "Axis Sally" serenaded the troops with carols—including the ever-popular "I'm Dreaming of a White Christmas"—and boasted that Germany had turned the war around. Eight Panzer Divisions had broken through on December 16 in the Ardennes on a 40-mile front, threatening Antwerp. News of Hitler's surprise offensive aroused fears of a similar blow on the Italian front, in particular the loosely defended IV Corps sector above Leghorn and Pisa. The rugged Apuan Alps front was lightly defended on both sides—not a matter of undue concern—but the Allied command was suddenly made aware that the Tyrrhenian coastal plain and the Serchio Valley were natural shooting galleries for a pincers movement aimed at Leghorn. Without that port, it would be impossible to adequately supply the Fifth Army in the vastnesses of the Apenines. Leghorn was defended by one division, the 92nd, under Army command which, as Colonel Wondolowski put it, "was rather widely extended over a broad front."[27] It was, in fact, divided and on opposite sides of the 13-mile mountainous Apuan massif. Moreover, IV Corps had no reserves.

Intelligence reports coming across General Truscott's desk were indeed alarming. Enemy troop movements were reported at Piazza on the upper Serchio and Castelnuovo just above the 92nd's Serchio positions where Italian Alpine units were also concentrating. Partisans and POWs reported that bridges and roads were being rebuilt—reports confirmed by aerial photographs. In the west end of the Po Valley, the 34th Infantry and 137th Mountain Divisions were available as reserves. Reliefs underway elsewhere on the Fifth and Eighth Army fronts suggested that three other divisions might soon be free for deployment.

The first heavy snowfall blanketed the Valley on December 23. Worried, Truscott attached the 339th Regimental Combat Team to IV Corps. The men from the 85th were rushed down Route 65 to close at noon of the following day in the Prato area as Corps reserve. Prisoners spoke of a "program" being set for December 28; others set the date as the 26th. A priest passed on a report from agents behind the enemy lines that the Germans planned an attack in the Serchio sector on December 27.

A projected Christmas Day attack by the 92nd's 365th Infantry on the Lama di Sotto Ridge, which overlooked the Serchio Valley, was called off on Christmas Eve. General Almond was told that the 92nd was to hold its positions at all costs. Another 85th Regiment was attached to the 92nd along with the 19th and 21st Brigade of the 8th Indian Division. Other support units—a chemical mortar battalion, two tank battalions, five artillery battalions from II Corps—assembled in the Lucca area some 15 to 20 miles south of the 92nd's defenses in the Serchio. IV Corps took charge of the whole lot, while the South African 6th Armoured Division reverted to Army control.

Buffalo soldiers were thin on the ground. The 366th Infantry minus its 2nd Battalion occupied the coastal area with the 371st on its immediate right. On the 9-mile Serchio front, the 92nd Reconnaissance Troop held the tiny mountain village of Bebio; the 366th's 2nd Battalion—Company I on the right, Company G on the left—held the remaining ground east of the Serchio on a line slightly north of Sommocolonia. West of the river, Companies C, A, and B, 370th Infantry, faced the enemy in the vicinity of Molazzana. The 370th's 2nd Battalion, recently returned to the Division from combat duties with the Brazilians on Monte Belevedere, was held in reserve between Barga and Gallicano. On Christmas Day, the battalion (less Company G, serving as an anchor on the Regimental left) moved under cover of darkness to the high ground west of the Serchio to prepare a defensive position on the heights south of Gallicano. Only two platoons from the 366th were left in Sommocolonia.

General Crittenberger, IV Corps Commander, made a personal reconnaissance of the Serchio Valley on Christmas Day. He met with General Almond and his assistant division commander, Brigadier General Wood, who assured him that their troops would make a determined stand if the Germans attacked down the valley. "It was perfectly apparent on Christmas Day," General Crittenberger later said, "as it had been for several months, that at no place along our front [80 to 90 miles defended by the Brazilians, Task Force 45, and the 92nd] would these troops, thinly spread, be able to withstand without reinforcements, a concentrated German effort. It was immediately evident . . . that . . . [stopping] the

German offensive depend[ed] entirely upon the speed with which we could get effective reinforcements into that area."[28] Crittenberger was clearly skeptical of the capabilities of the 92nd. Despite the hurried buildup of reserves and expectations of a German offensive, no reinforcements were sent up to the thinly held 92nd defensive positions. Instead, Crittenberger sent for two 8th Indian Division Brigade commanders who were then in Pisa. At eleven o'clock on Christmas night, Crittenberger ordered the Indians to take up positions astride the Serchio behind the 92nd.

At 0450 on December 26, west of the Serchio near Molazzana, Company A, 370th, reported receiving heavy machine-gun fire. The 92nd Recon at Bebbio, nine miles across the valley to the east on the far-right flank, reported small-arms and artillery fire in Sommocolonia. On the Lama di Sotto Ridge, some 2,000 feet above the village, a red and blue flare burst into the skies over enemy lines. It was followed by an uneasy calm as all firing on Sommocolonia ceased at 0500. Thirty minutes later, enemy troops, Austrians and Italians (some dressed as partisans), appeared in a draw north of the town, driving some 100 Buffalo soldiers and partisans back into town, where they were surrounded by 0730. An hour later, a wounded partisan reported 300 enemy engaged in the hand-to-hand, house-to-house fighting. A second E Company platoon was sent in as reinforcement. Lieutenant John Fox, a forward observer of the 366th Cannon Company, adjusted artillery fire just in front of his own post. "That round was just where I wanted it," he said. "Bring it in 60 more yards." Those were his last words as the shells landed and destroyed the Germans at his door.[29]

Meanwhile, over 200 of the enemy from the veteran Austrian-German Mittenwald Battalion, led by Italian guides familiar with the area, scrambled down sheltered draws between Bebbio and Scarpello to split the 92nd Recon. The troop was ordered back to its command post at Coreglia. Completely outflanked, it soon became clear that Sommo-colonia could not hold out. The defenders were ordered to withdraw. They managed to fight through the encircling Germans, who were falling back to the Barga Ridge. Of the 60 Buffalo soldiers, only 17 got out; the rest were killed or wounded.

On the west side of the Serchio, the 370th fought off enemy attacks on Calomini, Molazzana and Vergemoli. The enemy occupied a church at the east end of Calomini, capturing G Company's machine gun and mortar sections.

This mountain hamlet, perched atop a steep hill, was surrounded by 0830. Promania, just outside Molazzana, was occupied by the Germans as Companies A and C fended off repeated attacks. Reinforcements were requested. Company F was given the job, but by late morning the First Battalion's situation had improved. Company F was then sent to the other side of the Serchio to assist the 366th's 2nd Battalion. By 1500, G Company reoccupied Calomini. The enemy had been pinned down west of the Serchio, subjected to heavy shelling and mortar fire. His efforts slackened as the day drew on. Still, as Colonel Sherman of the 370th realized, his First Battalion was under considerable strain. Requests for reinforcements had to be denied; they were urgently needed across the river. Colonel Sherman decided to tighten up his defenses. Antitankers at Vergemoli were moved back to Trassilico to better protect the left flank. When the enemy broke through east of the river, outflanking the 370th's 1st Battalion, the men were ordered to withdraw to a new line on the heights south of the Gallicano stream. They did so under the cover of darkness, occupying their new positions by dawn.

The situation on the east side of the river worsened. After a massive artillery barrage, the enemy attacked at the 366th Infantry positions around Barga at 1400. Company G fell back in disarray despite the heroic efforts of a handful. When Pfc. Trueheart Fogg spotted an enemy squad setting up its machine gun, he moved out despite artillery and mortar fire to kill the crew with his BAR. Another enemy machine gun pinned him down while enemy infantry went after him. Fogg stood up, wiped out the second machine-gun crew, ". . . saving his platoon from almost certain annihilation."[30] The fall-back of G Company left a 500-yard gap promptly exploited by a German infantry company. Other elements of the 366th's 2nd Battalion withdrew to avoid being outflanked and isolated. The enemy now had what looked like a free run at the 370th Regimental Command Post in the river town, Fornaci. Every available man in the area was rounded up to meet the threat. A platoon from F Company, 370th Infantry, was called over from west of the Serchio. Three tanks fired straight up the river road and stood off the enemy several hundred yards north of the town. As General Crittenberger told it, the defense of Fornaci "was as good a piece of business as I saw during the entire fight."[31]

That afternoon, General Crittenberger visited Colonel Sherman's CP. He okayed Colonel Sherman's defense plan, including the reinforcement of the 2nd 366th Battalion by F Company of the 370th. General Crittenberger informed Sherman that reinforcements from the 8th Indian Division would take up positions behind the 92nd. Sherman, sure that his men would stand fast, asked only that a motorized Battalion from the 19th Indian Brigade take up positions on the right flank to block further encirclement. The request was granted, but when the battalion's commanding officer arrived, he declared that he was under the command of the 19th Indians, no one else. Moreover, the beleaguered 370th was told that the Indian battalion would not arrive until after dark.

The controversy was resolved, but not on very satisfactory terms for the troops on the spot. The battalion would remain controlled by the 19th Brigade but with the mission of reinforcing the right flank. The Regimental Command Post was withdrawn to Osteria. With nightfall, the enemy slacked off and no ground was lost.

Dawn came, and so did new enemy attacks—now focused on the east side of the river. Barga had to be evacuated by noon. Tiglio, a tiny village across a small valley from Barga was taken by white-clad German mountain troops. Coreglia was abandoned. The 366th 2nd Battalion reformed on a new line near Pedona, two and one-half miles south of the Christmas defense line on the Serchio. The enemy made no substantial gains on the west bank. Colonel John J. Phelan, 370th Regimental Executive Officer, gathered the shattered remnant for a last stand as enemy troops roamed through the hills on either side. The line held.

Air strikes—over 200 sorties on the 27th—coupled with fresh troops finally stopped the German drive down the Serchio. Major General Dudley Russell, Commander of the 8th Indian Division, assumed command of the sector. He ordered all troops of the 370th to join the 1st Battalion on the west side. Within two days, the Germans were pushed out of Barga. Patrols probing the Serchio found few Germans remaining. Sommocolonia was reoccupied on December 30. By New Year's Day patrols had entered Bebbio, Gallicano and Molazzana against little opposition, merely a rattle of small-arms fire. The Indians were withdrawn and the 92nd Division again assumed command of the front from the Ligurian Sea to the eastern slopes of the Serchio.

After the war, in April 1948, Hans Roettinger, Chief of Staff of German Army Group C, wrote: "The attack in the Serchio Valley . . . was meant only as a reconnaissance in force. . . . The aim was to get our own forces back to their line of departure. A more extensive attack into the depth of the enemy [Allied] front would have necessitated a much larger force than was at the disposal of the High Command of Army Group C."[32] The Germans, however, clearly achieved more than they dreamed of: panic among the rear echelons in Leghorn and within the Fifth Army high command. The Fifth Army was thrown off balance by the shifts in forces to meet the enemy's Serchio thrust. On December 28, Clark postponed the projected push for Bologna; two days later, Alexander called the whole thing off. The offensive would wait until spring. Meanwhile, the snows fell.

NOTES

[1] Wondolowski, *History of the IV Corps*, p. 437.

[2] Linklater, *The Campaign in Italy*, p. 410.

[3] Alexander, *Report Supreme Commander*, p. 10.

[4] Harpur, *The Impossible Victory*, p. 127.

[5] General McCreery was a bit unfair. The Italians fought well and honorably in the Spring offensive,

[6] Alexander, *Report Supreme Commander*, p. 9.

[7] Von Senger, *Neither Hope nor Fear*, p. 280.

[8] Alexander, *Report Supreme Commander*, p. 20.

[9] Frost, *Once a Patricia*, p. 363.

[10] India, *The Tiger Triumphs*, p. 178.

[11] Mowat, *The Regiment*, p. 251.

[12] Frost, *Once a Patricia*, p. 366.

[13] Mowat, *The Regiment*, p. 257.

[14] Ibid., p. 258. [15] Ibid., p. 262. [16] Ibid., 266.

[17] Frost, *Once a Patricia*, p. 368.

[18] Kay, *From Cassino to Trieste*, p. 302.

[19] Ibid., p. 304.

[20] Ibid., pp. 312–13.

[21] India, *The Tiger Triumphs*, pp. 178–79.

[22] Kay, *From Cassino to Trieste*, p. 321.

[23] Ibid., p. 332.

[24] Mowat, *The Regiment*, p. 280.

[25] Ibid., p. 283.

[26] Frost, *Once a Patricia*, p. 383.

[27] Wondowlowski, *History of the IV Corps*, p. 447.

[28] Ibid., pp. 452–53.

[29] Hargrove, *Buffalo Soldiers in Italy*, pp. 64–65.

[30] Ibid., p. 68.

[31] Wondowloski, *History of the IV Corps*, p. 456.

[32] Goodman, *A Fragment of Victory in Italy*, p. 72.

XXI

WINTER WAR

That winter the snow fell and the Italians said it was the worst year of the war. Food shortages, fuel shortages and the everlasting cold plagued farm and city. Partisans behind the lines felt betrayed by General Alexander's order, broadcast on November 13: "Cease operations organized on a large scale." Since partisans had already organized on a large scale, Fascist and German retaliations increased—most notoriously at Marzabotto, where some 1,800 perished. Comedian Bob Hope joked that "a slit trench [was] a G.I. outsized boot without laces." Bill Mauldin visited an aid station on Highway 65 some four miles below Bologna late that winter and caught a glimpse of what life in a "boot" was like: "[A] guy with a heavy beard and red, sunken eyes came in with a pain in his chest and a deep cough." Pneumonia, said the docs. He had been "lying on a muddy embankment for six days and six nights without being able to stand up or take his shoes off." It had rained every day, and dropped below freezing during the night. The G.I. had stayed at his outpost "until his coughing got so bad his buddies were afraid he would die or tip off the Germans to his position, and so they made him come up to the aid station."[1]

At a distance, the winter war seemed a stalemate. The *Fifth Army History* states, "no activity . . . disturbed the lines [blanketed in snow] since the end of October when General Clark halted the fall offensive," except "routine" patrols and "an occasional limited-objective attack launched by our troops or by the enemy." Dispatches may well have read, "All Quiet on the Italian Front," evoking for some the irony of Erich Maria Remarque's World War I novel. At the aid station, Mauldin caught the mood among the troops: "We said that everybody in the states seemed to think the Americans and Germans in Italy were dancing beer barrel polkas and all the war was in France."[2]

It wasn't, of course. But recent fighting had been inconclusive. Many felt that the war in Italy was a bum deal. Morale was off in both the Fifth and Eighth Armies. The Canadians were disgruntled, grim. A reinforcement draft in January helped somewhat to mitigate the "miserable stagnation" of "[t]hose winter days in the Senio line."[3] New Zealanders, too, were unhappy with their government's replacement scheme. "It's about time they started doing something more than talk about replacing the three year men," one letter griped. Another felt the scheme to be "so much hot air."[4] Among the Americans, Representative Clare Boothe Luce did not help matters when, returning home from a December visit to the Italian front, she declared that the troops in Italy were "forgotten men." In particular, she added that the men of the 34th Division had spent more than a year at the front and ought to come home.

Mail from home echoed her words, but to no great advantage. It was rough to get a letter saying, "How glad we are that you are in Italy, where there is no fighting," after a patrol had fended off an enemy raid, or just after an enemy artillery stonk. As Blue Devil staff sergeant, Mitchell Jasiniski, from New Bedford, Massachusetts, put it: "They talk like they know more than we do about the war. Those letters about coming home are bad. They get us all excited over nothing. They shouldn't write that stuff."[5]

Truscott, now in command of the Fifth Army, was well aware of the morale problem. General Keyes, II Corps commander, had already raised the issue. He had looked into the disciplinary and morale status of the 34th Division and found it wanting: An "inordinately large percentage of Court Martial cases have been for misbehavior before the enemy, disobedience of orders, aggravated AWOL, and related offenses." The division had a high "exhaustion" rate. Among the older, or original, officers and men there was "a deep conviction . . . that they have done their part in this war, that they should be permitted to return to the United States and the struggle left to those who have not been absent from home for two years." Keyes concluded that certain 34th Division personnel should be withdrawn from combat and returned to the States if the division was to remain in Italy. He also added that "no member of the United States Army should be required to serve overseas longer than three years."[6]

Keyes's proposal was clearly impractical. Largely because of the immense buildup of overseas forces in 1942, the Army would have had to rotate 100,000 men a month with shipping—not to mention other factors—still limited. Moreover, as Truscott observed, there was no real morale problem in the rear echelons. The War Department in 1944 had established a rotation policy at a rate of about one percent a month. Unhappily, more than three years would be required to return home the 35 percent of the 5,000 men remaining in the 34th who had gone over initially. Still, as General Bolte, the hands-on commander of the Red Bulls, remarked in response to Representative Luce, few soldiers spent an entire year up front. There was a good deal of turnover in a combat outfit. (By the end of the war, the 34th—surely the workhorse division of the 5th Army—had 500 days on the front line.) Bolte promised to transfer any man who survived a year of front-line service to a rear-echelon job.

Truscott saw no reason why combat troops could not be replaced at the end of 30 or 36 months. However, he also felt that the 34th's "difficulty is entirely one of discipline and command responsibility." He had observed, he tartly remarks in his biography, ". . . a tendency on the part of senior officers to explain all deficiencies away by placing the blame on the junior officers." This is wrong, he averred. "Command failures do not stem from the lower ranks, although they may exist there. Usually they originate among the higher echelons and are merely reflected downward." In the present instance, he pointed out that the morale in comparable outfits—the 3rd, 1st and 9th Divisions—was excellent. If there were officers in the 34th who had lost their effectiveness, Truscott said, General Bolte ought to take "immediate corrective measures."[7]

Bolte responded promptly, demonstrating that he had a firm grip on the 34th. Discipline was tightened; men were retrained; marksmanship re-tested. Bolte spent hours each day visiting front-line units and talking with his men. Truscott, too, tackled the "forgotten front" syndrome with an imaginative fervor. Taking a leaf from Ernie Pyle's reporting, the Fifth Army PR section put out press releases, all aimed for hometown papers, on small-unit actions, dangerous patrols into enemy territory, and feats of courage—naming individual soldiers. As Truscott remarked, too many war correspondents preferred the comforts of Rome to the discomforts of the Apennines. Folks back home learned what their guys were doing in that distant and forgotten theater and responded with the kind of mail soldiers appreciated.

All along the Italian front, commanders restored morale in analogous ways. Towards the end of 1944, in many places there had been a breakdown in supplies. At one period, for example, the men of the British 78th

Division had only one pair of cotton socks, which were always wet, and some were still wearing summer khakis. By mid-December, as the armies settled down, matters improved. Front-line 78'ers got socks, four pairs at least, as well as a variety of winter gear, including sleeping bags, windproof outer clothing, even skis and snowshoes in some instances. Forward positions got fresh rations every day. Colonel Horsfall of the Royal Irish Fusiliers even disputes the historians' characterization of that winter as the worst of the war. It may have been true, he said, for the supply columns on the long hauls with the mules, ice, snow and rain. "But in the line we did not fare too badly, and we kept comparatively dry on the mountain tops in the snow."[8] South Africans up in the Apennines donned white "oversuits and hoods, took to snowshoes," and found the new equipment "admirable." One stated: "There was no reason for any man to be unduly cold except when his task at the time called for his exposure and this was mainly when on patrol."[9]

On the Lombardy plain, where snow mingled with icy rain, commanders also contended with apathy, especially among the low-spirited Canadians. Lieutenant Colonel Cameron of the Hastings, for example, when his men were rotated for rest, refitting and retraining, instituted a Spartan regimen. Much to their surprise, the men were not only set to physical "hardening" exercises but to parade-ground drill, all spit-and-polish. Men and junior officers complained, of course. But, as Farley Mowat tells us, this did not last. "Day by day, the old face of the unit began to reappear, its lines hardening, its contours emerging clear-cut . . . Pride was returning"[10]

Back on line, Cameron concentrated on restoring combat confidence. Contact between companies, especially at night, was intensified; sentries and outposts were kept on their toes. Patrols were sent out against carefully picked objectives to reduce possible setbacks. Success spurred assurance. Sniping was encouraged, with scores posted daily—a contest that did wonders for combat spirit. The situation inspired a certain ingenuity. The Germans were well placed enough to roll Teller mines down the river embankment into sand-bagged houses occupied by the Canadian Patricias. A Patricia corporal, L.L. Cosford, liberated a truck inner tube and cut it into a gigantic rubber band, which he hitched to a forked tree as a catapult for grenades. His CO was skeptical, afraid that the grenades would blow up on his platoon. But he allowed a test shot with a rock, and the sling gave it a proper heave-ho. Others followed.

Cosford was then given a go-ahead, promptly launching live grenades in the middle of a group of Germans curiously examining the rocks.[11]

Before settling down to the deadly business of prodding at the enemy's outposts and defensive lines, the British Eighth Army cleared out two troublesome German bridgeheads on the wrong side of the Senio. The 714th Jaeger Division held ground roughly five miles northwest of Ravenna, which might make for a counterattack springboard aimed at the city. To the southwest on the Canale Naviglio between Cotignola and Franarola, the 278th Infantry Division's salient south of the Senio lengthened the front and required more troops on line than the Eighth Army could spare. So, General McCreery took advantage of the cold and clear weather to clear up the situation. Canadian 5th Armoured Division tanks rolled over the frozen ground on January 2 with air support and pushed the Germans to just below the southern edge of Lake Comacchio. (Later, the Italian Cremona Battle Group would take over the sector.) The next day, V Corps sent troops across the Naviglio to straighten out the line there. Both operations were successfully wound up by the 5th of the month.

Early in February, the Hastings and Patricias moved back on line after a short rest near Mezzano, a dreary flat marshland where German bodies still lay, fodder for wandering bands of half-wild pigs. Patrols alternated sloshing about in muck or slogging across frozen ground within the mile-deep no-man's-land. The Germans still held a strongpoint, Casa Baroni, on the banks of the Fosso Vecchio. In the early hours of February 3, the Patricias launched a company-strength raid on Casa Baroni under covering artillery, 3-inch and 4.2-inch mortar and heavy machine-gun fire. When a section of the leading platoon entered the first house, it blew up. German mortars zeroed in on the rest of the platoon as they attempted to dig our their comrades. Bodies were gathered under a Red Cross flag at daylight. Two officers were wounded, as well as 36 others; six men were killed and one was missing. So ended the Patricias' last major attack. At the end of the month, the Canadians, after twenty months of service in Sicily and Italy, moved to Western Europe, where they joined the Canadian First Army.

On February 25, the 8th Indian Division replaced the Canadians north of Bagnacavallo astride Route 16, the road running northwest from Ravenna to Ferrara. To their left, the 43rd Gurkha Lorried Brigade had been holding a 5,000-yard sector for a fortnight under the command of the 56th London Division. It was a lively sector, to say the least, as patrols and raids were nightly occurrences.

On the 23rd, the Gurkhas had occupied the near flood bank. Both sides dug into the bank. At night, footbridges were swung across the river and the Germans crept silently into the tunnel entrances of the inner bank. Less than five yards of earth separated the foes. When the enemy rushed the Gurkhas, the hillmen rose up with their curved, broad-bladed knives in hand. As their historian records the moment: "The death scream of a German cloven to the chin caused the man behind to falter, and in that split second's delay the kukri took another life."[12] Three days later, however, the Germans had their revenge when their mortars and artillery smashed into the so-called "Bastion," a strongpoint near a flood-gap blown earlier into the near bank of the Senio. Gurkhas were buried beneath collapsed earthworks, and the enemy overran the position. Gurkhas snatched the position back; the Germans took it away again. And so it went, until the Gurkhas were relieved at the end of the month. They handed over three miles of secure flood bank, established at a cost of three hundred men, but the Germans still held the Bastion.

The 8th Indians felt themselves a bit more fortunate—the Canadians had already cleared the outer slope of the flood bank. Still, their nights were made hideous not only with the clatter of machine guns, the crump of mortars and grenades but also by the Germans' latest missile, a short-range rocket with a two-hundred-pound warhead. It wasn't very accurate, but its blast was devastating.

On a battalion front of a few hundred yards, the Indians' historian avers, ". . . during the more or less static phase of the Senio tour, the average daily expenditure of ammunition amounted to eighty thousand small arms rounds, two hundred PIAT bombs, two hundred grenades and eighty three-inch mortars."[13] On March 13, the Jaipurs raided an enemy outpost, killing 27 Germans at a cost of one Jaipur killed and ten wounded. The Jewish Brigade, attached to the 8th Indian, surprised ten Germans asleep in another house, and accounted for them all. Germans in company strength struck at the Frontier Force Rifles without success. Otherwise, the Indian sector remained quiet

Both sides fluttered one another with paper bombs. Allied literature usually was simple stuff, mostly safe-conduct passes in three languages and signed by General Alexander. German material was more colorful—

leaflets portraying a bucolic land of bread and wine and buxom maidens behind the German lines on one side; on the other, fearful slaughter overseen by a grinning death's-head. Urdu leaflets were fired into British lines and English ones among the Indians more often than not, which suggested German intelligence was not up to snuff. The leaflets became souvenirs, each new issue eagerly sought by collectors.

The winter war along the Senio was very much an infantryman's war. Sniping was ubiquitous; anyone poking his head above the banks in daylight, instead of using a periscope, risked losing it. Grenade duels, machine-gun and mortar exchanges haunted the night. Soldiers learned not to throw grenades from established positions but from random spots. The London Irish, 56th Division, held the near side of the Senio flood bank, but German posts dug in on the inner side dominated both sides of the river.

One particular post bothered the Irish. It nestled in a "bund," a semicircle bulge slightly higher than the rest of the flood bank. There were no ready approaches not well covered by the Germans. Therefore, the Irish tunneled into the bund at its juncture with the main bank—and found themselves in an unused enemy dugout. Rather pleased, they decided to hit the Germans at three in the afternoon when, it was thought, they might be off-guard. Promptly at 1500, 25-pound shells hit the far bank to keep German heads down. A corporal, five riflemen and two Pioneers went over the top under cover of a smoke screen and were soon joined by the raiding party. It was over in a minute—five Germans captured, one killed and several wounded. The bund now belonged to the Irish.

Weather conditioned a good deal of the activity on the Italian front. Snow fell on January 6 in the afternoon over the New Zealand sector, which ran some 6,000 yards northeastwards from just south of Route 9, to the left of the 56th Division at Felisio. By the next day, the intermittent snow fall had covered some six inches. After a heavy frost, silent movement was virtually impossible across the crusted snow. Frosty nights and fine cold days succeeded one another until the middle of the month, when it rained and turned misty. This was followed by frost, fine days which thawed the roads, another five to six inches of snow, and then thaw.

Civilians, though often reluctant to leave their homes, were evacuated from areas under enemy observation, from buildings housing headquarters and from a zone some 3,000 yards deep behind the main defenses. Italians in Faenza were not compelled to leave, but no more were allowed in town. Despite enemy shelling that pulverized houses and farm buildings, some civilians contrived to remain. The New Zealanders transported an estimated 1,000 of them, along with 500 cattle and assorted other farm animals from their zone.

Both sides patrolled aggressively. Early one morning, the Maoris spotted some Germans headed for Palazzo Laghi and sent out a patrol to investigate. Six prisoners were taken and questioned. They revealed that they expected a runner with news of their relief. He was snared by the use of the German password. The Germans were ordered to return, so the Maoris pretended to be that patrol, hoping thereby to reconnoiter the river for crossings. But the seven-man patrol was met by small-arms fire, which wounded three, and the remainder sensibly quit. Though the Germans' snow clothing was said to be so white that it was easily detected, eight Germans in snow gear and on snowshoes gained the outbuildings at Galanuna, where they fired a bazooka and grenades at a house occupied by a Kiwi patrol. The Germans were finally driven out by artillery, mortar, machine-gun and small-arms fire that wounded three of them.

Another Maori night patrol made three attempts to reach the stop bank from Palazzo Laghi three times, but the men were thwarted each time by minefields and machine-gun fire. The next night, a patrol probed and crawled through a minefield to reach the bank a bit farther upstream. They got a good look at the river, 30 to 35 feet wide, five feet deep. Two mines exploded, and German machine guns opened fire. The Maoris fought back, launching grenades at the enemy on the opposite side of the riverbank, then withdrew under covering fire. It was that sort of warfare—where the Germans retained undisputed possession of the Senio stop banks, a situation recognized in General Freyberg's announcement of February 2: "The Division was to patrol and lift mines on its front, but it was not to occupy permanent positions forward of those already held; where possible it was to keep standing patrols on the Senio stop bank during the hours of darkness."[14]

Deserters drifted across the winter line, offering useful information about opposing units and German morale. Five deserters from the 9th Panzer Grenadier Regiment surrendered to the New Zealanders in mid-February, saying that others of their company would do the same were it not for fear of the minefields. One was a Soviet national of German stock who had fought with the Russians, Germans, and the partisans. (He claimed that he had been caught up by the Germans after being wounded with the partisans.) Another deserter was a Reich German; three were Poles. Of 73 enemy passed through V Corps' POW cage between January 26 and February 25, 51 were deserters; more than half of these were Poles,[15] Alsatians and Yugoslavs. (Fear of reprisals against deserter families had ceased when Poland and Silesia were "liberated" by the Russians.)

Italian deserters from Mussolini's two divisions facing II Corps' left flank reported that most of their battalions were staffed by German supervisors, officers and non-coms, who were harsh and insulting. They threatened "drastic measures" against deserter-families. Those with homes in the North were afraid to desert out of fear of reprisals against their loved ones. Posters, it was said, promised death to the remainder of a squad if one saw fit to desert. Many, nonetheless, did not hesitate when the opportunity offered to drop their guns and take advantage of "Safe Conduct" passes. Numerous deserters joined partisan bands in the hills. Out of 93 Italian prisoners from the Italia, Monte Rosa and Marco Divisions in January, 76 were deserters.[16] German prisoners said that following the roll-back of the Bulge and the failure to stop the Russian drive, morale had slumped badly. Many, they said, were waiting to desert. But throughout the Wehrmacht there was a fanatical minority as well as a hard core of tough and seasoned veterans prepared to fight to the end.[17]

Freezing cold and snow blanketed the front up in the Apennines, where Highway 65 was said to be "a skating rink." Snow limited patrolling beneath the ever-vigilant eyes of the enemy in the Spaduro–Monte Calderaro sector occupied by the 78th Division. It was all too easy to spot movement against a white background on a clear night. German bombardments were inhibiting and effective, consistently cutting communications lines. Signal linesmen groped for ends in the snow—two feet deep on the hillsides and waist deep in the ravines—mending breaks as best they could, under constant shellfire. The Germans probed the lines wherever and whenever possible.

On the night of February 8, B Squadron of the 56th Recce on Salara heard men approaching up the valley, one shouting in good English, "A Company. Don't shoot." But the sharp-eared Brits heard others speaking German and opened fire. The Germans fired back, hollering, "Come out and fight." But in the morning, the Germans left, leaving two killed and having wounded one British officer and four men. Despite the snow, a Fifth Army Communiqué reported: "Our patrols were active."

Blue Devils of the 88th's 351st Regiment volunteered for a "Ranger

Platoon," led by a Los Angeleno, Lieutenant Ralph Decker. Held up by two enemy machine guns in a farmhouse, Decker dashed forward and obliged the crew to surrender. While searching the house, Decker found an enemy-occupied dugout. When the Germans refused to come out, he tossed two grenades inside, then planted 60 pounds of explosives on top. Blowing it up, he then withdrew his patrol.

Firefights were often fierce. Lieutenant Linnsey L. Wheeler's five-man Blue Devil patrol was challenged by a German sentry posted outside a farm building. Wheeler got him with a burst from his tommy-gun, knocked out another as he charged out of the building and killed a third in a hand-to-hand encounter. A man was wounded by a mine as the patrol withdrew. Wheeler sent his men back and remained with the wounded man until help came, Another patrol, it was said, came within six miles of Bologna. It was pinned down for seven and a half hours by machine-gun and mortar fire until pulled back with no prisoners taken and after suffering several casualties.

Patrol was the name of the game played out that winter all along the Italian front. Many were contact patrols between companies. To keep in touch with the Natal Mounted Rifles of the South African 6th Armoured, a telephone wire was stretched across the Setta River. Each night, the patrol from Company K, 363rd Infantry, 91st Division, would make its way to the wire, attach a hand-powered telephone and wait until the Rifles patrol arrived and attached its set. This saved wading a cold river. On some nights, the moonlight or "artificial moonlight"—the giant lights directed over enemy lines—was so bright against the snow that the Germans resorted to using smoke to screen their movements.

Shortly after the 363rd moved into the Monterumici–Tomba sector, a German patrol set up a loudspeaker to greet the Regiment, ". . . we know you have been through a lot." After some music and lame jokes, the Germans signed off, wishing the 363rd "a lot of luck—you will need it in 1945," and promised to return the next night for a New Year's celebration. When the broadcast opened, it was rudely interrupted by exploding hand grenades. An eight-man patrol moved to outflank the broadcasters, but the enemy escaped through a draw. Buck private Herbert Vaughn complained, "If they hadn't thrown hand grenades we'd have had music all night."[18]

The Allies also used loudspeakers, to coax deserters: "Attention! Attention! Soldiers of the 576th Regiment in the 305th Division—you over there, listen. . . . Why are you still lying out here in the cold? Why do you risk your lives? . . . Germany is losing the war. . . . Do you want to sacrifice yourselves for a lost cause? Do you want to be killed—at this point, so shortly before the end? . . . [I]f you stay in your foxhole stubbornly and apathetically you will eventually be killed off by our artillery. A number of your comrades are with us already. . . . There are always opportunities to desert . . . and if you arrive in the early morning you may come just in time for breakfast."[19] One German who surrendered in response to this broadcast by Sergeant Klaus Mann, son of the famous novelist, said that the men in his unit had discussed deserting together but decided not to for fear of reprisals against their families.

Raids were conducted by patrols of platoon strength or more in order to secure prisoners, or to clear out bothersome German positions. In mid-February, after a rest period in Montecatini, the 363rd Infantry relieved the 34th Division's 133rd Infantry of its position east of Monte Belmonte and the escarpment in the Indice Valley.

The river's waters had recently receded, leaving a foot of gooey mud and the debris of war—cardboard shell containers, German antitank and Schu mines at odd angles, crashed plane parts, dead branches, small tree trunks and a partially covered German body. The Germans—troops from the 576th Grenadier Regiment, 305th Division—were well placed in fortified houses and dugouts on hills overlooking the Indice. It was an active sector as patrols probed enemy positions for information and prisoners. Hill 358 stuck out between the Indice and Zena Rivers rather like a sore tooth. Prisoners and deserters provided a good deal of information about enemy dispositions, including news of a projected attack from the German bunkers and machine-gun posts on the hill just above the houses occupied by Company E.

Rather than wait on the Germans, Captain Edmund J. Carberry decided that offense was the best defense. Lieutenant Robert G. Benckart, whose platoon got the job, broke his men up into three ten-man squads for a set-piece attack on February 26—two forward, abreast, and one in reserve. Benckart worked through three German bunkers, rounding up some ten prisoners in all. These were delivered to Staff Sergeant Norman Rodrigues, who marched them back through a spate of German mortar fire with an empty .45 pistol. He'd used up his ammunition in the attack. German machine-gunners, however, exacted a toll: several men were wounded, one sergeant killed. When it was clear the platoon could not hold on, the men were ordered back. Nine, however, were cut off in the German bunkers; there they remained for a day, firing German guns and directing artillery and mortar fire on targets they spotted from the hilltop. After dark, two by two, the men slipped back down the hill under covering fire from Allied artillery and mortars.

After a reshuffle of the companies on line, two major raids were launched on March 8. At 2130, a reinforced B Company patrol set out for a group of houses on the 363rd's right at the junction of the Indice and the Balino. As they approached their objective, a trip-wire set off a flare, bringing down enemy mortar shells. Having lost the element of surprise, the patrol withdrew with no casualties. On the left, a second patrol from Company L moved out at 2250 and, after clearing a minefield, pushed on along a ridge to the north. At 0400, encountering no enemy, the patrol was told to return. Two hours later, fourteen K Company men under Lieutenant Edwin Eells moved to take enemy bunkers on the west side of Hill 358 and thirty-one Company I men under Lieutenant Jeremiah Dow went for those on the east side of the hill. They were spotted by the enemy almost immediately, who threw in a mortar concentration that cut communication lines and held up the raiders. Both parties moved uphill under cover of friendly fire. But Dow was hit and one man was killed as his group attempted to move forward as enemy artillery joined enemy mortar fire. The Germans, who had Dow's group under machine-gun fire, also hurled potato-masher grenades down on the hapless Americans.

Lieutenant Eells and eight of his men gained the crest of Hill 358 and found the bunkers empty. Moving north, they asked for smoke to cover them as it got lighter, but their radio was out of order. Taking cover in a draw, they were attacked by some 15 Germans. As they crawled back, down a small stream, Lieutenant Eells and Staff Sergeant Osborne E. Amburg were caught out in the open. Eells was killed and Amburg hit above the knee. The group, strung out about 50 yards, lay all day in knee-deep water, successfully hidden from the enemy. Amburg bandaged his leg as best he could. working to keep it from getting too stiff to use. "It was the longest eleven hours and forty-five minutes I ever spent," Staff Sergeant Joseph Moisa later said.[20]

At 1845, Amburg got Lieutenant Eells's personal belongings, and the men began to move downstream. Several Germans appeared and succeeded in cutting off Amburg, who nevertheless succeeded in covering the withdrawal of the other seven men. One German cut loose with a machine pistol, and although shots hit between Amburg's legs and all around him, he was unscratched. He tossed grenades. When it got very still Amburg began to slither away. Then someone said, "Hands up." When Amburg turned his head, he saw a gun pointed at him from some three feet away. Amburg showed his wound and gestured that he couldn't walk.

He was dragged to a nearby bunker where he counted nine Germans, four wounded, one seriously, by grenades. After dressing his leg, the Germans took him to a command post, where he was questioned. Amburg gave his name, rank and serial number. But he wasn't wearing stripes and he was carrying Eells's effects. Despite the confirmation of his dog tags, the Germans insisted that he was an officer. He was passed back to the rear and questioned several times on the long walk back through the German lines. On the other side of Bologna, Amburg was questioned again. This time the Germans threatened to shoot him if he didn't talk. He was never mistreated, he said later, only threatened.[21] Following hospital treatment, he joined other POWs in camp near Mantova. When the Fifth Army broke out into the Po, the POWs were moved by bus at night to a camp some twelve miles from the Austrian border. Eventually Amburg was liberated by a patrol of the 85th Division.

Meanwhile, in the Apennines, the snow continued to fall.

NOTES

[1] Mauldin, *Up Front,* p. 218.
[2] Ibid., p. 215.
[3] Mowat, *The Regiment,* p. 289.
[4] Kay, *From Cassino to Trieste,* p. 385.
[5] Delaney, *Blue Devils in Italy,* p. 179.
[6] Truscott, *Command Missions,* pp. 461–62.
[7] Ibid., pp. 462–64.
[8] Horsfall, *Fling Our Banner to the Wind,* p. 212.
[9] Murray, *First City/Cape Town Highlanders,* p. 51.
[10] Mowat, *The Regiment,* p. 288.
[11] Frost, *Once a Patricia,* p. 397.
[12] India, *The Tiger Triumphs,* p. 164.
[13] Ibid., p. 185.
[14] Kay, *From Cassino to Trieste,* p. 376.
[15] So many Poles in German service crossed over to join their countrymen, both in Italy

and France, that the Polish Corps, despite some 25,000 casualties, ended the war numerically stronger than at the beginning.

[16] Wondolowski, *History of the IV Corps,* p. 402.

[17] Kay, *From Cassino to Trieste,* p. 379.

[18] Strootman, *History of the 363rd Infantry,* p. 139.

[19] Ibid., pp. 157–58.

[20] Ibid., p. 166.

[21] Ibid., p. 168.

XXII

WINTER ENCORE

Over in the IV Corps sector, the 92nd Division again assumed responsibility for the front that stretched from the Ligurian Sea to the eastern slope of the Serchio Valley. In addition to "Power" patrols, which amounted to small-scale attacks, and "Stealth" patrols—reconnaissance, wire cutting and some demolitions—the Buffalo soldiers resorted to weapons "shoots"—which prisoners acknowledged as nerve-wracking. As a Captain in the German 101st Cavalry Reconnaissance Battalion put it, later: "Your massed fire from very heavy machine guns [the "shoots"] was terrific. They were not only casualty producing, but very demoralizing." A 92nd Battalion commander, well aware, by virtue of POW interrogations, of that effect on the Germans, conducted several "shoots" in which *all* weapons were fired. "Shoots," he pointed out, also had a practical purpose. Indeed, they checked that "every man had a firing position and—given the snow and ice—ensured that weapons were in working condition." And, too, he added, ". . . the Battalion gained a certain confidence just from hearing the Battalion shoot as a unit, and from a realization of the volume of firepower an infantry battalion has when all weapons are firing."[1]

Nonetheless, not all was well with the all-black division. Nine successive straggle-collection lines were set up from November 1944 to the end of the war, netting 2,182 stragglers.[2] No doubt, as General Truscott observed, the Buffalo soldiers "were the product of heredity, environment, education, economic and social ills beyond their control."[3] Forty-three percent of the men were in category IV and 29.4 percent in category V of the Army General Classification Test. Still, many Buffalo soldiers did very well in combat. Other black combat units also racked up excellent records. Segregation was a fact in the U.S. Armed Services as in its society then. Officer candidate schools, however, were not segregated. Nor was the Mediterranean theater, where black and white soldiers intermingled on duty, in clubs, and at rest centers, Red Cross facilities and elsewhere.

Black officers assigned to the 92nd, however, often felt abused, seeing only a limited potential for advancement. Of the 774 officers in the division as of December 1944, 538 were black. Most of the top brass was white, although two of the four artillery battalion commanders and several infantry battalion commanders were black. Truscott argued that "command failures . . . usually . . . originate among the higher echelons and are merely reflected downwards." The 92nd Division was no exception in this respect. Before the division went overseas General Edward M. Almond told his superiors that his division would fight. Privately, however, he had mixed feelings, shared by other white officers in the division, most of whom were Southerners. Relations were strained between white and black officers. White officers blamed the division's poor performance on its men, saying that they lacked aggressiveness as well as intelligence. The fatal flaw, however, was the lack of trust between the men and their officers. If you do not trust your men, you cannot lead them; if they do not trust you, they will not follow.

The 92nd's positions in early winter 1944 were overshadowed by the enemy, who held the Strettoia hill mass overlooking the coast and the 3,000-foot Lama di Sotto Ridge thrusting from the north like a giant finger pointed at Barga and the Serchio. During January, 166 prisoners were taken, 70 percent of the total taken by the Fifth Army during that period. Intelligence reports indicated that German troops were being replaced by Italian fascists in the Serchio sector—"the introduction of the 2d Bn, 1st Berseglieri Regiment . . . to replace the 2nd Bn., 286th Inf. Regiment east of the Serchio seems certain now."[4] An increase in desertions from the German 281st Regiment on the coast suggested that enemy morale was shaky. Staff planners saw in this an opportunity to take Strettoia, which would open the way to Massa and bring Allied artillery within range of the German naval base at La Spezia, and to take the Lama di Sotto Ridge, which overlooked the Serchio Valley down to its junction with the Lima near Bagni di Lucca. Once on the ridge, American troops would overshadow enemy defenses that hinged on Castelnuovo. In addition, it was hoped that success would offset the disheartening consequences of the Christmas breakout down the Serchio.

The attack in the Serchio opened first on February 4 with little enemy resistance as C Company, 366th Infantry, occupied Gallicano on the east bank and the 2nd Battalion, 365th, entered Castelvecchio and Albiano, villages at the base of the Lama di Sotto Ridge. The next day, the 366th gained a half-mile in the hills west of Gallicano, opening the road from the hilltown of Calomini to Vergemoli. Company B, after two tries against intense small-arms and mortar fire, was unable to gain the crest of Monte Faeto, the 1,500-foot peak that dominates the hills bulging in the curve of the river below Castelnuovo. However, over the next three days gains were scored up the side of the mountain west of the river. There were no major counterattacks and the front here was stabilized.

West of the river, the enemy appeared to have been surprised. Italian fascist troops interspersed among the 148th Grenadiers folded, enabling the 3rd Battalion, 365th Infantry, to gain more than a mile from its line of departure on February 5. Within a few short hours, the battalion was well up on the right side of the Lama di Sotto, occupying the village of Lama, high ground beyond Sommocolonia southwest of Lama, and on Monte della Stella to the northeast. During the next day, the 2nd Battalion moved north across the southwest slope of the ridge under increasing mortar and artillery fire to consolidate its line with the 3rd Battalion. Meanwhile, Company K drove off several counterattacks aimed at Monte della Stella.

On the night of the 7–8th, the 1st Battalion relieved the 3rd when the Germans mounted a series of concentrated counterattacks to regain the ridge. The first, in company strength before daylight, failed under an artillery concentration. Then the entire 2nd Battalion, 286th Grenadiers, struck the Monte della Stella salient on three sides, forcing Allied troops back some 500 yards. Further attacks throughout the following day were to no avail.

On the 10th, the 365th committed two of its battalions and another from the 366th in an effort to retake the ridge. German machine-gun and mortar fire lashed the hillside, but the Italians once again gave way, yielding 55 prisoners, and the Buffalo soldiers were back on the ridge. Then the Germans intensified their efforts, infiltrating into Lama. Three enemy attacks were driven off on the 11th, but a fourth—of some two hundred Germans—forced a withdrawal. When the Serchio sector again settled down, the enemy still held the Lama di Sotto Ridge, but the 365th Infantry had advanced its positions by three-quarters of a mile.

At 0600 on February 8, Generals Truscott, Crittenberger, Almond and some members of the 92nd divisional staff gathered to watch as tanks and infantry moved out across the broad no-man's-land on the coastal plain. On the right, two battalions of the 371st Infantry tackled the sawtooth Folgorito Ridge above Seravezza. Shrubs and small trees clung to precipitous rock and shale slopes that the Buffalo soldiers took, in some places, almost straight up as the Germans waited behind barbed wire and carefully sown minefields in gun emplacements hewn out of solid rock. Air support, as Truscott reported, was "continuous and excellent."[5]

Unfortunately, Company G was strafed by friendly fighter-bombers, knocking the company commander and enough others out to force a reorganization. Company F took over, capturing 25 prisoners and killing and wounding a good number of the enemy. Over the next two days, the 371st struggled to maintain its foothold against counterattacks by the 285th Grenadiers and reinforcements from the Kesselring Machine Gun Battalion. Stubborn Buffalo soldiers held their 800-yard gain out of the thousand or so hoped for, at a cost of four officers and 17 men killed, 4 officers and 104 men wounded and missing.

"Things fall apart; the center cannot hold." William Butler Yeats's famous line could serve as the perfect communiqué from the 370th Infantry, attacking in a line of battalions along the curve of the Strettoia Hills. Just west of the coastal highway, the first hill, designated X in the attack plan, capped a series of terraces at 450 feet; a thousand yards to the north, Y rose 600; inside the curve, Z, nicknamed the "Ice Cream Cone," also peaked at 600. Hill Y was occupied first, at 1405; X was taken by the 2nd Battalion a short time later.

The Germans, however, were quick on the mark. The 285th Grenadier Regiment was brought forward out of reserve to bolster the sector's defending 281st Grenadier Regiment. Artillery fire blocked a German counterattack on Hill Y, but this was followed at 1700 by a shattering "inferno-like" mortar barrage. Two American officers were wounded and the company commander killed. Some of the men withdrew to Hill X; others scattered to the rear. By 2000, no American troops were left on Hill Y.

Over the four days of the operation, Company K remained, intact, on the eastern slope of Hill X. On top, however, the 2nd Battalion commander had difficulty holding on, never mind preparing for an attack the next day. He had 80 men on hand, and all the officers he could spare were busy rounding up stragglers. Over the next day the battalion managed to establish a defensive position. Another attempt was made on the third day to gain Hill Y with the reserve 3rd Battalion. Enemy artillery and mortar fire disrupted the attack, but the 3rd Battalion, 371st, passed through to secure a foothold on Hill Y. Battalion Commander Lieutenant Colonel Arthur H. Walker was killed by mortar fire at around noon. The barrage was a prelude to an enemy attack, repulsed on Hill Y but successful on Z. Disorganized, Company L was regrouped and returned to the Ice Cream Cone. The three hills were once again in American hands.

After a long, nervous night, Company L on Hill Y was attacked. A forward observer, 598th Field Artillery, with Company L later said he saw "two friendly infantrymen start to run; then all the company pulled out after them."[6] Exposed by the withdrawal of L Company, I Company on Hill Z followed suit. The 2nd Battalion of the 370th was ordered to take up a defensive line on the coastal plain along its original line of departure.

For all the troubles in the hills, the most severe opposition developed on the soggy flats of the coast. Task Force 1—Company C, 760th Tank Battalion, a platoon of the 701st Tank Destroyer Battalion, and the 3rd Battalion, 366th Infantry—moved out at 0500 following an intense artillery barrage and under heavy smoke cover. Tanks carrying infantry crossed the Cinquale Canal delta—the water about 30 inches deep and 90 feet wide there—without much trouble, despite the minefields. One tank hit a mine; another, last in line going around it, foundered in deep water. Still, at this point, there had been no casualties. As Task Force Commander Lt. Colonel Edward L. Rowny took comfort in this, the first fire of long-range heavies from the Punta Bianca naval guns near La Spezia hit his command group. "[W]hen I looked around there were only two others who had not been hit. The shell had killed seven. The entire mouth of the canal appeared to turn red with blood,"[7] he commented.

Tankers managed a dispersed formation as the infantry dismounted and dug. Colonel Rowny and a tanker sergeant cleared the dead and wounded to open a lane off the beach. Slowly, tanks and infantry—rein-forced by Company B, 370th Infantry—were deployed on an east–west line. Telephone lines were blasted out by shellfire. Radios went dead. "There did not seem to be a single patch of ground anywhere that was not covered by artillery fragments," Rowny later said.[8] Several soldiers digging in struck mines, which added to the wounded and demoralized the already depressed soldiers. During the night, the Germans made a feint at

Rowny's command post, but backed off. At dawn, Rowny looked around. "Only a handful of men were in their defensive positions. Several had been wounded and others had remained. The rest had drifted to the rear."[9] During the next afternoon, the 1st Battalion, 370th Infantry, moved in.

The bridgehead north of the canal extended some thousand yards along the beach and another five hundred inland. But tanks found it difficult to get off the beach. Paths were cleared, but some mines were planted so deep that after a number of tanks had passed over it a mine would explode, disabling yet another tank. Two counterattacks were driven off, but a third pushed back the perimeter. More troops were committed, ferried across the canal on tanks; but three tanks fell into deep craters and were drowned out of action. More tanks and men were lost in the minefields. Enemy machine-gun, mortar and artillery fire inflicted further losses.

Task Force 1 was ordered back south of the canal at 1930 the night of the 10th. By 0400 the next morning, the withdrawal was concluded. The enemy had suffered heavy losses, including 101 prisoners and 44 deserters. Allied losses were greater. The 760th Tank Battalion lost 16 medium tanks; the 758th Light Tank Battalion, 4; the 27th Armored Field battalion, 2 medium tanks. The 366th infantry's 3rd Battalion lost 329 men killed, wounded or missing. Altogether, the 92nd Division lost 47 officers and 659 men killed, wounded or missing in action.[10]

After high-level talks, the 92nd Division was reorganized along lines suggested by General George C. Marshall. The most reliable officers and men of the 365th and 371st Regiments were transferred to the 370th, which, in turn, transferred its unreliables. In a curious improvisation, the Nisei 442nd Infantry Regiment was brought back from France to join the division. Task Force 45's ex-antiaircraft gun crews, turned into infantry, formed the third regiment, the 473rd, of the reconstituted 92nd. The 365th and 371st were deployed on inactive sectors, while the 366th was deactivated and its personnel used to form two engineer general service units.

When General Truscott assumed command of the Fifth Army, he not only reviewed troop dispositions but also the plans for the renewed offensive in December. The plans called for a plunge on the II Corps front—linked with the British offensive—to go for Bologna by the shortest route, essentially down Highway 65. Given the heavy German fortifications, the unfavorable weather and terrain, it seemed to Truscott "an appalling undertaking."[11]

When Truscott mentioned his reservations and suggested a "maneuver" west of Highway 64, where the going was easier and where the same objective might be gained more quickly and at less cost, General Mark Clark was a bit testy. When Truscott argued for more flexibility in the spring, a readiness to exploit perceived enemy weaknesses east of Highway 64, as well as mounting the main attack west of Highway 65 as the shortest route to Bologna, Clark replied, "I cannot agree to a main attack generally along the high ground west of Highway 64."[12] Truscott, however, had concluded that the heights west of Highway 64 offered the best hope for a breakout into the Po Valley. Looking forward to spring, Truscott decided that the Belvedere–Torracia Ridge west of the Reno should be cleared to permit the use of Highway 64, reduce the exposure of the South African 6th Armoured Division's left flank and "to provide a more favorable avenue of approach to the Po Valley than the heavily defended route along Highway 65."[13] To do the job, Truscott had a newly-arrived instrument at hand: the American 10th Mountain Division.

Popularly known as ski troops, the 10th was intended as a "special" fighting formation, along with paratroops, rangers, OSS units and the like. It was the only outfit conceived by civilians, born of concerns raised by Charles Minot "Minnie" Dole, founder of the National Ski Patrol, and several of his friends. Citing the inevitability of mountain warfare, Dole urged President Roosevelt and General Marshall to form a specially trained outfit: "It is more reasonable to make soldiers out of skiers than skiers out of soldiers." When the Division was activated at Camp Hale on July 15, 1943, high in the Colorado Rockies west of the Great Divide near Leadville, it was a volunteer outfit. Recruits had to be vetted by the National Ski Patrol, the only civilian group ever designated a "recruiting agency" by the U.S. Army.

While the Patrol looked for skiing skills, qualifications were broad enough to scoop in outdoorsmen of every description, including cowboys, forest rangers, and woodsmen. Dole drummed up recruits at Eastern colleges and prep schools; the *Saturday Evening Post* ran a cover depicting a ski trooper in full battle whites that was used as a recruiting poster. Warner Brothers made a movie about the troopers, *I Love a*

Soldier, starring Sonny Tufts and Paulette Goddard. Skiing aficionado Lowell Thomas promoted the outfit on his popular radio broadcasts. Applications poured in, each with its three letters of recommendation, and 3,500 men were recruited.

The soldiers who drilled among 11,000-foot mountains that winter were an extraordinary lot. Crack skiers included Torger Tokle, world champion jumper (later killed in action), Olympic medalist Robert Livermore, Werner von Trapp of the *Sound of Music* family (recent emigrés from Hitler-occupied Austria), and college and prep-school men, a privileged group whose ranks included American paint heir Lee Glidden. The 10th Mountain Division was possibly the best educated and brainiest infantry outfit in the army. In an average of eleven other divisions, only 29.6 percent of the enlisted men scored 110 or higher in the Army General Classification Test, the qualification for Officer Candidate School. In the 10th's 86th Mountain Infantry Regiment, 64 percent scored 110 or higher; 13 percent scored 130 and up.[14]

For all the Ski Patrol's success in recruiting, volunteers did not fill out the 10th's complement of 15,000 so the Army resorted to an age-old practice. As Tony Ragazzine, a Youngstown, Ohioan (later killed in action), who had never been on skis before, told his "three letter" buddies in Hale, "I'm a volunteer all right." He'd been training for the Tank Destroyers in the south when their CO called out all the privates and told them: "You've just volunteered for the ski troops." Other draftees, many kids fresh out of high school from every corner of the United States, filled out the ranks.

For all that it was an elite outfit, however, the 10th was a division no one wanted. When Chief of Staff Marshall offered the 10th to various theater commanders, they declined, primarily because of its size—it was a Light Division without heavy-weapons companies—and its specialized training. Eisenhower's chief of staff, General Walter Bedell Smith, took one look at the 10th's table of organization and said: "All those mules? Hell no!" On D-Series maneuvers from March 25 to April 15, the ski troopers proved that they could withstand bitter cold, howling blizzards and the snow. But there were reservations. As Lieutenant Monty Atwater wrote Charles Dole: "A lot of our best skiers . . . still haven't got it through their heads that, from a military standpoint, skis are a means of taking firepower to places you can't take it on foot. It's a sad commentary on two winters of work that we still can't take out a unit the size of a battalion or a regiment and move it over the snow the way it should be done."[15]

As Allied troops fought in the hedgerows of Normandy, the 10th was transferred on July 21 to Camp Swift, Texas, for refitting and more training. Over two thousand officers and men were added to its roster and heavy-weapons companies were added to each battalion. More mules, too, joined up. Morale plummeted so badly that when a call went out for paratroop volunteers to replace losses in Normandy, so many ski troopers responded that the Division banned all transfers. When Lieutenant George P. Hays took over command just after Thanksgiving 1944, he was told by Army Commander General John Lucas that "there was some ill feeling and discontent . . . and too many men in the guardhouse."[16] But morale picked up as the division prepared to move overseas. It was now, officially, the 10th Mountain Division. Hays, who had won the Medal of Honor in World War I's Second Battle of the Marne, fought at Monte Cassino and commanded the 2nd Infantry's artillery on Omaha Beach, in the words of a compatriot "fitted the [Division] like a well-worn and well-loved glove."

Short of troops, General Clark had grabbed the 10th when it was offered while he was still in command of the Fifth Army. The division arrived in early January and occupied a quiet IV Corps sector between Bagni di Lucca and Vidiciatico, a hilltown at the eastern edge of a slope rising to Monte Belvedere. With high winds, poor visibility, waist-deep snow and ice-coated rocks, the rugged terrain seemed tailor-made for mountain troops. Oddly enough, proper equipment was not at hand. "Crampons and ice axes needed badly," one patrol leader complained, and others remarked that "snowshoes and skis would have been helpful."[17] Troopers joked that the only patrol on skis was run for *Life* photographer Margaret Bourke-White. The 10th's journal records only three patrols on skis.

Ordered by General Truscott to take the Belvedere–Torraccia massif and the high ground running northeast to just above Vergato on Highway 64 and on the Reno, Hays went to have a look at his immediate objective. "It was a formidable sight," he says in his memoirs. Belvedere and Monte Gorgolesco rose some 3,800 feet, with little or no vegetation—for cover—on their approaches. To the left, a rugged cliff, its face ripped as if by giant claws, rose 1,500 feet above the Dordagna to a series of peaks running south to north some three and a half miles, and ranging from 3,000 to almost 5,000 feet above sea level. "If I captured Mount

Belvedere while the enemy held Riva Ridge," Hays told Colonel Tommy Tomlinson, "the enemy would have observation over all my troops and . . . mortar and artillery fire would cause . . . terrific casualties."[18]

Tomlinson, commander of the 86th Regiment, sent out patrols to seek ways to the top. Shattered ice filled steep ravines and old snow, crusted as hard as marble, clung to 75-degree slopes. Where winter winds had blown the rockface clear, stones crumbled. It was, as climbers say, "poor rock." Tomlinson reported that patrols could find no way up. Hays retorted, "You say your men are mountain climbers. Now, let's see how good they are at climbing this mountain."[19] Tomlinson sent his men out for another look, and they found four possible approaches "provided there was no enemy opposition."

Hays decided on a night attack. His Operations Officer however showed him a Fifth Army study that said night attacks were not only extremely hazardous but should only be attempted by experienced troops. Hays asked when the report was published; about three months earlier, he was told. "Well," Hays said, "don't you think by now the enemy has a copy?" The officer agreed. "Well, he wouldn't expect a night attack, and we should be successful."[20]

As darkness settled over the valley on February 18, teams of climbers fanned out along the base of Riva Ridge, coils of rope slung over their shoulders and clusters of pitons and snap links on their belts. They drove steel pitons into the rocks, hooked on snap links, and threaded them with nylon ropes. Long before the last piton had been driven in, troops from 1st Battalion and F Company, 86th Mountain Infantry, had begun their climb. Sub-zero temperatures chilled sweat-soaked bodies. Rifles, ammunition and mortar tubes slung on their backs threw climbers off balance. Hearts froze as bits of shale and loose rock spat on the men below. Surely, the Germans heard that. They didn't, and the enemy—the 2nd Battalion, 1044th Grenadier Regiment, in the process of being relieved by elements of the 232nd Fusilier Battalion—was taken by surprise. As one German officer later admitted, "We didn't believe your men could climb anything that awkward." At daybreak, Riva Ridge was the Allies', without the loss of one man.

Still, the Germans did not let it go at that. Throughout the next day and night, the ski troopers fought off seven counterattacks. Food and water ran out. The engineers erected an aerial tram for the evacuation of the wounded. On Pizzo di Campiano,the northernmost peak, Lieutenant

James Loose's A Company platoon established a defensive perimeter so close to the enemy that he could hear their mortar crew chief give orders. Frank Fairweather, grazed in the head, threw back two German "potato mashers," one of which had landed in his lap. Bazooka man Dale Archibald fired into a German dugout, killing several of the enemy. When he entered it later, he found a phonograph with an Al Jolson record on it. Also, there was a record of "Lily Marlene," and the troopers played it from time to tine to taunt the Germans.

On the second night, Loose's men had run out of grenades and were low on ammunition. "We're going to tell the artillery to bring it in real close," he warned his men. Forward observer Lieutenant Frank Gorham called for a pre-registered concentration; then Loose told the artillery to back it up two hundred yards. Artillery commander Colonel Albert H. Jackson could not believe what he heard. "Do you realize that you are asking for fire exactly on your position?" Loose replied, "I do, but if we don't get artillery support, you'll have nothing to support."[21]

While the 86th's 1st Battalion contested Riva Ridge with the Germans, the 87th, 85th and the 3rd Battalion, 86th, tackled Monte Belvedere and the next peak northward, Monte Gorgolesco. General Hays told his commanders what he wanted: "No small arms fire to be permitted by our troops. They could only use hand grenades and bayonets." The troops were to avoid enemy fire. There would be no artillery barrage. "In other words," he said later, "the night attack was not an attack at all. It was simply slipping through and around enemy positions to gain the high ground behind them, so as to deal with the enemy at daybreak."[22]

At eleven o'clock on the night of the 19th, the 87th's 1st and 2nd battalions advanced along the Valpiana Ridge, northeast up the western slope of Belvedere while the 85th's 3rd went up Belvedere's eastern slope and the 1st headed for Monte Gorgolesco, about a half-mile away. (When the 85th reached Hill 1053, a mile and a quarter eastward and about that distance short of Operation Encore's first main objective, Monte della Torraccia, the Brazilians were to attack their old bête noire, Monte Castello, and move northeast to protect the 10th's right flank.) The three-mile Belvedere–Torraccia massif was held by the 232nd Grenadier Division's 1045th Regiment, while its 1043rd defended the Monte Castello–Reno sector.

Green as they were, the 10th's troopers went up in the dark with M-1 rifle chambers empty. The night before, they had marched eight miles on foot into assembly areas along the line of departure at the base of the Belvedere–Gorgolesco massif. Lead elements of the 87th had advanced some 800 yards, when enemy outposts along a line of bunkers and fortified houses erupted with small-arms and machine-gun fire. Extensive minefields caused some of the first casualties among the troopers and their partisan guides. The freezing cold was a mixed blessing. Some mines were frozen—but so was the ground, which made probing for mines almost impossible.

By 0430, the 87th's 1st Battalion reached Belvedere and began clearing a spur of the main ridge running to the north towards Valpiana. The 2nd swung west towards Riva Ridge, knocking out a strongpoint in the village of Polla. German counterattacks were repulsed on the 20th as the 87th consolidated its position. By dark on the 22nd, the Regiment completed its task: partisans occupied Rocca Corneta. And the line across the Dordagna Valley from Belvedere to Riva Ridge was secure.

Belvedere's summit was occupied by the 85th's 3rd Battalion in the face of heavy artillery and mortar fire at daybreak. Company I had been pinned down by enemy fire. Captain Walter A. Luther went around the flank to knock out the enemy position. He was killed by a sniper, but his men were able to make the top. C Company Sergeant Robert Fischer was hit by a sniper high on the slope of Gorgolesco. He was dying in the arms of Mac Mackenzie when his friend Hugh Evans came up and tried to bandage the wound. Fischer cried out,"Oh, God. Please not now. Please not now!" Evans, a mild-mannered fellow, was enraged. He charged up the hill, leading a small group of men, firing his grease gun and throwing grenades. Ten minutes later, eight Germans were dead and twenty others had surrendered. Evans had won the Silver Star and Gorgolesco was in Allied hands.

Moving along the ridge beyond Gorgolesco, the 85th met increased small-arms and mortar fire. Company-strength counterattacks and several small enemy thrusts were fought off. The 85th's 2nd Battalion passed through the 1st to continue the attack towards Monte della Torraccia. On the right, the 3rd Battalion, 86th, worked across the eastern slope of the ridge against light opposition to occupy Mazzanca, a farm overlooking the slopes falling away and rising towards Monte Castello to the northeast. G-85 occupied Hill 1053, triggering the Brazilian attack on Castello the following morning.

During the night, G Company fended off a counterattack from elements of the 4th Mountain Battalion, 1044th Regiment. Lieutenant Colonel John Stone reported in the morning that his 2nd Battalion had driven off seven counterattacks; a few hours later, he reported that he was out of ammunition, food and water, sustaining casualties from a battalion-strength counterattack from elements of the 741st Light Regiment, the first unit of the 114th Jaeger Division committed in the sector. They had been joined by troops from 1st Battalion, 1043rd Grenadier Regiment, until then held in reserve by the Germans. Mules brought up fresh supplies the next night.

At the end of the day, the 2nd Battalion had edged along to the eastern slope of Monte della Torraccia. Meanwhile, the Brazilians converged on Monte Castello, the 1st Battalion, 1st Brazilian Infantry, attacking northeast from just beyond Mazzanca; the 3rd, striking north. By late evening, the Brazilians were mopping up scattered pockets of resistance on the mountain. East of Castello, the 11th Brazilian Infantry captured the village of Abetaia. Over the next two days, the Brazilians consolidated their positions, advancing on Monte della Casellina, a mile east of Monte Castello, and subsequently outflanking and capturing La Serra, slightly over a mile east of Torraccia, in the face of heavy machine-gun fire. A bayonet and grenade assault on several pillboxes climaxed this phase of the Brazilian attack.

On Monte della Torraccia, the Germans held on for dear life. Whoever held the mountain would control the sector east to Highway 64 and the Reno River. Without it, the 10th could not move on to its next objective, a range of hills directly above Vergato. The Germans pounded the 2nd Battalion positions with heavy artillery and mortar concentrations. From positions two to three hundred yards beneath the summit, men from Companies E and F charged straight up, only to be driven back time and again. To one observer, the line of walking wounded back to the aid station seemed unending. German guns would fall silent whenever Allied aircraft appeared overhead, bombing and strafing enemy positions. Coming in as close as 600 yards, Spitfires and P-47s of the 57th and 350th Fighter Groups and the 8th South African Air Force Wing flew a total of 412 sorties in support of the Belvedere–Torraccia attack.

Down to 400 men, again dangerously short of supplies, the 2nd Battalion was relieved on the night of the 23rd. Following an artillery barrage the next day, the 86th's 3rd Battalion overran the crest of Monte della Torraccia. "It was a nightmare," Thomas O'Neil of I Company, later recalled. "Only about thirty percent of our men made it to the top. The rest were either killed or wounded by the mines and mortars. . . . Once we got to the top, we were told to dig in. The Germans were counter-attacking and firing right in on us. It was very frightening."[23]

The Germans made one last attempt, on the 25th, to drive the mountaineers off the mountain. Enemy light field howitzers fired a thousand rounds. A German captain, taken prisoner along with 36 men, later said that he had expected to walk in after that barrage.[24] Instead, the assaulting units of the Mittenwald Mountain Battalion were almost completely destroyed. Enemy units—members of the 74th Light Regiment and the Reconnaissance Battalion of the 114th Jaegers—were thrown in piecemeal after forced marches from the rear. And though they continued to mount attacks on the northeastern slopes of Torraccia over the next few days, the battle for the Belvedere–Torraccia massif was over.

On February 28, the Brazilians took over the western wing of the 10th's zone with the 10th Antitank Battalion and the 10th Recon now on Riva Ridge under their operational control. The Brazilian 1st Infantry's defensive positions ranged from Rocca Corneta, beneath Riva Ridge, across Belvedere and Gorgolesco to emplacements just short of Monte della Torraccia, held by the 86th. The balance of the Brazilians held a sector east of the 87th which had replaced them on the forward slope of Monte Castellina.

On March 3, after a spate of bad weather, the 86th and 87th attacked north through the "Tenth Corridor"—the gap between the two Brazilian units—towards a series of mountains running east–west, slightly south of Vergato. Monte Terminale, at 3,330 feet and almost a mile north of Torraccia, was cleared early on, but Company E ran into stiff resistance in Iola, just beyond the mountain.

Two Germans stepped out of a house and were gunned down. When the bodies were examined, the troopers discovered—to their horror—that the "Germans" were women in German uniforms. God knows why, except that the enemy may have forced the uniforms on them.[25] The Germans were cleared out, house by house, at a cost of nearly an entire platoon killed or wounded. Thirty prisoners were taken, including the commanding officer and most of the staff of the 2nd Battalion, 721st Light Regiment.

Farther west, in Company A, a 170mm round bounced through a mortar section and went through a stone fence, but did not explode.

"Sometimes, you get lucky," Bart Wolffis, the section leader, said.[26] Ski-jump champ Torger Tokle was not so lucky. He went to help a bazooka man take out a machine gun and was killed when an incoming shell set off the bazooka rounds. His Company A buddies were so angry that they took out the German position, no prisoners, and reached their objective in half the time expected. By nightfall, the 86th was two miles north of its line of departure.

The 87th made good progress, too, taking Monte della Vedetta and establishing a road block at Pietra Colora, a two-mile gain northeast of its line of departure at the forward base of Castellina. Both regiments resumed their advance the next day. The 86th cleared Sassomolare at noon, moving another mile north to take its last objective, Monte Grande d'Aiano, the western anchor of a range running east to Vergato. The 87th took Monte Acidola, north of Pietra Colora, at midday; shortly after 1600, Madonna di Brasa, a height overlooking the town of Castel d'Aiano. Meanwhile, its 3rd Battalion struck east from Pietra Colora to seize Monte della Croce. Subsequently, they were relieved by the Brazilians, who had been advancing on the 10th's right. Mopping up hamlets between Rocca Pitigliana and the Reno north of the Marano, the Brazilians moved northeast to outflank the town of Castelnuovo. Taking the town, Brazilian troops also moved just west of Highway 64, a mile beyond, to overlook Vergato.

On March 5, the 10th committed the 85th on the right of the 87th, which attacked Castel d'Aiano the same day. Operating on a narrow, one-mile front, the 87th sent its 2nd Battalion around to the left to take the high ground immediately above the town and to cut off the roads running northwest. Covered by the 1st Battalion, the 2nd, spearheaded by tanks, headed for the town. Elements of the 29th Panzer Grenadier Division, rushed up from reserve to block the 10th's advance, fought fiercely, but to no avail. "The town was an utter ruin," Marty Daneman recalled later. "Few buildings weren't heavily damaged or destroyed. Broken glass, half-demolished furniture, and broken masonry littered the cobblestone streets and alleys. A jeep, all four tires flattened by shrapnel, rested in the middle of the town square amid the rubble."[27]

On Monte della Spe, just east of town, the 85th's Company B troopers fought hand to hand with 29th Panzer Grenadiers. Lieutenant John Creaghe, the company exec, led a group of seven men to clean out enemy pockets and took charge of defensive positions on the left flank during the first of four counterattacks, despite wounds in the arm, leg, chest and eye.[28] During the night of March 5–6, the enemy struck back at the 1st Battalion on Monte della Spe. One hundred mounted the fourth attack but were driven back by Company B—for good.

Frustrated, the Germans retaliated with harassing artillery fire but little else. The 2nd Battalion made a flanking attack against Monte della Castella and found its approaches well covered by enemy fire. Evasive action enabled Company E to take the south peak and move northwest, where they encountered a trench system. Friendly fire was called for; the Germans surrendered after bazookas knocked out two houses. The next day, E Company continued its advance, taking the northernmost peak, Monte Spicchione, without opposition. Company F occupied Hill 985, the eastern peak, and Company G occupied Tora and established a defensive position in the saddle between Spicchione and Della Spe.

General Hays wanted to continue the attack. He sensed that the Germans were weakening. Over the past few days, the Germans had fallen back from ridge line to ridge line over much of the Division's front, rarely counterattacking as expected, and yielding up a good number of prisoners. Moreover, the Division was still short of its ostensible objective: a range of hills anchored on the left at Monte Grande d'Aiano and arching north of Castel d'Aiano and Monte della Spe with its apex at the town of Tole. Once on this line, the 10th would have been on the down slope to the Po Valley. But Truscott called a halt. To go on, he feared, would alert von Vietinghoff, who then might develop defensive positions bracketing Highway 64 as formidable as those on Highway 65.

In three days, the 10th had taken approximately 1,200 prisoners and occupied 35 square miles of enemy territory. Belvedere–Torraccia cost the Division 203 killed, 686 wounded and 12 missing. Phase II of Operation ENCORE cost 107 killed, 417 wounded and 25 missing. Over the next few days, the Brazilians shifted the balance of their troops to the 10th's left, while the ski troopers extended their lines to the sector held by the 1st Armored Division. The 10th now held a six-mile front on the inner ring of the defensive range still in German hands from Monte Grande d'Aiano to the hills edging Highway 65.

NOTES

[1] Goodman, *A Fragment of Victory,* p. 80.
[2] Ibid., p. 106.

[3] Truscott, *Command Decisions,* p. 474.

[4] Ibid., p. 85.

[5] Truscott, *Command Decisions,* p. 471.

[6] Goodman, *A Fragment of Victory,* p. 97.

[7] Ibid., p. 99.

[8] Ibid., p. 102.

[9] Ibid., p. 103.

[10] Ibid., p. 106.

[11] Truscott, *Command Decisions,* p. 453.

[12] Ibid., p. 478.

[13] Ibid., p. 466.

[14] Burton, *The Ski Troops,* p. 136.

[15] Ibid., p. 138.

[16] Hays, *Memoirs,* p. 31.

[17] Anon., *Combat History of the Tenth Mountain Division,* p. 8.

[18] Hays, *Memoirs,* p. 33.

[19] Burton, *The Ski Troops,* p. 151.

[20] Hays, *Memoirs,* p. 36.

[21] Whitlock, *Soldiers on Skis,* pp. 84–85.

[22] Hays, *Memoirs,* p. 35.

[23] Whitlock, *Soldiers on Skis,* p. 102.

[24] "History of the 86th Mountain Infantry," mimeographed, p. 20.

[25] Whitlock, *Soldiers on Skis,* p. 112.

[26] Ibid., p. 113.

[27] Ibid., p. 123.

[28] *85th History,* pp. 25–26.

XXIII

INTO THE VALLEY

On March 18, General Clark conferred with his army commanders and staff. Battle plans were ironed out for the effective coordination of the final offensive. The enemy was to be crushed once and for all. The attack, declared Operation Instruction Number 4, 24 March 1945, was to be driven "home . . . so that the maximum number of German troops will be destroyed or captured."[1] "[W]e were," Allied Theater Commander Alexander later reported, "no longer thinking merely of the capture of Bologna, nor, indeed of any objective on the ground, but of more wide-sweeping movement which would encircle as many of the Germans as possible between the converging blows of the two armies."[2]

Clark, however, still had his mind set on the Fifth Army's making the main effort west of Highway 65 to capture Bologna. Moreover, he had reservations about the Eighth Army. Not only had it lost the Canadians, but, as General McCreery put it, "he really thought the Eighth Army had had it. . . .[I]t was not only worn out but had not the will to fight any more."[3] Truscott was willing enough to have the Fifth make the main effort, but he did not want "Clark . . . to interpose a restriction" which would make it impossible to exploit what he perceived as German weaknesses along the high ground west of Highway 64.[4] McCreery, annoyed, spoke to Alexander. What happened behind the scenes no one knows but, in the end, as McCreery later explained, "both Truscott and I did it our way while confirming sufficiently to Mark Clark's plan to avoid any direct conflict with his directive."[5]

Clark's orders called for the Eighth Army to open the offensive on April 10 (later advanced to April 9). After broaching the Santerno, McCreery's forces were to move either northwest towards Budrio to aid the Fifth Army's drive on Bologna and the Po or, if the situation were favorable, to go northeast through the Argenta Gap towards Ferrara. That city, just south of the Po, was on the shortest route to the last possible German defense line on the Adige River. The Fifth Army was to attack on April 13 with "the mission of debouching into the Po Valley with a secondary mission of capturing or isolating . . . Bologna." Truscott was to join the Eighth Army at the earliest possible time in order to complete the encirclement of the German armies south of the Po. Then, the two armies would cross the Po and capture Verona.[6]

The winter halt had improved the Allied situation in Italy. Eighth Army historian Eric Linklater asserts that its "battle-worn divisions were rested and restored, replenished and reinforced, and their morale was high. Manpower was abundant, new weapons had arrived, and a huge reserve of ammunition had been accumulated."[7] Not only did the Allies enjoy overwhelming supremacy in the skies but they also had a two-to-one preponderance in artillery and three-to-one in armor, including self-propelled antitank assault guns. More than 7,000 new officers and enlisted men were assigned to the Fifth Army's nine divisions (and the equivalent of another) as "overage," an advancement on future replacements to enable some in-the-field training before the offensive opened. In "repple depots" were 21,000 officers and enlisted replacements, 2,000 black soldiers for the 92nd Division, 5,000 for the Brazilian Expeditionary Force and 1,200 Nisei for the Japanese-American 442nd Infantry Regiment. Behind German lines were 50,000 well-supplied—500 tons of materiel delivered in March alone—partisans assisted by sixty mission teams.

While these preparations were going on, General McCreery got the shock of his life: a letter from General Anders, commander of the Polish Corps, saying that, in the light of what had occurred at Yalta over February 4–11, "I can see little but the necessity of relieving those of my troops now in the line. . . ." Roosevelt and Stalin, with Churchill's reluctant acquiescence after the fact, had delivered—despite fancy words about "free elections," etc.—Poland to the Soviets. "We had marched thousands of miles together," Anders said. "We had fought great battles together and had suffered thousands of casualties. We had come from the torture of the Russian labour camps to the brink of a battle which would seal our claim to be allowed to go home. Suddenly we are told, without ever being consulted, that we had no home to go to."

Anders met with Alexander, Clark and McCreery to explain that he could not ask his men to risk their lives for nothing. All three commanders were sympathetic. Alexander urged patience, saying that the British wanted a free and independent Poland. Clark felt that the Polish soldiers could "still find a ray of hope in President Roosevelt"; he said of Anders, "I know the great confidence the Polish soldiers have in their commander, and I also know that they would accept any decision coming from you without hesitation." McCreery, who, Anders expected, would try to talk him around with excuses, simply spoke to him as one soldier to another. "He told me very quietly that if I took away my Polish Corps I would leave a ten-mile gap. Then he asked me to put myself in his position and suggest how this ten-mile gap . . . could be filled."

Anders was shaken. McCreery, he knew, had virtually no reserves. If the Poles did not fight, Anders thought, they might not only ruin the Allied victory but also forfeit their continuing fight for independence. "I knew in my heart what I had to do," Anders said. "I told McCreery that we would fight on."[8]

If McCreery had a bad moment, the Germans surely were on edge with the approach of spring. Yet, despite a pervasive dread, the Germans still possessed certain strengths. General von Vietinghoff, who had replaced Kesselring as the commander of German forces in Italy, was among Germany's best. He had no less than twenty-three divisions—among them crack outfits such as the 1st and 4th Parachute, a Panzer and several Panzer Grenadier Divisions—all up to strength under his command. In addition, Mussolini's Salo Government fielded four more divisions, making it roughly 27 divisions against 20 on the Allies' side. One must keep in mind, too, that it was not then considered feasible to attack against prepared positions with hope of success, at least not without having a numerical superiority of three to one.

Historian Linklater has calculated the Eighth Army's offensive strength in infantry as 1.6 to 1.[9] Though morale was no longer what it had been, the men of the Wehrmacht were stubborn enough to fight. Paradoxically, as one German veteran put it, a "love–hate" attitude kept the Germans fighting; they were "motivated by . . . hatred of Hitler, who . . . had deceived and disappointed them, and by their rage over the Allied bombing of the Fatherland, over the uselessness of the sacrifice they had willingly made year after year, and over the senselessness of the war."[10] It is a paradox, echoed in Von Senger's remark that "troops who had seen the light were more dependable than the misguided followers of Hitler. He who looks his destiny in the face will understand the adage: *Nec metus nec spes*—Neither fear nor hope."[11] No wonder Alexander was moved to aver, "We were not fighting rubbish."

Enemy lines, however, were stretched thin. The Italian boot widened at the hip, stretching German defenses out from the Ligurian coast just above Viareggio to the Adriatic just above Ravenna. Vietinghoff recognized, as Kesselring later put it, that "forces just sufficient in the mountains were lost in the plains" and that "the strategic value of the west flank was very small"—though the armament industry there was "a consideration that ruled out any question of its immediate evacuation."[12]

In recognition of these realities, Kesselring's staff drew up plans for a pull-back to the much shorter Alpine defense line anchored on the Adige River, the entire operation to be triggered on the code word *Herbstnebel* (Autumn Fog). Yet, this was not an option open to Vietinghoff. General Alfred Jodl, Chief of the Armed Forces Operational Staff, made this clear in a spring telegram to Vietinghoff: "The Führer expects now as before . . . to defend every inch of the North Italian area . . . ." To drive the point home, Jodl warned of "the serious consequences" for not carrying out Hitler's orders "to the last word."[13]

Meanwhile, the Allies needled the enemy, taking advantage of a spate of fine weather to bomb all Po River crossings, railway yards, roads, bridges and supply dumps. The destruction of vehicles and gasoline shortages compelled the Germans to rely increasingly on horses and oxen to move their equipment—commandeering farm wagons, urban buses and civilian cars. Selective German spotter planes were allowed to scout dummy positions in the Adriatic sector that, along with increased activity in Ravenna, might suggest an Allied landing by sea along the coast. In response, one of two motorized divisions in reserve was moved from the Germans' center to near Venice, a waste of invaluable resources.

On April 5, the Fifth Army launched a diversionary attack with supporting fire from the Royal Navy up the Ligurian coast towards Massa (captured on the 10th). General Lemelson promptly reinforced this sector with the 90th Panzer Grenadiers, another draw-down of German reserves away from much more critical sectors. This attack may have precipitated Vietinghoff's decision to fall back from the Senio line to stronger defenses on the Santerno. It was a sensible move. Had it succeeded, Allied plans would have been upset and the offensive postponed. On the evening of April 6, the Germans laid down a heavy barrage all along the Eighth Army front to break up the Eighth's troop concentrations, destroy gun positions and cover a withdrawal. At the last minute, the German High Command canceled the operation at Hitler's behest—but not in time to prevent the waste of a good deal of ammunition

Just as Truscott prepared for the spring offensive, clearing the Germans off Monte Belvedere and the heights west of Highway 64 above Vergato, McCreery prepared the way for an advance through the Argenta gap towards Ferrara. At night on April Fool's day, the 2nd and 9th Commandos boarded forty Fantails on Lake Comacchio. They were to attack the Comacchio Spit, a needle thrust out into the lake towards several islands. But the lake was low, and the Fantails got stuck in the mud.

The commandos were transferred to storm-boats, manhandled over the mud. But by then it was realized that the commandos could not reach the spit before daybreak; nevertheless, they landed under a heavy barrage and a curtain of smoke. Meanwhile, the 43rd Royal Marine Commandos attacked the Spit by land. By the 4th the Spit had been taken, along with 800 prisoners; the following day, the Special Boat Services captured the islands. Then the 56th Division attacked across the Reno, captured 700 prisoners and occupied the "Wedge"— the triangle between the Reno and the southern shore of Comacchio. McCreery gained an edge for a thrust at the Argenta Gap. The Germans moved several units eastward in expectation of landings at the head of the Adriatic.

Soft breezes and sunshine announced another spring day on April 9. "And a beautiful day it was," writes 78th Division historian Cyril Ray, "firm underfoot for men and machines, cloudless overhead for our aircraft."[14] For the Germans, as nervous as they may have been, despite the intermittent machine-gun fire, the occasional mortar round or incoming shell, it appeared a routine morning. One might even take it easy, seize the day as Horace urged, as a "gift of chance/So much to the good."

Eighth Army troops, however, were busy. All along the Senio banks during the early hours, men were quietly withdrawn several hundred yards back, under the cover of "normal" harassing fire. The Germans hadn't a clue as the morning slipped away with a few bomber sorties—enough to keep up appearances of normality. Then, at 1350, as Geoffrey Cox recalled, ". . . there, distantly as if the sky were a vast metal sheet being shaken till it vibrated, came the hum of four-engined planes in mass."[15]

For an hour and a half, 825 heavy bombers dropped 175,000 fragmentation bombs behind enemy lines on artillery areas and places where

German reserves might rally. Medium and fighter-bombers flew sorties against prearranged targets: enemy HQs, gun sites, mortars, ammunition and supply dumps, and anything caught moving. A thick yellow haze, accented by billowing black smoke from burning buildings, blossomed over enemy lines. Then came a twenty-minute lull, followed by the expected artillery bombardment of the Senio flood banks.

Were these three-quarters of an hour of hellfire not surely the prelude to an Eighth Army attack? Time to get out of bunkers and foxholes to confront the attackers? But the ten-minute silence was followed by a stream of fighter-bombers strafing and bombing all along the line. And so it went, repeated five times, until about 1900 when the fighter-bombers screamed overhead once again. While the Germans hunkered down, expecting another bombardment, the men of the Eighth, from Highway 9 to the Comacchio, rose out of their slit trenches. Flame-throwing tanks directed long streams of fire on German positions on the flood banks. McCreery's men were on the move.

Within twenty minutes, the New Zealand Maoris were across the Senio, and by 2000 all four New Zealand battalions were moving forward under advancing barrages. To their left, north of Highway 9, the Poles, farther back from the flood banks—"the dirtiest bit of the river," Cox says, "[a]ll curves and high banks and stiff with mines"[16]—got off to a slow start. It didn't help matters when, during the preparatory bombardment, several medium bombers dropped their loads short, causing heavy losses among the waiting troops.

General McCreery, who witnessed the incident through his binoculars from his command post, was horrified. He would not have been surprised if General Anders—in light of what had happened in March—had said, "Enough is enough! We are pulling out!" The gallant Poles, however, rallied in quick time. Fighting desperately to establish themselves on the far bank, they asked the New Zealanders if they might use Kiwi bridges—set up in remarkably short order—for their tanks, which then crossed the river, enabling the Poles to break out of their bridgehead. Later, when medium bombers were again on order, General Anders told McCreery, "Don't worry. I'll have them. They are not likely to make the same mistake twice."[17]

The New Zealanders expanded their salient across the Senio during the night. A Tiger tank rumbled past Kiwis crouched on a side road. One got up and chased the monster, firing his PIAT at close range, blowing up the tank from the rear. And so it went with several other tanks. One with four soldiers riding on top surrendered when confronted by a corporal with a sten gun.

By midnight, the advancing brigades had reached their first objective, 4,000 yards beyond the river. To their right, the Eighth Indian's 19th Brigade ran into trouble. The 6th/13th Frontier Force Rifles carried the near slope but were caught in the trough by machine-gun fire. Sepoy Ali Haidar and two others were all of one platoon to cross the stream. While his comrades gave him covering fire, Haidar hurled a grenade at the offending gun—some thirty yards distant—and charged. Wounded by a "potato masher," he closed in and destroyed the nest. Without pause, he went for another, where four machine guns were posted. Struck twice, he fell, but then managed to crawl forward, pull the pin of a mills bomb with his teeth and toss it among the Spandaus. Staggering on, though weakened by a loss of blood, Haidar went at the gunners until the two survivors surrendered. The Rifles then went forward. Haidar recovered and won the Regiment's first Victoria Cross.

On the 21st Brigade front, the Mahrattas and Punjabis met a hail of steel slashing the crest and inner slopes of the near flood bank. Mahratta-led companies were decimated, and survivors took cover on the near bank. Again, one man made the difference. Sepoy Namdeo Jadhao made the far bank with two wounded comrades. He half-carried, half-dragged them, one at a time, back up the inner slope to safety. Then he dashed for the nearest machine gun, dropping his sten gun when a bullet tore his hand, and wiped out its crew with a grenade. He silenced two more enemy posts in quick succession, then waved his fellows forward. Inspired by his example, they ferreted the Germans out of their boltholes, clearing the banks. Haidar, too, received the Victoria Cross. The valor of these two men had indeed, as the Division's history put it, "altered the fortunes of the day."[18]

On the Division's left flank, the Punjabis were pummeled by German guns placed to enfilade a bend in the river. Unscathed by the preliminary bombardment, the Germans rose out of their warrens to tackle the Punjabis at the water's edge. "Men drowned in each other's grasp. Machine-gunners were yanked from their tunnels feet first and killed rabbit fashion,"[19] it was recorded. By midnight, the Punjabis were mopping up across the flat fields beyond the Senio. Sterling and Selkirk bridges were thrown across in less than the eight hours allowed in Divisional attack plans. By first light, tanks were across, roving between the Senio and the Santerno at the behest of the infantry. By mid-morning, April 10, situation reports were encouraging. The air was full of aircraft. Too full for some—several heavy bombers misplaced their loads, causing heavy casualties among New Zealanders and Indians forming up for the next advance. Still, German armor was in retreat before the Poles, south of Highway 9. The Indians were on the Lugo Canal, probing for a thrust to the Santerno. The Jaipurs entering Lugo, where a monstrous statue of Mussolini loomed in the marketplace, were greeted by the mayor with a white flag in one hand, a bottle of wine in the other. The New Zealanders were well ahead—thrust, as Cox put it, "like an aggressive forefinger, reaching out for the enemy's throat along the line of the Santerno."[20]

Commanders are chary of exposed flanks: getting cut off by the enemy is a soldier's nightmare. Though the New Zealander commander, General Sir Bernard Freyberg, might reasonably assume that the enemy to his right and left were too occupied to hit his flanks, he could not be sure that this was the case. Nonetheless, Freyberg did not hesitate. The Kiwis would cut the enemy's throat at the Santerno.

Moving out from the road line just short of the Santerno at daybreak, April 11, four battalions abreast, the New Zealanders attained the near stop bank without difficulty. The 24th Battalion even discovered a large section of the river undefended. The Germans' vaunted withdrawal capability clearly had been crimped. By 0830, the 24th and 25th Battalions each had two companies across and digging in. Still, the Germans did manage to take advantage of the dry, twisting river bed wherever it touched the canal that had straightened the flow of the river.

The Maoris were held up, as was the 23rd, by stiff opposition on the Division's right flank. Mid-afternoon, the Maoris struck for the river. Private J. Kira, the first man across, destroyed two machine-gun posts and knocked out a sniper. Soon, his comrades were a good five hundred yards beyond the Santerno. Three Germans singing "Lili Marlene" came down the road in a horse-drawn cart loaded with rations. "The Maoris considered the soup unpalatable but liked the black bread," their historian reported.[21]

That night, the 25th Battalion lost some ground to a German counterattack, but quickly regained its forward momentum. Sappers worked through the night; armor crossed the river at dawn. Striking beyond the Santerno on April 12, the New Zealanders reached the outskirts of Massa

Lombarda before dark. Meanwhile, the 8th Indian Division drew up on their right, despite difficulties experienced in crossing the Santerno, where motorized flame-throwers reportedly "proved temperamental and accomplished little." Lashed by machine guns, the water, one officer said, "looked like a miraculous evening rise of fingerlings."[22] On the far bank, the Germans struck back with a vengeance, leaving only two out of the left-flank Gurkha platoon and eleven on the right. The Gurkhas then flanked out at right angles to allow the British Royal Fusiliers to open up the bridgehead. Tanks soon followed, to take on a troop of Tigers and save the day. On the Division's right, North Irish Horse tanks ranged right, *sans* infantry, to gain some six thousand yards. By evening, the Indians had joined up with the New Zealanders.

Like the Indians, the Poles on the New Zealand right had a rough time after the initial surprise at the Senio. German counterattacks kept coming as the Poles moved towards the Santerno. Enemy tanks crossed the river embankments in three places. "And that was a surprise," platoon leader Kazimierz Cichy told war correspondent Marek Swiecicki." We were lying in an open field, and along comes tank after tank and fires at us until we wanted to cry. What could we do? It wasn't right to retreat . . . difficult to stay. . . . But the lads . . . took to their grenades. . . . One tank caught fire, and then our antitank guns began to let it rip. The blighters had to turn back."[23] Marek reported that the Germans exhibited either "savage determination or utter apathy," while the Poles were gripped by a growing passion—"a cold, inexorable certainty of victory."

In the attack on the Santerno, amid the crocodiles and tanks moving into clouds of smoke and fire, the infantry appeared, in Marek's phrase, "a little insignificant." Yet, as he adds, it was the infantry that "destroyed the force of the German resistance and obstinacy."[24] On the morning of April 14, the Poles crossed the Santerno all along the line.

To the north, the 56th Division carried out a second amphibious assault across the flooded ground south of Comacchio and moved towards the Argenta Gap. Its success, along with that of the 8th Indian Division, forced the German 42nd Light Division to withdraw from a salient at Alfonsine, enabling the Italian Cremona Group to occupy the town and advance along Highway 16 to the Santerno against light opposition. Behind a screen of armor, Germans scrambled tanks, horse-drawn and motor vehicles packed with men and gear in an effort to get out of

Massa Lombarda unscathed.

Attacking mid-afternoon on April 12, the New Zealanders knocked out the tanks and occupied the town itself shortly before midnight. By then, the Germans were falling back to the next river, the Sillaro, six miles distant, the New Zealanders hard on their heels. Early in the morning of the 14th, the New Zealanders crossed the Sillaro. On the left flank, enemy fire from Sesto Imolese drove elements of the 22nd Battalion back behind the eastern stop bank. Shortly after sunset, the battalion crossed the river again. Meanwhile, the enemy had moved in its 278th Division, a fresh outfit of "no distinction," as Cox observed, but one less for the offensive now underway in the mountains to the west. Though the New Zealanders would take another day or so to break out, a bridgehead across the Sillaro was established that night. Thanks to the gains scored by the New Zealanders and the Indians, the 78th Division could now strike for the Argenta Gap and the shortest run to the Po.

NOTES

[1] U.S. Army, *Fifth Army History*, Vol. IX, Ann. B.

[2] Alexander, *Report, Supreme Commander*, p. 32.

[3] Harpur, *The Impossible Victory*, pp. 126–27.

[4] Truscott, *Command Decisions*, pp. 478–79.

[5] Harpur, *The Impossible Victory*, p. 145.

[6] Ibid., pp. 177–81.

[7] Linklater, *The Campaign in Italy*, p. 417.

[8] Anders, *An Army in Exile*, pp. 249–54.

[9] Linklater, *The Campaign in Italy*, p. 425.

[10] Burtscher, *A Report from the Other Side*, p. 53.

[11] Von Senger, *Neither Fear nor Hope*, p. 296.

[12] Kesslering, *A Soldier's Record*, p. 260.

[13] Harpur, *The Impossible Victory*, p. 152.

[14] Ray, *Algiers to Australia*, p. 199.

[15] Cox, *The Race for Trieste*, p. 70.

[16] Ibid., p. 78.

[17] Harpur, *The Impossible Victory*, p. 159.

[18] India, *The Tiger Triumphs*, pp. 188–89.

[19] Indians, p. 190.

[20] Cox, *The Race for Trieste*, pp. 89–90.

[21] Kay, *From Cassino to Trieste*, p. 432.

[22] Indians, pp. 191 and 192.

[23] Swiecicki, *Seven Rivers to Bologna*, p. 64.

[24] Ibid., pp. 65–66.

XXIV

AS GALLANT AN ARMY
AS EVER MARCHED

Heavy fog rolled over the airfields south of the Fifth Army's front on April 12, the due date for the American offensive. Truscott planned to open the attack with a preliminary IV Corps operation to capture the Green Line along a mountain mass that, roughly, arched eastward from a series of hills above Castel d'Aiano through the 2,500-foot Rocca di Roffeno and Monte Pigna to Monte Montino and Monte Pero and down to Vergato in the Reno valley. When IV Corps reached the Green Line, abreast of the South African Sixth Armoured Division, II Corps would join the offensive. Fog grounded aircraft again on the 13th, the day the radio announced the death of President Roosevelt.

Truscott was determined that IV Corps would have air support, so it was a nervous group of officers who gathered in his Command Post at Traversa in the Futa Pass the next morning. The attack was set for 0800. One after another, each fighter base reported, "Fogged in. Visibility zero." A good deal of coffee was consumed before General Darcy, answering the telephone, called out, "Grosseto. Can see end of runway. They're taking off." The assembled brass cheered; Truscott called Crittenberger, IV Corps commander, to tell him: "The attack is on—0900."[25]

The heavy bombers droned over high in the sky at 0830 as 10th Mountain troopers and 1st Armored tankers waited for their orders to go forward. They were followed by fighter-bombers—459 sorties in flights of four—against gun positions, strongpoints, troop areas and other defensive emplacements. As soon as the planes were gone, at 0910, the artillery—over 2,000 pieces ranging from the 10th's 75mm pack howitzers to the Fifth Army's 8-inch howitzers—opened up for 35 intense minutes. Replacements wondered how anyone could survive; veterans knew the Germans would be there, waiting.

At 0945, April 14, the 85th Mountain Infantry, on the left, moved off Monte della Spe, dropping into a bowl-shaped valley, the Pra del Bianco, to attack a cluster of hills to the northwest. The 87th, on the right, attacked a tiny village, Serra Sarzana, where they were held up for fifteen minutes by an artillery barrage. Machine-gun and small-arms fire from hills on their left kept them pinned down. Starting out at 1030, the 86th, on the Division's right flank, reached the valley floor northeast of Della Spe, where they were halted by mortar fire from Hill 903 in the 87th's zone of attack. Movement along the 10th's main axis—a secondary road taking off to the north and the Po Valley from the lateral Castel d'Aiano–Vergato road—depended on the success of the 85th in the hills above the Pra del Bianco.

When L Company, 85th, crossed the LD that morning, it met little in the way of hostile fire. But out in the open fields of the Pra del Bianco, where the dust haze had cleared away, the company rushed through a mortar barrage. While the company was deployed along the road running through the basin, a German threw a "potato masher" from a nearby house at Staff Sergeant Frank Mitkowski, who tossed it back, prompting the surrender of eight Germans. Herding the prisoners up Hill 913, he made them point out enemy positions, but friendly fire forced them back.

By noon, the company was moving on to the hill. To their left, the advancing I Company was meanwhile being chopped to pieces by Germans on the southwestern end of Hill 913 who had somehow survived or evaded the air and artillery bombardment. Lieutenant Keith J. Evans, I Company's weapons platoon leader, was killed when he stepped on the release string of a stock mine. Platoon leader Lieutenant John D. Mitchell was killed by a sniper. Another platoon leader, Lieutenant Robert Dole, had just dragged his mortally wounded radioman to a shell hole when he was hit by machine-gun fire or shrapnel. As the company pressed on, two medics were killed trying to get to the wounded below Hill 913. Lieutenant Dole was finally brought to the rear, near death, and spent 37 months in hospital recovering—though he never regained full use of his right arm. (He would later become Republican Majority Leader of the U.S. Senate and the 1996 Republican nominee for President.) By the afternoon, I Company suffered so many casualties in its attack on the hill that K Company was passed through to continue the assault.

Captain Otis F. Halvorson, G Company commander, was killed by machine-gun fire while scouting enemy positions along the foot of Hill 909. At midday, the company was well up on the hill, but its second platoon was pinned down by enemy machine-gunners. That morning, John Magrath, a nineteen-year-old from Norwalk, Connecticut, where he had learned to ski on the local golf course before joining the ski troops, had been placed in charge of the Company Headquarters group of runners, in line to make his sergeant's stripes.

After bringing his men across the Pra del Bianco, Magrath went forward to contact the second platoon. Spotting a machine gun nest, he charged it, killing two Germans and wounding three others. Discarding his rifle, he picked up the enemy machine gun and, firing as he went across an open field, knocked out two more machine-gun positions. He then circled around another, destroying it from the rear. After that, he tackled a fourth position with like results. Freed up at this point, the second platoon topped the hill and cleared two houses, while the rest of the company pulled up, taking Hill 909 by 1355. That afternoon, Magrath volunteered to go around the platoons for status reports. On his way back to company headquarters, dug in on the rear slope, he crossed an open field and was killed by a mortar round. He was the 10th's only Medal of Honor winner.

G Company was ordered into battalion reserve. E and F Companies continued the attack along the ridge, occupying Hills 913 and 898 and slowly fighting their way to Hill 810. This enabled the 87th's 1st Battalion troopers in Serra Sarzana to move on Torre Iussi, where bitter house-to-house fighting slowed the attack. Ordered to bypass Torre Iussi, the 2nd Battalion moved on to clear Hill 903 while the 86th came up out of the valley on their right to take Rocca di Roffeno. At 1900, General Hayes ordered his men to "button up" for the night, excepting the 87th's 2nd Battalion, which was then on the way to Monte Pigna.

By late afternoon, the success of the 10th had secured the left flank of the 1st Armored, which moved its 14th Armored Infantry towards Suzzano, a village in the hills just west of Vergato, where the Battalion prepared for an attack on Monte Pero. Troop A tanks and infantry, meanwhile, tackled Vergato itself at 1830. On the way in, one tank ran over a mine that injured three crew members and burned the tank. Three tanks entered the town during the night as infantrymen fought house to house, even room to room. By daylight, about half the town was taken, but it took the rest of the day to clean out snipers. Even at that, a few remained as late as the morning of April 16.

Meanwhile, on Hill 909, G Company repulsed a vicious counterattack just before buttoning up for the night. A twenty-minute barrage preceded the attack the next morning, April 15, at 0700. The 86th's 2nd Battalion moved out from Rocca Roffino and entered Amore, a battered cluster of stone houses, a thousand yards to the north at 0950. Moving east, the troopers picked up a ridge running to Monte Mantino, which they occupied at dusk without opposition. At the center, the 87th captured Monte Pigna at 0810.

Resistance was spotty; the 87th took the next series of hills so rapidly that the enemy "surrendered in droves."[26] Tackling Monte delle Croci, however, the 87th came under a heavy artillery barrage and fierce machine-gun and small-arms fire. Nevertheless, they were on top of Croci twenty minutes after the assault began. Meanwhile, other units of the 87th captured Monte Le Coste, farther north, against scattered opposition. The 87th was now within striking distance of Tole, a village on a spur that commanded a network of secondary roads down the valleys of the Lavino and Samoggia rivers. One could say that from Tole it was downhill all the way to the Po Valley.

On the Division's left, the 85th still faced determined opposition, which effectively pinned down the mountaineers shortly after they jumped off. Still, the 3rd Battalion, on the left, managed to fight forward some eight hundred yards to the northwest. There they dug in, waiting for the 2nd Battalion to draw up on their right. During the night, however, the Germans had infiltrated to the right rear of the 2nd. With fire from an adjoining hill, the enemy was able to slow the battalion's advance. Though some ground was gained, the battalion reserve, G Company, was committed midday to close a gap that had opened up between the two battalions. While E and F Companies attacked northeast to parallel the 87th's advance on Monte Pigna, G Company struck for Hill 762, over a thousand yards to the north. "The sun was exceptionally hot," a company account later recalled. "The men broke out in a sweat moving downhill. The oppressive silence was broken only by the sound of feet crunching along the leaf-covered slope. . . . Hill 762 . . . [beyond a roll of] green hills, tree-studded, and dotted with starkly outlined houses . . . seemed an incredible distance away."

When the men broke out onto an open down slope, they were hit from three sides by machine-gun and rifle fire. Company Commander Lieutenant Beck was among the first hit. Radio contact was lost when the radio man was hit. One group made it to a cluster of farm buildings, where they fought the Germans in and around the buildings for most of the remaining daylight. Twenty men made it to a draw at the foot of Hill 762 some three hundred yards distant. They then unfortunately came under friendly fire, which killed four men and wounded seven others. Pfc. Edward A. Nickerson made his way back through a field of fire to the company CP, set up in a farmhouse to report. Contact was reestablished with Battalion; friendly fire was lifted and redirected to better effect. Lieutenant Beck then dragged himself several hundred yards to the CP. Pfc. Gogolin volunteered to go back to the Battalion's aid station for litters and litter teams.

Finally, the company was told to withdraw under the cover of darkness. Pfc. Nickerson with a fellow volunteer, Pfc. Sutton, returned to the draw to guide the survivors back. Fifteen German prisoners carried the wounded on litters. Others hobbled back as best they could. The rest of the company brought up the rear. A little after 0100, the men returned to their old foxholes, "and for the first time in nearly forty-eight hours of fighting," it was reported, "the 36 remaining men . . . were able to sleep, and were thankful that in the morning they at least would wake up."[27] In two days, Company G lost 119 men: twenty-three killed, 95 wounded and one missing. The 85th as a whole lost 98 killed and 364 wounded.

By dark on April 15, the 10th was well beyond the Green Line, the Brazilians filling in smartly on its left flank, and the 1st Armored on the right had taken Monte Pero. Late that afternoon, fighter-bombers capped waves of heavy and medium bomber runs with a series of sorties in the Monte Sole sector. They followed this up by dropping tons of flaming napalm on known enemy strongpoints across the II Corps front. At 2230, after an intense artillery barrage, the 6th South African Armoured Division and the 88th Division attacked towards Monte Sole and Monterumici. Throwing ropes of Cordex across minefields and detonating them, the South Africans cleared their approach up Sole. With five men, Lieutenant G.B. Mollet dashed through the last minefield without waiting for it to be cleared. One man was killed, but the South Africans were on top of the mountain just before 0100, April 16. By 0300, two platoons were on top, and by 0430 Monte Sole was all South African.

Over the following two days, the South Africans cleared the mountains around Monte Sole and advanced roughly two and a half miles north. They lost 70 killed and 300 wounded, with enemy casualties estimated at over 500, including more than 70 dead counted.

On their right, the 88th Division was stopped at daylight by the cliffs of Monterumici and defensive fire from the caves on the mountain face. For three days, the Germans held on. On the 16th, General Kendall told his officers that the division had suffered light casualties, fewer than a hundred, and that it "must go where the Krauts are and take our objective."[28] That the Blue Devils did.

Staff Sergeant Billy J. Edmundson, leading his squad in an attack against several machine-gun nests, had the bad luck to step on a mine. Though seriously wounded, he kept shouting instructions to his men, pointed out targets and fired rifle grenades, killing four and wounding five German gunners. By 0910, April 17, there were four companies on Monterumici. Colonel Fry, now Assistant Divisional Commander, called a line company to say, "Things are breaking. Must put on the heat." Then, a half-hour later, the Blue Devils were ordered to break off contact with the enemy. The division was to shift to II Corps' flank, between the South Africans and the Reno River.

Two hours after the South Africans and the 88th jumped off, the 91st, astride Highway 65, and the 34th Divisions to the east followed suit. On the right flank, the Italian Legano Combat Group made a good deal of a fuss to fool the Germans about II Corps' intentions and were prepared to follow up any German withdrawal.

Highway 65 was the shortest way to the Po. Here the Germans expected the Fifth Army to make its main attack. Monte Adone to the east and the hill masses on the west of Highway 65 were crucial to their defense of Bologna. Once in Allied hands, II Corps would have an unimpaired view of the Setta and Savena Valleys. Naturally, the Germans were determined to hold the ground, successfully slowing the advance of the 91st and 34th Divisions. Doggedly, however, the 91st pushed the enemy back on both sides of Highway 65.

Though the outcome was never in doubt, the G.I.s faced a good many nerve-wracking moments. Company I, 363rd Infantry machine-gunners had only a limited supply of ammo and two grenades when the Germans counterattacked at 2300 on April 17. They fired most of what they had left as the enemy attacked. Pfc. Morell P. Murray threw one of the grenades, wounding one attacker and momentarily frightening the rest off. Then they came back. Murray had rolled up some mudballs, which he threw. By the light of the moon, the Germans thought them grenades, and ran back out of range. Then they came on again. Murray's fellow gunners fired; he tossed his last grenade. Finally, the attack abated.

"Next morning," gunner Ben C. Kelly reported, "there were nine Germans lying where we could see them very well."[29] At 1142, April 18, three members of the 361st Infantry's I&R Platoon, with a partisan guide, raised the American flag on 2,161-foot Monte Adone. Two Germans asleep in a nearby dugout awoke and surrendered—the last of their lot on the mountain. Three days of fighting had cost the Division 432 casualties, 230 on April 17 alone.

April 16 marked the 500th day of combat for the 34th Division. General Bolte committed the 168th Infantry, holding the 133rd and 135th in reserve, with the 2nd Battalion on the right, striking for the Sevizzano Ridge, and the 3rd on the left, going for the fortified church at Gorgnano. Tankers found it impossible to navigate the narrow trails on the approach to the ridge. Repeatedly, the Germans drove back the attacking infantry.

On the right the Red Bulls, backed by tanks, were able to surmount Gorgnano Hill but they could not dislodge the enemy from the church rubble. Artillery was called in—24,479 pounds worth—driving the Germans out of the ruins before the day was over. April 17, as it was for the rest of II Corps, was a day of bitter fighting for the Red Bulls. Driven back a thousand yards from the destroyed church, the enemy, lodged in a fortified cemetery, knocked out two Allied tanks, driving the infantry back to the church. But that night the Red Bulls battled to the summit of Sevizzano Ridge, obliging the enemy to abandon the no-longer-defensible cemetery.

On the 18th, the 1st Battalion was committed; two companies waded waist-deep in the Cavinzano River to take yet another hill, Poggio Corniala. With only slight casualties, the Battalion captured over 100 Germans and killed or wounded as many. The Red Bulls had breached the enemy defenses, and by the 19th they were ready to move on to Bologna.

Pressure on the Germans mounted on the Eighth Army front as well. Advancing behind tanks along Highway 9, the Poles, with the 10th Indian Division on their right, entered Imola on April 16, where posters in very good Polish proclaimed, "Hurrah for the Polish Guns." Outside one building, however, they were greeted by a ragged group, right hands raised, shouting "Seig Heil! Sieg Heil!" The Germans, the Italians in the Municipal office explained, had taught the inmates of the local lunatic asylum Hitlerite slogans and had turned the women's wing into a brothel. This "brothel in a lunatic asylum with mad women as prostitutes" amazed war correspondent Swiecicki, who could hardly believe his eyes.[30] On the 17th, the Poles took thousands of prisoners beyond Castel di San Pietro and were within ten miles of Bologna.

On the 14th, the New Zealanders to the Poles' right had crossed the Sillaro, taken 557 prisoners and "wrote off," in Cox's phrase, "the greater part of the depleted 278th Division." Two days later, the Kiwis came up against the much tougher 4th Parachute Division, across the Gaiana River, little more than a ditch crossing the Ravenna–Bologna road. They were old enemies, having dropped on the New Zealanders in Greece and Crete, fought them at Cassino and in front of Florence.

During the night of April 18–19, the New Zealanders mounted their last set-piece attack of the war with the 9th Brigade on the right and the 43rd Gurkha Lorried Infantry Brigade on the left. They went in after an immense artillery barrage and the flame-throwers. Charred enemy corpses littered the ground, mainly paras who had crept forward to surprise the Kiwis on the near stop bank. The Kiwis and Gurkhas pressed forward. Tanks crossed before 0400. Three hundred prisoners were taken and the attackers were well on their way to the Indice River, the last river before Bologna, and the base for the Genghis Khan Line designed to save the city. But the Maoris crossed on the 20th with hardly a fight. The Genghis Khan Line was broken; the 4th Paras existed only as isolated groups of fanatics—bitter and desperate.

To cut the Germans off at the pass, the Eighth Army needed to get to the Po River. To do so by the shortest and quickest route, it needed a slender isthmus, two to three miles wide and four miles long, between the flooded marshes of the Reno, which, curving like a horseshoe above Bologna, reaches the sea north of Ravenna near Lake Comacchio. Argenta was the place to stop the British, and the motorized infantry of the 29th Panzer Grenadier Division swung over from northeast of Bologna to do the job.

On April 14, the 78th, the Italian Cremona and the 56th Division, left to right, were converging on Bastia and Argenta. The area had been turned into a vast minefield. Fortunately, the Italian partisans had discovered paths through which they guided British troops. On the 15th, the 56th Division advanced through the water-logged plain; though one regiment was halted by the lack of roads and by the minefields, another occupied Bastia the next day.

The 11th Brigade of the 78th took the lead and headed four miles up Highway 16. On reaching the outskirts of Argenta, where a canal, the Fossa Marina, cut eastward across the town, the brigade met the stubborn enemy. After dark, the Lancashire Fusiliers crossed the canal, fighting hand to hand, leaving the waters streaked with blood and blotched with corpses. By midnight, the Fusiliers had established a bridgehead, two companies strong and 200 yards deep. Sappers, working under shellfire, put up an Ark bridge and three tanks were soon across to help throw back three counterattacks. Divisional artillery laid on devastating supporting fire that caught large numbers of Germans in the open as the 29th Panzer Grenadiers carried out a relief of the original defenders.

Over the next two days, the 78th contested the Germans for Argenta, now mere rubble (cleared on the 17th), and the road north. On the 18th, the Royal West Kents were two miles beyond Argenta, but as the Argylls struck for the next town, the Germans knocked out four of their supporting tanks. Enemy artillery and mortar fire harassed the Argylls as they struck home with bayonets. Then, slowly but surely, the British beat back the Germans. Kangaroo Force, armored troop carriers of the 4th Hussars loaded with London Irish and backed by Sherman tanks, took three undemolished bridges, an officers' mess, a battery of 88s, a battery of 14-centimeter guns, a miscellany of other guns and over 200 prisoners. Striking northwest in the darkness of April 18, the Buffs foot-marched eight miles to Benvigante, outstripping the armored. The 78th Division was through the Argenta Gap—and the British 6th Armoured was ready to pass through for Ferrara, some ten miles north on Highway 16.

When and where would the Germans break?

While McCreery hoped to snare the Germans by an end run to Ferrara and the Po River just beyond, that would not necessarily bring about an end to the fighting. Nor did it guarantee that the Germans might not break out and gain the Adige, the defense line of the Alpine redoubt so feared by the Allies. Vietinghoff again on April 14 had requested permission to withdraw to the Po. It was refused on April 17. By then, the 10th Mountain Division had captured Tole, entering, in Von Senger's phrase, "a terrain that had always caused me anxiety," a country of "gentle and uncultivated slopes descending towards the Po, where armor could at once be operated."[31]

Truscott immediately took advantage of the terrain, switching 1st

Armored's Combat Command A from the Reno Valley to the 10th's left flank. Cutting over behind the 10th's advance, the tankers attacked down the valley of the Samoggia on April 18. Truscott also released his reserve, the 85th Division, to IV Corps. Crittenberger used it to relieve the 1st Armored in the Reno Valley. The 88th Division was inserted on the South African 6th Armoured's right, freeing the Africans for a drive down the Reno as the 85th moved up into the mountains to the west and on the 10th Mountain Division's right flank.

The mountain troops were moving down the Lavino Valley, clearing the heights on both sides as they went. Aware that his front was crumbling, General Steinmetz decided the hell with waiting for permission to fall back. But he was too late; the Americans appeared to be everywhere. As his troops withdrew in the dark, they had to abandon much of their heavy equipment. Harassing American artillery fire cut up his left-flank battalion so badly that it was next to useless. Vietinghoff hastily committed the last of his reserve—a regiment of the famed 90th Panzer Grenadier Division. But they arrived too late to plug the widening gap in the Fourteenth Army front on the ridges between the Samoggia and Lavino Rivers. By the afternoon of April 19, the mountain troops were on those ridges overlooking the Po Valley. The next day they rushed down the slopes onto the plains of the Po. "We ran down across an open field," a trooper later recalled, "bullets spitting all around us. No one was hurt, though one guy had a bullet hole in his jacket. We were out on the flats. It was exhilarating." "It was a grand rush," recalled another. "[T]he next thing you know we were riding—riding tanks!"

The mountain troopers were the first American soldiers to break out into the Po. They may have also been the last ever to mount a cavalry charge. "I was looking down into the valley in front of us," Dan Kennerly, a machine-gunner in M Company, 85th, recalls, "when I saw these horsemen come through." These were the 10th Recon, all too eager to catch up with the Germans, who had thrown up a line of machine guns in a peach orchard. "It was kind of like a movie," says Jim Nutt, one of the 176 horsemen, "charging down into the valley and all." The Germans had a field day. "It was just complete chaos," says another witness, Jim Hoff; "the shells came in and horses started bucking and stampeding, and men and horses were going down everywhere."[32]

Perhaps not an auspicious beginning for what became a grand rush for the Po River. While the 10th approached the Po Valley, the 90th

Panzer Grenadiers moved to the left to attack the 1st Armored Division, then retreated out into the valley, away to the left of the mountaineers. This cleared the way for them to close in on Ponte Samoggia on Highway 9. After a visit to the 10th's Command Post the day before, General Truscott bet General McNarney a bottle of Scotch that the mountaineers would reach Highway 9 out in the valley by 1300 on the 20th. He lost by about an hour. Pfc. B.L. Lessmeister, lead scout for Company A, 86th, crossed the highway at approximately 1430 that afternoon. General McNarney returned his prize with a request that it be given to the first man who had crossed the highway. Doubting that the soldier would ever be found, Truscott sent the bottle on to General Hays, who presented the bottle to the lad, a man from Montrose, Missouri, soon after.

General Hays, hard on the heels of his advancing troops, arrived at Ponte Samoggia some time around 1600. He was about to lunch when General Truscott dropped in and asked what he was doing. "I'm just relaxing. I have no orders." "This is no time to relax," Truscott said, somewhat cryptically. Shortly after, General Crittenberger showed up and, when Hays repeated his conversation with Truscott, took a look at a small-scale map. He pointed out a bridge over the Panaro River at Bomporto, and told Hays to capture it. Hays called in his Assistant Division Commander, General Duff, and ordered him to form a Task Force—a tank company, a platoon of tank destroyers, a signal platoon, a company of engineers and the 2nd Battalion from the 86th infantry—and move on Bomporto, twenty miles away, north of Modena, as fast as he could. He was to bypass all towns and any enemy resistance. The rest of the Division would follow and mop up. When Hays told Crittenberger the next morning, April 21, that he thought Task Force Duff would take Bomporto that night (it was taken intact at 1600) he asked, "What do you want me to do then?" "Go to the Po River," Crittenberger replied.[33]

Task Force Duff then spearheaded the 25-mile drive to the Po River, setting out at dawn on the 22nd with the remainder of the Division following up and clearing out the enemy. Late in the day, just before the Task Force reached the river, the lead tank ran over a mine. No one was injured in the tank. But General Duff, who had spotted the mine and ran forward to warn the driver, was seriously wounded.

For most of the rest of the Division, the move to the Po became a high-speed chase. Prisoners became so numerous that Hays told his troopers to disarm the Germans and send them back down the road where they would be collected, every ten miles, by the MPs. When G.I.s asked where the Germans were, the excited Italians along the roadsides said. "*Tedeschi tutta via!*" (Germans are all gone!)

Robert Livermore wrote his wife, "I was witness to the most exhilarating experience a soldier can have, the enemy retreating in confusion . . . .[I felt] drunk with the power of the machine that rushed forward through flat, canal-crossed wheat fields, orchards and gardens—through little villages of cheering paisans offering eggs, vino, throwing flowers, cheering, "*Bravo! Viva! Liberatore! Salvi!*"[34] One day, recalls another mountaineer, "we rode on tanks; the next, on anything on wheels, or hoof—captured Kraut trucks, Volkswagens, motorcycles, bicycles, carts pulled by oxen, horses, on horse back . . . I swear I saw one guy in a cutaway G.I. can on wheels, whipping his horse like Ben Hur in a chariot race."

The 10th's arrival on the banks of the Po was unexpected—and not only by the Germans. Motorized assault boats for crossing had been assigned to the 88th Division. Hays had no orders to cross and, while the 10th waited for some form of transportation, the Germans scurried across the river as best they could. Von Senger's HQ staff was dissolved into several groups. "I had to decide whether to be taken prisoner with my corps HQ staff while still south of the Po," he later said, "or whether to cross the river." At dawn on the 23rd, Von Senger and his group found a ferry still in service at Bergantino, some 15 miles downriver, as the crow flies, from where the 10th sat poised for its crossing. The access road to the ferry was blocked by burning vehicles; Von Senger had to leave his car behind. Fighter-bomber attacks made it impossible to cross in daylight. Many officers and men took advantage of the low level of the water to swim across. Von Senger does not say whether he swam or not, but he did cross in "the morning twilight"[35]—and marched twenty-five kilometers to Legnano to spend the night. On the 24th, he crossed the Adige, and set up temporary headquarters in San Stefano before withdrawing farther over the Pasubio Pass to a remote mountain village, Ronchi.

Boats arrived sometime during the morning of the 23rd. At noon, A and B companies of the 87th crossed the river with flak shells exploding four feet from the water—six men to a boat paddled by four engineers, who then paddled back to pick up another load of infantrymen. There were no casualties. George Hurt, one of the first men on the north bank, reported, "Nothing happened. There were some German dugouts there, but there was nobody around."[36] (Hurt was later wounded when his squad took out a machine gun some three-quarters of a mile to the north.) The 126th Engineers, however, suffered some casualties on the south bank by shellfire as they were constantly exposed, loading up the assault boats. German guns across the river were finally silenced by fire from the British 176th Lowland Medium Artillery Battery, which had hop-skipped across the valley, at times in advance of the infantry, in an example of British–American cooperation. Battery commander Lieutenant Colonel Freeth had lost his radio man in a German shelling. Walter Galson, an 87th radio man, volunteered to relay his calls, which he did until badly wounded.

General Truscott crash-landed his cub plane while the 87th and the 85th became the first Allied troops to cross the Po. "What are you doing, George? You know I do not have any troops to support you if you are attacked across the Po River." Hays explained to Truscott that his men had just captured some 500 Germans who had just arrived on the north bank. He had also learned that a lot of German troops were crossing downriver, and he planned to have them picked up as they landed. But Truscott ordered him to establish a firm bridgehead instead.[37] By then, Hays had two regiments over and a third on the way. The 86th completed its crossing the next morning when the 85th Division, which had caught up, also crossed after a heavy barrage. It landed just in front of the perimeter foxholes of G-85. "Scared the hell out of us. When we got out of our holes along come these guys, marching in close formation down the road. I dunno who was more surprised, them or us."

The breakout of the 10th Mountain Division into the Po Valley was the beginning of the end for the Wehrmacht in Italy. At 0600 on the 21st, the Poles entered Bologna; the 34th Division entered at 0800. The partisans' presence was already evident—"firing into the air in sign of triumph," Marek Swiecicki reported, "increasing indescribably the confusion among the ravens and jackdaws circling in clouds above the houses."[38]

The Germans had withdrawn and Fifth Army Headquarters had signaled the partisans to take over the city. "When our troops entered," *19 Days from the Apennines to the Alps* reports, "they found the Italian regulars policing the streets and rounding up known *fascisti* who were trying to masquerade as citizens."[39] The Italian Legnano Group also occupied the city.

Bypassing the city, the South Africans gained some 22 miles and on the night of April 22–23 ran into a stiff exchange with the Germans at Finale Emilia. They killed over 100 and captured 160, at the cost of two killed and 14 wounded. Large numbers of the German 1st and 4th Paras, 65th and 305th Infantry, were cut off by the South African success at Finale. Perhaps of greater importance was what the scene of battle revealed on the morning: in the 600 yards between the canal and the Panaro River an officer counted the remains of 100 cars, 50 trucks, a half-dozen self-propelled guns and a dozen 88s. In nearby fields were dozens of 105mm guns, Spandaus, Schmeissers and Faustpatronen.

Relieved of duty in Bologna, the 34th picked up Highway 9 at Modena and swept west to Piacenza, taking the town on the 28th after a bitter fight in which it changed hands twice. Meanwhile, the partisans captured Genoa on April 21 and were fighting in Milan and Turin. The Brazilians came out of the mountains and turned west along the edge of the Apennines to cut off Germans attempting to escape north along Highway 12. The 88th Division crossed the Po on the 25th to win a race for Verona—beating the 85th, on its right, in a sixteen-hour dash. From Verona, it moved on to take Vicenza and to sweep up into the Alps along the valley of the Piave, before swing west towards Trento. On the Blue Devils' right, the 85th plunged into the Alps towards Belluno. The 91st crossed seven miles downriver on the 25th, starting a sweep that would carry the Division past Vicenza on the Treviso, where it met the British Armoured 6th five days later.

The British Eighth Army, too, was on the move. "Once the Argenta Gap had been forced," says the historian of the Royal Ulster Rifles, "the battle became a route and even at the River Po there was virtually no resistance."[40] The British 6th Armoured Division passed through west of the 78th, and the 8th Indian came up to reinforce the pursuit of the Germans along Highway 16.

Early in the morning of the 23rd, the 5th Royal West Kents passed over a bridge west of Ferrara held by the Indians. Advancing with Churchill tanks, the Kents were the first of the Eighth Army to reach the Po. Ten minutes later, and few miles west, 6th Armoured patrols were also at the river's edge. By mid-morning the next day, the New Zealanders were at the Po above Bondeno. "The crossing went perfectly at night," says Cox, "except that the floating tanks sank ignominiously."[41] The 6th

Armoured also gained the far bank against little opposition on the Kiwis' right. Meanwhile, the 56th Division swept the ground to the northwest of the Comacchio, crossed the Po, and ultimately were at Venice.

East of Ferrara, the 78th Division ran into the enemy's last flare-up, not so much because the Germans still wanted to hold on to ground south of the Po but because they could not escape to the north. After three hours of close, bitter fighting, the Irish Brigade slowly drove back the 29th Panzer Grenadiers who were holding on to Saletta, a tiny village some three miles south of the Po. At dusk, the 9th Lancers cornered the remaining tanks of the 26th Panzers. Far into the night, under a bright moon, tanks fought tanks, and the Lancers, Cyrl Ray avers, "won its biggest regimental victory since El Alamein."[42] The Grenadiers lost ten Mark IV tanks to one of the Lancers. The countryside was littered with German dead, guns and equipment of all sort, ten Mark IVs, ten other tanks and four self-propelled guns destroyed by the Grenadiers.

Since the 78th Division had been preoccupied, the honor of leading the British V Corps across the Po on April 24 went to the 8th Indians. On April 25, Leutnant General von Schewerin surrendered the remains of his LXXVI Corps (and his champagne) to the 27th Lancers. By then, 14,000 prisoners jammed V Corps cages.

Crossing the Adige possessed few difficulties, except for the rain, yet another exhausting bridge-building job and the general nastiness of parachutist rearguards on the far side. Wanting bicycles for their escape, the enemy had shot down half the men in one village on the road east, past Padova, liberated by partisans, to Mestre, cleared after a brief fight by the Kiwis and the 56th.

At Churchill's urging, President Truman gave the go-ahead for the capture of Trieste and the province of Venezia Giulia. "The great thing," Churchill said, "is to be there before Tito's guerrillas are in occupation."[43] Alexander was to inform Tito of his intentions, and on the April 30 he ordered the New Zealanders to get on with the task of taking Trieste. "No roadblock, no crater checked [the armored cars]," says Cox, "as they raced forward at thirty-five miles an hour, their wireless masts swaying like saplings, their [tires] sizzling on the wet road surfaces, their commanders upright in the turrets, earphones over their soft black berets."[44]

The Kiwis met the Yugoslavs at Monfalcone on the evening of May 1, after an 80-mile run from the banks of the Piave. After some palavering with the local Yugoslav commander, General Freyberg decided to push on to Trieste, occupied by both forces on the 3rd. But the Germans surrendered to the Kiwis, fearing capture by the Yugoslavs.

In Trieste, as Cox points out, the Kiwis "were not only in a new area, but in a new era, the post-war era of the emerging Cold War."[45] Meanwhile, the British 6th Armoured Division, having met the 91st Division in Treviso, sent mobile columns to Udine and Belluno. On the 2nd, the 6th Armoured sent troops to Tarvisio, Caporetto, and found Tito's troops in Cividale di Friuli. "I am very glad you got into Trieste, Gorizia and Monfalcone in time to put your foot in the door," Churchill wired Alexander. "Tito, backed by Russia, will push hard, but I do not think that they will dare to attack you in your present position."

Churchill was prescient. Not only did no such attacks occur, but the wisdom, as he put it, of having "a solid mass of troops in this area"[46] ultimately paid off. Though the Yugoslavs and their Communist partisan comrades promptly disarmed pro-Italian partisans, arrested six of their leaders (subsequently smuggled to freedom by the Kiwis) and ruled Trieste as an autonomous area within Yugoslavia, the Allied presence won out. On June 5, Tito backed down. Venezia Giulia was to be occupied by the Americans and the British. Residents deported to Yugoslavia were to be returned. Bogdan C. Novah estimates that 2,100 were never returned; most perished without trial.[47] Still, Venezia Giulia remained Italian—no small thanks to the valiant New Zealanders.

On the north bank of the Po River, the 10th Mountain Division expanded its bridgehead and reconnoitered routes towards Verona. Colonel William O. Darby, famed commander of the Rangers, replaced General Duff as Assistant Division Commander. Hays ordered him to take over Task Force Duff. But the Task Force could not move until the river was bridged and its armor could cross.

Shortly after midnight on April 25, the 1st Battalion of the 85th started out for the airport at Villafranco, nearly 40 miles to the north. The mountaineers bypassed Mantova, occupied by the partisans, and reached the airport just before ten o'clock. Task Force Darby joined them several hours later and set off for Verona at 2000 hours. Hays was ordered to head into the Alps towards the Brenner Pass. "I had the choice of two routes," he later said, "up Highway 12, which followed the Adige River . . . or up the east side of Lake Garda. I chose the later, as I thought we could make faster progress."[48] Since the 85th Division had already entered Verona, Task Force Darby swung west to the shore of the lake.

Battalions were to leapfrog, one on foot as fast as it could go, while another came up by truck and then took over.

The 87th's 3rd Battalion took over from Darby's troops at Lazise and, after a brief but bitter firefight, yielded to the 85th's 2nd battalion at 1600 on April 27, just above Garda. Intermingled within a line of tanks, the 85th force-marched—G Company in the lead—seventeen miles to Malcesine, where the 86th's 2nd Battalion took over at 0200 on the 28th. Meanwhile, the Germans had blown the tunnels north of the town and the mountaineers were "ducked" around to carry on towards Torbole.

On the 30th, Company K of the 85th crossed the lake in DUKWS, landing at Gargnano, the site of Mussolini's villa. (The dictator had been captured and murdered by partisans on April 28 and his body, along with that of his mistress, now hung—heels-up—in Milan.) Artillery loaded on a boat headed up the lake capsized and sank with all hands. Lieutenant Colonel John Freeth of the British 178th Medium Battalion of Royal Artillery loaded his guns on some fishing boats in the Malcesine harbor. Their wheels hung over the sides.

This was *their* kind of country, and the mountaineers worked the hills above Garda, around the tunnels, towards Torbole and Nago. At tunnel No. 5, German artillery in Riva, at the head of the lake, fired three rounds; one exploded just inside the entrance, wounding fifty and killing five troopers. Torbole was taken after a bitter house-to-house fight; the town was a mass of rubble before the fight was over. German artillery and tanks forced Allied troops in Nago to pull back to the edge of town. Riva was taken on the last day in April.

On May 1, Colonel Darby came up to Torbole to confer with the 86th Regimental staff about the next phase, an attack north to Trentino and Bolzano. After the meeting, he stepped outside the hotel and climbed into his jeep. An 88 shell hit a nearby building, killing Darby and the 86th Regimental Sergeant Major, John Evans. They were among the 10th Division's last casualties, and among the last in the armies fighting for Italy to fall.

On April 26, 1945, the Russian Army had broken through the outer defenses of Berlin, and in the early-morning hours of April 30 Adolf Hitler committed suicide. Allied armies on the north German plain were mopping up the remnants of the Wehrmacht in the west.

On May 2, the Germans in Italy surrendered.

NOTES

[1] Truscott, *Command Decisions*, p. 486.
[2] *Combat History*, 10th., p. 50.
[3] Anon. *Attack*.
[4] Delaney, *Blue Devils in Italy*, p. 194.
[5] Robbins, *The 91st Infantry Division*, p. 278.
[6] Swiecicki, *Seven Rivers to Bologna*, p. 76.
[7] Von Senger, *Neither Fear nor Hope*, p. 299.
[8] Whitlock, *Soldiers on Skis*, pp. 146–47.
[9] Hays, *Memoirs*, pp. 49–50.
[10] Burton, *The Ski Troops*, p. 173.
[11] Von Senger, *Neither Fear nor Hope*, pp. 300–301.
[12] Whitaker, p. 159.
[13] Hays, *Memoirs*, p. 55.
[14] Swiecicki, *Seven Rivers to Bologna*, p. 112.
[15] U.S. Fifth Army, *19 Days from the Appenines to the Alps*, p. 80.
[16] Graves, *The Royal Ulster Rifles*, p. 298.
[17] Cox, *The Race for Trieste*, p. 120.
[18] Ray, *Algiers to Australia*, p. 222.
[19] Churchill, *The Second World War*, Vol. VI, p. 552.
[20] Cox, *The Race for Trieste*, p. 9.
[21] Ibid., p. 15.
[22] Churchill, *The Second World War*, Vol. VI, p. 552.
[23] Cox, *The Race for Trieste*, p. 223.
[24] Hays, *Memoirs*, p. 56.

Acknowledgments

We cannot know how much we learn
From those who never will return,
Until a flash of unforeseen
Remembrance falls on what has been.
　　　　　　　—Edwin Arlington Robinson

This account of the fighting north of Rome in 1944 and 1945 cannot match what the poet calls "a flash of unforeseen remembrance" but perhaps it will suggest something of what we can learn from those who fought there. At least, it will provide some measure of our—and this book's—debt to them.

The book, too, owes much to the writers who preceded me in illuminating one aspect or another of the war in Italy. Their contributions are clear and I am grateful.

Over the years I have benefited from many conversations, shared remembrances, with World War II veterans from many different units. If some who fought in Italy feel that I have overplayed the role of the 10th Mountain Division, I can only say: It was my outfit.

While writing the book I gained immeasurably from arguments, conversations and thoughtful suggestions from Maurice "Speed" Murphy, a sergeant who once kept this GI in line and is now a valued friend. Dr. James W. Ruff, who served with the 34th Division, became a devoted correspondent these last few years. He has a somewhat different view of the Italian campaign, which has kept me on target.

Steven Smith displays his talent as publisher with this attractive volume. Donn Teal's fine editorial hand worked marvels with my manuscript. To both, thank you.

And to my wife, Harriet, my love for her everlasting patience and encouragement.

PICTURE CREDITS

All photographs unless otherwise credited are from the National Archives, U.S. Army Signal Corps collection. The maps on pages 418–421 are from *The Fifth Army History.*

Bibliography

Adleman, Robert H., and Walton, Colonel George. *Rome Fell Today.* Boston: Little, Brown and Company, 1968.

Alexander, Field Marshall Earl. *Report, Supreme Commander, Mediterranean, to the Combined Chiefs of Staff on the Italian Campaign, 12 December to 2 May, 1945.* London: His Majesty's Stationery Office, 1951.

Alexander, Field Marshall Earl. *The Alexander Memoirs 1940–1945.* London: Cassell, 1962.

Anders, Lt. General W. *An Army in Exile.* Nashville: The Battery Press, 1981.

Anon. *Attack: Company G, 85th Mountain Infantry.* N.d., n.p. Denver: 10th Mountain Resources Center, Public Library.

Anon. *Combat History of the Tenth Mountain Division.* Fort Benning, Georgia, n.d.

Anon. *History of the Third Battalion, 337th Infantry, Eighty-Fifth Division.* Nashville: The Battery Press, 1979.

Battaglia, Roberto. *The Story of the Italian Resistance.* London: Odhams Press Limited, 1957.

Berenson, Bernard. *Rumour and Reflection.* London: Constable, 1952.

Bond, Harold L. *Return to Cassino.* New York: Doubleday & Co., 1964.

Bowlby, Alex. *Countdown to Cassino: The Battle of Mignano Gap, 1943.* New York: Sarpedon, 1995.

Burdon, Randall Matthews. *24 Battalion.* Wellington, N.Z.: War History Branch, Dept. of Internal Affairs, 1953.

Burton, Hal. *The Ski Troops.* New York: Simon and Schuster, 1971.

Burtscher, Hans. *A Report from the Other Side.* N.p. Denver: 10th Mountain Resources Center, Public library, 1992.

Casella, Luciano. *The European War of Liberation: Tuscany and the Gothic Line.* Florence: La Nuova Europa, 1983.

Churchill, Winston S. *The Second World War,* Vols. I–VI. Boston: Houghton Mifflin Company, 1948.

Clark, Mark W. *Calculated Risk.* New York: Harper & Brothers, Publishers, 1950.

Cox, Geoffrey. *The Race for Trieste*. London: William Kimber, 1977.

Cray, Ed. *General of the Army*. New York: W.W. Norton Company, 1990.

Delaney, John P. *The Blue Devils in Italy: A History of the 88th Infantry Division in World War II*. Washington: Infantry Journal Press, 1947.

Fisher, Ernest F. *Cassino to the Alps*. Washington: Center of Military History, United States Army, 1977.

Forty, George. *Fifth Army at War*. New York: Charles Scribner's Sons, 1980.

Frost, C.S. *Once a Patricia: Memoirs of a Junior Infantry Officer, World War II*. St. Catherine, Ontario: Vanwell Publishers, 1988.

Fry, James C. *Combat Soldier*. Washington: The National Press, Inc., 1968.

Gelhorn, Martha. *Faces of War*. London: Rupert Hart-Davies, 1959.

Goebbels, Joseph. *The Goebbels Diaries*. London: Hamish Hamilton, 1948.

Goodman, Paul. *A Fragment of Victory in Italy: The 92nd Infantry Division in World War II*. Nashville: The Battery Press, 1993.

Graves, Charles. *The Royal Ulster Rifles*. [Moxborough, Yorks]. Royal Ulster Rifles Regimental Committee, 1950.

Hargrove, Hondon B. *Buffalo Soldiers in Italy*. Jefferson, N.C.: McFarland, 1985.

Harpur, Brian. *The Impossible Victory*. New York: Hippocrene Books, 1981.

Hays, Lt. General George P. *Personal Memoirs*. Typscript. Denver: 10th Mountain Division Resources Center, Public Library.

Horsfall, John. *Fling Our Banner to the Wind*. Kineton, Warwick, Great Britain: The Roundwood Press, 1978.

Hougen, John H. *The Story of the Famous 34th Infantry Division*, Nashville: The Battery Press, 1979.

Howard, Michael. *The Mediterranean Strategy in the Second World War*. New York: Frederick A. Praeger, 1968.

Howe, George F. *The Battle History of the 1st Armored Division, "Old Ironsides,"* Washington: Combat Forces Press, 1954.

Huff, Richard A., editor. *A Pictorial History of the 36th Division*. Nashville: The Battery Press, 1979.

India, Defence Department, Director of Public Relations. *The Tiger Triumphs: The Story of Three Great Divisions in Italy*. London: His Majesty's Stationery Office, 1946.

Jackson, W.G.F. *The Battle for Italy*. London: B.T. Batsford Ltd., 1967.

Kay, Robin Langford. *Italy: Volume II: From Cassino to Trieste*. Wellington, N.Z.: Historical Publications Branch, Department of Internal Affairs, 1967.

Kesselring, Albert. *A Soldier's Record*. Novato, Calif.: Presidio, 1989.

Lett, Gordon. *Rossano*. London: Hodder and Stoughton, 1955.

Linklater, Eric. *The Campaign in Italy*. London: Her Majesty's Stationery Office, 1977.

Llewellyn, S.P. *Journey Towards Christmas: Official History of the 1st Ammunition Company, Second New Zealand Expeditionary Force, 1939–45.* Wellington, N.Z.: War History Branch, Department of Internal Affairs, 1949.

Lucas, James. *The British Soldier.* London: Arms and Armour Press, 1989.

Macmillan, Harold. *War Diaries: January 1943–May, 1945.* New York: St. Martin's Press, 1984.

Mariano, Nicky. *Forty Years with Berenson.* New York: Alfred A. Knopf, 1966.

Mauldin, Bill. *Up Front.* New York: Henry Holt & Company, 1945.

Mauldin, Bill. *The Brass Ring.* New York: W.W. Norton & Company, 1971.

Moraes, João Baptista Mascarenhas de. *The Brazilian Expeditionary Force.* Washington: U.S. Government Printing Office, 1966.

Moran, Lord. *Churchill: Taken from the Diaries of Lord Moran.* Boston: Houghton Mifflin Company, 1966.

Mowat, Farley. *The Regiment.* Toronto: McClelland and Stewart, 1955.

Murphy, Thomas D. *Ambassadors in Arms.* Honolulu: Univerity of Hawaii Press, 1954.

Murray, Lionel G. *The First City/Cape Town Highlanders in Italy, 1943–1945.* Cape Town: Cape Times, 1945.

Norton, Frazer D. *26 Battalion.* Wellington, N.Z.: War History Branch, Department of Internal Affairs, 1963.

Orgill, Douglas. *The Gothic Line.* New York: W.W. Norton & Company, 1967.

Origo, Iris. *War in Val d'Orcia.* Boston: David R. Godine, Publisher, 1984.

Origo, Iris. *Images and Shadows.* London: Century Publishing, 1970.

Orpen, Neil. *Victory in Italy.* Cape Town: Purnell, 1975.

Parkinson, C. Northcote. *Always a Fusilier.* London: S. Low, 1949.

Pringle, David James. *Chirnside: 20 Battalion and Armoured Regiment.* Wellington, N.Z., War History Branch, Department of Internal Affairs, 1957.

Puttick, Sir Edward. *25 Battalion.* Wellington, N.Z.: War History Branch, Department of Internal Affairs, 1960.

Ray, Cyril. *Algiers to Austria: A History of 78 Division in the Second World War.* London: Eyrie and Spottiswoods, 1952.

Robbins, Robert A. *The 91st Infantry Division in World War II.* Washington: Infantry Press, 1947.

Salvadori, Massimo. *Storia della Resistenza Italiana.* Venice: Istituto Tipografico Editoriale, 1955.

Schultz, Paul L. *The 85th Infantry Division in World War II.* Washington: Infantry Journal Press, 1949.

Sevareid, Eric. *Not So Wild a Dream.* New York: Atheneum, 1987.

Shepperd, G.A. *The Italian Campaign, 1943–45.* New York: Frederick A. Praeger, 1968.

Shirley, Orville C. *Americans: The Story of the 442nd Combat Team.* Washington: Infantry Journal Press, 1948.

Starr, Chester G. *From Salerno to the Alps: A History of the Fifth Army, 1943–1945.* Washington: Infantry Journal Press, 1948.

Stevens, George Roy. *Fourth Indian Division.* London: McLaren, 1945.

Strawson, John. *The Italian Campaign.* London: Secker & Warburg,1987.

Strootman, Captain Ralph E. *History of the 363rd Infantry.* Washington: Infantry Journal Press, 1947.

Swiecicki, Marek. *Seven Rivers to Bologna.* London: J. Rollo Book Co., 1946.

Tompkins, Peter. *A Spy in Rome.* New York: Simon and Schuster, 1962.

Trevelyan, Raleigh. *Rome '44.* New York: Viking Press, 1981.

Trevelyan, Raleigh. *The Fortress: A Diary of Anzio and After.* London: Buchan & Enright, Publishers, 1985.

Truscott, Lt. General L.K., Jr. *Command Missions.* Novato, Calif.: Presidio Press, 1954.

Tutaev, David. *The Man Who Saved Florence.* New York: Coward McCann, Inc., 1966.

United States Army. *Fifth Army History,* 9 vols. Florence, Italy: L'Impronta, 1945–47.

United States Fifth Army. *19 Days from the Apennines to the Alps.* Nashville: The Battery Press, Inc., 1987.

Von Senger und Etterlin, General Frido. *Neither Fear Nor Hope.* Novato, Calif.: Presidio Press, 1989.

Wallace, John E. *The Blue Devil "Battle Mountain" Regiment in Italy.* Nashville: The Battery Press, 1977.

Warlimont, Walter. *Inside Hitler's Headquarters.* New York: Praeger, 1964.

Wedemeyer, General Albert C. *Wedemeyer Reports.* New York: Henry Holt & Company, 1958.

Whitlock, Flint. *Soldiers on Skis.* Boulder, Colo.: Paladin Press, 1992.

Wilhelm, Maria de Blasio. *The Other Italy.* New York: W.W. Norton & Company, 1988.

Wondolowski, Peter S. *History of the IV Corps.* U.S. Army War College, Carlisle Barracks, Pennsylvania, 1948.

Woodruff, John B. *The 85th Moutain Infantry Regimental History..* Mss. Suitland, Md.: National Archives, n.d.

General Index

Index of Military Units

If, after the Fascist government's collapse, Italy had fallen quickly into Allied hands, Churchill's dream of an Anglo-American penetration into central Europe (ahead of the Russians) might have become reality. Instead, German armies occupied the country and used successive mountain and river lines to stall the Allied advance. Nine months after the invasion in September 1943, Rome was occupied by the Allies on June 4, 1944. For the next eleven months, until the last week of the war, the Allies fought to reach the Po River, the last viable enemy line of defense.

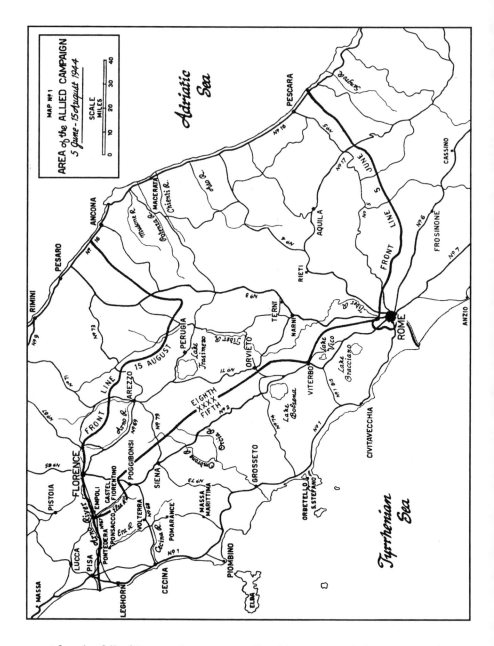

After the fall of Rome, the summer of 1944 was spent fighting past Lake
Trasimeno and the Arezzo Gap to Florence.

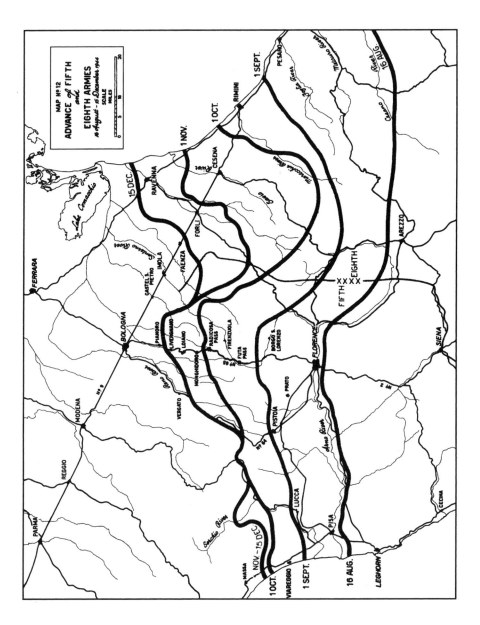

This map illustrates how, through difficult and costly advances, the Allies *almost* got to Bologna by winter.

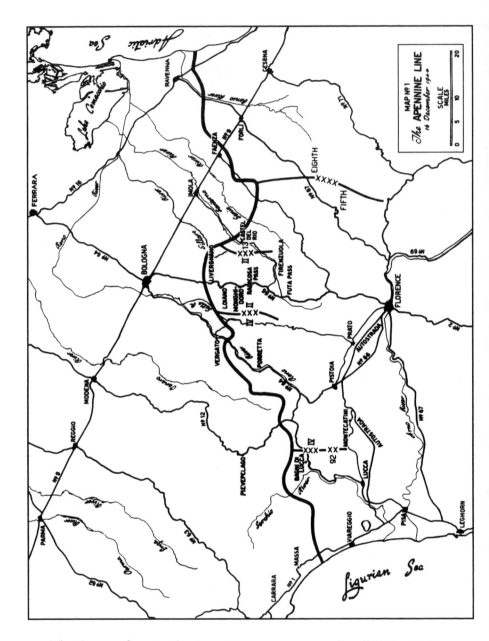

The German front in the Apennine range, commonly called the Gothic Line. The Germans held here throughout the winter—sometimes, as along the Serchio River, launching limited counterattacks.

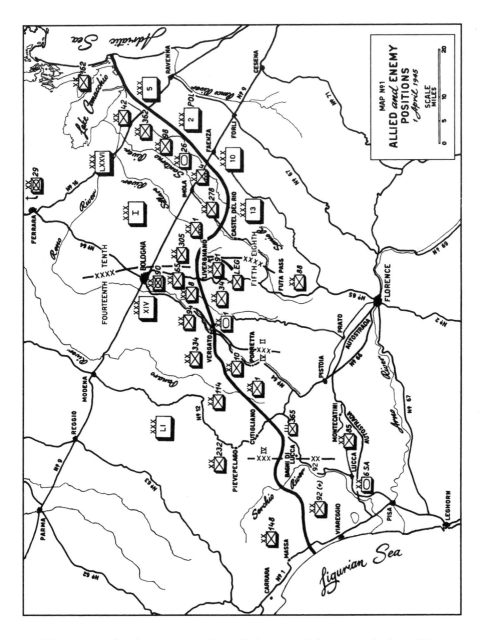

Dispositions for the spring push on Bologna and thus into the broad Po River Valley. Once the Germans had been pushed out of the Apenines, they had no way to stem the mobile flood of Allied forces.